A TRAVEL GUIDE TO
JEWISH RUSSIA & UKRAINE

A TRAVEL GUIDE TO JEWISH RUSSIA & UKRAINE

By Ben G. Frank

PELICAN PUBLISHING COMPANY

Gretna 2000

Library of Congress Cataloging-in-Publication Data

Frank, Ben G.
   A travel guide to Jewish Russia & Ukraine/ by Ben G. Frank.
      p. cm.
   Includes bibliographical references and index
   ISBN 1-56554-355-6 (pbk: alk. paper)
   1. Jews—Russia (Federation)—History. 2. Jews—Travel—Russia
(Federation) Guidebooks. 3. Russia (Federation)—Description and
travel. 4. Jews—Ukraine—History. 5. Jews—Travel—Ukraine
Guidebooks. 6. Ukraine—Description and travel. I. Title. II.
Title: Jewish Russia and Ukraine III. Title: Jewish Russia and
Ukraine
   D8135.R92 F72 1999
   9479—004924—dc21   99-27260
                                                                          CIP

Maps and cover art by Joseph Honig

*Information in this guidebook is based on authoritative data available at
the time of printing. Prices and hours of operation of businesses are subject
to change without notice. Readers are asked to take this into account when
consulting this guide.*

Manufactured in Canada

Published by Pelican Publishing Company, Inc.
1000 Burmaster, Gretna, Louisiana 70053

*To my wonderful grandchildren, Randall Stuart Frank
and Rebecca Naomi Frank, who also trace their roots
to their great, great-grandfather and great, great-grandmother
and beyond, who came from Russia and Ukraine
to these blessed American shores.*

Contents

Acknowledgments

Writing is a lonely craft, and the hours of research that go into the creation of a volume, especially a travel book, could never be endured without the encouragement and help of family, relatives, friends, colleagues, fellow journalists, historians, administrators, and officials. This *Travel Guide to Jewish Russia and Ukraine* could never have been realized without them.

Many people contributed to this book. But a few years ago, a number of individuals brought me to the point of even attempting the enormous task facing any writer who tries to fathom mysterious Russia.

One certainly was the late Jewish journalist Joseph Poliakov, who in a review and in discussion told me how could I write about Jewish Europe, without including Russia and Ukraine. Another who immediately saw the crucial need and potential of this volume and who believed in this project from the very beginning was Amir Shaviv, assistant executive vice president for special operations of the American Jewish Joint Distribution Committee. His interest and help never lagged. A third key person, Raphael Rothstein, national director of marketing and communications for Israel Bonds, guided my approaches to style and interpretation and often read parts of the manuscript. A source of inspiration-plus was Allan "Geli" Gelfond, senior financial resource development officer of the Jewish Federation of Metropolitan Detroit. He never let me falter, and often voluntarily forwarded ideas, suggestions, and information. Among those who helped me through the entire project was Jerry Goodman, executive director of the National Committee for Labor Israel and founding director of the National Conference on Soviet Jewry. He cited current sources and refreshed my memory of events in the struggle for Soviet Jewry.

It would be remiss of me not to thank the organizations whose patient staffs were there when I needed them. They are the American Jewish Joint Distribution Committee (JDC), Chabad Lubavitch, The Jewish Agency, the Charles and Lynn Schusterman Family Foundation, International Hillel, and the World Union of Progressive Judaism.

I am very grateful to Scott Richman, desk director, Former Soviet Union programs at the JDC office in New York. He is extremely knowledgeable regarding Russia and Ukraine, as well as the former Soviet republics. Material, listings, photos, and above all advice and skill to navigate the new and wonderful Jewish communities—they were all freely passed on to me. His very capable assistant, Margo Klein, added to the professionalism of this department.

I want to thank Ralph Goldman, honorary executive vice president, American Jewish Joint Distribution Committee, for his illuminating interviews.

In Russia, two very supportive people stand out as being instrumental in interpreting the complexities of Jewish life in Russia's capital. They are Michael Steiner, director of the Moscow office of the JDC, and his very able assistant, Sveta Perlmutter. After I had been long gone from Moscow, they helped with answers to important queries, far and above the call of duty. I owe them both a debt of gratitude.

In Moscow, too, Lev Krichevsky, journalist and professor, who covers the former Soviet Union for the Jewish Telegraphic Agency, aided me in understanding the Russian and Ukrainian scene today. Victoria Motchalova, director of Sefer, Moscow Center for University Teaching of Jewish Civilization, helped me understand Jewish academic life.

In St. Petersburg, I want to thank Natasha Gordina, office manager, and her JDC staff, and Leonid Kolton, director of Hesed Avraham Welfare Center, who answered my questions and supplied information on the Jewish community of St. Petersburg.

In Kiev, I thank Ksenya Avdeeva, formerly of the JDC office, who helped with her knowledge of the community, and Asaph

Jagendorf, then of the JDC office in that city, now of Jerusalem, who was very thorough in guiding me and explaining this historic capital of Ukraine.

In Israel, my thanks must go to Asher Ostrin, director of the FSU (Former Soviet Union) programs of the JDC, who added to my knowledge with an analysis of current events as well as updated information for me. Charles Hoffman, author and JDC area director for the Volga and Ural Mountain region of Russia, gave unstintingly of his precious time by reading several of the chapters in this volume and offering insightful comments, especially on my chapters on Ukraine and Kiev. Also helpful was Marina Fromer, JDC area director for Moldova and southern Ukraine and director of library programs.

In Russia, three rabbis came to my aid in interviews there, and in e-mail correspondence. They are Rabbi Berel Lazar, chairman of the Rabbinical Allaiance of the CIS, Rabbi Menachem Mendel Pewzner, spiritual leader of the Choral Synagogue in St. Petersburg, and Rabbi Pinchas Goldschmidt, chief rabbi of Moscow. They were extremely patient with my many, many questions.

In Ukraine, Rabbi Yaakov D. Bleich, chief rabbi of Ukraine, and Rabbi Moshe Azman, vice president of the Kiev Jewish Community and chief rabbi of the Central Synagogue, both of Kiev, met with me on a number of occasions and introduced me to other members of the community for source material. Their staffs in Ukraine and their colleagues in the U.S. were always on call for clarification and information.

Also in Ukraine, Rabbi David Wilfond, the Reform Movement of Judaism rabbi in Kiev, spent much time sharing with me his experiences as an American rabbi in the city and surrounding area. His interest did not stop after I visited him; we kept in touch via fax and e-mail.

Two special guides not only helped me tour their home cities, of which they are both very proud, but also forwarded information, especially changes or moves of institutions and groups. They are Alla Markova of St. Petersburg and Galina Ryltsova of Moscow. They are excellent and extremely knowledgeable guides, and they understand the needs and anxieties of travelers.

Back in the U.S., Rozaline Kleyman, writer and public relations person, of New York, helped me with research and photos and briefed me on her observations of Kiev, which she also visited in 1998. Winston Beigel of New York City, expert in communications, read and edited several chapters.

My thanks go again to Francoise Bartlett, of Chappaqua, New York, an editorial advisor and consultant who read and edited several chapters and made suggestions; to Joseph Honig, of Valhalla, New York, designer and graphic artist who designed the cover and maps; to Elizabeth Ackley, of Stormville, New York, who keyed in my manuscript; and to brothers Matt Golden and Ross Golden, of Chappaqua, New York, two computer experts who helped me organize my computer files and guide me through the new technology.

For gathering information and historical background, especially on Russia and Ukraine, a difficult task, I am forever grateful to the entire staff of the Chappaqua Library: Mark Hasskarl, director; the reference librarians—Martha Alcott, Carolyn Jones, Paula Peyraud, Jane Peyraud, Carolyn Reznick, Michele Snyder, and Maryanne Eaton; and staff members Marilyn Coleman, Mary McGrath, Peggy Gaillard, Judy Lauder, and Joan Kuhn.

Rita Tavel Fogelman, director of West Nyack Free Library, was very helpful in checking facts and historical background, for which I thank her.

While my entire family helped, I must cite cousins Manual and Natalie Charach of West Bloomfield, Michigan, who not only shared their impressions of St. Petersburg and Vladivostok with me, but took time out of their busy schedule to supply me with maps, photos, and even books. Encouragement always came from my brother, Dr. Ivan C. Frank, and sister-in-law, Malke Frank, as well as cousin Audrey Silverman, who helped with family research.

I am certainly grateful to the following individuals who shared their vast knowledge of Soviet and Russian affairs and the history of Jews in Eastern Europe and Russia: Ambassador Herbert Donald Gelber, who helped me make sense of the complexities of international affairs; Dr. Yaffa Eliach, author and pioneer scholar in Holocaust studies; Jack Wiener, a psychoanalyst in New York, who suggested perspectives regarding Russian psychology; Joseph Rosen, international financial technology consultant at Enterprise Technology Corporation of New York; Yitzchok Fuchs, CPA and international tax expert in New York; Dr. Maurice and Mrs. Marcia Cohen, of Chappaqua, New York, both of whom offered valuable suggestions, read the manuscript, and helped me stay the course; Felix Krasnopolsky, of New York, formerly of Kiev, senior computer programmer, Dmitriy Galin of New York, formerly of Odessa, computer programmer, and Galina Nazarova, of Chicago, formerly of Grozny, translator, all of whom helped me with translations as well as research; Michael W. Ellmann, international securities analyst, New York; Jules Vachon, international financial advisor, New York; Arthur Vinen, formerly of Kiev, now of Florham Park, New Jersey; Dr. Joshua Fogelman, who helped me with sources; Mrs. Linda Zlotoff, member of the Paul Zuckerman Campaign Leadership Series of the Jewish Federation of Metropolitan Detroit, who shared her views of Russia and Ukraine with me; Richard Berman, of Bedford, New York, who was kind to send me much material; and Sarai Brachman, program director of the Charles and Lynn Schusterman Foundation, who helped me with information and photos.

I want to thank travel professionals Bo W. Long, general manager, the Americas, for Finnair and his able assistant, Michelle.

I can only hope that I am not omitting any name. If I am, I apologize. I am especially indebted to the unnamed helpful residents in post-Communist Russia and Ukraine who pointed me in the right direction.

I offer praise and appreciation to Dr. Milburn Calhoun, publisher and president of Pelican Publishing Company, and the entire staff of Pelican. This is our third book together and, as in the past, Dr. Calhoun supported and saw the need for *A Travel Guide to Jewish Russia and Ukraine.*

I owe a special debt of gratitude to my editors at Pelican, especially Nina Kooij, who understands the demanding pressure on an author to meet deadlines and who helped make this book possible. Jim Dunn, my editor at Pelican on this book, guided me all the way through the arduous task of checking facts and revisions and did yeoman service in editing the manuscript. I thank him.

My deepest thanks, of course, go to my family.

My late parents, Nathan M. Frank and Sonya Winerman Frank, and my wife's late parents, Rabbi Solomon Spitz and Jeanette Joskowitz Spitz, were from the former Russian Empire. They inspired my wife Riva and me to learn more and keep alive the traditions of the Jewish people, and this certainly encouraged us to seek out details of our roots. It is also an amazing reward for a father to have two sons who can aid him in such a momentous project. I am deeply indebted to my journalist-writer son, Martin N. Frank, for spending long hours editing the manuscript. I also owe a debt of gratitude to my lawyer son, Monte E. Frank, who represented me in launching the endeavor. Our children and grandchildren, Martin, Jodi, and Randall Stuart, and Monte, Leah, and Rebecca Naomi have been a source of strength to me.

Finally, any author knows how at times, especially as deadline approaches, pressure can become burdensome on one's wife—or husband. As for my wife, Riva, her love and devotion, her encouragement and steadfastness, not only kept my resolve moving on track, but also reinforced what we both knew—that this was a worthwhile project not only for this generation, but for future generations.

Introduction

"Russia, like a bear after a long winter, was awakening within me."

Those bearish desires to visit this massive land grew inside me too, just as they had for Andréi Makine, author of *Dreams of My Russian Summers.*

I soon discovered what many before me had felt; that even if you do not go to that vast country today, one way or another, mentally or physically, you will eventually journey to Russia, either as a jet or cruise ship passenger, or as an armchair traveler.

This is especially so if your parents, grandparents, or great-grandparents, like mine, were born in the Russian Empire which, before 1917, included Poland and the Baltic countries. You will want to see this land where they lived, this land of the tsars, land of the Reds, land of post-Communism, this land which slightly more than a century ago contained the largest Jewish community in the world.

I also heard an additional inspiring inner voice that moved me and that I hope will inspire you, the reader: "There are still Jews in Kasrilivke," that little Jewish town, that *shtetl* which is all Jewish towns. Despite seventy years of communist oppression, Judaism had not died in Russian and Ukrainian provinces, towns, cities, and villages such as Zhitomir, Vinnitsa, Tomashpil, Berdichev, Kiev, Moscow, St. Petersburg, and Odessa—places whose very names quickly retrieve from memory those stories of the Sholom Aleichem town and city.

With the 1991 fall of Communism, desire became reality. I made several trips to Russia and Ukraine and wrote *A Travel*

Guide to Jewish Russia and Ukraine for the person searching for their roots, for the tourist who wants to see the world, for the businessperson, for the armchair traveler, for those interested in Russia and Eastern Europe, and for those people who want to know more about Jewish communities around the world.

Like countless others, I had lived through the Cold War and marched under the banner "Save Soviet Jewry." Now I discovered that any visitor to the former USSR with even the slightest feeling of history can witness the miracle of the revival of Jewish life in the land from whence many of our grandparents and parents emigrated.

This practical, anecdotal, and adventurous journey through historic Jewish Russia and Ukraine, including synagogues, kosher restaurants, cafés, and museums, plus cultural and heritage sites, will guide the visitor to the Jews of Russia and Ukraine.

With this volume, you can also embrace Russia's fantastic history. You can inhale its culture, its Byzantine sites, its mysterious cities, its art and music, and its wonderful collector's paradise of museums, such as the Hermitage in St. Petersburg. You will learn about the Kremlin Wall, the May Day reviewing stand, expansive Red Square, Pushkin's statue in Moscow, the Potemkin Steps in Odessa, and the green hills of Kiev. View them now without fear; they beckon you.

My wish for travelers or armchair travelers is that they know what Russia has been, what it is today, and what it might be tomorrow. Despite its plunging into a deep economic depression, Russia is still with us.

For the Jewish, and for the non-Jewish tourist, too, meeting the Jews of Russia can be an inspiring aspect of your trip; it can be spiritually and mentally rewarding. Since 1991, the Jews of Russia and Ukraine have been liberated, free to attend religious services, to send their children to a Hebrew day school, to read a Hebrew newspaper, to light the Sabbath or Chanukah candles, and to emigrate and not worry about retribution.

There are functioning synagogues, Jewish community centers, Hillel houses, kosher restaurants, and Hebrew day schools. No this is not London, Paris, or New York, with the well-equipped, mammoth Jewish community centers, for example, that dot the landscapes there. Russian institutions are modest, at best. After decades of "Let My People Go," of pleading and praying for their release, the Jews of Russia and Ukraine were reunited with Jews all over the world, and now they are building their own religious and cultural centers. Today, Jews can meet openly with Jews.

Before 1989, I had hesitated to go behind the Iron Curtain. But with the crumbling of the Berlin Wall and the sudden implosion of the USSR, I felt I had to get there. I wanted to report to you, my readers, on the status of the Jewish people in the land of our fathers and mothers, our grandfathers and grandmothers.

Other forces greater than even the bearish awakening of seeing Russia moved me. I felt I wanted to continue in the path of my near-namesake, Benjamin of Tudela, that twelfth-century Spanish Jewish rabbi who traveled throughout the then-known Jewish world, reporting on Jewish communities, their size, their community structure, the location of their synagogues, their rabbis, and their relations with their country of residence and the citizens therein. After writing *A Travel Guide to Jewish Europe* (2nd edition, Pelican Publishing, 1996), which covered Europe up to the Soviet border, I felt I wanted to move further east.

In the new millennium, the largest Jewish community in the world is located in the United States of America. A century ago the "greatest Jewish center of the Diaspora" was part of the vast Russian Empire.

If you are interested in the roots of your family, you probably want to know about the Russian Jewish community—how it lived, how it survived, its contributions, its writers and artists— in short, its people and its history. This volume, like *A Travel Guide To Jewish Europe,* gives you the background and description of Russia and Ukraine in the last five hundred years, the time of Jewish involvement. I follow my pattern of discussing aspects of Russian and Ukrainian Jewish history at various general sites and at various Jewish and non-Jewish sites in the former Soviet Union, whether they be Babi Yar, in Kiev; the Choral Synagogue in St. Petersburg; the Kremlin Wall in

Moscow; a small but excellent kosher apartment-restaurant in Moscow; the famous steps in Odessa; or one of the other interesting sites to be found and enjoyed.

The cities, towns, and villages of Russia and Ukraine are virtual "yellow pages" of American Jews, whose last name is often the name of a town or a derivation of an immigrant ancestor's name. There are Kamenets, Podolsky, Tapolsky, Tulchin, Chmielnik, Nemirov, and Lutsk or Lutsky, just to name a few.

For the first time in nearly a century, American Jews have an opportunity to travel to the former Soviet Union, to their roots. You can visit the towns where your grandparents lived; and where they were buried. Fortunately, not all synagogues or cemeteries were destroyed by time, by the Communists, or by the Nazis. True, sometimes the boundaries of your province may have changed. For example, a large chunk of today's Ukraine was in Galicia, which before 1917 was ruled by Austria, then Poland, and is now part of Ukraine. An enormous amount of records from tsarist times exists. Assisted by archivists or private research companies, you can trace your family history. In many cases, Jewish organizations and leaders are willing to help. You will find resources in this book for the search of your roots.

Russia and Ukraine today are accessible. They are not "on the other side of the moon." Never before, in thousands of years, has Russia been so close, so open to the world. Five cities in the Ukraine have direct flights every week to Israel. One ship leaves Odessa each week for Israel. Red tape is gone. Controls on where you can or cannot visit are gone. The woman who sits in the hall on your floor, who outwardly used to collect your hotel key when you went out, but in reality spied on you, is gone or she is just collecting your key. Relax! "Big Brother" no longer gazes on you, nor do KGB cameras spy.

No one had to tell me of my roots. Most American Jewish mothers and fathers or grandparents emigrated from what was the old Russian Empire, an empire that included Ukraine, Belarus, parts of east Poland, and Russia. I, for one, am the son of "an Odessa mama," whose name, Sonya, is as Russian as Elizabeth is English.

My parents were young when they arrived in America, and

The author's maternal grandmother and her children were photographed in Odessa, Ukraine, probably around 1916. Grandfather is not in the picture for like many, many others, he had left for Canada to find a cantorial position and would bring the family over later. From left to right are: (first row) Aunt Ann, Sonya (the author's mother), Grandmother Zlota, and Aunt Lil; (second row), Aunt Clara and Uncle Mischa. Uncle Mischa would later run away and join the army and disappear forever. The family emigrated to Canada in the early 1920s. (Photo credit: Audrey Silverman)

This is a view of part of the town of Tomashpil, in the Ukraine, the birthplace of the author's father. The town was a shtetl. *There are still a half-dozen Jews living here.* (Photo credit: Michael Katz)

they never really went into great detail about Russia, though I am told that as a baby I knew all the Russian songs, and sang them pretty well; after all, I am the grandson of a cantor who sang in the finest synagogues of Odessa before World War I. My mother was born in Odessa, that unique, almost Mediterranean port city. Before coming to America, she and her mother and sisters hid in the cellar from the Bolsheviks, she once told me. Their diet often consisted of only bread and garlic. The family talked about a brother who, as the story goes, ran away to join the army, and vanished forever in that void of World War I and the Russian Civil War. My grandfather, the cantor, had sailed for Canada in 1914, and the family was to be reunited immediately. But World War I and the Revolution interfered, so my grandmother sent her oldest daughter, my Aunt Clara, to find him. She was then all of seventeen. But that is another story. The family eventually was united in 1921 in Winnipeg, Canada, and later moved to Pittsburgh, where I was born.

My father is from a *shtetl* called Tomashpil, a five-hour drive southwest of Kiev, and south of Vinnitsa. An infant when he left Tomashpil, he obviously had little recollection of this Ukrainian childhood *shtetl* that to this day has about a half-dozen Jews.

Most people I talked to want to know more of their own background story. The reasons are obvious.

Travel within Russia is better than ever. New private airlines fly on time. For example, I found Finnair to be comfortable and convenient, with immediate connections in Helsinki to St. Petersburg and Moscow. The airline Transaero can fly you to many Russian cities. People enjoy the train experience of the beeline overnight from St. Petersburg to Moscow. City subways are efficient; art in the Moscow subway stations is a must-see.

Despite the economic meltdown, the financial crises, and the devaluation of the ruble, as well as inflation, the dollar still goes a long way in Russia. The country is not falling apart. Sure, there are difficulties, but things are coming together, albeit slowly.

There is crime in Russia. But there is less chance of being held up at gunpoint in Moscow than in some U.S. or European

This is Tomashpil, Ukraine, the birthplace of the author's father. Some visitors say the area has not changed much since the days when the Freiden (or "Frank," as it became in America) family emigrated, probably around 1908. (Photo credit: Michael Katz)

cities. Safe travel principles are valid in every metropolitan Russian city, just as they are in Manhattan or in Chicago. In this book I have included some tips for the traveler to Russia.

Hotels are improving. They are better managed and at least one person behind the reception desk speaks English. Gourmet restaurants in the Russian capital have proliferated and have even reached New York prices. The food in the first-class hotels and restaurants is excellent.

To travel to Russia and Ukraine, a tour group, or several couples together, may be the ideal situation. Fortunately, there are good guides who can show American tourists the general and Jewish sites. I have listed several near the end of chapters on St. Petersburg, Moscow, and Kiev.

You too will realize that Russia and Ukraine are wonderful destinations for the Jewish and non-Jewish tourist. If there ever was a country where tourists—once they push aside the mystique, the rumors, the old images, and the distance—will expand their horizons in our global village, this nation is certainly it. Once a traveler decides not to psychoanalyze Russia but to view it as an experience and inhale the atmosphere, he or she will not only gain knowledge but will also understand the world better. Remember, this country is one-ninth of the world's landmass.

The best reason to visit Russia, though, is the chance to observe a fascinating society with rich culture and traditions as it goes through a period of monumental change. A walk around the Kremlin cathedrals and museums, a ballet performance at the Bolshoi, a concert at the Conservatoire, and a tour of the Tretyakov Art Gallery are still the real joys of Moscow, to say nothing of the spectacular Mariinsky Theatre and Hermitage Museum in St. Petersburg. "Such treats will be good for the spirit and soul," stated the *Financial Times* of September 1998.

It is true that these are lean times in the former Soviet Union. But now Russian citizens, if they have the money, can purchase almost anything they need. Under Communism, one could hardly find anything. In Russia and Ukraine, tourists will certainly find ample food. However, except for the first-class establishments, it may mean a great deal of fried food, potatoes, pancakes, and soup. Kosher meals will satisfy the traveler. And at every meal, bread. As the Russians say, "bread is the beginning of everything." You may even find food you will like outside of the big cities. The best meal I had on one wintry trip to Russia was in a small hotel in a former capital of Russia, Vladimir, where soup was the order of the day.

For the first several years after World War II, Europe, which had been in ruins, rose as a phoenix, but still suffered economic hardship. But people still visited Paris, London, Rome, and Amsterdam. Tourists realized that cities were in poor physical shape, their citizens tired and hungry and weary, but the beauty and history were still there, and that is why they flocked to these areas. Russia may be in a similar situation today. Besides, as historian John Lawrence said, "Russian chaos is seldom quite as bad as it looks."

The Russian poet Tuitchev said that Russia could not be known by the mind alone, that no ordinary yardstick can measure her. She has a unique dimension. In Russia, one can only believe.

The Russians have a wonderful custom: Before embarking on a journey, they sit down on their suitcases in a closed room. They remain seated for a few minutes in silence, without looking at each other. Then on to the journey. Perhaps for you, too, Russia, like a bear after a long winter, is "awakening" within you.

So, let us begin. As the Chinese say, the journey of a thousand *li* begins with the first step.

A TRAVEL GUIDE TO
JEWISH RUSSIA & UKRAINE

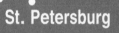

St. Petersburg

MOSCOW

RUSSIA

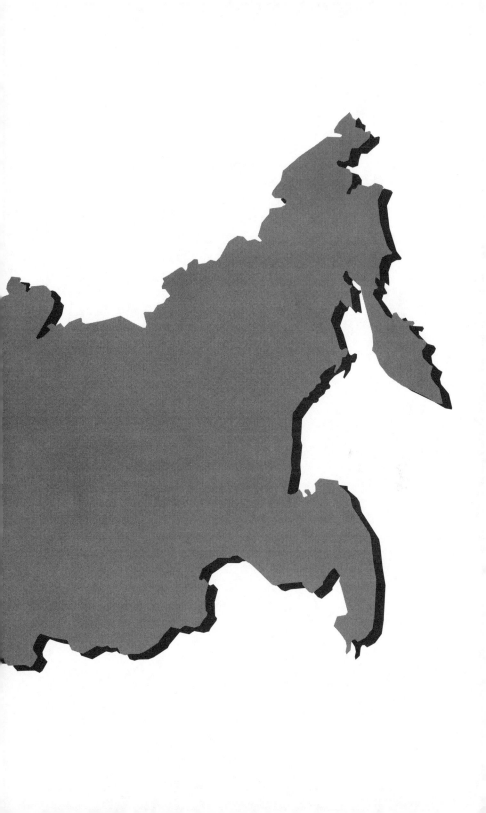

Russia
Never an end in sight

One day Larisa Feodorovna went out and did not come back.
. . . She vanished without a trace and probably died somewhere, forgotten as a nameless number on a list that afterwards got mislaid, in one of the innumerable mixed or
women's concentration camps in the north.

Boris Pasternak, *Dr. Zhivago.*

"In the 1970s I attended a seance and I asked the ghost, 'Will
I be alive when the Soviet regime collapses?' The ghost
answered 'Yes.' I laughed and laughed. Neither I nor anyone
else in the room believed it."

Victoria Motchalova, as told to the author.

"And where do you fly to, Russia? . . ." The carriage bells break
into an enchanted tinkling, the air is torn to shreds and turns
into wind, everything on earth flashes past, and, casting worried, sidelong glances, other nations and countries step out of
her way.   Nicholai V. Gogol, *Dead Souls.*

"Russia, it's not a country, it's a whole world. You travel and
travel and there's never any end in sight," declares a character
in Ilya Ehrenburg's novel, *The Storm.*

Indeed it is so.

Russia covers 6.5 million square miles, one-ninth of the world's
total land area. It measures 6,000 miles west to east—ten time
zones—and 2,800 miles north to south.

Russia, with a population of 148 million people, is three-quarters the size of the former Soviet Union. Canada, the world's second-largest nation, would fit almost twice inside the borders of today's Russia.

Only two countries, Turkey and Kazakhstan, include territory in both Europe and Asia. The European part of Russia could easily swallow the next five largest European nations, while Asiatic Russia alone could neatly hold both China and India, the second- and third-largest nations on that continent.

Russia borders on eight European countries and three Asian nations: Norway and Finland to the northwest; Estonia, Latvia, Belarus, and Ukraine to the west; Georgia and Azerbaidzhan to the southwest; and Kazakhstan, Mongolia, and China along the southern border.

While it is true that Russia inhabits three global neighborhoods—China, the belt of former Soviet Republics, and Europe—size and population are not the only factors that count in the twenty-first century. Russia contains the world's largest and most unique supply of untapped natural resources. It boasts that it possesses some 40 percent of the world's natural gas reserves. For years it was the largest producer of oil and second-largest producer of gold. No one knows exactly how much untapped wealth it will discover.

Read Russian history or talk to Russian scholars, and you will realize that this rough land and harsh climate, alongside the theme of violence and the threat of violence, played and will continue to play a large part in Russian history, points out David Remnick, editor of the *New Yorker*, who adds, "the Russians had inherited a legacy of terror, xenophobia and lawlessness. Even today no political decision is made in Russia without setting off an explosion of conspiracy theories."

"I know of no nation which has collected more injustices for itself than has Russia," says Daniel Rancour-Laferrier in *Slave Soul of Russia.*

In her book, *Aleksandr Blok: A Life,* Nina Berborova called Russia "the land of frustrated destinies."

"No people on earth were so long-suffering and so devoid of sense as the Russians. Their patience knew no bounds. Any abominations, any filth dished out to them, they would lap up with nothing but reverent gratitude toward their beloved bene-factor," the great Russian author Aleksandr Solzhenitsyn wrote in his novel, *Lenin in Zurich.*

The words "stoic," "suffering," "mysticism," "resiliency," and "survival," keep popping up in descriptions of Russia and her people. Russians have been beaten down by foreigners and by their own rulers, by the Turks, by Ivan Grozny, by Peter the Great, by Nicholas I, by the tsarist police, by the Bolsheviks, and by the German occupation. "All this seems to have instilled into them such a deeply rooted fear of authority," notes A. Anatoli (Kuznetsov), the author of the novel *Babi Yar.*

A crisis is nothing new for Russia. "The Russian people tend to put up with difficulties for a long time before suddenly exploding. There is smoldering discontent just beneath the sur-face," wrote Librarian of Congress James Billington.

"It is a strange and peculiar history," commented novelist Alexei Tolstoy regarding his country. "Great bursts of ideas, vast enterprises of worldwide scope," a theme repeated by Yuri Luzhkov, the mayor of Moscow, in the *New York Times,* on February 23, 1999. "Russian life has never been continuous but is a kind of series of outbursts followed by periods of doing nothing."

"Impossible," points out author Harlow Robinson, "to make sense of what is not a sensible country. One has to embrace all of Russia's impossible contradictions, her mystery, her preten-sions and charm."

The country remains unpredictable. It is capable of wild swings from left authority to right strongman rule. Do we need more proof than the collapse of the mighty Union of Soviet Socialist Republics? "That an ostensibly advanced industrial nation and superpower should collapse without any large-scale military defeat, after 45 years of peace, and essentially from internal causes, is unheard of in modern history," wrote Martin Malia, author of *The Soviet Tragedy: A History of Socialism in Russia, 1917-1991.*

The reasons for the demise of the USSR are endless: the internal decay, the corruption of the Communist Party bosses, the fact that the military and civilian economy could not keep up with the U.S. in pouring out huge amounts of funds for such ventures as "Star Wars" missile defense system, the entrance of Mikhail Gorbachev and *perestroika* and glasnost, and the fact that Gorbachev did not send Red Army troops or tanks to squash protestors—all these were factors in bringing down the Berlin Wall and the Communist way of life in the East European regimes, and helped destroy the Soviet Union.

There are those who believe that without Mikhail Gorbachev, the Cold War might never have ended. Some say Gorbachev and company did not really understand the depth of Soviet structural weakness or have a clear vision of where his reforms were leading. They thought that *perestroika* and glasnost would revive the system; but in reality, it discredited the myths that held it up, according to historian Martin Malia. A Russian proverb got it right: "A dead fish rots from the head." In *Cold War: An Illustrated History, 1945-1991,* State Department analyst Raymond L. Garthoff said of Gorbachev's role in the abrupt end of the Soviet Union: "He may not have done so alone, but what happened would not have happened without him; that can not be said of anyone else."

The dramatic events of August 1991 flash before us. The Russian tanks pouring into Moscow in a poorly planned and botched coup attempt. Reports coming on the airwaves that Gorbachev was ill and incapacitated at his dacha in the Crimea. Russian Federation President Boris Yeltsin standing on a tank in front of the Russian parliament building in the center of the city and mounting a courageous defense of democracy. The coup leaders hesitating to attack the crowds around the White House, (the Russian parliament building). The troops not firing on the demonstrators. Then, within a few days, the coup leaders giving up, and an exhausted Gorbachev flying back to the capital. "The sinister plot of the drunken adventurers had completely transformed the political scene," pointed out author Ronald Grigor Suny in *The Soviet Experiment.* In the eyes of the public, the Communist Party and its ideology had been completely discredited. Gorbachev, in effect, was out, and the Communist Party dissolved.

In that summer of 1991, three young people, one of them

Jewish, were killed by an armed personnel carrier moving toward the White House in support of the coup. At the ceremony honoring them a few days later, Zinovy Kogan, head of the Congregation of Progressive Judaism, also known as the Progressive Synagogue, Hineini, of Moscow, would recite the Kaddish, the mourner's prayer, probably the first time in the long tortuous history of Russia that a Jewish prayer was uttered at a public gathering.

The Red flag over the Kremlin came down for the last time on December 25, 1991, when Gorbachev read his farewell address on television. Communist Russia ceased to exist. In its place came a peaceful anti-Communist Revolution. Perhaps we should call it the Third or Fourth Russian Revolution of the twentieth century, depending on how you count. Actually, the years 1986-1991 often are referred to as the "Gorbachev Revolution."

Two years later, viewers the world over saw the scorched remains of the Russian White House after a siege was ordered by Boris Yeltsin, then president of Russia. Just before the shelling, President Yeltsin had dissolved the Communist-dominated Parliament and a showdown began. He had called Parliament an armed "Communist-fascist mutiny." Russian army artillery then blasted the building, setting it on fire, and the Parliament faction, which had resisted, surrendered. President Yeltsin would lead Russia in its transition to democracy and in its attempt to jump-start capitalism. He went on to win a significant presidential election in 1996. But the financial battery energizing the economy went dead two years later, and Yeltsin's health and popularity plummeted. And yet he held on.

Nevertheless, gone is the "dictatorship of the proletariat," gone is the police state, gone are state control and censorship of the press, gone are the indiscriminate arrests, gone are the fixed elections. The Russians may stumble. They certainly will slip and slide, but as far as can be told, almost everyone agrees they never will return to the old Soviet regime. As they look on the present, you can be assured Russians are keeping an eye on the past, a past that so terrifies them.

This is not your usual Western European nation, steeped in

democratic tradition. Forget any enlightenment, or any basis of English law. Muscovite Russia could not summon a tradition of Russian law. A foundation of Western-style legal order never existed. That is why, when visiting the former Soviet Union, and when talking to Russians or Ukrainians, Jews included, one must always keep in mind that this country, except for a few months, has never experienced representative government, never defended freedom of the press, nor completely allowed freedom of religion. The state possessed overwhelming power, and individuals were forced to depend on it. Paternalism reigned.

Always remember as you experience this country, that its development as a civil society was interrupted by the Bolshevik Revolution and seventy years of Communist dictatorship and terror. As Jack F. Matlock, former U.S. ambassador to Russia, wrote in the *New York Times Book Review,* on April 11, 1999, "When the Communist dictatorship collapsed under the weight of its own contradictions and irrationality, Russia was left more backward socially and institutionally than it had been in 1914. Developments since 1992 can be properly understood and assessed only with that heritage in mind."

It has been said the Russians always seem to be weak, always seem to struggle, always seem to be afraid, always seem to fear rebellion, and at the same time always seem to be ready to revolt against a Moscow or St. Petersburg autocratic center.

"Russia may remain stubbornly true to its authoritarian traditions. The Russian government will probably continue to make domestic and foreign policy without the people's participation and to foist executive decisions on a largely powerless and apolitical population," according to Albert Weeks, writing in *Foreign Affairs.*

While one could debate the strength of democracy in Russia today, we still must be thankful that the police state has disappeared. Television and radio stations and newspapers are free to report the truth. People do not cower or cringe at officialdom. Political demonstrations take place. People are not arbitrarily arrested and sent to the gulag. People vote in free elections.

But Russia and Ukraine are places where "everything is suddenly up for grabs, at least until the future reveals itself," wrote reporter Stephen Holden in the *New York Times,* May 1, 1998.

At the end of the twentieth century, Russians are still restless. They are haunted and humiliated by their loss of empire. The unfortunate Russian people have always been exploited by the ruling classes, including the elite members of the Communist Party hierarchy of 1917 to 1991, who reigned supreme with special department stores, special food stores, special privileges, special cars, and dachas (country houses), all in the name of the "dictatorship of the proletariat." Some pigs were more equal than other pigs, as author George Orwell noted. And the corruption that existed among Soviet officials continued with the downfall of the USSR; the shift to capitalism made many government officials rich overnight.

Even more than one hundred years ago, people who wanted to show how good it was to live in the West would use Russia as an example of a non-democratic nation. Did not Marquis de Custine, French observer of the Russian scene, write that if one really wanted to understand liberty, one should visit Russia? "If ever your sons be discontented with France, try my recipe, tell them to go to Russia. It is a journey useful to every foreigner; whoever has well examined that country will be content to live anywhere else."

Short of war, there are few things worse for any country than to be hit with an economic depression. Severe financial crisis can destroy a government—witness Russia in 1917 and Germany in 1933. The decade of the 1990s has seen an economic downturn in the former Soviet Union worse than the Great Depression of the 1930s in the U.S. "After Communism, few people have ever suffered in peacetime as rapid and extensive a decline of power and standard of living as did the Russians after the collapse of Communism," wrote James H. Billington.

The bubble burst in Russia on August 1998, "choking off the banks, wiping out savings and sending the ruble on a new downward spiral," noted Serge Schamemann, correspondent, in the *New York Times Magazine,* December 27, 1998. The ruble lost two-thirds of its value in a single week that August. Major banks went into bankruptcy; imports ceased; many foreign businesspeople left; and many investments were wiped out. Russia was broke. Yet they managed to get through the winter of 1998-99. Still, for the government to hold on, Russia will have to meet the International Monetary Fund's requirements for debt-relief programs.

Hanging over the Russian people today is economic stagnation. A complete collapse of Russia would "threaten the U.S. in many ways," wrote foreign correspondent Jane Perlez in the *New York Times,* January 26, 1999. She cited Russia's increasing its output of nuclear arms, a turn toward authoritarian rule, and an inability to control uprisings in neighboring countries.

"You can't eat democracy," some Russians say. It does not take long for an electorate to become disillusioned. Even today, there is a growing disrespect for authority and a rise in political assassinations. The gap between rich and poor widens. Rubles intended for workers disappear without a trace, as local officials siphon them off for themselves, it is alleged. By the end of 1998, many workers had not been paid in two years. Burnout, malnutrition, lack of medical facilities, and non-payment of wages were all a part of the political scene in the late 1990s. There have been numerous reports of corruption in high places. Privatization in Russia has become a fierce and ugly battle for power and economic position, a battle that has put severe strains on the economy, said some. It was not clear if privatization would continue and at what pace, though the government promises it, as well as reform of the tax system and payment of back wages.

We know Russians possess a well-known ability to endure both disappointment and hardship. After all, many Russians exclaim, there is very little they can do about it anyway. The dream of good living dissolved in August 1998, and life became scraping for enough money to get through each day. The middle class was hard hit and there are many Jews in the middle class.

What went wrong?

Were reforms too slow?

Was corruption too deep?

Had the International Monetary Fund and Western governments given bad advice or insufficient assistance?

Jeffrey Sacks, a professor of economics at Harvard University and economic advisor to President Boris Yeltsin from 1991 to January 1994, said Russia simply "lacked the historical knowledge and trained personnel to manage a market economy."

At century's end, Russia seems to flounder between some form of free-market capitalism and statism. Low birthrate and a declining life expectancy characterize the country. The average male life span is less than fifty-eight years in a nation where the diet and medical care have never matched Western standards. In Israel, men will live into their late seventies. Certainly tension and stress, perhaps more than even during the Communist era because of the anxiety caused by the economic plunge, have contributed to early deaths among males. Increased use of alcohol in a country facing an even bleaker life has also lowered the male life span.

A survey warns that by 2015 only 15 to 20 percent of babies will be born in a healthy condition. According to one expert with the Russian Parliament, there are now more than 4 million homeless children in Russia, more than after the 1917 Bolshevik Revolution and the ensuing Civil War. At the end of the twentieth century, according to the *New York Times*, "living standards in Russia were falling even more rapidly than previously believed, with almost one in three people now residing in poverty. In the 1990s, more than 44 million of Russia's 148 million people live below the poverty level, defined as less than $32 a month, and 8.4 million are without jobs." And *Agence France Press* reported that 2 million Russian children lack families and almost two-thirds of those live in the street.

Along with domestic problems and economic meltdown, the Russians are angry when left out of the loop of international affairs. "Sensitive" is a key word in understanding Russia. True, they do not have the power they once heralded. They seem to say, "We may not be a superpower, but we are important and you should listen to us." When NATO expanded and took in the Central European countries of Poland, Hungary, and the Czech Republic, "the Russian political elite took this as a sign of indifference to Russian sensitiveness at best, and the beginning of a campaign to exclude, isolate, and humiliate the new Russia at worst," wrote Michael Mandelbaum, director of the Project on East-West Relations at the Council of Foreign Affairs, in his book *The New Russian Policy*. Russians may not have wildly waved their sabers when NATO expanded, but there is no doubt that they felt threatened. Over the past ten years, Russia has suffered "wounded pride" at its loss of international status. Much that has guided its foreign policy in 1999 is an attempt to regain at least their diplomatic status as a major power.

Russians resent what they perceive as the U.S. doing as it wishes, without any "strong international checks and balances, at a time of Russian weakness," writes Jane Perlez in the *New York Times*, January 26, 1999. The war in Serbia in the spring of 1999 caused a chill in the West's relations with Russia. Public opinion in Russia was pro-Serbian and anti-NATO.

Not since the Soviet days had there been such growing tension between Russia and the Western alliance as there was over the bombing of Yugoslavia by NATO. Russian sympathy for the Serbs brought out Russian rhetoric against bombing, as well as anti-West voices in the former Soviet Union. Yet President Boris Yeltsin's government signaled it had no intention of getting involved militarily in the conflict. On the contrary, Russia moved to the forefront—with U.S. prodding, no less—to broker a political settlement, and tried to convince the two sides to come to a peaceful compromise. Russia's wounded pride was salved somewhat as the Russians moved once again to a high state of world diplomacy. "Constructive Russian diplomacy was crucial to avoiding a bloody ground war and securing a just peace," opined the *New York Times*, on June 19, 1999. After the war ended a few weeks later, the U.S. and Russia began to patch up differences and put their relations on an even keel.

"While the first post-Soviet years saw a generally pro-Western tilt in Moscow's intentional dealings, Russian foreign policy has become less accommodating or predictable than it was," wrote Gary C. Hufbauer, of the Council of Foreign Relations. One student of Russian history told this writer the word to use in describing the foreign policy of Russia is "pretentious." But Russian thoughts of provoking the West may be tempered for now not only by their weak military forces, but also because Russia needs financial aid from the U.S. and European countries.

Still, Russian experts such as Michael Mandelbaum caution us not to put Russia on the "back burner." It may be unstable and unhappy, but it is an enormous nation with a large nuclear arsenal, and her neighbors, such as Ukraine, Belarus, and others, look at Russia with a suspicious eye. It took the *Financial Times* of September 8, 1998, to point out that "Russia is on Europe's doorstep . . . and political turmoil in Russia, if it were to follow economic collapse, could bring the threat of social disturbances, mass emigration, or environmental disaster."

Michael Mandelbaum, writing in the May/June 1997 issue of *Foreign Affairs,* argues that "in the wake of the Cold War, the two most important countries for the United States are Russia and China. The reasons for their importance are plain; their size, their economic potential, and their military power. Despite important differences between them, these two nuclear armed, formerly Orthodox Communist countries, pose the same challenges for the U.S."

In the foreign policy arena, diplomats fear an anti-American bloc grouping Russia and one or more of the other Eurasian players; China, Iran, or even France or Germany. Some talk of an alliance of Russia, China, and Iran. Only the twenty-first century will reveal the players. But make no mistake about it—weak or strong, Russia will be a player on the world court. Did not Russian General Aleksandr Lebed say, "the universe will shake once again from the deeds of Russian arms?"

Nations are worried that Moscow will not tighten controls over weapons-grade nuclear materials and expertise. They are concerned that Russia may not be able to stop nuclear leakage to rogue states or terrorists. Russia controls more than 10,000 nuclear weapons and sells arms to anyone who comes up with the cash, it has been reported. In 1999, the U.S. offered to increase its financial aid to Russia to minimize the threat posed by Russian nuclear arms. The money would be used to dismantle warheads and other weapons, and to redirect Russian scientists and scientific institutes into civilian pursuits, according to the *New York Times* of January 19, 1999.

There are many who believe that the future stability of Europe now rests heavily on the consolidation of democracy and free markets in Russia. As writer David Hale put it, "Russia still deserves Western assistance as a defeated but potentially dangerous nuclear power." But he added: "The West, however, has yet to create an effective framework to aid a country whose political institutions are still reeling from 70 years of command economy, mismanagement and a corrupt redistribution of state assets after Communism's collapse."

Still, it seems that the U.S.—realizing that it has a stake in Russia's economic well-being, has decided not to let Russia become a "global financial pariah." That would be too risky, as the *Economist* noted on April 17, 1999.

No one can predict the future of this volatile country. No one knows where it is going. As Michael Wines wrote in the May 2, 1999 issue of the *New York Times,* "Nobody knows what Russia will be in the long run." But after all is said and done, we had better not count Russia out.

A resilient Russia in the past has dodged calamities, and all the predictions of the pundits sometimes do not count when one is dealing with this huge country, especially the politics in this nation when the prime minister may be gone tomorrow. Nor can one predict the outcome of the Duma elections in December 1999 or the presidential elections set for May 2000. Remember, as many have noted, nothing in Russia is simple. Winston S. Churchill had it right when he described Russia as "a riddle wrapped in a mystery inside an enigma."

One of the characters in novelist Alexei Tolstoy's *Road to Calvary* says, "And yet, Russians are an inquisitive lot . . . impressionable. And with heads on their shoulders, too. All they need is knowledge to find the way out of all this Byzantine mire." Many believe they will find that way out.

Meanwhile as Viktor Shenderovich, creator of the popular satirical show, *Puppets,* told the *New York Times,* on October 6, 1998, "as long as no one is shooting at us or sending us to labor camps, as long as we can find food for our children, we just live life as we have always lived . . ." Millions of people in the former Soviet Union get up in the morning, work all day, come home late at night, and go to sleep. They try to live normal, meaningful lives. It may take fifty years or a century for Russia to rise again. But in the meantime, Russia's relations with its neighbors will depend on what kind of country Russia itself becomes, Michael Mandelbaum tells us in his book, *The New Foreign Policy.*

Let us recall that while the Soviet Union was oppressive to all of its people, it was the Jewish community that not only survived but also witnessed its liberation and its redemption as the new Jewish community of Russia, a community American Jews have fought for, have aided, have rescued, and have rejoiced at its new-found freedom. Russian Jews certainly should not be forgotten now.

For years now Europeans have argued that if one must know Russia, one must go to Russia. So, let us begin with an introduction to the Jewish communities that we shall meet on our trip to Russia.

Suggested Reading:

Anatoli, A. (Kuznetsov), *Babi Yar.* New York: Washington Square Press, 1970.

Beizer, Mikhail, *The Jews of St. Petersburg: Excursions Through a Noble Past.* Philadelphia: An Edward E. Elson Book, The Jewish Publication Society, 1989.

Ben-Ami, (Arie L. Eliav), *Between Hammer and Sickle.* Philadelphia: Jewish Publication Society, 1967.

Conquest, Robert, *The Great Terror.* New York: Macmillan, 1973.

Dawidowicz, Lucy S., *The War Against the Jews: 1933-1945.* New York: Holt, Rhinehart & Winston, 1975.

Figes, Orlando, *A People's Tragedy: A History of the Russian Revolution.* New York: Viking, 1997.

Florinsky, Michael T., *Russia.* New York: 2 Vols., Macmillan, 1961.

Freeze, Gregory L., editor, *Russia: A History.* New York, Oxford: Oxford University Press, 1997.

Gilbert, Martin, *Holocaust Journey: Traveling in Search of the Past.* New York: Columbia University Press, 1997.

Goodman, Susan Tamarkin, *Russian Jewish Artists in a Century of Change, 1890-1990.* Munich, New York: Prestel-Verlag, 1995.

Hosking, Geoffrey A., Russia, People and Empire, 1552-1917. Cambridge, MA: Harvard University Press, 1997.

Isaacs, Jeremy and Taylor, Downing, Cold War: An Illustrated History, 1945-1991. Boston, New York: Little, Brown & Company, 1998

Malia, Martin, The Soviet Tragedy: A History of Socialism in Russia, 1917-1991. New York: The Free Press, 1994.

Mandelbaum, Michael, editor, The New Russian Foreign Policy. New York: Council on Foreign Relations, 1998.

Moynahan, Brian, The Russian Century: The Birth of a Nation. New York: Random House, 1994.

Radzinsky, Edvard, The Last Czar. New York: Doubleday, 1992.

Ro'i Yaacov, Jews and Jewish Life in Russia and the Soviet Union. Ilford, England: Frank Cass & Co., Ltd.,1995.

Suny, Ronald Grigor, The Soviet Experiment, Russia, the USSR and the Successor States. New York, Oxford: Oxford University Press, 1998.

Wasserstein, Bernard, Vanishing Diaspora: The Jews in Europe Since 1945. Cambridge, MA: Harvard University Press, 1996.

Wiesel, Elie, The Jews of Silence, A Personal Report on Soviet Jewry. New York: Schocken Books, 1987.

The Russian Jewish Community:
New and thriving!

"I am still very optimistic regarding the Jewish community in Russia. The recent terrible attack on the synagogue and the economic and political crisis are only bringing more and more Jews out of the closet and closer to the community. So yes, I am still as optimistic and I still think Russian Jewry will become one of the strongest Jewish communities in the world."

Rabbi Berel Lazar,
chairman of the Rabbinical Alliance of the CIS.

Several times a day, even during the dark "black days" of Stalinist repression, even during the deep Russian winter, Rabbi Getcher Wilensky would walk up the hill to the then half-century-old synagogue on Archipova Street, open the door of the Moscow house of prayer, and as the day wore on recite the morning, afternoon, and evening prayers.

On the Sabbath, a small number of Moscow Jews, as well as the usual Jewish congregants who served as KGB spy informers, greeted Rabbi Wilensky. He never missed a day during the decades when just entering a synagogue was considered cause for suspicion.

This synagogue never closed. Prayers were always rendered. Judaism did not die in Soviet Russia, and that fact allowed this synagogue to function as a showplace for tourists and dignitaries.

But even though the flame of Judaism never blew out, it was

reduced to a flicker. Jews secretly studied Hebrew, passed *samizdat* secret publications from one hand to another, and clandestinely listened to the Voice of Israel, the Voice of America, and Radio Liberty to absorb uncensored news.

Sometimes the curtains were drawn to hide religious observances. Sometimes they were very open, as on the dramatic occasion when Secretary of State George Shultz attended a Passover Seder in a Soviet Moscow apartment. Soviet Jews wanted the whole world to see that celebration.

Sometimes Jews stood in front of the Interior Ministry raising cardboard signs. The words on the signs demanded the right to emigrate. But their posters were ripped apart by tough, black-jacketed KGB agents. These tactics are no longer used.

Welcome to the new Russian Jewish community. Throughout Russia, Hebrew schools and Jewish universities flourish; Lubavitch communities thrive; soup kitchens feed the needy; and hundreds of kosher butcher outlets serve the community. In addition, Jewish and Yiddish clubs, day nurseries, concerts, Israeli centers, and active Jewish organizations and societies build an infrastructure for a community of more than a million Jews, including those in Ukraine.

Each year, a Jewish Book and Cultural Festival takes place across the vast mass that is Russia, with tens of thousands in attendance. They participate in storytelling sessions, comedy hours, book displays, concerts, poetry readings, and dance recitals. What more evidence of a revival of Jewish life is there than the free display of books with Jewish themes? An annual book fair is called OFEK, a Russian acronym for "Community Festivals of the Jewish Book," which also translates into the Hebrew word for "Horizon."

More than 15 tons of matza were imported in the late 1990s by Lubavitch alone; once, even the baking of unleavened bread was banned in certain cities by the Soviets.

Actually, if you observe any Jewish activity in the former Soviet Union, you can be sure that it is only during the last decade that such an event could take place, or the event may be a first. One example of such an event, as well as an example of the new freedom that Jews feel in Russia, occurred one day in

Moscow to Scott Richman, the American Jewish Joint Distribution Committee's desk director for the former Soviet Union. He tells of an incident that occurred at the Moscow airport as a delegation he was leading was returning to the U.S. Ten extremely enthusiastic Hillel students, who had met the delegation, had come to the airport for a "send-off." "Inspired by the moment," Richman related in an interview with the author, "the students began singing 'Heveinu Shalom Aleichem' at the top of their lungs. I was waiting for the KGB to come swarming down. This was, after all, in the middle of the Moscow Airport. But nobody came. Nobody said anything. I don't know if anybody was looking. But could you have imagined such bold behavior just five years ago? I couldn't. These students had no fear, so they proudly asserted their Jewish identity—for Moscow and all the world" to see.

In Kiev, a Passover Seder was being held in the hall of the former Communist Party Headquarters. When the door of the building was opened to greet the prophet Elijah, an old man walked up to the leader and said he didn't believe in opening the door to the Messiah. To which the leader replied: "If someone were to have told you 10 years ago you would be celebrating the Seder in the former Communist Party Headquarters building, would you have believed it possible?"

In the March 11, 1994 issue of the newspaper *Forward*, Natasha Singer wrote, "barring a political cataclysm, however, Jewish institutional and cultural life is slowly entrenching itself in cities and small towns across Russia." That was 1994. Some six years later Jewish life was definitely "entrenched."

Statistics show that today there are 132 Jewish welfare societies, 40 Jewish day schools, nearly 200 supplemental schools, and nearly 30 Jewish preschool programs operating in the former Soviet Union. More than 50 universities and institutes with Jewish studies programs dot the land.

No longer are Russian Jews trapped behind the Iron Curtain. They are free to decide where they want to live—Israel, Germany, the U.S., or anywhere, for that matter. That brings up the crucial question that reporter Walter Ruby, writing in the *Long Island Jewish World*, February 4, 1994, asked: "Why are

Russian Jews choosing to stay put in an unstable and explosive environment supercharged with anti-Semitism when the doors of the former Soviet Union are wide open and a haven in the Jewish homeland is so readily at hand? And why are many of those who are choosing to leave rejecting Israel in favor of the U.S. and Germany?"

His conclusions then, which in effect could be applied to the present, are that a considerable percentage of the more than 1.5 million Jews in the former Soviet Union are now "much better off financially."

Many of these young people stress that this is their home. Many tell you that, as strange as it may sound, they feel at home in Russia; and yes, they love Russia. They add that anti-Semitism exists everywhere; that they see fascist slogans on the streets of St. Petersburg, swastikas in Germany, and swastikas on Long Island, New York.

One basic reason Jews are staying put is that being a refugee or emigrant is one of the most difficult aspects of life; it is not easy to pick up and leave familiar surroundings and become an alien in another land. They obviously have an affinity for Russian culture. As long as they see an opportunity to make a life for themselves, they will remain. Community and family ties also help bind them, of course.

As staff writer Faygie Levy notes in her article in the *Jewish Exponent* quoting from the statement of Yosef I. Abramowitz, president of the Union of Councils of Soviet Jews, "there are many Jews whose Jewish identity is not very strong and who still see themselves as Russians of Jewish ancestry and who have a stake in the pro-democracy movement. But also on a human level, it's difficult to move." He added that some stay behind to take care of elderly relatives, a wonderful Jewish value.

One observer of the Russian Jewish scene said that in the 1940s and 1950s grandparents knew that their grandchildren would not have it better than they did; but now, they know that their grandchildren will have a better life. Russian Jews have aspirations too, he added.

People often exclaim that the ones who did go to Israel in the beginning of the exodus consisted of the top Jewish lay leaders, including scientists and academicians, leaving a leadership gap. The goal remains to find good leaders, leaders who will keep this community united, who will further organize and galvanize this Russian Jewish community. While the Jewish population is aging—estimates say that 30 to 40 percent are pensioners—there are new Jewish leaders slowly moving into the untested waters of the Russian economy in areas such as media, business, banking, import-exports, and service in the government.

Jews, (some were part Jewish) were among the most prominent Russian politicians associated with economic reform. Many of them are out of office for now, while some were out and have returned. Others are out today, but could be back tomorrow, knowing the nature of Russian politics. For example: **Grigory A. Yavlinsky** is a leading reform economist, head of the Yabloka Party, and probably a presidential candidate in the 2000 elections. **Anatoly Chubais** is a liberal reformer, an advocate of privatization, and indeed a former privatization chief. **Boris Y. Nemtsov,** former governor of Nizhni Novgorod who became the first deputy prime minister in charge of economic reform, is of Jewish origin. He was forced out of the government when the economy collapsed, and Yevgeny Primakov took over as prime minister. **Yakov Urinson,** fifty-two, was promoted from deputy economics minister to head the ministry and to become deputy prime minister, but he was also forced out in the financial crisis of 1998. **Sergei Kiriyenko** was Russia's prime minister in April 1998, and is of Jewish ancestry. Thirty-five years old, he was first placed in the top post by President Boris Yeltsin, then removed. He was described in the press as a "hard-working technician." **Yevgeny Primakov** was named prime minister at the end of 1998, and then forced out in the spring of 1999. Primakov has never spoken about his childhood and has never acknowledged being Jewish. The recently published *Russian Jewish Encyclopedia* and numerous sources in Tbilisi, the Georgian capital where Primakov spent his childhood, say the former prime minister is of Jewish descent, and once had a different, Jewish-sounding last name.

Another word which has come into use in the new Russia is

oligarchy. In Russia, it is used to describe an influential group of Russian businessmen who control the country's leading corporations. Some of them have inordinate influence in government. Some experts say they are not "robber barons," for they take their money out of the country and place it in Swiss banks.

With the fall of the Soviet Union, there obviously existed a power vacuum, and these men stepped right in to fill it. Most of the so-called "oligarchs" are Jewish. In the old Communist days, Jews were not at the top of the Communist Party or in fields such as the foreign ministry or the KGB. Jews were involved in banking, the media, and entertainment. That experience moved them into the post-Communist free market economy, where they used their acumen to gain a foothold in Russian businesses and enterprises formerly owned by the state. As one observer of the Russian scene put it, to think in creative terms in corporate strategy is alien to Russians.

Vladimir Goussinsky and **Boris Berezovsky** are closely connected with the nation's political elite. Berezovsky, a Jewish media, oil, banking, and real-estate tycoon, had a great deal of power because of his close ties with the Yeltsin family when he served as former executive director of the CIS, the Federation of Russian States. In 1999, he was dismissed from that post, and it is unclear what his political future will be, although there are always rumors of a comeback by Berezovsky.

On the other hand, Goussinsky is active in the Jewish community, where Berezovsky was not. As president of the Russian Jewish Congress (RJC), Goussinsky emerged in 1999 as a major Jewish community leader. He also maintains ties with the country's most powerful political leaders. A banker and businessperson, he owns a television network, NTV, and a newspaper. As head of the RJC, Goussinsky, along with the group's executive director, Aleksandr Osovtsov, have hit out at anti-Semitic actions. Goussinsky's television network extensively covered the anti-Semitic remarks of Communist Party Duma member Albert Makashov and Communist Party leader Gennadi Zyuganov. Goussinsky also asked Western governments to cease contact with Zyuganov and others in the Communist Party until they renounced anti-Semitism.

The stereotypical charges leveled by communists and extreme nationalists that Jews control banks and the mass media have gained increased credence in the former Soviet Union. A suspicion of Jews lingers below the surface of Russian politics. "The presence of Jews in high places, more than during any time under the tsars or since the Revolution of 1917, is something that some Russians are depicting as sinister," according to Alessandra Stanley of the *New York Times*, who added, "frustrated with the wrenching economic and social upheaval that followed the collapse of Communism and the Soviet Union in 1991, and spurred on by politicians willing to tap their resentments, many people are returning to a traditional scapegoat, the Jews."

"When economies go bust, when there is a decrease in people's living standards, extremist sentiments in society rise," Aleksandr Shishlov, a Duma member, told the Philadelphia *Jewish Exponent* on April 1, 1999. "Poverty is the best soil for growing communism, nationalism and anti-Semitism."

And that is exactly what happened in 1998 and on into 1999. Anti-Jewish rhetoric, Nazi-style demonstrators, synagogue bombing, and desecration of cemeteries have sown fear among many Jews in Russia. In 1999, the Israelis and the Clinton administration, as well as the American Jewish Committee, the Anti-Defamation League of B'nai B'rith (ADL), the National Conference on Soviet Jewry, and others, voiced concern about the rise of anti-Semitism in Russia. Then-Prime Minister Yevgeny Primakov assured an ADL delegation that his government would take "a very strong stand against any manifestations of nationalism, including anti-Semitism," according to Dr. William Korey, writing in the April 5, 1999 issue of *Near East Report*. "As a whole, the Russian people are not anti-Semitic," according to Shishlov. "But there are some crazy people, and the only way they can survive is to be anti-Semitic."

"By the early summer of 1999, despite the rise in anti-Semitism, Jews did not panic, they would not be cowed," wrote Walter Ruby, journalist, in the *Jewish Exponent* of April 1, 1999. He pointed out that "there is no reason for panic," arguing that "there is little likelihood that the self-styled national patriots will gain sufficient strength to take power here or to threaten the physical safety of Russian Jews."

There are three major international Jewish organizations that head up the drive to aid and galvanize the Russian Jewish community. They are:

The American Jewish Joint Distribution Committee. Almost since its inception in 1914, the Joint Distribution Committee (JDC) has been helping Jews in Russia and Ukraine. During the Russian Civil War, for example, a JDC employee was killed by guerrillas as he traveled to communities in war-torn Ukraine to help feed Jews.

Asher Ostrin, director of the FSU Program for the JDC, tells of another happening. A Kiev Jew once told Ostrin that when he was six years old, a truck came through the *shtetl* where his family lived. A sack of flour was delivered to every home that had a mezuzah. Written on the sack of flour was the name, "Joint." The man turned to Asher and said, "My mother made me promise if I ever met someone from the 'Joint,' I would say thank you." Asher then relates that the man looked up to Heaven and with his hands outstretched, cried, "Mama, I said it."

The "Joint," as it is known, plays a key role in aiding Russian Jewry. The JDC is defined as the major organization serving Jewish communities Abroad. It receives its funds mainly from United Jewish Appeal-Federation campaigns.

In Russia, "the Joint" offers seminars to train people for key leadership roles and also brings delegations from all walks and professions to the U.S. and Israel to study and gain experience, so they can effectively lead the Russian Jewish community. Remember that until 1991 in the Soviet Union there were no leadership or teacher training courses, no schools of social work, and only one rabbinical seminary, and that was in Budapest, Hungary. In addition, the JDC helps sponsor two very important programs of special interest to American Jews.

The first, the Buncher Program, provides a three-week training program in Jerusalem, and is funded by the Pittsburgh philanthropist Jack Buncher, who began the program 10 years ago. The program trains Russian Jewish service leaders.

Potential leaders are identified with the assistance of the JDC and the local Jewish community leadership. Those chosen have to pass psychological and practical tests before they can begin their training.

The second, the Melton Program, prepares senior educational professionals who spend six months in Israel in intensive training in Jewish education. The program is sponsored by the JDC, in cooperation with the Melton Center for Jewish Education of the Hebrew University of Jerusalem. Since the program's inception in January 1993, 74 people have graduated, and the majority have returned to Russia and Ukraine to work in the Jewish community.

There is hardly a Jewish institution in the former Soviet Union that does not receive financial and social services aid from the JDC, whether it be synagogue, welfare center, community center, or day school.

In large cities in Russia and Ukraine, about 35 percent of the Jewish population are senior citizens. In small towns, the figure is from 50 to 60 percent. The recent economic downturn has severely hit Jewish retirees. A pension of $25 or $35 a month would barely buy medicine, clothes, and food, and when prices went up six times in rubles, as they did in the summer of 1998, one can see how large an effect this would have on pensioners. JDC points out that it is aiding 150,000 elderly Jews in 600 different locations in the former Soviet Union.

One often hears that a tradition of philanthropy does not exist in Russia and Ukraine. There, the concept of charity is said to have a "capitalist tinge," and it is difficult to persuade the community to donate money. However, in St. Petersburg, the Jewish community today has encouraged philanthropy among Russian Jewish businessmen.

In Moscow, as we shall see, because the JDC supports and aids Russian Jewry, it has formed a welfare council that allows that body to decide on the distribution of much-needed funds.

A phenomenon floats over Eastern Europe and Russia, and it is this: There probably are as many Jews in Russia today as there were when the mass exodus to Israel began in 1989. How is that possible? The fact is young people are coming out of the woodwork each day and identifying themselves as Jews.

Over and over again, one hears examples of talented people declaring that their mother was Jewish, but they were never exposed to Jewish culture. Thousands and thousands of jews have been left untouched by the rebirth of Jewish life in the former Soviet Union.

During the Soviet era, many tried to hide their Jewishness and/or intermarried. Today, there is no fear to say, "We are Jews." True, they may not be Jews according to *halacha* (traditional Jewish law), which says that to be Jewish you have to be born of a Jewish mother. Difficulties occur when one tries to define who is a Jew. For purposes of returning to the Jewish state freely, you can emigrate if at least one grandparent was Jewish. Yes, you can return to Israel and live there. But being recognized as a Jew is another matter, because Orthodox law is paramount there.

Since the state of Israel was established in 1948, close to 1 million Russian Jews have emigrated to the Jewish state, according to a Hebrew University study. People speaking the Russian language in Israel are now the country's largest single ethnic group, overtaking Arabs and Israelis of Moroccan descent. Russians in Israel now comprise one-seventh of the population. In the 1999 Israeli election, the Russian vote was sought and fought over; the Russians can make a difference in a contest.

The Jewish Agency provides valuable educational services. Hebrew courses and education regarding the birth of Israel, its struggle for independence, its life today, and the celebration of holidays are offered. While aliya (the emigration of Jews to Israel) is its main goal, the Jewish Agency does not just fill out forms, but sponsors activities that educate, instruct, and show Russian Jews a meaningful life.

More than one hundred Israeli *schlichim* (messengers or emissaries), work in about 30 cities throughout the former Soviet Union. A special program called Naaleh has been set up, in which about two thousand teenagers a year fly to Israel for a year of study and to check out the possibility of settling in the country. Until 1999, aliyah had been dropping. According to the Jewish Agency, in 1990, 187,000 Jews left the USSR. In 1991, it dropped to 147,000, and in 1992 to about 65,000. In Moscow, in an interview with the author, Alla Levy, chairwoman of the Jewish Agency there, said that from 1993 through 1997, aliyah consisted of about 60,000 persons a year leaving Russia for Israel. In 1998, it dropped to less than 50,000.

But with the collapse of the economy in the latter part of 1998 and into 1999, 3,687 Russians emigrated in January and February of 1999, compared to 1,877 men, women, and children during the same period of 1998, reported the Jewish Agency.

Most Jews from the big cities—Moscow, St. Petersburg, and Kiev—are staying put. The people who are leaving are those from the small towns and cities. Jews and non-Jews who work with computers or are engineers, businesspeople, or teachers, were doing well financially until the crash of August 1998. By the end of 1998, numerous inquiries were directed by Jews to Jewish Agency offices regarding emigration to Israel.

The Jewish Agency also organized celebrations of Israel's fiftieth anniversary in 1998. Events included entertainment for children, a lottery for a free 10-day trip to Israel, dancing, singing, and fashion shows on three different stages in Moscow's Hermitage Park, according to Lev Krichevsky, JTA wire service correspondent. The agency also offered a disco and exhibitions. "The healthy turnout for the event demonstrates the pride that many Muscovite Jews feel for Israel," he wrote, following his interview with Alla Levy. By the way, the site of the celebration was Hermitage Park, which is located across the street from the Moscow Police Headquarters, another miracle.

The Russian Jewish community joins in numerous activities. Alla Levy noted that that many Russian Jews appeared to be more enthusiastic about the Jewish state's jubilee than Israelis themselves, according to Krichevsky. Jubilee celebrations for Israel were held throughout Russia. Photo exhibits about the history of Israel and non-stop showings of documentaries about Israel were included. Job opportunities in Israel were detailed. Representatives came from Jerusalem, Beersheba, and Haifa. A late-night disco provided entertainment.

The third organization, **Chabad (Lubavitch),** is a very committed organization that has sent rabbis throughout the former Soviet Union and has established and re-established synagogues, yeshivas, schools, and kindergartens.

Unlike the Jewish Agency and the Joint Distribution Committee, Chabad concentrates on religions matters, although they also enter the welfare field. About 90 to 100 Chabad rabbis offer spiritual guidance in about 55 different cities in the former Soviet Union, and are helping build an infrastructure in the community. Chabad is active in the organization known as the Federation of Jewish Communities of the CIS. In these Russian towns and cities, Chabad sponsors more than 35 summer camps, helps feed needy Jews at soup kitchens set up in local synagogues and centers, has established schools and orphanages, sponsors educational programs including lectures, and also sponsors magazines and publications.

Two schools of thought regarding Russian Jewry are on people's minds. One is optimistic, and says that Russia will find its way out of its deep economic slump and malaise. Judaism will blossom anew. In the meantime, because of the situation they are in, Jews should be helped, seen, visited, and encouraged to live a Jewish life. They should also be watched. As the *Jewish Week* newspaper wrote in an editorial on September 4, 1998, "In the 1970s and 1980s, the world Jewish community came together in an unprecedented way to help a Soviet Jewish population held in bondage by the totalitarian government in the Kremlin. While it was the fall of Communism that ultimately freed the Jews, an aroused international Jewish community provided a measure of protection for many. It succeeded in giving human rights a prominent place in the American diplomatic agenda. It may take a similar coming together to deal with the crisis now unfolding in Russia."

The other opinion says that Jews are in danger, that the Jew in Russia will be a scapegoat, with all the attendant consequences. As has been previously mentioned, there are already signs of this anti-Semitic activity. People who hold this view say that all Jews should leave for Israel and other destinations. Included in this group are some American Jews who say Jews should leave Russia as quickly as possible.

But is it not true that Jews should be able to live where they desire, with freedom, without persecution? They and they alone, however, should make the decision as to where they will live.

The fact that the down economy does not hit young people as hard as it does their parents is one reason young Jews stay. Big cities are considered cities of opportunity. In the last analysis, Jews will mold their own destiny by leaving or remaining.

Today the American Jewish community must continue watching out for its brothers and sisters. Israel should also continue to follow events with concern.

During the Communist era, Jews and Russians were poor, but life was stable. It was predictable. It is when we enter the unknown that there is fear, as there is today. "Things that were stable or safe in the past, such as banks, food, could vanish," said Michael Steiner, director of the Joint Distribution Committee in Moscow. From 1919 to 1991, nothing changed; costs for housing, food, medical care, and education were set in stone. Today, there is a lack of security and much greater unemployment, he adds.

No longer are jobs permanent. No longer are monies safe. No longer is there assurance that tomorrow morning when one wakes up the same government will be in place. Democracy must also provide food for the table.

A rising tide of political violence and anti-Semitism will mean a rise in emigration. If the rule of law and civil society breaks down, guarantees of safety and human rights of minorities will go by the wayside. This is the great danger to the Jewish community.

Generally, it is felt that in the days ahead, there may be unrest and instability, but no pogroms. State-sponsored discrimination is gone. Doors are open for Jews in the highest branches of academia, business, and government.

Some newspapers, nationalist groups, and church officials have taken up anti-Semitic actions since the Soviet Union dissolved in 1991. The national government has largely failed to stop offenders, and several local governments have even lent support to these fringe groups.

Anti-Semitism is not new to Russia. Economic downturn leads some to proclaim that problems are caused by Jews in the government, the banking industry, and the media. It is the well-known scapegoating and grassroots anti-Semitism.

Vladimir Zhirinovsky, a rabid anti-Zionist and anti-Semite, and a member of the Duma, is not alone anymore. In the early 1990s, Zhirinovsky, who is reported to have had a Jewish father, Volf Edelshtein, according to David Remnick, editor of the *New Yorker*, shocked the world with his anti-Semitic utterances.

In 1997, a report on anti-Semitism in the former Soviet Union was issued by the Washington-based Union of Councils for Soviet Jews. It noted that in Russia, the state-sponsored anti-Semitism that killed, imprisoned, exiled, and terrorized Soviet Jews for nearly 75 years has been replaced by a more diffused type of prejudice. Earlier, the organization had pointed out that the threat to Russian Jews comes from organized Jew-haters who feel that those who commit these hate crimes will not be arrested and prosecuted by the government.

But in mid-1998, anti-Semitism reared its ugly head when the economy declined. Anti-Semitic remarks in the Duma and the murder of Galina Starovoitova of St. Petersburg, a leading Russian reformer and outspoken critic of extremists as well as a longtime supporter of Jewish causes, fanned the flames.

Russia has a legal statute banning the incitement of ethnic strife. Anti-Semitism has been on the increase ever since the mid-1980s, when President Gorbachev's program of glasnost unleashed all types of grass-roots chauvinism. But it still remains on the fringes of society. "For all the scare talk, Russia's neo-fascist groups are still small and marginal," wrote Celestine Bohlen in the *New York Times* on March 2, 1999. Yet, anti-Semitic rhetoric by ultra-nationalist groups may heat up for the Duma elections in 1999 and the 2000 presidential election.

Future of Russian Jews

The future of Russian Jews is tied up with the future of Russia. Here also, there are two sides of the equation. Most Jews, such as Yuri Edilstein, a Soviet refusenik, and in 1999 a member of the Israeli cabinet, do not believe anti-Semitism is state supported. But the question is, will the government move to quash anti-Semitic outbursts, such as made frequently by members of the Duma?

One Communist said on national television that Jews were "bloodsuckers," and in other interviews added that jewish participation in government, business, and mass media should be subject to a special quota.

Some don't believe there is any future for Jews in Russia and Ukraine. If the economy is good, they will assimilate; if it turns bad, they will face extreme danger, says former refusenik Marina Furman, who compared Russia to Germany in the 1930s, when the scapegoat was also the Jews. In the 1920s and early 1930s, the German economy collapsed and Jews were blamed. Ukrainians and Russians will do the same, goes this conventional wisdom.

There is no doubt that the Russian Communist Party has shown open evidence of ultra-nationalism, including its cousin, anti-Semitism. As noted, in 1998 its leaders refused to officially censure some of its members for anti-Semitic remarks. This implies that there is an endorsement of publicly stated anti-Jewish sentiments.

Throughout the 1990s, incidents of political violence have occurred, and the culprits were rarely caught.

In 1998, Micah Naftalin, national director of the Union of Councils for Soviet Jews, a U.S.-based group that monitors anti-Semitism in the former Soviet Union, noted that because of "a very serious escalation of anti-Semitic behavior," the group had to set up a new infrastructure to monitor human-rights abuses in various provinces throughout Russia and Ukraine. By mid-1999, a number of Jewish groups, including the National Conference on Soviet Jewry, began reacting to the increased level of anti-Semitism in Russia. The conference, for instance, was monitoring the situation and sending out reports on the status of Jews in the former Soviet Union.

But Russian Jews are not a community that will fold easily in the wake of difficulty. They have gone the proverbial whole nine yards, from being the largest and probably the greatest Jewish intellectual and religious center since the Golden Age of Spain to the mass emigration of millions to the U.S. and Israel, including most of the leaders of the Zionist movement and the State of Israel. This is a Jewish community that suffered not only pogroms but also a Holocaust never before witnessed by humankind. Finally, it has seen Stalinist brutality almost wipe out Judaism, and now, in the twenty-first century, it is witnessing the revival of Jewish life in this land.

And we must never forget that for one hundred years and more Jews have been part of a Russian nation that suffered unbelievable losses in two world wars, a civil war, and a brutal dictatorship that snuffed out the lives of even more untold millions. Jews do not live in a vacuum; there is no ghetto, not even really a Jewish neighborhood. Jews are part of the world's largest nation.

Which leads this writer to express the following. It is true that aliyah from Russia and Ukraine is running about fifty thousand to sixty thousand a year, and that in 1999, because of a rise in anti-Semitism, more Jews are studying Hebrew and inquiring about emigration to Israel as their right. But that does not mean this Russian and Ukrainian Jewish community (together, they are still the third-largest Jewish community in the world) will disappear. Over the past few decades, I have traveled far and wide to Jewish communities throughout the world. In those countries, there was talk of dire demographic studies, of Jews leaving for Israel, of observers saying and writing that this or that Jewish community is dead. I never believed any of it, and neither should you, dear reader. The Russian

Jewish community will be with us for a long time. History has enabled our generation of Jews to be able to see with our own eyes the rebirth of a community with a great Jewish heritage. It will be a community that will continue to contribute to world Judaism.

A Brief Jewish History

For most of their history in Russia, Jews have been on the wrong side of the fence. Their life in Russia, at least until 1991, was marked by religious persecution, denial of civil rights, burdens of heavy taxes, painful expulsion, and pogroms, according to author Fran Markowitz, in her book *A Community in Spite of Itself.*

Tsarist policy to the Jews was a policy of destruction verging on economic and cultural annihilation, points out Solomon M. Schwarz in his book, *The Jews in the Soviet Union.* Add to that the losses in World War II, Stalin's "black years," and the denial of human and religious rights, and the picture of the problems Russian Jews have faced is almost complete.

Despite the discrimination, the suffering, the nervousness, and the depression that have been cited as a natural trait of Russians in general and Russian Jews in particular, it can be said that at least up to the Communist era, Jews not only survived but maintained the highest religious and cultural traditions. Five million Jews produced a galaxy of "golden age" writers, artists, religious, and Zionist leaders. Need we mention Sholom Aleichem, Marc Chagall, the Ba'al Shem Tov, the Gaon of Vilna, David Ben-Gurion, and Chaim Weizmann?

Today, the U.S. and Israel contain the two largest Jewish communities in the world. But a mere century ago, the greatest

Jewish center of the Diaspora, the largest and densest concentration of Jews in the world, was situated in Russia, where Jews comprised about 4 percent of the population.

Russian Jewry contained 4 times more Jews than in the Hapsburg Empire, 10 times more than Germany, and 100 times more than France. At the end of the nineteenth century, 1.3 million Jews resided in Austria-Hungary, 600,000 in Germany, and 40,000 in France, according to Albert S. Lindemann.

Of that massive Jewish community, a number of families traced the homes of their ancestors to parts of Russia even before the Russians arrived on the scene. Legend has it that part of the Lost Ten Tribes of Israel lived in Armenia in 721 B.C.

As in other sections of Europe, Jews followed the Greek settlers to the Crimea and set down around the famous Black Sea port cities of Sevastapol and Kerch, beginning around the fourth century. We know of Hebrew inscriptions in the Crimea. As the Roman Empire declined, however, Jews moved into the interior of Russia.

In our chapter on Kiev, we shall see that in the eighth century the Khazars, a Finno-Turkish tribe that had migrated through southern Russia, converted to Judaism. Vladimir, grand prince of Kiev from 980 to 1015, converted to Christianity in 987.

Trouble started, however, when Greek Orthodoxy, imported from Byzantium to Russia, brought with it a "hatred and contempt for the Jews" that lasted far into the Romanov dynasty, according to Chaim Potok, author, in his book *The Gates of November: Chronicles of the Slepak Family.*

In Russian history, there is no shortage of anti-Semitic quotes by Russian rulers, including Ivan IV, who said Jews "have led our people astray from Christianity, and have brought poisonous weeds into our land, and also wrought much wickedness among our people." "Both the Orthodox Church in Russia and Catholic Church in Poland propagated extremely negative images of the Jews that fed into popular stereotypes," points out Ronald Grigor Suny in his book, *The Soviet Experiment, Russia, the USSR, and the Successor States.*

The traveler rightly questions how such a large Jewish mass

ended up in Russia, especially since they were not even tolerated in Muscovy?

During the Middle Ages, a large group of Jews came from Germany and eastern lands to Poland, Lithuania, Belarus, and Ukraine. They fled from Western Europe because of the Crusades, which murdered them, and the Black Plague of 1348-49, which struck them down. Another group emanated from the lands of the Khazars, relates the *Encyclopedia Judaica*.

After Poland and Lithuania took over what was still the territorial bulk of Russia and Ukraine, a huge wave of Jewish emigration enveloped Poland, as well as Ukraine, in the middle of the sixteenth century, especially in the provinces of Volhynia and Podolia. This mass movement laid the foundations at the close of the century for most of the Jewish communities of Ukraine, Belarus, and Russia.

Russia expanded in the seventeenth century. It incorporated Ukraine and vast Siberian lands, as well as territorial gains in the Baltics. Especially during the reign of Catherine II (1762-1796), the Russian Empire annexed most of Poland, Crimea, and the northern Caucasus. That annexation brought a huge population composed of Jews as well as Poles, Tartars, and large groups from the Caucasus.

"There were few Jews in Russia prior to the three partitions of Poland by which Russia automatically acquired the Jews who lived in the annexed areas," states Isaac Levitats in *The Jewish Community in Russia, 1772-1884.*

Along with these partitions and annexations of Poland by Germany, Austria, and Russia—in 1772, 1793, and 1795—the Russians moved southward and westward on into the eighteenth century. With these additions, Russian rulers not only inherited the largest Jewish population in the world, they became their "masters."

Most tsars treated the Jews badly. Even though Catherine the Great realized that Jews were needed to help settle her southern territories, even though she allowed them to move into the vast southern Ukrainian lands, especially the Crimea, and even though she thought herself an enlightened supporter of religious freedom and special privileges to Jews, she, too, restricted Jews' political and economic rights. She also imposed higher taxes on her Jewish subjects and kept them penned in a massive landmass stretching from the Baltic Sea to the Black Sea. We know that territory as the "Pale of Settlement."

For several hundred years in next-door Ukraine, the Polish nobles used Jews as estate managers to collect taxes, and to run the inns, distilleries, and general stores. These so-called "plum jobs," however, would backfire. The way the peasants saw it, Jews served as the hated agents of Polish lords, and since the lords were usually absent, the Jew was on the firing line when that hatred erupted into violence.

Although the tsarist regime discriminated against the Jews and severely restricted their rights of residence, it did not always interfere too deeply in the religious and cultural affairs of the Jewish community. Many Jewish bodies enjoyed a national and religious semi-autonomy, organized principally within the framework of the Kehilah, the "Jewish Community Council."

"This situation allowed the Jewish community of tsarist Russia to develop a meaningful, Jewish life and culture in spite of discrimination and persecution," according to author Joshua Rothenberg in his book, *The Jewish Religion in the Soviet Union*.

The tsarist government never abandoned its secret hope of a mass conversion of Jews. Did not Konstantin Pobedonostsev, advisor to the tsar, assert that one-third of the Jewish people would die, one third would emigrate, and one-third would assimilate (convert) into the Russian population?

If the Russians really wanted the Jews to assimilate, all they had to do, Isaac Levitats tells us, was grant them "full emancipation," as was offered in nineteenth-century Europe. This they never did.

While they attempted to "normalize" the Jewish population on the one hand, tsarist officials would cancel out these measures with harsh rules to crush the "stubborn and recalcitrant lot," once and for all, according to Solomon M. Schwarz, in his book *The Jews in the Soviet Union*.

This restrictive policy, however, supported a bag of contradictions. The tsarist government still had to prove Jews were second-class citizens, and the way to do that was to isolate the

Jews. And that is exactly what Russian rulers did. The law establishing the Pale of Settlement was sent by Catherine the Great to the Senate on December 23, 1791.

"Jews could assimilate into Russian life fully only by ceasing to be Jews, but continually met obstacles when they tried to live as Jews equal to Russians," notes Suny. Not until the first decade of Communist rule (the 1920s) would Jews be allowed to assimilate if they desired.

The Pale of Settlement

The tsars did everything in their power to keep Jews fenced into newly incorporated non-Russian lands. They set up the enclosure called the "Pale of Settlement," a vast ghetto in western and southwestern Russia and eastern Poland and Lithuania. The Pale, which contained over 90 percent of the Jewish population, was not "your usual crowded dark urban ghetto." It was "a permanent apartheid," declares author Orlando Figes. The idea was to keep the Jews, one-ninth of the population, out of Russia.

"The Pale was a larger area than France or Spain. Encompassing 25 provinces, it stretched from the Baltic Sea to the Black Sea, an area of about 750,000 square miles, i.e., 40 times as large as Israel," writes author Albert S. Lindemann. Approximately five million Jews lived in this entrapment of 2,000 towns and cities. Out of bounds to Jews, unless they obtained special permission, were St. Petersburg, Smolensk, Moscow, Kharkov, and Kiev. In 1897, Jews amounted to 11.6 percent of the population of the Pale.

Impoverished Jewish craftsmen, artisans, apprentices, innkeepers, and petty merchants lived in the Pale. And they indeed were poor. Twenty-two percent of all Jews received welfare from the Jewish community, according to historian Martin Gilbert.

Orthodox Jews made up the bulk of Russian Jewry. The mother tongue of nearly 97 percent of these Jews was Yiddish. Orthodox Jews generally fought against any form of enlightenment. "Behind the stubborn attitude of Jewish Orthodoxy was the absolute conviction that secular education was bound to lead Jews to heresy and baptism," observes Levitats.

The Russians forbade Jews from living in rural villages, and those that resided there already were expelled if they did not own their homes.

Millions of Jews would emigrate over the years from the towns of the Pale, mostly to the U.S., Britain, Palestine, and even Argentina, where Baron Hirsch attempted to settle Jews.

A few successful Jewish capitalists managed to hang on, but most Jews survived as small traders. Most historians agree that despite the poverty and pressures of life in the Pale, the years 1835 to 1914 saw a great flourishing of Jewish literary, cultural, political, educational, journalistic, religious, and spiritual activity.

"Kidnappers of Children"

Jews of Russia have always faced inequalities. For instance, Jews were forced to supply proportionately more army recruits than the native population. This one injustice certainly helped propel the vast emigration of Russian Jews. Their children, yes, children, some even under the age of 10 years, were drafted into the Russian Army, certainly not to raise the armed strength of the Empire, but obviously to decrease the Jewish population through assimilation.

More than 75,000 Jewish children were conscripted into the tsar's army between 1827 and 1854, when Tsar Alexander II abolished this decree, according to Rabbi Baruch A. Poupko, writing in the *Jewish Chronicle* of Pittsburgh.

The need to fill the army quota had adverse effects on the Jewish population. Unfortunately, the Jewish community created a breed of "child snatchers," whose sole occupation was to snare children and haul them into conscription centers.

Specially trained press gangs, known popularly as kidnappers or *khappers,* searched through the villages and hamlets and seized youngsters in their homes. The burden fell to the poor and working class, according to author Isaac Levitats. In short, Jew had to coerce Jew; rich Jew fought poor Jew. Since one-half of the Jews lived in cities, one-third in towns, and one-sixth in villages, notes Jewish historian Simon M. Dubnow, some parents hid their children in other villages, some parents hid their children in the woods, and some let their children mutilate their own bodies intentionally to avoid military service. These young kids would amputate fingers or blind themselves. Some mothers would hold her son's finger under the carving knife of a clumsy operator, according to Dubnow. The Russians believed barracks life would breed a new generation of Jews who would discard their nationality and become "Russianized." Perhaps they might even be baptized. But these children and teenagers apparently "would not betray the faith of their fathers. They would divorce their young wives prior to entering services so that their wives would not be doomed to permanent widowhood."

Overall, the bulk of Russian Jews did not fight back against these cruel measures of the tsar and the bureaucracy. A pacifist attitude clearly dominated the *shtetl.* "Talmudic conditioning for the entire two thousand years of the Diaspora urged the Jew to adopt a passive posture when it came to his own defense. Survival in exile became associated with non-aggression, and for centuries Jews would permit themselves to be burned, murdered, and otherwise assaulted in an enduring persecution," says author Sol Gittelman. The spirit of the ghetto told the Jew to hide if possible. It was futile to attempt to raise your fist in defense, and furthermore, it was against the strictures of the Talmud.

The sky brightened somewhat with the rise to power of a new tsar, Alexander II, the "Tsar Liberator." This era of liberalization brought about by Alexander II also meant the emergence of some rich Jews, industrialists, and bankers in the central towns of Russia. They accumulated funds from the wine trade or from commerce with the West. The Wissotzky firm of tea merchants, for example, was one such successful company, and is now known throughout the world. One-third of the sugar industry was controlled by Jews before the Revolution. Its leading sugar magnates were the Brodsky family, whom we shall meet in Kiev.

Only for a short time, under Alexander II, did Russian Jews feel like human beings. If Alexander II had not been killed, he probably would have reformed the Russian political system. But on March 1, 1881, a fateful day in Russian history, Alexander II was murdered. Immediately, rumors spread that Jews played a major part in the killing of the tsar. The assassination, however, was an excuse for anti-Jewish legislation, says the late Jewish historian Salo Baron.

The terrorist group that killed the tsar included only one Jewish person, a woman named Hessia Helfman. She was sentenced to death, together with five other revolutionaries. Helfman's contribution had consisted merely in providing shelter for her fellow conspirators. Because she was pregnant at the time, her execution was delayed and she died in the Peter and Paul Fortress in St. Petersburg after the birth of her child.

The murder of the tsar triggered four years of pogroms and led to severe restrictions on Jews' privileges, privileges that had been few at best. The government immediately endorsed by legislation a quota system in the universities that was later termed *numerous clausus,* and which consisted of restrictions and limitations on the number of Jews admitted to universities. Jews also could not acquire any real estate outside towns and could only engage in agriculture if they leased the land. Hit with such restrictive treatment, known as the May Laws of 1882, more than one million Jews would emigrate over the next 20 years.

Where Shall We Go?

After the assassination of the tsar, pogroms began. Many believe these pogroms were instigated by the government and stimulated by a rise in anti-Semitism. The word "pogrom" is Russian for a violent mass attack carried out against a section of the community.

Tens of thousands of highly enterprising people left Russia during the last two decades of the nineteenth century. Still, by 1897, slightly more than 5 million Jews remained as a "vast, under-utilized store of intellect, energy and obsessiveness."

Where to put all that energy? Which way to go? To the revolutionary parties? To the Jewish socialist workers of the Bund (see below)? To Zionism? To Orthodox Judaism? Or finally, to emigrate to Western Europe, Palestine, or America? Every family had to make a choice.

Jews would join the leadership of all Russian opposition movements in larger numbers in proportion to their population. That Jewish liberation in Russia was impossible unless tsardom was overthrown was the prevailing feeling of many Jews. They believed they were scapegoats and that their freedom lay in the downfall of the tsarist regime. But they also could turn toward Jewish nationalism, toward expanding their culture in a Jewish homeland, toward the creation of a new Yiddish literature and a reborn, modernized Hebrew. But, depressed by the restrictive laws, many Jews did not believe in the possibility of Jewish equality before the law in Russia, so they emigrated.

The Bund

Before the 1917 upheaval, the desperate economic conditions and the draconian laws to which the Jews were subject by the tsarist authorities, especially after 1882, gave birth to an important Jewish labor movement, called the Bund, the Jewish General Workers Union.

Founded in Vilna in 1897, the Bund proclaimed itself a Jewish Socialist party. It was committed to defending the special interests of Jewish workers, says author Robert S. Wistrich. These Jewish Social Democrats, who were Marxists and anti-Zionists, felt that only socialism would stamp out anti-Semitism.

In 1898, the Bund played an important part in the founding of the Russian Social Democratic Party, parts of which would later become the Bolshevik and Menshevik parties. The Bund would provide many of the most important Social Democratic leaders, including Pavel Axelrod, Leo Deutsch, Julius Martov, Leon Trotsky, Lev Kamenev, and Grigorii Zinoviev, just to name a few.

Deutsch and Axelrod, whom historian Bertram W. Wolfe calls "Russified" Jewish intellectuals, were among the founders of Russian Marxism, along with Plekhanov and Martov. The latter, after a brief period as a member of the Jewish Bund, broke with it to become Lenin's chief collaborator in the Petersburg League. Later, however, Martov and Axelrod would go over to the Menshevik movement when the party split into Bolshevik and Menshevik factions in 1903. Indeed, Jews would play a much larger role in the Menshevik movement than in the Bolshevik.

It was called the great Party schism of 1903. The dispute, which involved the Russian Social Democrats and the Jewish Bundists, took place over the latter's claim to recognition as an extra-territorial organization for Jewish workers on a national rather than regional or local basis.

Lenin attacked the separation of the Bund. He turned down the idea that the Jews were a separate people. The Bolsheviks argued that the idea of a Jewish nationality—itself a reactionary idea—contradicted the interests of the Jewish proletariat.

This resulted in the Bund's withdrawal from the Russian Social Democratic Party at the group's 1903 convention. The Bund left in a huff because the congress refused to recognize it as the sole representative of the Jewish proletariat.

The withdrawal of the Bundist delegates from the conference and from the Russian Social Democratic Party had important consequences. By pulling out its five delegates (along with two delegates from the Union of Russian Social Democrats Abroad), the Bund gave a small voting majority to the Leninists, according to Solomon M. Schwarz. The Leninists then became the "Bolshevik" (majority) party, as opposed to the "Menshevik" (minority) party. The split between the two also occurred because Lenin wanted a tightly knit organization of professional revolutionaries, while the Mensheviks preferred a somewhat broader and looser association. Involved, too, in the dispute was the issue of control of Party publications. Whatever party one sided with, however, in 1905, the scene was set for what some have called the First Russian Revolution of the twentieth century.

1905

The Revolution of 1905 was "a dress rehearsal" for the big productions of 1917. The disastrous war with Japan in 1904 and "Bloody Sunday"—the day Father Gapon led thousands of innocent civilian petitioners in St. Petersburg to alleviate their conditions, only to be met with a hail of bullets from Russian troops—caused the upheaval of 1905.

But the waves of terrorist counterrevolution at the end of the year, and the series of pogroms in 1906, made the earlier anti-Jewish rioting in 1903 appear insignificant. Now, horror and bloodshed reached new heights. From 1881 to 1917, city after city in Russia witnessed pogroms, including Mogilev, Minsk, Gomel, Bialystok, Lodz, Kiev, Zhitomir, Vologda, Simbirsk, Odessa, and Kishinev, notes Chaim Potok. He adds that in one week in October 1905, 300 pogroms occurred in Russia. Army veterans, Cossacks, and Black Hundreds (a group of revolutionary anti-Semites who staged pogroms) wreaked vengeance upon Jews in the streets of Minsk, Brest Litovsk, Lodz, and other cities. Nearly 50 anti-Jewish pogroms broke out that October in cities such as Odessa, Kiev, Kishinev, Simferopol, Romny, Nikolayev, Yekaterinoslav, Kamenets, Podolski, Yelisavetgrad, and Orsha. Hundreds of Jews were killed.

Edvard Radzinsky, author of *The Last Czar,* writes that while the police sometimes tried to halt pogroms, they were actually printing proclamations against Jews and stirring up the population.

The Far Right issued *The Protocols of the Elders of Zion,* a book written like a mystery. The publication stated that mankind has suffered a series of calamities because of the Jews and the Masons, whom the Jews controlled, the reactionaries proclaimed.

The government always explained the persecutions of Jews, including pogroms, by emphasizing that they were a reaction against the participation of Jews in the Russian revolutionary movement.

The terror and fear got so bad that in February 1905, 35 Jewish communities signed a petition that said, "The measures adopted for the last 25 years toward the Russian Jews were designed with the deliberate end in view to convert them into a mass of beggars, deprived of all means of sustenance, and of the light of education and human dignity." The signes stated that it was "impossible to continue such a life."

They wanted to be free.

Zionism

The Jews of Russia saw Zionism as the only possible solution to the Jewish question, according to Sh'marya Levin, who was one of the outstanding intellectuals and artistic figures of Russian Jewry who settled in Palestine. From 1881 and onward, the Chibbat Zion, the Lovers of Zion, founded in Russia after the death of Tsar Alexander II, had urged Jews to settle in Palestine, and in 1882, the town of Rishon Le Zion was founded by Russian Jews who also settled in Mishmar Hayarden, Ness Tziona, Yesud Ha'Maala, Petah Tikva, and Gedera.

Zionism drew large numbers to its ranks. However, it is truly amazing that while Zionism was actually legal in tsarist times, meetings were raided by police, and many Zionist leaders were sent to Siberia.

Without question, the Revolution of 1905 served as a catalyst for emigration. The signers of the 1905 petition knew in their hearts that more bloodletting was yet to come in the form of pogroms, pogroms that would accelerate the departure of a new group. The 5,000 settlers who came to Palestine in the 1880s and up through 1904 and who settled in towns were known as the Bilu Movement, part of the First Aliyah. Zionism had found a considerable response among the Russian Jewish masses in the Pale of Settlement.

The new group consisted of the emigration of Russian Jews who would lay the ideological and social basis of the Jewish state. We call this group the Second Aliyah, the 40,000 Jews that arrived in Palestine between the years of 1904 and 1914. Even though it was only a trickle, this emigration of *chalutzim* (pioneers) who had departed for the Holy Land became the backbone of the World Zionist Organization, or WZO, and the basis of its mass support, as well as its increasingly socialist outlook. But as early as September 1, 1919, Bolshevism closed down Zionist headquarters and suppressed its publications. Zionism in effect was outlawed in 1919-1920, but it took about 10 years for the Communists to complete the total physical shutdown of the movement, although spiritually, the Soviets would never succeed. Emigration to Palestine was almost nonexistent from the USSR.

Zionists writers such as Achad Ha-am of Odessa called for a Jewish spiritual and cultural revival. Leon Pinsker, who also hailed from Odessa, wrote: "We do not count as a nation among the other nations and we have no voice in the council of the peoples."

In 1897, the first World Zionist Congress in Basel, Switzerland, which was attended by many Russian Jews, gave birth to "a totally new kind of life into the public affairs of the Jewish people as a whole," wrote author David Vital in the *Times Literary Supplement* of August 29, 1997. Zionist leadership was "not self perpetuating and self selected, but democratic and responsible and bent on operating on the largest possible scale."

The headquarters of Zionism may have been in Vienna, but the masses were in Odessa, Zhitomir, Pinsk, and Minsk.

Actually, Theodor Herzl (1860-1904), the father of modern Zionism, with his majestic appearance, his formality, his education and knowledge, even his beard, had the aura of a messiah to Russian Jews. Still, the Jews of Russia would challenge Herzl when he accepted Great Britain's offer for Jews to settle in Uganda. Led by Chaim Weizmann (1874-1952), and Menachem Mendel Ussishkin (1863-1941), the Zionists of Russia defeated that proposal.

To Russian Zionists, no country other than Palestine could offer a genuine home for the Jewish people. Western Jews may have favored Uganda, but the Jews of Eastern Europe stood firmly against the idea.

Besides Weizmann and Ussishkin, these Zionists included Nachman Syrkin (1867-1924), Ber Borochov (1881-1917), and A.D. Gordon (1856-1922). In 1900, Poale Zion was formed. It combined socialist and Zionist views. The Poale Zion believed that Jewish workers had to align themselves with the WZO and the Socialist International. Syrkin and others called on Jewish youth to come to Israel.

By 1918, Russian Zionists embraced about 1,200 local Zionist groups, and some 300,000 members. It had become a huge mass movement of Jews throughout the world. By far, one of the most inspiring ideologues, and the one who added an idealistic push, was A. D. Gordon, who took over some ideas from the early Russian socialists, as well as from Tolstoy. He propagated a new brand of Zionist socialism that was to replace the class struggle by the idea of mutual love and devotion to a "religion of labor."

Gordon and others influenced the generation that came to Palestine from Russia and Poland and who were known as the

Second Aliyah. They arrived as Zionist dreamers, workers with a democratic socialist outlook. They, and those that followed them, were the *chalutzim*. The aliya was honed by centuries of wishing for a return to Israel. This Second Aliyah was the backbone of the modern State of Israel. These idealistic men and women called on Jews to shed their ghetto clothing. They said Jews had to become farmers, road builders, truck drivers, and laborers. If they would do this, members said, Jews would not only build a Jewish state, but they would also build themselves. "We came to The Land of Israel, to build and to be built by it," were the words of one early pioneering song. These Poale Zion, these workers of Zion—they drained the swamps, planted forests, paved highways, established *kibbutzim*, and *moshavim* (cooperative agricultural settlements), and set up factories and cooperatives. At the same time, they founded self-defense units, such as Haganah. In 1948, the Haganah itself became the Israel Defense Army. Overnight, they staked out isolated agricultural settlements and set up Jewish towns. They organized themselves into one huge labor unit, called Histadrut, which not only supplied the workers, but also offered up capital to build the country, where private enterprise dared not venture.

Russian Zionist Ideology in Europe, 1881-1917

Most of these pioneers believed, as did Zionist theoretician Ber Borochov, that the Jew in Europe lived in an inverted triangle. The top layer consisted of businesspersons and professionals, whereas at the bottom of this inverted geometric figure were the workers, with the obvious conclusion that to build a state, the triangle had to be righted, with a few businesspersons at the top and a huge mass of Jewish workers at the bottom.

Ber Borochov, a founder of Poale Zion, which, as noted, synthesized socialism and Zionism, preached his "proletarian Socialist-Zionist ideology" throughout Russia. Other Russian Zionists included Joseph Vitkin (1876-1912), who issued an appeal to Jewish youth to join the Socialist Zionist ranks in Palestine, Berl Katznelson (1887-1944), Joseph Sprinzak

(1885-1959), and of course, Joseph Trumpeldor (1880-1920). Trumpeldor we shall meet when we visit Odessa. The Second Aliya was followed by the Third Aliya, which arrived in the 1920s and 1930s. Most of these emigrants, however, came from Eastern Europe, especially from the large Jewish community of Poland. The Communist regime had simply cut off emigration from the USSR.

This is not to say that every Jew coming to Israel was a socialist pioneer. Many Jews came as businesspersons and artisans and populated cities such as Tel Aviv, Haifa, and Jerusalem. Many religious Jews joined the Zionist cause. Rabbis Yehudah Alkalai (1798-1878), and Zevi Hirsch Kalischer (1795-1874), "preached Zionism as a solution to the persecution of the Jews," according to Yaffa Eliach, in her prize-winning book, *There Once Was A World, A Nine-Hundred-Year Chronicle of the Shtetl of Eishyshok*. An outstanding spokesperson for Zionism was Rabbi Samuel Mohilever (1824-1898), of Glumbokie, near Vilna, a leader of Religious Zionism who encouraged the establishment of the Zionist movement called Mizrachi. Rabbi Isaac Jacob Reines of Lida (1839-1915), who founded the Mizrachi, and others espoused Jewish religious tradition in the future Jewish state; that is, "the Land of Israel for the people of Israel based on the Torah of Israel."

During the first 25 years of the existence of the State of Israel, Russian-born Jews who had lived under tsarist rule played a leading part in the state's political, economic, and cultural life.

The first four presidents and the first four prime ministers of Israel were all born in the Russian Empire. In 1960, for instance, of the 73 members of the Knesset who gave their birthplace in *Who's Who in Israel*, 52 had been born in tsarist Russia, 9 in Israel, 5 in Germany, 3 in Rumania, 3 in Austria-Hungary, and 1 in Bulgaria. Some of those born in the Pale of Settlement were David Ben-Gurion, prime minister, 1948-1953 and 1955-1963; Chaim Weizmann, first president of Israel, 1948-1952; Yitzhak Ben Zvi, second president, 1952-1963; Zalman Shazar, third president, 1963-1973; Moshe Sharett, prime minister, 1954-1955; Levi Eshkol, prime minister, 1963-1969; Golda Meir, prime minister, 1969-1974; Ephraim Katzir, fourth president,

1973; Hayym Laskov, chief of staff, 1958-1961; Menachem Begin, prime minister, 1977-1983; and Pinchas Sapir, minister of finance, 1954-1955 and 1969-1975.

World War I

Pistol shots "heard around the world." Those are the words the commentators used when they reported that Archduke Franz Ferdinand d'Este was assassinated in 1914 by a Serbian nationalist who opposed Austria's Hapsburg rule.

On August 2, 1914, in St. Petersburg and other cities, Russians took to the streets and shouted for joy at the new war. "For Faith, Tsar, and Country," they yelled with passion. The cheering later would turn into tragic tears at the enormous amount of lives lost in the conflict. The war's consequences would be appalling.

The Russian army, which moved against the Central Powers into East Prussia, (now East Poland), was "poorly trained, incompetently led, and inadequately equipped," wrote author Jay Winter in the *The Great War and the Shaping of the 20th Century*. In fact, at the Battle of Tannenberg and Masurian Lakes, in East Prussia, two Russian armies were completely destroyed and 30,000 were left dead, with 100,000 taken prisoner. The rest ran for their lives. Led by Generals Paul von Hindenburg and Erich Ludendorff, Germany had achieved a great victory, as the Russian army had walked into a brilliantly constructed trap. Indeed, one of the Russian generals, Alexander Samsonov, committed suicide over the debacle. But the victory was as much a sign of Russian ineptitude as of German military prowess.

The army retreated back to Russia. Obviously, the Germans wanted to break the will of the Russians. They pushed for a single-front war, and when they finally achieved it, the Romanovs were out and the Bolsheviks were in.

The war may have been won and lost on the Western Front, but the carnage in the east was unbelievable. The total Russian losses after 10 months of war alone amounted to 3,800,000 men. The Russian Empire would go on to lose over 6 million soldiers.

The Jews who lived in the Pale of Settlement, as well as in Poland, Galicia, and Bukovina, found themselves situated on the main battlefields of the eastern war zone, according to the late Jewish historian Lucy S. Dawidowicz.

Jews were expelled from their homes in western Russia. Six times the Russians advanced into Galicia. As Russia's army advanced, it arrested, tortured, deported, and killed Jews. Then the process would be repeated as the Russians retreated. Yet 240,000 Jewish soldiers fought for Mother Russia in the First World War.

World War I was a catastrophe for the Jews. Thousands fled from combat zones and wandered in the snows "driven like cattle by platoons of Cossacks," says author Brian Moynihan. We know now that the First World War helped bring on the catastrophes of the first half of the twentieth century, the Russian Revolution, the Russian Civil War, social disintegration, totalitarianism, more wars, and the Holocaust.

People demanded an end to the fighting, wrote W. Bruce Lincoln in his *Red Victory: A History of the Russian Civil War.* In March 1918, with the conflict still going on, the Russians pulled out of the war when they signed the Treaty of Brest Litovsk. The new Red government had accepted harsh terms of surrender.

In 1917, all restrictions that had been placed on Jews during the tsarist years were abolished. Zionist youth groups flourished; Hebrew journals and books were published.

Overt manifestations of anti-Semitism began to disappear. Anti-Semitism dropped to its lowest point in the middle of the 1930s. This was the period of "Communist romanticism," and "internationalism."

Until 1930, Jews generally enjoyed civil rights and liberties they had never experienced in Russia. "These were the years, at least at the beginning of the decade of the 1920s, of the rebirth and flowering of Yiddish culture in the Soviet Union, the period when the Soviet government granted the Jews the same cultural rights as other nationals," according to Ben Ami (Arieh L. Eliav), author of *Between Hammer and Sickle.*

But most Jews did not buy into the Communist system. Ayn Rand, whose real name was Alisa Rosenbaum and who has been described as "the most driven of American literary anti-Communists," was born in St. Petersburg in 1905. Her father was a pharmacist, "whose profession had been determined by the quotas set for Jews at the city's university," according to Claudia Roth Pierpont, writing in the *New Yorker* magazine of July 24, 1995. She had been present in her father's shop the day the Bolshevik soldiers broke in and affixed a red seal to the door, declaring his life's work the property of the Soviet people. The day she obtained a visa in 1926, wrote Roth, "one of the guests [at a party] made a request that she held on to for years. 'If they ask you, in America, tell them that Russia is a huge cemetery, and that we are all dying slowly.'"

Anti-Semitism, however, had a checkered career in post-Revolutionary Russia. Noted author Maurice Samuel wrote, "it cannot be denied that during the early years, especially during Lenin's years of rule, anti-Semitism disappeared from view in Russia." "The Russian Revolution raised great hopes among the Jews of Russia. At long last they would be set free and would enjoy the same rights, privileges, and opportunities as the rest of the population," writes author and journalist B. Z. Goldberg. The Revolution, however, would fail them.

Led by the zeal of dedicated Jewish communists, Soviet officials destroyed the traditional community institutions that had shaped Jewish culture during the preceding centuries. They closed houses of worship. They condemned the Hebrew language and Zionism. Ironically, these Jewish communists would be among the first to lose their lives in the great Stalinpurges of the late 1930s.

Yevrektsiia

Yevrektsiia, the Jewish section of the Communist Party, made Jews conform to the new Soviet state, writes author Fran Markowitz. Until it was closed down by the Communists, Yevrektsiia not only caused much damage, but it changed the face of Russian Jewry. Its job was "to impose the proletariat dictatorship among the Jewish masses," says the *Encyclopedia Judaica*. Between 1932

Here is a gymnastics class at a JDC-sponsored school in 1923 in the USSR. (Photo credit: American Jewish Joint Distribution Committee)

Childen play at a JDC summer camp in 1922 in the USSR. (Photo credit: American Jewish Joint Distribution Committee)

and 1940 only one-fifth of Soviet Jews were being educated in the Yiddish language, and the Soviets had already stopped supporting Yiddish culture.

Joshua Rothenberg says that the role of this Jewish section of the Communist Party "in religious persecution and in the arrest of the Jewish clergymen is a dreary episode in the history of Soviet Jewry."

"The Soviet Union soon restricted and controlled organized religious life in the country. The Communists had a professed desire to erase religious beliefs from the consciousness of the Russian people," Rothenberg added. That is why hundreds of rabbis, ritual slaughterers, and other clergy were arrested and deported to far-away places in the 1920s.

According to Jewish historian Zvi Gitelman, 650 synagogues were shut down, and more than 1,000 Jewish schools were closed during the years of 1922 and 1923 alone.

"In tsarist times the Russians had been contemptuous of the Jews. How they feared and hated them; blamed the Revolution on them; and saw them as conspiring to destroy the entire Christian world," writes author Chaim Potok in *The Gates of November: Chronicles of the Slepak Family*. From the late 1930s on—except for a short break during World War II—the Communists eliminated Jews from more and more vocational fields.

As Solomon Schwarz noted in his 1951 work *Jews in the Soviet Union*, "the democratic Jewish community was destroyed in 1919-1920 and nothing of it has since been revived . . ."

"Discrimination against Jews in the Soviet Union is a combination of all the basic forms of discrimination existing in other countries of the Diaspora, and includes official discrimination. There are percentage norms limiting acceptance to higher educational institutions and limiting employment opportunities," wrote Professor Mikhail Zand, who was allowed to leave the USSR in the 1970s.

Birobidzhan

One of the experiments floated by the Communists in the late 1920s and early 1930s was hailed as the Jewish workers' paradise. Known as Birobidzhan, it was to be a Jewish republic. The concept never made it to fruition.

And yet, even a few years ago, travelers arriving at the railroad station in Birobidzhan were moved when they viewed the large sign over the building on which was written in Yiddish, in large Hebrew letters, the name "Birobidzhan." Some even went so far as to say they were under the spell of those letters, and felt they were on Jewish soil.

The sign may have been there, but the "paradise" was still an illusion, as it always had been. The author George St. George called this Jewish autonomous region, with the city of Birobidzhan as its capital, an "ethnographic oddity, later modified to geographical and historical oddity." However, the Soviets trumpeted Birobidzhan as the great event in the history of the Jewish people.

It has been described as a "shell game." It was big on talk and small on reality, said Rabbi William M. Kramer, writing in the *Heritage Southwest Jewish Press* of November 7, 1997.

Although it was referred to in publications as early as 1928, it was not until 1934 that Birobidzhan became a Jewish Autonomous Oblast (region). The dream was to settle 100,000 Jews there. Nearly 70 years later, the area has been relegated to the status of a footnote in twentieth-century Jewish History. The percentage of Jewish residents there never rose above 20 percent.

Still, in the 1920s, two decades before the establishment of the State of Israel, the notion of a Jewish "homeland" appealed to many.

Situated in the southern part of the former Soviet Union Far East, and near the border of China, Birobidzhan is located in a rigorous climate, where the winters are long, dry, and cold, and the summers are hot and rainy. Containing about 14,000 square miles, it occupies a very sensitive military area. The Soviets wanted to stop Chinese and Korean emigration, especially after the Japanese invaded Manchuria in 1931, and the settlement in Birobidzhan fit the USSR's strategic need to settle the border.

The name "Birobidzhan" is derived from two small tributaries of the Amur, the Bira and the Bidzhan. Covering the size of an area the size of Connecticut and Massachusetts combined, Birobidzhan is situated in one of the farthest and coldest regions of Siberia, a region that had an unsavory reputation as a vast penal colony. By 1941, 30,000 Jews out of a population of 114,000 lived there. In 1948, 20,000 more Jews arrived. At one point, 128 elementary schools, with Yiddish as the language of instruction, thrived there, as well as a Museum of Jewish Culture, "a daily Yiddish newspaper, a medical school, a music school, and 27 Jewish collective and state farms," according to Potok.

Ben Ami wrote that there is no doubt that Stalin and his cohorts had decided that the whole plan of settling Jews on the Chinese border in an autonomous Jewish region was basically wrong and should not be allowed to develop.

In 1958, the head of the USSR, Nikita S. Khrushchev, admitted failure of the region housing 300,000 Jews. He blamed the failure on "Jewish individualism."

By 1959, Max Frankel of the *New York Times* wrote that Yiddish was not taught in the schools, no Yiddish films were shown, and no Yiddish books were printed. In that same year, 14,269 Jews out of a population of 162,836 called Birobidzhan home. About 2,000 Jews are said to live there now.

The "Black Years"

Birobidzhan was not the last suggestion for creating a Jewish republic in the USSR. There was also a suggestion to put such a settlement in the Crimean peninsula, between the Black Sea and the Sea of Azov. That never came about, but its repercussions were felt, as the Communist Party claimed this request by various Jewish leaders was an anti-Soviet plot by Russian Jews who were allegedly "in cahoots with American imperialists."

After World War II, and until Stalin died, Jews lived under a Soviet reign of terror and cloud of fear. Instead of allies, the U.S. and Russia became enemies.

In 1948, the situation of Soviet Jews worsened. The Jewish Anti-Fascist Committee was disbanded. The actor and Jewish community leader Solomon Mikhoels was murdered. The

Yiddish press was shut down. Jewish publishing houses were closed, and Jewish library doors were locked.

By the early 1950s, the 3 million Russian Jews were engaged in medicine, economics, industry and technology, teaching, and art, says Fran Markowitz, author of *A Community In Spite of Itself.* And then came the "Doctor's Plot."

A group of Jewish doctors were accused of poisoning or killing prominent Soviet leaders, and of being Zionist agents. Ilya Ehrenburg, an outstanding Soviet Jewish author-journalist and an apologist for the Soviet state in those years, was stunned by the spewing of anti-Jewish hate on street corners. Later he commented that although "our people had matured spiritually, nonetheless events of 1953 show that the 'thinking reed' stops thinking at times."

After World War II, "the Jews of the USSR were isolated as a result of decisions by the Soviet authorities to obliterate their cultural and religious characteristics and force them to melt into the larger Russian population," wrote Jerry Goodman, founding director of the National Conference on Soviet Jewry and who served at its helm for 16 years. Goodman made this statement in a paper published in *Jewish Civics: A Tikkun Olam/World Repair Manual.*

During the "Black Years" of 1948-1953, almost all remaining Jewish institutions were closed down. The synagogue stood as the only existing Jewish institution in the country. The production of Jewish religious items, prayer shawls, phylacteries, Torah scrolls, mezuzahs, prayer books, and Jewish calendars, was not permitted until the late 1980s, according to Joshua Rothenberg. "Objects for Jewish rituals now found in the Soviet Union either date from the Tsarist period or were left there by foreign tourists as gifts," Rothenberg added.

The USSR would become the "largest producer and disseminator of anti-Semitic materials in the world . . . [which was] a serious threat to the status and security of Jews," said U.S. State Department documents at that time.

Some Jewish organizations operated underground, even though that very practice was also now forbidden. These Jewish groups, however, continued to care for the welfare of the community, preserving Jewish life and caring for the poor and the sick.

Only during the Khrushchev years did the world begin to hear "the thin, small voices of Jews who were still alive behind the Iron Curtain," writes Chaim Potok. The Soviets, despite their intentions, had not made Jews forget that they were Jews.

Israel

Meanwhile the USSR was the second power in the world to recognize Israel. This action was surely motivated to undermine British control in the Middle East.

In 1948, the Jewish people were reborn in their own homeland. The State of Israel was declared on May 14 in a museum in Tel Aviv. At the United Nations, as we noted, the USSR was the second nation to recognize Israel. The U.S. was the first.

On May 14, 1947, the Soviet delegate to the UN General Assembly, Andrei Gromyko, had called for the establishment of separate Jewish and Arab states in Palestine, if the two peoples could not be brought to agree on the establishment of an independent bi-national state. Emphasizing the present tragedy of the "hundreds of thousands of homeless Jewish survivors in Europe," and the fact that nothing was being done by the nations of the world to relieve the misery of the displaced Jews, Gromyko said that the Jews had a right to establish a state of their own "in view of the ugly fact that not a single country in Western Europe did anything between the two world wars to protect the Jews from Nazi oppression."

Jewish historian Salo Baron says that the leaders of the USSR expected, as did most outside observers, that the new state would be quickly overrun by the Arab armies and that a British mandatory country would be replaced by an Arab state. One theory states that Soviet leaders also thought that, because of the socialist leanings of the country, Israel at very least would not rush to join the American bloc. Much conventional wisdom then, and even today, held that the Russians backed a Jewish state to eliminate Great Britain from Palestine and enable the USSR to penetrate this strategic Near and Middle East. The tables were turned, however, when the Jews, fighting for their lives, turned back an Arab alliance of nations. Israel won its war of indepence in 1948, in part having been supplied with Czech arms, obviously with the tacit approval of the Soviets. From then on, however, Stalin viewed the Soviet Jewish population's enthusiasm for Israel as tantamount to disloyalty to the USSR. By the time Nikita S. Krushchev reached power in the 1950s, the foreign policy of the Soviet Union was definitely pro-Arab, and the Soviets not only began to arm the Arab states with massive modern weapons, but also supported those nations in the international arena.

Before the Six-Day War of June 1967, Israeli diplomats who could move around the Soviet Union and could bring in some cultural and educational materials, "created the first links to a fragile Jewish world," in the USSR, notes Jerry Goodman.

There is no doubt that Israel was sending *shlichim* (literally "messengers") behind the Iron Curtain, including the Baltics and Russia itself. In 1952, the author, spending a year of work and study at Kibbutz Kfar Blum (a cooperative agricultural settlement), was told that a key member of the kibbutz who spoke Latvian was on a "special assignment." Everyone assumed he had returned to the Baltic countries to be in touch with Jewish communities. A few decades later, thousands of Baltic Jews, as well as Jews from the USSR, would emigrate to Israel.

The Israel Delegation to the Youth Festival held in Moscow in 1957 was probably the first occasion of personal contacts between Jewish youth from Israel and the USSR. Jews from throughout Russia came to see the Israelis.

In the Six-Day War, the Soviet authorities unleashed a violent anti-Israel and anti-Zionist campaign in the mass media. Twenty years later, one Russian Jew told me he remembered a sharp rise of anti-Semitism among his fellow students during that short war. The Soviets began to mobilize public opinion on behalf of the Arab states.

Despite widespread hostility, Russian Jews took pride in Israel's victory, and this stimulated a new wave of Zionist sympathy among the younger generation, according to Goodman.

When the USSR broke off relations with Israel in 1967, "Jews had to defy the Soviet state to become involved with the Jewish state. This occurred despite the fact that most of them were ignorant of Jewish history, life, traditions and customs after five decades of Soviet efforts to choke Jewish life," Goodman added.

Over the next 20 years, the "nascent Zionist movement remained a challenge to Soviet hegemony over the many different peoples within its borders," says Goodman, adding, "encouraged by advocates in the U.S. and other countries, and supported by Israel, the Jews struggled for years to attain their rights." He maintains that the struggle would come to be an "open wound" for the USSR, "causing it to bleed for years." He wrote that the "advocacy campaign would help erode the Soviet system and become a factor in its eventual collapse." It also brought hundreds of thousands of Jews to Israel, the U.S., and Western Europe.

But in those days, the plight of Soviet Jewry was known as "the greatest misfortune" facing world Jewry, declared Ben Ami in *Between Hammer and Sickle*. "The situation of Soviet Jewry is complex, difficult, tragic, and unprecedented," he added, noting that something could be done because there were many Jews in the Soviet Union who were anxious not to sever ties with their people.

In the 1960s Jews were tried for economic crimes, for crimes of embezzlement, and for speculation. More than 500 trials took place in the early 1960s. Very often nationalistic, anti-cosmopolitanism slogans served as a poor cover for crass anti-Semitism, which was steadily gaining ground in government circles.

Between July 1961 and March 1963, about 110 death sentences were handed down for economic crimes. Of these 110, at least 68 were given to Jews. The 68 were shot, and their property was confiscated by the government, according to Martin Gilbert.

In 1963, the Central Party leadership permitted Ukrainian writer Trefim Kichko to publish *Judaism Without Embellishment,* an anti-Jewish tract which provoked more citizens of Jewish origin to apply for exit visas.

We must remember that until 1967, it was virtually impossible for Jews to leave the Soviet Union. Even from 1967 to 1971, fewer than 5,000 Jews actually departed, and their permits were issued for family reunification and repatriation—not because of their right to leave and go to their homeland, Israel.

"Prisoners of Zion"

The right to move from the USSR and emigrate to Israel or any other destination was enshrined in international documents and covenants to which the Soviet Union was a signatory, and was also protected in the Constitution of the Soviet Union. This did not prevent the authorities from arresting Jews on trumped-up charges or threatening them with arrest for alleged crimes, including "hooliganism" or "parasitism," if they were unemployed after having sought to emigrate to Israel.

Martin Gilbert tells us that "many of those imprisoned were subjected to extreme brutalities, near starvation and solitary confinement in sub-zero temperatures." They were thrown into prisons and camps throughout the USSR.

Some of these Jews were allowed to leave after much pressure from the West. But others were picked up, arrested, tried, and imprisoned. Jews were sent to psychiatric institutions, again after they too applied to go to Israel. Here again, international protests lessened their punishment.

In June 1970 a number of Leningrad Jews were arrested for publicly protesting the refusal of Soviet officials to grant them visas for Israel. In December of that year, a group of young Jews, mostly from Riga, was sentenced to death or long imprisonment for planning to seize a Russian plane to escape and reach the Jewish state. Two were sentenced to death, and others to prison terms ranging from 4 to 15 years. A worldwide storm of protests, including some from Communist parties and newspapers in the West, preceded the appeal of the condemned into the Supreme Court of the Russian Republic in Moscow. In 1971, the death sentences were commuted to 15 years hard labor, and some of the other sentences were reduced.

Soviet Jews had been agitating for the right to leave for Israel, and in 1971, some of the barriers were lifted. There was also a growing advocacy group not only among American Jews, but also in the U.S. government and in some nations in Western Europe.

In 1971, the USSR did an about-face, and Jewish emigration to Israel was permitted. Between January 1970 and April 1976, more than 118,000 Soviet Jews were given permission to leave the Soviet Union. Of these, 110,000 settled in Israel—mostly traveling via Vienna. Thirty-five thousand Jews left in 1973.

"Under the Helsinki Agreement of August 1975, the Soviet Union agreed that the requests which were lodged by old and sick people for their reunification of families must be considered as urgent and must be treated in a positive and humane spirit," points out Gilbert.

For the next 15 years, as Soviet policies toward its Jews fluctuated according to domestic and foreign policy considerations, harassment of those demanding the right to depart was the norm, especially when relations with the U.S. declined.

Throughout the two decades of the struggle for Soviet Jewry, allowing Jews to emigrate to the Jewish state was similar to a spigot being turned on and off by the Communists as international pressure mounted or lessened. When the gates finally widened in 1989 and opened completely in 1991, a large percentage of the Jewish community decided that they no longer wanted to remain on Russian or Ukrainian soil.

At the same time, more than 1.5 million Jews stayed in Russian and Ukraine, with 100,000 in St. Petersburg, a Jewish community we shall now visit.

Suggested Reading

Allen, W. E. D., *The Ukraine, A History.* New York: Russell & Russell, Inc., 1993.

Baron, Salo, *The Russian Jew under Tsars and Soviet.* New York: The Macmillan Company, 1964.

Ben-Ami, (Arieh L. Eliav) *Between Hammer And Sickle.* Philadelphia: Jewish Publication Society, 1967.

Ben-Sasson, H.H.A, *History of the Jewish People.* Cambridge, MA: Harvard University Press, 1976.

Dawidowicz, Lucy S., *The War Against the Jews: 1933-1945.* New York: Holt, Rhinehart & Winston, 1975.

Dubnow, Simon M., *History of the Jews in Russia and Poland, From the Earliest Times Until the Present Day, Vols. I, II,* and *III.*

Philadelphia: The Jewish Publication Society of America, 1916-1920.

Dubnow, Simon M., *History of the Jews, From the Congress of Vienna to the Emergence of Hitler, Vol. V.* South Brunswick, NJ, London: Thomas Yoseloff, 1973.

Ehrenburg, Ilya and Grossman, Vasily, editors, *The Black Book: The Ruthless Murder of Jews by German-Fascist Invaders Throughout the Temporarily-Occupied Regions of the Soviet Union and the Death Camps of Poland During the War of 1941-1945.* New York: Holocaust Publications, 1981.

Eliach, Yaffa, *There Once Was A World, A Nine-Hundred-Year Chronicle of the Shtetl of Eishyshok.* Boston, New York, London: Little, Brown and Company, 1998.

Figes, Orlando, *A People's Tragedy: A History of the Russian Revolution.* New York: Viking, 1997.

Florinsky, Michael T., *Russia.* New York: 2 Vols., Macmillan, 1961.

Gitelman, Zvi, *A Century of Ambivalence: The Jews of Russia and the Soviet Union, 1881 to the Present.* New York: Schocken Books, 1988.

Goodman, Susan Tumarkin, *Russian Jewish Artists in a Century of Change, 1890-1990.* Munich, New York: Prestel-Verlag, 1995.

Kurzweil, Arthur, *From Generation to Generation: How to Trace Your Jewish Genealogy and Family History.* New York: HarperCollins Publisher, 1994.

Levitats, Isaac, *The Jewish Community in Russia, 1772-1844.* New York: Octagon Books, 1970.

Lindemann, Albert S., *Esau's Tears: Modern Anti-Semitism and the Rise of The Jews.* New York: Cambridge University Press, 1997.

Markowitz, Fran, *A Community in Spite of Itself.* Washington and London: Smithsonian Institution Press, 1993.

Meltzer, Milton, *World of Our Fathers: The Jews of Eastern Europe.* New York: Dell Publishing Co., Inc., 1974.

Moynahan, Brian, *The Russian Century: Birth of A Nation.* New York: Random House, 1994.

Pares, Sir Barnard, *A History of Russia.* New York: Alfred A. Knopf, 1968.

Potok, Chaim, *The Gates of November: Chronicles of the Slepak Family.* New York: Alfred A. Knopf, 1996.

Reid, Anna, *Borderland: A Journey Through the History of Ukraine.* London: Weidenfeld & Nicolson, 1997.

Riasanovsky, Nicholas V., *A History of Russia, Fifth Edition.* New York, Oxford: Oxford University Press, 1993.

Ripp, Victor, *From Moscow to Main St., Among the Russian Émigrés.* Boston: Little, Brown and Company, 1984.

Rothenberg, Joshua, *The Jewish Religion in the Soviet Union.* New York: Ktav Publishing House, 1972.

St. George, George, *Siberia; The New Frontier.* New York: David McKay Company, 1969.

Scammell, Michael, *Solzhenitsyn: A Biography.* New York: Norton, 1984.

Schwarz, Solomon M., *The Jews in the Soviet Union.* Syracuse, NY: Syracuse University Press, 1951.

Schwarz, Solomon M., *The Russian Revolution of 1905, the Worker's Movement and the Formation of Bolshevism and Menshevism.* Chicago: Chicago University Press, 1969.

Vitukhin, Igor, *Soviet Generals Recall World War II.* New York: Sphinx Press, Inc.,1981.

Wiesel, Elie, *The Jews of Silence, A Personal Report on Soviet Jewry.* New York: Schocken Books, 1987.

Wistrich, Robert S., *Anti-Semitism, The Longest Hatred.* New York: Schocken Books, 1994.

St. Petersburg
A Special City, A Special People

"No one is forgotten, nothing is forgotten"
                          Olga Berggolts, Russian poet.

A young Orthodox Jewish lady with a lilting soprano voice chants the most beautiful rendition of the Sabbath song, "Sholem Aleichem," I have ever heard in my life. She appears at a Friday afternoon pre-Sabbath program sponsored by Hesed Avraham, a Jewish charitable center in St. Petersburg. Senior citizens were mesmerized—people who look like my grandmother and grandfather and perhaps yours, too; people who, having lived in the former Soviet Union, had dared not openly express any form of Judaism for 50 or 60 years. Now they recite in Hebrew the blessings over wine and bread, an act unthought of even a decade ago.

The Lubavitch movement sets up a "*sukkah* mobile" that is parked for three days on the Nevsky Prospekt, the avenue made famous by Dostoevsky and Gogol. Hundreds of Jews come into the *sukkah*, holding a *lulav* and *ethrog*, and say the blessings. You will see similar scenes of Jewish revival in this city on the Neva, whether you visit in summer or winter.

Imagine, young boys hurrying to the synagogue to say their evening prayers in a house of worship that in reality under Communism was off-limits.

Welcome to St. Petersburg, Russia's second-largest city, the

91

mother of the Russian Revolution, the country's largest port, and home to approximately 5 million people, including about one hundred thousand Jews.

Indeed, large groups of people visit St. Petersburg in the summer, the long days and short nights of the summer solstice. The middle of May to the middle of July is the optimum time to visit St. Petersburg. "The Russian summer is a brief one, but the people make the most of it," wrote author Charles A. Stoddard, in his book *Across Russia, from the Baltic to the Danube*, more than one hundred years ago. "The days are long and beautiful; it is the time of the White Nights."

During summer settings of the sun, Sabbath does not begin till around eleven P.M., and the prayers ending the day of rest on Saturday night do not occur until around midnight.

But eventually, the days will shorten and winter will arrive. Business travel to Russia from November on is heavy, and to some, the snow season remains the realistic time to see the sites. Witness the psychologist who insisted that I should visit Russia in winter. How else could I inhale the crisp, cold air and feel the life of the country down deep in my bones, unless I walked alongside men bundled up under their Russian-style fur-lined hats and greatcoats and Russian women with babushkas and heavy lined coats. Remember that this city is located on the same latitude as southern Alaska and the middle of Hudson Bay. With such a location, there is not much light in winter.

I do not advise the traveler to take an icy bath in the lakes of the city, where in November it was only 17 degrees Fahrenheit, and daylight hours can range from ten A.M. to four P.M. Here winter bathing is a traditional Russian pastime for swimmers who call themselves "walruses," and who can be seen taking dips on some weekends. The average temperature in January is 18 degrees Fahrenheit.

Because of the climate and its location, St. Petersburg has often been called a "city of introversion," "of split personalities," and at the same time a city of "ideas, exuberant and vibrant, fermenting in an extreme individualism." The city captivates every visitor.

Travel literature correctly describes beautiful St. Petersburg as a "city with its window facing westward," a "city which echoes empire," a "city known as a cradle of the Russian Revolution," a "city of Peter the Great," a "city of the tsars," and "a city of majesty with its palaces, and its dreamlike streets." Dostoevsky called carefully planned St. Petersburg "the most fantastic and international city in the world." It will hold you in its spell.

Whatever the season, quick impressions will remain in your mind. You will compare St. Petersburg to Paris or Vienna. You will think you are floating in Venice. Is this city not called "The Venice of the North"? About nine hundred small rivers and four hundred bridges intersect the city. The colors of the buildings will shine forth—sometimes dark red, sometimes green, sometimes yellow, sometimes blue. Factor in those granite-faced banks along the Neva River known as embankments or quays, and your eyes will glow as they scan this attractive metropolis. Keep in mind that here stands the city of Anna Karenina and Vronsky, of Raskolnikov in Dostoevsky's *Crime and Punishment,* of writers and poets such as Pushkin, Chekhov, Bely, and Brodsky, of the musical and dancing artistry of Prokofiev, Shostakovich, Tchaikovsky, Nijinsky, Nureyev, Baryshnikov, and Pavlova. This is a city with museums, theaters, and concert halls that inspire. A visitor to St. Petersburg is never far from the city's 20 or more theaters and concert halls.

The traveler to St. Petersburg should never experience a boring day or night in this capital of culture. There is a rich tradition of design, art, and ballet in Russia. At the beginning of the century, Russian artistic talents as symbolized by Diaghilev and Nijinsky were greatly admired. New talents are here again in today's St. Petersburg. One can attend a performance of the Kirov Ballet at the Mariinsky Theater (formerly the Kirov), or the Mussorgsky Theater of Ballet, or the Opera (formerly the Maly Theater).

The City

Founded in May 16, 1703, the city has been known by many names. Its first official name was the Russian form of the Dutch for Saint Peter's City, "Sankt Pieter Burkh", which became Sankt-Peterburg. Russians, however, have always associated the city with its founder, Peter the Great, not his patron saint, and have called it Petersburg, or more colloquially, "Pieter," according to writers Robert A. Maguire and John E. Malmstad, in *Petersburg*, by Andrew Bely.

In World War I, due to anti-German feelings, Petersburg changed its name to Petrograd, meaning "Peter's city" in Russian. The town fathers wanted to get rid of the German ending, "burg." Ten years later, in 1924, when Communist leader Vladimir Ilyich Lenin died, the municipality took the name "Leningrad." With the fall of Communism in 1991, the people of the city, in what probably was their first "free" referendum, changed the name of the city to St. Petersburg—after Peter the Great.

When Peter I, the Great (1672-1725) came to power in 1689, the country's only seaport was Archangel, located on the White Sea and icebound for half the year. After defeating the Swedes in the first part of the eighteenth century, Russia gained control of the isthmus between Lake Ladoga and the Gulf of Finland. In 1703, here, at the mouth of the Neva River, Peter started building the metropolis that was to be "a window into Europe," as well as a capital "free from the influence of Moscow." In reality, Peter needed a seaport and naval base on the Baltic, and for that reason alone, some say, he built his new capital.

One can see immediately why St. Petersburg owes much of its greatness to the Neva River, which remains frozen four to five months of the year. The city itself was built on a marshy delta where the Neva River ends its 42-mile run from Lake Ladoga, from whence it rises, and empties into the Gulf of Finland, an arm of the Baltic Sea. The Neva takes its name from the Finnish *neiva* or *newo*, meaning "swamps." The main channel of the river flows through the center of the city. Smaller branches divert and form islands and canals whose banks are lined with stucco houses built in the simple, grand style of the classical eighteenth century.

Only by the sea could Russia obtain direct contact with that European civilization that was so necessary for her to become a modern state, notes historian Sir Barnard Pares in *A History of Russia.* Before Peter came to power, Russia's population could be counted as largely illiterate and rural. A civilized infrastructure had to be set up before a modern culture could be established. Even though it would take a great deal of time and lives, Peter started the process of remaking medieval Muscovy into modern Russia.

Many factors were stacked up against Peter the Great building a capital on his chosen site. It was waterlogged and could not be reclaimed without draining the swamp, and decades of pile driving would be required before the weight of buildings could be supported. Subject to floods, the future city could not be supplied from the surrounding countryside, explains historian John Lawrence, in *A History of Russia.* A monument to its founder it may be, however, "its charms invite us to overlook the thousands of lives lost in its creation," argues historian John Keep. Thieves and criminals as well as noblemen had to pitch in to build the city. Every noble and merchant was forced to build a house in the new city, according to traveler and author, Charles A. Stoddard.

Peter forbade stonemasons to work anywhere else in Russia, and he levied a tax, paid in stone, on carts and barges coming to St. Petersburg. Just by looking at the city, one can tell he hired foreign architects, among them Italians, Germans, and Frenchmen. The capital became a showplace of baroque and neoclassic architecture.

The government was moved from Moscow in 1712 and installed in St. Petersburg. For nearly three centuries, the city would become a fortress against Swedes, Lithuanians, Poles, Finns, and finally the Germans, all of whom attempted to conquer not only St. Petersburg, but also Russia itself. They all failed.

St. Petersburg became a special city and its people a special people, says Harrison E. Salisbury. By 1905, the capital had grown into a bustling metropolis, with 1,635,000 residents. The old capital, Moscow, in the words of Pushkin, paled "like a purple-clad widow before a new empress." In the post-Communist era, the queen would go on to sparkle as the "bastion of progressive politics."

A Brief History

Empress or not, the city witnessed five momentous events that would not only shatter Russia and change the course of its history, but also much of the world. Each traveler to this city on the Neva should keep these happenings ready for instant recall.

The first was the assassination of Tsar Alexander II in 1881. His untimely demise in St. Petersburg ended any chance of reform. "Alexander II, who deserved to be honored and loved by every Russian for the great blessings which he conferred upon his people, was the victim of that bloodthirsty and insane nihilism which still terrorizes Russia and makes the life of the present sovereign a hideous nightmare," wrote Stoddard in his 1891 book, *Across Russia*. The tsar's death ushered in an era of reactionary policies, including pogroms. With his demise came two inept rulers.

Tsar Alexander III vented his wrath on the Jews and was behind the issuance of *numerous clausus* and the land exclusion law. Both Alexander III and his son, Tsar Nicholas II, were hostile to Jews, to say the least.

Nicholas II had the support of monarchist organizations, such as the Union of the Russian Peoples, an organization that Orlando Figes defines as "an earlier version of the Fascist movement." These people hated Jews. The tsar blamed the Jewish people for the disturbances of 1905. Nicholas II, who was 26 years old when he succeeded to the throne, also believed the Jews "responsible for subverting the entire empire." "So long as I am Tsar, the Zhyds of Russia shall not have equal rights," he is reported to have said. The anti-Semitic Black Hundreds "knew only one way to solve the Jewish question—kill the Jews, notes Simon M. Dubnow in his *History of the Jews in Russia and Poland, From the Earliest Times Until the Present Day, 1920*.

The assassination of Alexander II also began the process of vast Jewish emigration that would last about 40 years. It brought several million Jews to America, and eventually thousands would participate in creating a Jewish state in Palestine.

This massive Jewish emigration became "one of the most extensive movements of people in modern times," says

Lindemann, in *Esau's Tears: Modern Anti-Semitism and the Rise of the Jews.*

Between 1881 and 1914, nearly three million Jews headed for the United States, approximately two hundred thousand to Britain, and about sixty thousand to Palestine. More would have come to America, but in the early 1920s, the U.S. closed its gates to emigration.

From 1881 to 1917, Russia passed through an exceedingly black period for Jews, often described as the worst decades in Jewish history since Chmielnicki's Cossacks slaughtered Jews in Ukraine, in the uprising that began in 1648.

Here we should mention Tsarina Alexandra and her depraved holy man Grigor Rasputin. A half-mad empress and a "diabolic holy man" held the fate of Russia in their hands, notes Potok. With Nicholas at the front commanding his army in the First World War, Alexandra and Rasputin literally ruled the country. "A charlatan who pretended to stand close to God and the Russian people, Rasputin had, for more than a decade used his strange, hypnotic ability to stem the bleeding of Russia's hemophilic tsarevitch, Aleksei, to gain the Empress's unreserved confidence," W. Bruce Lincoln declares in *Red Victory: A History of the Russian Civil War.* Even though Rasputin had no use for Jews, historian Salo Baron points out in *The Russian Jew Under Tsars and Soviets,* we cannot attribute the misfortune of Jews to the evil influence of this man whom he calls a drunkard, a lecher, and a horse thief. Historian Pares maintains Rasputin was a "violent opponent of any diminution of the autocracy." Protected by the imperial couple, Rasputin gambled and dabbled in intrigue in St. Petersburg until he was assassinated in 1916. Still, the Romanovs "sank further into infamy" until the Revolution arrived in 1917—a revolution caused in large part by World War I's demand on the government and people.

The second point to remember as you tour St. Petersburg is Russian involvement in the First World War. For Russians, the call to arms emanated from this city. Few nations would suffer like Russia in World War I. About 13 million combatants were killed on five continents during the war, with the Russians losing about half of that number. Not only was the Russian monarchy doomed, but the emperors of Germany and Austria were also toppled because of the war. Except for the Great War, Lenin, Trotsky, and the other Bolsheviks, many historians believe, probably would have remained exiles. And even if there would have been a Russian upheaval during peacetime, it may not have resulted in a Communist takeover.

Our third cataclysmic event we know as the Russian Revolution of February 1917, which eight months later resulted in the Communist October Revolution, a phenomenon which we shall explore later in this chapter

But in March 1917, "for the first time in Russian history, Jews acquired full civic rights," notes Florinsky. The February revolution of 1917 could have laid the groundwork for a democratic Russian government. Rid of tsarism, minorities were free. Jews were emancipated. Discriminatory laws and practices were discarded. Jews achieved complete legal equality with the rest of the population. St. George says the Jewish professionals and the intelligentsia obviously welcomed the change. "A large number of early revolutionary leaders were Jews, a fact that was widely used by counterrevolutionary forces for propaganda purposes." However, while Jews were involved in the Revolution, and many were Bolsheviks, most stayed on the sidelines.

St. Petersburg became a center of organizations of all parties and factions of Russian Jewry. In fact, in June 1917, the Seventh Conference of the Zionist Organization of Russia was held in St. Petersburg.

An interesting anecdote was that Yitzhak Sadeh was called the "Jewish Garibaldi," after the Italian patriot who founded the Red Shirts. Sadeh would go on to organize the Jewish Palmach commandos, who played a decisive role in Israel's War of Independence. A general, essayist, boxer, wrestler, and football player, Sadeh came to Petrograd as a social revolutionary officer during the Russian Revolution.

Moreover, in 1917, a Jewish battalion under the command of Joseph Trumpeldor was formed, and was made up of Jewish soldiers of the local garrison. Around this battalion a self-defense unit was organized that protected Jewish lives and property from February through October 1917. We shall meet up with Trumpeldor again in Odessa.

The Provisional Government never lasted. Alexander Kerensky, prime minister of the Provisional Government in 1917 until the Bolshevik takeover, had come into power at a time of the greatest crisis of the country since Napoleon invaded Russia. He could not keep his promises, he couldn't obtain financial support, and he couldn't avoid military defeat, for the Central Powers were very much involved in the war in the summer and autumn of 1917. Subversion was unnecessary. Lenin and Trotsky did not make the Revolution, "they merely presided over a set of events arising from the Provisional Government's disastrous decision to go on with the war," according to authors Jay Winter and Blaine Baggett, authors of *The Great War and the Shaping of the 20th Century.* "The Provisional Government lacked the aura of legitimacy that a popular election might have conferred upon it," says historian Robert Service.

The Bolshevik Revolution radically changed the lives of not only the Russian people, but in the long run, the lives of millions around the world.

As a result of the Communist takeover, the capital was moved back to Moscow in March 1918, and once again power was transferred to the older city. Petrograd not only began to feel the physical loss as designated capital, but also began to worry about its own future. For two hundred years, Peter and his successors had lorded the capital on the Baltic over Moscow. Now it was Moscow's turn to pay back the founder's city.

Since its founding, St. Petersburg had been Russia's geographical link with the Western world, especially after World War I, when Russia lost so much territory, including the Baltic provinces and Finland. The city became the most westernized of Russian metropolitan areas.

Moscow, on the other hand, was traditional Russia to the core. When they arrived in Moscow, the new Red rulers of the country moved from the Italian and French palaces into the somber medieval splendor of a Kremlin filled with the memories of the darkest age of Russian absolutism. "It is not impossible, although, perhaps not very plausible, that these gloomy semi-Asiatic surroundings had some effect upon the subsequent evolution of the doctrine and practice of Marxism-Leninism and have in some degree influenced the growth of that peculiar Byzantinism which may be regarded as a characteristic of the second Moscow period of Russian history," according to author and journalist Harrison E. Salisbury.

History tells us that the acting out of Stalin's bizarre intrigues would not be far off, especially for the people of the city on the Neva River. First, Zinoviev, the old Jewish Bolshevik of St. Petersburg, was demoted in 1927. Then came the purges of the 1930s. The purges, the fourth momentous event in the city's history, were unleashed because of the murder of Kirov, who had served as Communist Party boss of St. Petersburg and who had been sent to replace the dethroned Zinoviev. Stalin must have thought Kirov had gathered too much popular support during the latter's tenure in office, for on December 1, 1934, a young man named Leonid V. Nikolayev walked into Kirov's office in the Smolny Institute and shot him. Nowhere did the resulting terror strike more harshly than in St. Petersburg, then known as Leningrad. Over one hundred party leaders were executed immediately, according to Harrison Salisbury in *The 900 Days; The Siege of Leningrad*. Later, Zinoviev and Kamenev were blamed for the killing, and were put to death, although Stalin was probably responsible for Kirov's death. In the end, Stalin sentenced thousands of Leningrad citizens to death, in an unprecedented reign of terror.

The fifth momentous event to affect this city remains, of course, the World War II siege of Leningrad, resulting in the death of nearly one million men, women, and children due to German bombing, shelling, and the resulting blockade that caused the city to starve. It is called the "900 Days," during which the people of Leningrad sacrificed nearly one-third of the population. But they never surrendered, and their resistance helped defeat the Nazi invaders.

The siege can not be described without pain, a pain that has not really subsided in the mind of each Russian. Clyde Haberman was correct when he wrote in the *New York Times* of June 26, 1998, that no one has to "teach the Russians about pain." "The Victory Monument of the 900 Days" is a fitting site

Marc Chagall (front row, third from left), is seen here early in his career, when he resided in St. Petersburg, joining a group of artists and writers at the Third International Children's Colony, founded by the JDC near Moscow, in 1923. (Photo credit: American Jewish Joint Distribution Committee)

to visit, and we shall see it later in our tour of St. Petersburg. In the Russian Civil War that followed the Communist seizure of power, Red Petrograd stood its ground and defended itself against White tanks with nothing but rifles, so the story goes. To honor Trotsky's role in the defense of Petrograd, he was awarded the Order of the Red Banner, the first such order of its kind. To recognize his status as the hero of the city of Gatchina, where much of the fighting had taken place, the town was renamed Trotsk. Ironically, it was the first Soviet town to be named after a living Communist, even though Stalin accused Trotsky of Bonapartism.

As we know from history, it was "the pot calling the kettle black," so to speak. At one time or another Stalin would unleash murder and terror over St. Petersburg, Russia, and the Jewish community.

Let us now turn to some notable Jews who were part of the scene here and whom we shall now meet as we visit this and other cities in Russia.

Notable Jews

Marc Chagall (1887-1985). Though he lived in France for many years, Marc Chagall's roots of course go back to Vitebsk in Belarus. Chagall, widely regarded as the greatest modern Jewish artist, arrived in St. Petersburg in the winter of 1906-07 and found a job as a retoucher with the photographer Yaffe, who was also an artist. The sculptor Ilya Guenzburg gave him a letter of recommendation to Baron David Guenzburg, who in turn offered him a stipend. Chagall painted signs for various shops in St. Petersburg and even worked as a salesman for a while. Later, a St. Petersburg patron hired Chagall as a personal valet so he could live in the capital and study at various private schools. After a sojourn in Paris, he returned to Russia in 1914. In the summer of 1915, he went back to Vitebsk, where he married Bella (Bertha Rosenfeld). During the war, he remained in Petrograd until the early spring of 1917. He and Bella lived in a flat at **7 Perekupny Pere'ulok.** The building still stands. Following the October Revolution, Chagall traveled back to

Vitebsk. He helped found the Moscow Yiddish State Theater in 1919. That same year, he participated in an exhibition of revolutionary art held in the Winter Palace. Today, a number of his paintings are on display in the Russian Museum in St. Petersburg. Chagall paid a last visit to Leningrad in 1973.

Simon M. Dubnow (1860-1941), noted historian of the Jews of Poland, Lithuania, and Russia. Before Dubnow, there were hardly any historians of the Jews of Eastern Europe. A political activist, he arrived in St. Petersburg in June 1880 and continued his education until 1922. In *The Jews of St. Petersburg: Excursions Through a Noble Past,* author Mikhail Beizer says that it would be hard to find a St. Petersburg publication from 1880 to 1920 "that did not contain one of Dubnow's literary or polemic articles." His attitude toward the Bolsheviks was negative. He was worried about the participation of Jews in the Red Terror, and fled Russia in 1922. He was murdered by the Germans on a Riga, Latvia street in 1941.

Boris Pasternak (1890-1965), poet and novelist and, as the *Encyclopedia Judaica* states, "one of the truly great Russian poets of all time." Pasternak was reared in a cultured Zionist home of a famous painter and friend of Leo Tolstoy. The son "drifted spiritually into the world of both Russian populism and Russian Orthodox mysticism," according to Baron. He was "one of the very few Soviet Jewish writers whose work is essentially Christian in spirit." Some say his historic novel *Doctor Zhivago* reveals Pasternak's total estrangement from Judaism and his faith in the superiority of Christianity, although Pasternak never converted. In 1950, when Pasternak was awarded the Nobel Prize for *Doctor Zhivago,* the Soviet government refused to give him permission to fly to Stockholm and receive the prize.

Simon An-sky, (1863-1920). Semyon Akimovitch Rapoport wrote under the pen name of An-sky. A renowned Russian and Yiddish writer, An-sky was a former *narodnik,* or populist, and a member of the People's Will Party. Born in 1863 in Vitebsk, the city of the great Jewish artist Marc Chagall, An-sky, like many of his contemporary Jewish revolutionaries, "went out to the people." He wrote on Jewish themes. His most famous work is *The Dybbuk,* a play that has become a classic. An-sky helped organize the Jewish Museum in St. Petersburg. He left Russia for Vilna, and then went on to Poland, where he died in Warsaw on November 9, 1920. The world Jewish press mourned his demise.

Travel Tips

Whether you land at the airport or walk down the gangplank of a luxury cruise ship, it doesn't take much time to realize that St. Petersburg is badly in need of repair. The municipality is simply out of money, it is reported. Some tourists and observers call Russia a "Third World Country," and therefore discount immediately the inherent beauty of its cities and countryside. They see much that is crudely patched together. They see dilapidated housing. They see ill-clad Russians. They see rusting ships, rusting cranes, and rusting cars. They are amazed that this rundown city was part of the world's second-greatest military power. But that does not, and should not, stop the tourist from visiting the Hermitage, Catherine's Palace in Pushkin, the Great Palace in Petrodvorests (Peterhof), the Nevsky Prospekt, Smolny, and other eye-catching sites. It has been said St. Petersburg is about power, past and future, and the sites you see will bring that atmosphere to your heart and soul.

Whether they walk down the Champs Élysées or the Nevsky, seasoned travelers know that they should exercise caution. Here are some tips for the traveler to St. Petersburg, for instance.

In St. Petersburg, or in any other city, it is always advisable to stay in the normal tourist areas and not to travel to out-of-the-way places without the benefit of a reputable tour guide.

Always travel with a companion.

Don't leave any of your belongings unattended in public areas.

Be generally aware of people and activities around you.

Do not accept packages from anyone you don't know.

Keep a low profile. Dress and behave conservatively, and remove excessive jewelry.

Do not drink local water. Drink bottled water.

Make sure you have your visas, hotel vouchers, and passport in proper order.

Sites

Nevsky Prospekt. "There is teeming life on the Nevsky," wrote the famous Jewish novelist Isaac Babel. It seems that all Russia promenades on the Nevsky, the city's Champs Élysées. So, you, too, can saunter on this, the main street of St. Petersburg, this large, great, busy boulevard, which the poet Aleksandr Blok thought "the most lyric street, the most poetic in the world."

"There is nothing more beautiful than the Prospekt, at least in Petersburg," said Nikolai Gogol. However, for Trotsky, it was merely "the main artery of the bourgeoisie."

The Nevsky runs to Znamenskaya Square, where the railway station is located. Here one boards trains to Moscow, Tver, and Novgorod.

This famous and fashionable thoroughfare measures 115 feet wide and 2.75 miles long; it is the longest street in the city. St. Petersburg was laid out according to the most up-to-date Western theories of city planning, with perfectly straight streets and boulevards. The Nevsky was named in honor of Alexander, the son of Yaroslof, the Prudent, known as the "Liberator of Russia." Born in 1221, he pushed back the Swedes and Teutonic Knights. He is said to have wounded the king of Sweden on the banks of the Neva in 1240. He then took the name of Nevsky, which became Alexander Nevsky, according to writer Charles A. Stoddard. When you walk down the Nevsky, you may see few people smiling. This in a land that is not known for people walking around with smiles on their faces all the time. If some persons are laughing, they must be in the under-thirty group, for the older generation does not laugh too often, it is said. The young Russian wants to enjoy life, to dine out, to dance, to drive a nice car, to do more than just survive, as he or she may have done in the past.

Pushkin Apartment Museum, near Nevsky Park, Moika 12 Embankment, St. Petersburg. Russian literature was born here on the shores of the Neva. This city is the home of Aleksandr Pushkin(1799-1837), considered the nation's greatest poet. His statue is located in Arts Square. This first great Russian writer and poet, this Pushkin, "is in the bread Russians eat, the wine they drink," according to poet Alexander Kushner. Deeply revered throughout Russia, he wrote the historic tragedy *Boris Godunov* and the verse novel, *Eugene Onegin.*

Speaking of Pushkin, we must note that this literary city boasts that it is the home of not only Pushkin, but also Fyodor Dostoevsky (1821-1881), and Nikolai Gogol (1809-1852), as well as Aleksandr Blok and Aleksandr Mayakovsky. Authors are not only read in Russia, they are loved. Poets and novelists are honored. The great Russian writers had little personal contact with Jews and were not familiar with Jewish life. Their description of Jewish characters was "stereotyped and lifeless," states Salo Baron, Jewish historian. These great Russian masters—Pushkin, Lermontov, and even the better-informed Gogol—wrote about Jewish poisoners, spies, and cowardly traitors, points out Baron. The great Russian writer Ivan S. Turgenev was but moderately friendly in his story *The Zhid.* In the final analysis, Gogol, Pushkin, Lermontov, Turgenev, and others all depicted Jews as repulsive characters.

The museum highlighting the life of Pushkin consists of 11 rooms, including displays of his documents, writing desk, canes, and the waistcoat he was wearing when he was killed at age 37 in a duel fought in the snow over the honor of his wife.

In June 1999, all Russia participated in the celebration of the two-hundredth anniversary of Pushkin's birth, for he truly is the backbone of Russian culture.

Museum of Fyodor Dostoevsky (1821-1881), Kuznechny Pereulok 5/2, St. Petersburg. William Phillips wrote in the 1996 *Partisan Review* that "Dostoevsky, in my opinion, was one of the greatest—if not the greatest—of novelists." Dostoevsky spent more than 30 years in St. Petersburg, where he created his greatest novels: *Crime and Punishment,* and *The Brothers Karamazov.* Dostoevsky, an anti-Semitic writer who was certainly unfriendly to Jews, nevertheless said in a letter written in February 1877 that, "I am by no means, nor have I ever been, an enemy of the Jews," according to Baron in his book, *The Russian Jews under Tsars and Soviets.* Mikhail Beizer quotes Dostoevsky's diary, where the writer said he was surprised to learn he was considered a hater of the Jews. "For in my heart, I have never felt this hatred. On the contrary, I say and write that everything that humanitarianism and justice require, everything that humanity and Christian laws demand, all this should be done for Jews." Still, Dostoevsky and author Ivan Aksakov exhibited anti-Semitic tendencies.

Beizer notes, however, that many Jews are in love with Dostoevsky. "One of the main reasons for this phenomenon may be that in Dostoevsky's novels (if we leave out the Jewish question) we encounter not rationalism, not faith, not expediency," but ethics; "not the cult of the strong, but an apologia for the weak." He adds: "a philosophy that is much more Judaic than Christian permeates all of Dostoevsky's works, for the Russian writer stresses soul." By the way, you can visit **Number 7 Pergevalsky Street,** where both Dostoevsky and Raskolnikov, the hero of *Crime and Punishment,* lived. A tour of the sites of *Crime and Punishment* is also offered. The museum includes documents, manuscripts, photographs, and maps illustrating places connected with Dostoevsky's life and characters.

Osip Mandelstam House, No. 70 Zagorodny Prospekt. Osip Mandelstam (1891-1938), was one of the greatest Russian poets of the twentieth century. His peers were Boris Pasternak, Anna Akhmatova, and Marina Tsvetayeva. He certainly belongs to the list of great Russian writers that includes Michael Bulgakov, Vladimir Nabokov, Evgeniia Ginsberg, and Alexander Solzhenitzyn. Born in Warsaw into a family of middle-class Jewish merchants, he attended school and university in St. Petersburg. He studied literature and philosophy in France, and in Germany, where he resided. He may have tried to run away from his Jewishness, but Beizer argues that there are definitely Jewish motifs that "expressed a perception and understanding of life that is peculiarly Jewish." Mandelstam, a Jew who openly admired the West, has never been wholly embraced by Russians as one of theirs, it is said. "Russian writers look at me with canine tenderness in their eyes, imploring me to drop dead," he once complained. Mandelstam described Stalin in a brilliant verse that cost him his life. Stalin was the "Kremlin mountaineer," wrote Mandelstam in a poem called "The Stalin Epigram." Mandelstam goes on to cite "the huge cockroaches" on Stalin's "top lip." Stalin alone goes boom, says the poem from *Osip Mandelstam Selected Poems,* translated by Clarence Brown and W.S. Mervin. This devastating poem about Stalin was recited to a handful of his literary friends. Someone squealed on him, according to Mark Taplin, author of *Open Lands: Travel Through Russia's Once Forbidden Places,* and the secret police arrested Mandelstam in May 1934. His wife Nadezhada went with him into captivity.

Exiled to various places, including Veronezh, he was allowed to return to Moscow a few years later. In 1938, he was picked up again by police and dispatched to Barracks No. 2 of the Vtoraya Rechka transit camp near Vladivostok. Here thousands of "enemies of the people" disembarked from the Trans-Siberian Railway and languished until they could be dispatched in slave ships across the Sea of Okhotsk to the dreaded Kolyma camps above Magadan. One of his fellow inmates was the dissident writer Evgeniia Ginzburg.

According to Clarence Brown in his book, *Mandelstam,* the official date of Osip Mandelstam's death was December 27, 1938, supposedly of "heart failure."Mandelstam's remains are thought to rest in a mass grave not far from the old camp perimeter. Today few come along the shady road that leads to the site, which was renamed after him by the Vladivostok City Council. Thanks to his widow, Nadezhada Mandelstam, much of his late work survived.

Joseph Brodsky's House, Pestel Street 27. This huge Moorish-style mansion is Joseph Brodsky's former home. Born during the Leningrad siege, Brodsky left school at 15 and began to write at 18. He taught himself English and Polish, and when still a young man, he impressed the poet Anna Akhmatova. In 1964, he was accused of "parasitism" and was sentenced to internal exile in the far north of the USSR. In 1972, he was put on a plane to Vienna, where he was met by his idol, W. H. Auden. Brodsky moved to Ann Arbor, Michigan, and later to New York City. He taught at Columbia University and Holyoke College. In 1987, Brodsky won the Nobel Prize for Literature and was named America's poet laureate.

Decembrists Square, (once called Senate Square), was named

The author is pictured in front of the "Bronze Horseman" statue of Peter the Great in St. Petersburg. (Photo credit: Ben G. Frank)

in honor of the revolutionaries and of the nobility who rose to power on December 14, 1825. This badly staged demonstration was quashed without any difficulty. In December 1825, after the death of Tsar Alexander I, a group of aristocratic officers wanted to install Alexander's brother, the more liberal Constantine, on the throne in place of his younger brother, Nicholas. Nearly all of these officers had fought in the war against Napoleon and were called the "Children of 1812." Having spent time in Paris at the end of the Napoleonic War, these officers returned to Russia with new customs, new manners, new ideas, and new impressions. High on their list was the aim of bringing new democratic institutions to Russia. "Their hope," writes Michael Scammell, author of *Solzhenitsyn: A Biography*, "was that the more liberal Constantine would promulgate an enlightened constitution for Russia limiting the monarch's powers and enshrining the rule of law." But Constantine had refused the offer and supported his brother Nicholas. The officers attempted a coup d'état. During the "interregnum," Nicholas I promptly crushed the rebellion by force, executed five of the ringleaders, imprisoned others, and exiled considerable numbers to Siberia. The cruel suppression of the Decembrists by the victorious tsar outraged the youth of Russia. Many became nihilists, and from the nihilists came the Bolsheviks, says Abraham Thomi, author of *Between Darknesss & Dawn: A Saga of Hehalutz.*

Bronze Horseman, Decembrists Square. (Also known by its prerevolutionary name, Senate Square). On their wedding day, young couples come here to place roses at the foot of the statue or pose in front of this massive and impressive statue of Peter the Great. You can't go far in this city without being reminded of Peter the Great (1672-1725), or of Catherine the Great (1729-1796), for that matter. That's probably why the most famous monument of Petersburg remains the equestrian statue of Peter the Great known as the "Bronze Horseman," immortalized by Pushkin's long poem of the same title.

The monument stands as a "symbol of the state in the shape of a massive horse, thundering on the heels of a defenseless man who is running away from it, and rearing on its bronze hooves over his head," according to poet Yevgeny Yevtushenko, who adds, "all the great Russian literature initiated by Pushkin can be seen as the ordinary person's defense against the state's bronze hooves."

Peter the Great has been seen as a ruler who created "a new Russia," all by himself. But there were chinks in his armor—his iron rule, his coercion, his oppression, and his heavy taxation. In fact, most of his subjects "sighed with relief when he died in 1725," declared author John Keep.

The monument was unveiled on August 7, 1782. It was inscribed "Peter the First, Catherine the Second," and was the result of many years' work by the great French sculptor Etienne Maurice Falconet (1716-1791). The tsar is riding up a rocky slope, his face turned to the Neva. He points with his right hand toward the area where he worked. The horse is balanced on its hind legs and tail, while its hoofs trample on a writhing snake. Falconet made the model in 1769 and supervised the work of casting it in 1775. Marie Collot, Falconet's pupil, created the head of the rider. Fyodor Gordeyev carved the snake. The enormous granite block that forms the pedestal is 46 feet long, 19.5 feet wide, and 16.5 feet high. This great rock, found in Finland, was known as the "thunder stone," because lightning had supposedly split it.

One can feel almost physically the strength and willpower of the laurel-crowned rider as he reins in his horse from a full gallop.

Catherine the Second, the Great, was interested in attracting Jewish persons and professionals She asked her officials to overlook the presence of those "useful" Jews who lived there with their families. "We tolerate them," she wrote to Diderot in 1773, "in spite of the law, pretending we don't know they are in the capital." She may have officially stopped Jews from living here, but she kept individual Jews in town. By the end of the eighteenth century, a substantial Jewish community had settled in St. Petersburg. Because of the partitions of Poland in 1773, 1792, and 1795, Catherine and Russia now ruled over the world's largest Jewish community.

When Peter the Great was in Holland, the story goes, the Amsterdam Jewish community wanted him to admit Jews into

Russia. But he claimed that "time has not yet come to bring these two nationalities together." He is supposed to have felt that if admitted, Jews would suffer from "the hostility of the Russian people." According to Levitats in *The Jewish Community in Russia, 1772-1844*, Peter said of the Jews, "They are rogues and cheats. It is my endeavor to eradicate evil, not to multiply it."

On the other hand, Peter, who created fear among all his subjects, saved a synagogue when he stopped an attack on Jews by ordering the execution of 13 ringleaders, and he allowed converted Jews to come to Moscow.

He also had a court jester, a Marrano by the name of Acosta, "whose biting satire helped the Emperor to expose to public ridicule some of the boyar's 'backward' mores," according to Salo Baron. Peter Shafirov (1669-1739), son of a converted Jew, rose to become a baron and negotiated several treaties for Peter the Great.

In her book, *Russia in the Age of Peter the Great,* Lindsay Hughes says that Tsar Peter "could not tolerate Jews or Jesuits."

Peter said that it would take three Jews to deceive one Russian. "Your position in the empire would be too miserable; you have the reputation of cheating all the world, but my children would be too much for you," he is reported to have said.

"Despite his courting of foreigners, Peter was violently anti-Semitic," according to Michael Florinsky. "I would much rather have Mohammedans or heathens than Jews. The Jews are scoundrels and rascals," said the man who was the first Russian ruler to travel widely at home and abroad.

In 1727, two years after Peter died, a decree was issued that Jews should not be admitted into Russia for any reason. Another decree in 1742 prohibited Jews from residing in Russia and ordered their immediate deportation unless they embraced the Greek Orthodox Church, points out historian Michael T. Florinsky. This Russian quarantine against Jews lasted well into the eighteenth century.

So-called Judaizers were discovered in Novgorod in 1470. People said that the Judaizers denied the Holy Trinity, maintained that the Messiah had not come, and claimed that Judaism was the only true religion. The name "Judaizers" was therefore a useful weapon in a religious movement which, it seems, was inspired by three Jews known as Skharia, Moses, and Samuel, who came to Novgorod in the 1470s.

Peter and Paul Fortress. Walk on the grounds of the Fortress of Peter and Paul, this Russian Bastille, probably the first structure built in this city. This building is a monument to repression. This Fortress of Peter and Paul contains the State Prison, the Cathedral of Saints Peter and Paul, the Mint, and the Old Arsenal with an artillery museum. All Russian emperors of the house of Romanov since Peter the Great (with the exception of Peter II), their wives, and the imperial grand dukes and grand duchesses are buried here in the imperial vaults.

This fortress has seen many a famous prisoner. As Jewish visitors stand on the ramparts of this fortress at the banks of the Neva, they might be surprised to learn that the founder and leader of the Chabad Chassidim, or Lubavitch, was once incarcerated here.

In 1798 and in 1800-1801, Shneur Zalman (1747-1812) of Liady, the founder and leader of the Chabad Chassidic dynasty and a leading disciple of Rabbi Dov Ber of Mezhirech, as well as follower of Ba'al Shem Tov, was thrown into prison here. The opponents of Chassidism, who were known as *mitnaggedim,* informed on Shneur Zalman's followers to the tsarist government. Shneur Zalman, (the Ba'al HaTanya), was accused of treason against the state. He had sent money to Palestine, and that act was interpreted as "helping the Turkish sultan." As if that were not enough, "the denunciation severely blackened the character of the Chassidic leader and portrayed him as immoral and opposed to the government."

Shneur Zalman was brought to trial in St. Petersburg, but was acquitted and released on the 19 of Kislev in 1798. The man who actually accused him was Rabbi Avigdor, the rabbi of Pinsk. The day of his release is celebrated by the Chabad Chassidim as the "Holiday of Deliverance." He was arrested again in 1801, on the same charge, and again released. His eldest son, Rabbi Dov Ber (1773-1827), became leader of Chabad and settled in the little town of Lubavitch. He was the grandfather of the late Rabbi Menachem Mendel Schneerson (1902-94), some of whose followers declared to be the Messiah.

As you walk through the prison, you may want to recall other prisoners who were incarcerated here. But first, let us note that you are standing in the oldest building in St. Petersburg. Also, don't be frightened at noon when the cannon goes off with a loud boom.

The spire of the Peter and Paul Fortress rises four hundred feet. Built in 1703, the citadel is located at the mouth of the Neva River, directly opposite the Winter Palace. Containing damp and gloomy cells, the fortress was also used as a military outpost and prison. Not a single prisoner escaped from the fortress occupied by revolutionaries. Here was the cell of Vera Figner (1852-1942), a revolutionary and sister of the famous tenor Nicholas Figner. Vera became a legendary figure for the communists. She had been exiled in 1904 and spent her time abroad lecturing about her experiences before the 1917 Revolution. Maxim Gorky (1868-1936) also served a sentence in this prison.

You can peek into the cell of Lenin's brother, Alexander I. Ulyanov (1866-87), who was imprisoned here before he was hanged for his part in an attempt to kill the tsar. Hessia Helfman, one of the conspirators who killed Tsar Alexander II, also died in the Peter and Paul Fortress.

The last prisoners held in the fortress were the rebellious sailors of the Kronstadt uprising in 1921, which was put down by brute force by the Communists, a decision made, we are told, by Leon Trotsky, who at that time was probably second only to Lenin.

In 1979 the bodies of the tsar and his family were discovered in a mass grave in Yekaterinburg. In 1991 the family bones were excavated, except those of the tsar's son, Alexis, and one of his daughters. Having been banished to Yekaterinburg, the tsar and his wife, Alexandra, and their five children were murdered in the cellar by their Red captors on July 17, 1918. Many cite this as an example of Red Terror. The head of the group of Bolshevik soldiers, Yakov Yurovsky, happened to be Jewish. When the country learned of the tsar's assassination, a rumor spread that Jews were responsible for his death. Supporters of the conspiracy theory rely on the fact that many of the early Bolsheviks were Jews, including Yurovsky. Of course, the murder by the Bolsheviks came on orders from Lenin in Moscow. Interestingly, over the years, various Russian Orthodox Church officials have spread a rumor in the form of a question: "Did Tsar Nicholas II and his family perish in a ritual murder perpetrated by a Jewish conspiracy? As Lev Krichevsky, JTA correspondent in Russia wrote in a dispatch, "no matter how strange the question might seem, it is listed on the agenda of a Russian government commission charged with investigating the death of the Tsar and his family and identifying his remains." But the fact that the church raised the question at all could be seen even today as testimony to the persistence of anti-Semitic beliefs among some members of the church's nationalist wing. Nemtsov himself, of Jewish origin, a former Russian deputy prime minister, headed a government commission that used historical and forensic arguments to dispel the version of the death that holds Jews responsible.

In 1997, the bones of Tsar Nicholas II, the last tsar, and that of his family, except his son Alexis and one of his daughters, were buried in the family crypt in the Cathedral of the Fortress.

Smolny Institute, Smolny, St. Petersburg. Actually, there are two Smolnys: The one we refer to here is not the marvelously built Baroque Church, but the Smolny Institute, located next door to this house of worship. The institute served as the command post for the October Revolution, or, as it should be known, the Communist Takeover. Lenin lived in the building for 124 days. Today, his rooms remain unchanged. The armchairs are still uncovered. The beds on which he and his wife Nadezhda Krupskaya and Trotsky slept are still made. In this building, Lenin proclaimed the Soviet state on October 25, 1917. Trotsky, born Lev Davidovitch Bronstein in 1879, "as second in command gave Lenin the most effective assistance," wrote historian Sir Barnard Pares.

For weeks in 1917, Trotsky/Bronstein never left Smolny. For 24 hours a day, he toiled for the Revolution. He labored to overthrow the Provisional Government. He ate, slept, and worked in his office. He and his wife lived in one room on the top floor. A poor artist's attic-studio, it was even partitioned to make good use of the space, according to writer Louise Bryant, in *Six Red Months in Moscow*.

Today, Lev Davidovich Bronstein is not a household name in the former Soviet Union. Yes, residents know who he is, "this accomplished revolutionary propagandist, brilliant orator and military leader" of the 1917 Bolshevik Revolution. Considered a demon of power, this great writer was perhaps the "greatest leader the Revolution ever produced." But in essence, he is really forgotten by the Russian people.

Some could go as far as to say no Jew in modern times, until the founding of the State of Israel, rivaled his power. "He is without question the most dramatic character produced during the whole sweep of the Russian revolution and its only great organizer," said Louise Bryant, in her book *Mirrors of Moscow*. As the chief rabbi of Moscow once put it, "it was the Trotskys who made the revolutions, but it was the Bronsteins who paid the bills."

Trotsky favored the armed uprising. This idol of the Reds, this first Soviet foreign minister, was adored by his disciples, according to Theodore Draper. Let us not forget that he was, as author Dimitrii Volkogonov points out in *Trotsky: The Eternal Revolutionary*, "one of the architects of the Soviet totalitarian bureaucratic system." Just for openers, he helped institute the Red Terror and smashed the sailor revolt at the Kronstadt naval base.

The son of a Jewish farmer in the southern Ukraine, Trotsky, then still known as Bronstein, was schooled in Odessa. He studied math at Odessa University, but gave up his studies to devote himself to revolutionary activities. He joined the illegal Social Democratic Party in 1896, and was arrested by the tsarist authorities in 1898 and sent to Siberia. He escaped to England in October 1902 and arrived on a forged passport issued in the name of "Trotsky," the name of the jailer, as the story goes. In London, he cooperated with Russian Social Democratic Party leaders Lenin, Martov, and Axelrod in editing that party's newspaper, *Iskra.*

At the Second Congress of the Russian Social Democratic Party in 1903, Trotsky attacked Lenin and supported the Mensheviks. He then became an independent socialist. Trotsky returned to Russia at the outbreak of the 1905 Revolution and became a leader of the Revolutionary Workers Council (Soviet) in St. Petersburg. Arrested, he escaped again and sailed to New York. There, Trotsky lived as an exile in the Bronx. We know that Trotsky rented a three-room apartment. Inexpensive by American standards, this domicile gave him the unaccustomed luxuries of electric light, a chute for garbage, and a telephone. In fact, he scraped a living together from writing émigré journalism and lecturing in English and German on the need for a world revolution. He ate in Jewish delicatessens and made himself unpopular with the waiters by refusing to tip them, on the grounds that it was injurious to their dignity. He also bought some furniture on an installment plan, two hundred dollars of which remained unpaid when the family left for Russia in the spring, just after the first revolution of 1917. By the time the credit company caught up with him, Trotsky had become foreign minister of the largest country in the world.

But let us not forget that Trotsky believed there was no future for the Jews as a separate people. He favored Jewish assimilation. He visualized the solution of the Jewish problem only through the socialist reshaping of society within an international framework. "He was quite aware of the fact that his Jewish origin was a political handicap," according to the *Encyclopedia Judaica.*

After the victory of November 7, 1917, when Lenin nominated Trotsky as the head of the first Soviet government, Trotsky refused. In his own words, he mentioned, "among other arguments . . . would it be wise to give into the hands of the enemies such an additional weapon as my being Jewish?"

Later, Trotsky was shocked at the anti-Semitic innuendoes of the campaign conducted against him in the late 1920s in Russia. He pointed to the anti-Semitic undertones of the Moscow trials in the 1930s case against Zinoviev, Kamenev, and others.

In the Civil War that followed the Communist takeover, Trotsky saved Petrograd from the Whites in 1919. Red Petrograd stood its ground and defended itself against White tanks with nothing but their rifles, so the story goes.

Ukrainian nationalists and the White Army never got over the fact that they were beaten by the Red Army, led by the Jew, Leon Trotsky. A Jew had inflicted defeat upon the White Army that was commanded by old Russian generals. It drove them "batty," wrote Thomi.

By 1923, Trotsky was involved in a "ferocious struggle with Stalin," who was by then the Party secretary-general. Trotsky's political life ended with his expulsion from Moscow into exile in 1927. He moved to Alma Ata, in a faraway corner of the Soviet Union in January 1928, then to Turkey in 1929, and then began his long period of exile in Mexico. "He was now a hardened, dedicated revolutionary with an impressionable record of accomplishment and sacrifice," author Theodore Draper points out. Trotsky exposed Stalin's dictatorship in his book, *The Revolution Betrayed*. On August 21, 1940, Trotsky was assassinated in Mexico by an agent who obviously acted on Stalin's orders.

Smolny would go on to serve as the Communist Party headquarters for Party Chief Andrei Zhadanov, who from this building directed the defense of Leningrad in World War II. Today, the building, located inside a small park, is the home of the administrative offices of the governor of the city of St. Petersburg.

Jewish Bolsheviks

While we are speaking of Smolny, it is fitting that we comment on, and record for history, other Jewish Bolsheviks.

"Not many Jews were Bolsheviks, but many of the leading Bolsheviks were Jews," says author George St. George. The propaganda term "Jewish Bolshevism" was coined by the Whites. It was later used by the Nazis in occupied Ukraine and Russia. Many Russians thought that their country's ruin was somehow connected with the sudden appearance of the Jews in high places and positions of authority formerly reserved for the non-Jews, writes Figes.

"Actually the proportion of Jews in Bolshevik ranks was smaller than in virtually all others," according to Albert S. Lindemann, in his book, *Esau's Tears: Modern Anti-Semitism and the Rise of the Jews*. He notes the Mensheviks contained a distinctly larger proportion of Jews. "Even accepting such all-encompassing definitions, however, it is beyond serious controversy that the overwhelming majority of Jews in Europe were not revolutionaries in the sense of favoring violent upheaval and that even among secular Jews in Russia only a minority actually identified with the Bolshevik Party before the summer of 1917."

It is true that some Jews welcomed the Bolshevik Revolution, for the Communists promised the world, but did not deliver. In the beginning, the Bolsheviks were the lesser of the two evils. Later, many came to the conclusion that as far as Jews were concerned, the Bolsheviks were worse than the tsar, although very few Jews had mourned the fall of the tsar. "Despairing of a future under the Tsarist regime, many young Jews turned to the Revolutionary movement," wrote journalist Robert Leiter, in the Philadelphia *Jewish Exponent.* "The Jews perceived the Soviets would put an end to anti-Semitism."

Thus, as important as it was, the role of Jews in the Russian revolutionary movement has been much exaggerated.

Most Jews preferred to join their own Socialist or Socialist Zionist party, or to remain politically uninvolved. Others followed Martov and Axelrod, two leading Menshevik ideologists, according to Bertram D. Wolfe, author of *Three Who Made A Revolution.*

There were many more intellectuals of Jewish origin among the Mensheviks than the Bolsheviks, and the few who were associates of Lenin, such as Trotsky and Kamenev, "were likely to be 'unJewish Jews,' non-professing, Russified, brought up outside the Pale," declares Wolfe, adding, "the bulk of the Jewish masses, in so far as they were politically organized, were to be found in neither wing, but in specifically Jewish movements," such as the Bund or Zionism. He claims that outside of the revolutionaries, the bulk of the Jewish masses were truly conservative.

These Communist Jews were no more Jewish than their non-Jewish atheist party comrades were. They did not speak for or identify with Jews, and indeed were often the enemies of Jews. In fact, Wolfe cites the example that when the Bolsheviks overthrew the Provisional Government, "there was not one among Lenin's associates with sufficient knowledge" of Yiddish to start up a newspaper.

"Trotsky's hostility to other Jews was not uncommon among Jewish revolutionaries; almost all had rejected Jewish belief and custom. They saw the rabbis as collaborators with the officials of the Tsar," according to author Albert S. Lindemann. Further, because many Jews stepped into the vacuum created by the disintegration of the tsarist bureaucracy, it now seemed to many Russians that Jewish government officials were everywhere, wrote author Chaim Potok in his book, *The Gates of November.*

Numbers did not reflect the actual Jewish participation in the rank and file of the Party. From 1922 to 1930, Jewish membership declined from 5.2 percent in 1922, to 4.3 percent in 1927, to 3.8 percent in 1930.

In the late 1930s most Jews were dismissed from important positions (especially the Party and the armed forces). Many of the cadres who took over were imbued with "anti-Semitic hatreds they had absorbed in their villages and urban hovels," according to author Abraham Brumberg, writing in the *Times Literary Supplement* of December 11, 1998.

"As time went on, the leadership, as well as the lower echelons, were gradually filled by non-Jews." Salo Baron points out that "most of the early Jewish leaders died a violent death at the hand of their fellow Communists."

Among the Bolsheviks, the best-known Jews are Trotsky, Zinoviev, Kamenev, Radek, Uritsky, Litvinov, Kaganovich, and Yoffe, men whose names keep popping up. For instance, three of the seven men comprising the 1923 Politburo were Jews: Trotsky, Zinoviev, and Kamenev. Within a decade, Stalin had driven Trotsky into exile, and killed the other two.

As Theodor Plievier wrote in his book *Moscow,* "Trotsky was murdered, Zinoviev executed, Kamenev executed, Bukharin executed, Rykov executed, and Sobolnikov executed, and Tomsky driven to suicide. Of the 15 members of Lenin's Politburo, only Andreyev, Molotov, Voroshilov and Stalin were alive when the Germans were at the gates of Moscow."

Since Trotsky has already been dealt with, listed here is information on other famous Jewish Bolsheviks.

Grigorii Evselvich Zinoviev, (1883-1936). A native of

Yelisavetgrad, his last name was originally Appelbaum. After meeting Lenin in 1903, he joined him during the 1905 revolution. Zinoviev became a prominent member of the Bolshevik Central Committee and became Lenin's closest assistant. He also followed Lenin to Switzerland, and was the principal architect and first chairman of the Communist International, as well as Bolshevism's leading advocate of world revolution. After the revolution, Zinoviev emerged as chairman of the Petrograd Soviet of Workers Deputies, and chairman of the Council of People's Commissars of the Union of Communes of the Northern Region. He was virtual dictator of Petrograd. Following Lenin's death in January 1924, he joined with Stalin and Kaminev to constitute a troika of party leaders. Together they drove Leon Trotsky into political isolation.

In 1925, he and Kamenev led the Leningrad Opposition, which tried to seize power in the party, but was defeated by Stalin, in alliance with Bukharin. After this, Zinoviev tried acting in alliance with Trotsky, but the two could not recover lost ground. After 1926, he lost all his main posts, and all importance. He is said to have kissed the boots of the Chekists (secret police) who led him out to be shot. Pleading for mercy, he died a horrible death.

Lev Borisovich Kamenev, (1883-1934). A leading Bolshevik, whose real name was Rosenfeld, he was also Trotsky's brother-in-law. In 1901, Kamenev joined the illegal Social Democratic Party and in 1903, he signed on with its Bolshevik faction. He was imprisoned several times by the secret police. Fortunately, he eventually lived in exile in Switzerland. In 1914, he returned to Russia and edited the Communist Party newspaper, *Pravda*. Picked up by the police, he was sent to Siberia, but he returned to Petrograd after the 1917 February Revolution.

During the debates in the Central Committee of the Communist Party, he and Zinoviev opposed Lenin's plan of seizing power by an armed coup. Kamenev wanted a coalition government of all socialist parties. After the Bolshevik Revolution, he became one of the most powerful figures in the Soviet Union as chairman of the Moscow Soviet, deputy chairman of the Council of People's Commissars, and a member of the Party's Politburo.

After Lenin's death, Kamenev and Zinoviev actively opposed Stalin. They were even expelled from the Party on several occasions, but were always readmitted. After the 1934 assassination of Sergei Kirov in Leningrad, which began the great terror wave of the purges, Kamenev became a prominent figure in the Moscow purge trials, in which veteran leaders of the Party were accused of conspiring to overthrow the Soviet regime. At his trial in August 1936, he confessed to all the charges and was sentenced to death. He was later executed.

To put it bluntly, **Lazar Moiseyevich Kaganovich** (1893-1991), was "bad." He is thought to have personally signed the death warrants of 36,000 people. Even in death he was loyal to Lenin and Stalin. In July 1991, sitting in his apartment, he was watching television news reporting on *perestroika,* and showing Mikhail Gorbachev and Boris Yeltsin. His maid heard him say, "It's a catastrophe." When she looked around, he was still sitting in front of the television set, but he was dead.

For a number of years, Kaganovich was the only Jew to occupy a top position in the Soviet leadership. He served as secretary of the central committee of the Communist Party and was close to Stalin. Only Kaganovich sat with Stalin. He was indeed "one of Stalin's principal allies in the struggle for Bolshevik power and the drive to collectivize agriculture." He helped bring about the great famine of 1932-34. According to author and journalist, Edward Crankshaw, Kaganovich believed that anyone who "stands in the way of salvation through heavy industry must be crushed." In 1930, he put down the peasant resistance to collectivization, deporting and starving millions. He organized the construction of the Moscow subway. After World War II, he crushed the nationalist resistance in Ukraine. In 1957, as a member of the anti-Party group of Molotov, Malenkov, and Shepilov, he was expelled from the Central Committee and dismissed from all government posts. He was put in charge of a cement works in Sverdlovsk, where he lived until he died.

Maxim Maximovich Litvinov, (1876-1951). Before the Revolution, Litvinov's name had been Finkelstein. Other aliases were Wallach, or just plain "Mr. Harris." Born in Poland, he was later attracted to Marxism. After the October Revolution, he immediately became a political representative of the new Soviet

Union. After a stint as ambassador to London, he had a successful diplomatic career. From 1930 to 1939, during the Stalin terror, he was people's commissar for Foreign Affairs. Stalin sacked him in 1939 for Molotov, whom Lenin once called "the best filing clerk in the Soviet Union." The Soviet dictator could not have a Jew in the foreign minister spot if he was going to make a deal with Nazi Germany, as he soon would do in August 1939. However, historian Edvard Radzinsky says Stalin kept Litvinov alive because he might be needed. It was to be so. When Hitler attacked the USSR, Litvinov was appointed vicecommissar for foreign affairs. During the May Day parade in Red Square, Stalin brought Litvinov out in the open on the reviewing platform of the Lenin Mausoleum. He had been "politically embalmed," says Whaley. He served as Soviet ambassador to the U.S. from 1941 to 1943 and again as deputy people's commissar for foreign affairs from 1943 to 1946.

The irony of it all was that Maxim Litvinov slept with a revolver under his pillow so that he could shoot himself if arrested, according to Chaim Potok.

Genrikh Grigorievich Yagoda (1891-1938), was head of the Soviet Secret police.

Nikolai Ivanovich Yezhov (1895-1940), replaced Yagoda as head of the secret police in 1938. Both Yagoda and Yezhov were executed by Stalin.

Moisei Solomonovitch Uritsky (1873-1918), was one of the leaders of the Cheka, the despised secret police force that later became the KGB. The Cheka and its successors arrested and executed millions of innocent Russians during Stalin's purges in the 1930s. It also established labor gangs to build dams and the gulag, the camps that held political opponents and dissidents.

Born into a merchant family in 1873 in the town of Cherkassy, Uritsky joined a group of revolutionaries in the early 1890s. A friend of Trotsky's, he was elected a member of the Party's Central Committee. In August 1918, another Jew, Leonid Kanegisser, assassinated him in his room in the general staff building. One version maintained that the act was a so-called plot by right-wing elements. Another story has it that

Kanegisser, a poet, was not part of a plot. He wanted to prove that Jews, as Jews, were not responsible for the "terror," despite the fact that many Jews were actively involved in it, especially in Petrograd, according to Mikhail Beizer, author of *The Jews of St. Petersburg: An Excursion through A Noble Past.*

Karl Radek (1885-1939), was a native of Galicia, a brilliant journalist, and an audacious and resourceful politician. He is the man portrayed in Arthur Koestler's novel, *Darkness at Noon.* At the beginning of the First World War, he joined Lenin in Switzerland and later traveled with Lenin through Germany back to Russia in 1917. At the end of 1918, he went to Germany to help start the so-called proletarian revolution, but was arrested and released. In 1923, he shared the discomfort of the opposition leaders and ceased to hold prominent Communist Party posts. For many years, he was the most effective writer in the Soviet press. At the show trial of January 1937, he gave incriminating statements about other Communist Party members. Some say he was not shot, but died in confinement shortly afterward. Conflicting accounts of his death linger till this day.

Revolutionary Sites

The Winter Palace and the Hermitage. It all started when Catherine built a pavilion onto her Winter Palace in St. Petersburg so she could hang her pictures. She called it her "hermitage." So the Hermitage became an extension of the Winter Palace. This palace served as the home of the tsars beginning in the eighteenth century, as well as the home of the Provisional Government in 1917. Over the years, Catherine and other succeeding tsars bought up valuable collections of art and placed them in the Hermitage.

The Winter Palace stands as one of the most beautiful baroque buildings in the world. "It grows out of the ground like a giant's wedding cake on a platter," wrote author Geraldine Norman in *The Hermitage: The Biography of a Great Museum.* Walk along its 27 miles of corridors and you will see more than 2.8 million works of art. The structure contains more than 1000 rooms and reception halls, with a total area of about 495,000 square feet. There are 1,945 windows, 1,786 doors, and 117 staircases.

More than 3 million people visit here each year. Currently only 5 percent of the Hermitage's enormous collection is on display. Edmund Wilson said that he got lost in its "somber old labyrinth."

Under Empress Elizabeth, B.F. Rostrelli built the Catherine Palace at Tsarskoe Selo (now Pushkin), and entirely rebuilt the Winter Palace, giving it the appearance that it has today.

The Winter Palace was completed in 1762, six months after Elizabeth's death, and was first used by Peter III and Catherine the Great. The latter was instrumental in starting the museum on its path to become the holder of one of the world's great art collections.

The Hermitage Museum is Russia's premier museum. It contains "one of the greatest collections in the world, on a par with the Louvre, the British Museum or the Metropolitan Museum of Art in New York City," writes Norman.

Here you will bask in the atmosphere of the great—Gaugin, Matisse, Renoir, van Gogh, and Picasso. Two of Leonardo da Vinci's 14 existing paintings are exhibited here. The second-largest collection of Rembrandt's paintings is represented. Thirty-six paintings by Reubens and the second-largest collection of French impressionists are shown here.

The museum was nationalized by the Bolsheviks, and expanded by commandeering extensive collections to fill the tsar's Winter Palace.

In World War II, two thousand people lived in a makeshift bomb shelter in the museum cellar. During the Leningrad siege, 32 shells and 2 bombs hit the museum, but it remained standing, "Suffering shattered glass and boarded up with plywood," says Norman.

Two momentous events occurred at the Winter Palace, at its southern facade that looks onto Palace Square. The first, "Bloody Sunday," was the peaceful 1905 march of Father Gapon and his followers, who were slaughtered by the tsarist troops. The second was the "storming" of the Winter Palace by the Bolsheviks in October 1917, also known as the Bolshevik Revolution.

"Bloody Sunday"

Between 1904 and 1905, strikes, protests, and discontent had spread throughout the Empire. News reports arrived from the Far East disclosing that the Japanese had defeated Russian land forces and that the tsar's fleet had been wiped out at Tsushima. On January 9, 1905, several hundred thousand Russians carrying icons and chanting prayers and led by the priest, Father Gapon, peacefully marched to the Winter Palace. Standing in Palace Square in front of the Winter Palace, they bore church standards and icons of saints and were armed with petitions calling for moderate reforms they wanted to give to the tsar at his palace. The soldiers guarding the palace opened fire. This killing of several hundred innocent men and women led to the 1905 Revolt, which has been called "a fateful moment in Russian history," and a "rehearsal for the Revolution to come," says Irving Howe in his book, *A Critic's Notebook*. It was a prelude to the full outbreak of revolution 12 years later. The firing of tsarist troops on Father Gapon broke at last the spell of the tsar over the Russian people.

There were also several Jews with Father Gapon: a first-aid nurse, a dentist, a pharmacy student, and a journalist. Pinchas Rutenberg found Gapon lying helpless on the ground; Rutenberg got Gapon to a friend's residence, where he then helped the priest escape abroad. (The Rutenberg-Gapon story was not over yet. After fleeing Russia, Rutenberg would return in 1917. He then became an assistant to a deputy prime minister. He also served as a deputy governor of St. Petersburg. As an assistant to Kerensky, who headed the Provisional Government, Rutenberg managed to rescue people from the Winter Palace during the Bolshevik seizure of the residence of the tsars.)

In October 1905, the tsar yielded to pressure and issued a manifesto, which promised "civil liberty on principles of true inviolability of person, freedom of conscience, speech, assembly and association." A duma, or official assembly, would be elected. Adult males in all classes of the population would be enfranchised. The October Manifesto held out the prospect of a new constitutional order in which both monarchy and society might develop along European lines.

The reforms did not go over well with rightist groups, who played a leading role in igniting pogroms. Their real violence was reserved for the Jews. There were 690 documented pogroms, with over three thousand reported murders, during the two weeks following the declaration of the October Manifesto. The worst pogroms were in Odessa.

The 1905 riots caused processions and rallies, even in the U.S. Repercussions echoed throughout the world.

At the end of 1905, Emperor Nicholas II crushed the first Russian Revolution of the twentieth century by dismissing the Duma. For the next 10 years, Russia, seething with unrest, was held together by an autocratic regime which might have lasted were it not for the First World War, which totally destabilized the country.

After serving six months in jail because of his association with Kerensky, Rutenberg went to Moscow, Kiev, and Odessa, "where he joined a French-sponsored, White Russian government that did not last long," according to the *Encyclopedia Judaica*.

Rutenberg came to the conclusion that there was anti-Semitism even in revolutionary movements, and so he went to Palestine in November 1919.

In Geneva, Gapon joined the Social Revolutionaries, a spin-off from the Social Democratic Workers Party, and later returned to St. Petersburg and betrayed members of the SR organization. The executive committee of the Party thereupon made it Rutenberg's responsibility to dispose of Gapon. In March 1906, Gapon was found hanging in a lonely and derelict country house outside of the city.

In 1920, Rutenberg settled in Paris. He would again appear in the limelight when he obtained a concession for the electrification of Palestine, a project he successfully accomplished. He died in Haifa in 1942.

By 1917, hunger plagued the city of St. Petersburg and beyond. Women stood in long bread lines. Finally, on February 26 by the old Julian Russian calendar, the frustration boiled over. The citizenry had reached the limits of endurance. A group of women textile workers on the Vyborg side of Petrograd would not stand in the bread line any longer and went off to rally their husbands and boyfriends in the nearby metal factories for a protest march to the center of the city. Thus began the Russian Revolution. (Actually, more civilians were killed by the crowds in the February Revolution than in the October Bolshevik coup.) Authority evaporated. Workers formed a soviet, a committee of workers' and soldiers' deputies. Three days later the tsar abdicated. Meanwhile, political parties mushroomed. People sang the "Marseillaise." The chant of "freedom, freedom," was heard in the streets of Petrograd. Eyewitnesses recalled the color red blinded everyone. Red flags were everywhere.

Filling the vacuum the collapse of the monarchy left were the Provisional Government and the Soviets. Soon to head the government was Alexander Kerensky, an obscure provisional lawyer who would ride the crest of the revolutionary wave to become prime minister of Russia. By that summer, however, more pogroms broke out, and Bolshevik leaders were arrested. By the middle of 1917, Petrograd was a terrible place in which to reside. In the end, the Provisional Government under Kerensky would fall to the Bolsheviks.

Even while the Russian army disintegrated, Kerensky launched an offensive against the Germans and Austrians to demonstrate the new regime's commitment to the Allies.

It would not take long for the second-most-famous event to take place in front of the Winter Palace, i.e., in Palace Square. We know it as the Bolshevik Revolution. Few historical events, however, have been more profoundly distorted by myth than those of the Bolshevik grab for power and the seizure of the Winter Palace. It was not a huge battle at all. It was a bloodless, small-scale event—no more than a military coup. It passed unnoticed by the vast majority of Petrograd residents. The city's restaurants and tramcars functioned normally during the hours the Bolsheviks were taking power. Only a few shots were fired. Salisbury notes that few citizens would have believed a revolt occurred. It was business as usual.

Lenin had brewed the coup d'état, wrote Salisbury. After a

discussion lasting nearly 10 hours, the committee, by a vote of 10 to 2, approved Lenin's clumsily worded resolution declaring that "armed insurrection is inevitable and (the time for it) fully ripe," according to Florinsky.

A politburo was set up of Lenin, Bubnov, Zinoviev, Kamenev, Sokolnikov, Stalin, and Trotsky. Trotsky was given the task of masterminding the planning of the insurrection.

The October Revolution

The October events were encumbered by trivia, petty rivalry, miscalculation, hesitation, ineptitude, posturing, and mistakes. Almost nothing was planned, and what did happen was often accidental. "The Bolsheviks blundered into power," wrote Salisbury in *Black Night, White Snow.*

It is interesting to observe that even at the height of the Communist Revolution, even at the seizure of the Winter Palace, Jews were always a topic of conversation. The following incident occurred in the Winter Palace, according to Salisbury:

The Cossacks were about to pull out from the Provisional Government side to go over to the Bolsheviks. To hold them back, Lt. Alexander Sineguba, head of the Engineering School, argued with the Cossacks.

"When we came here we were told everyone would be here, all the military schools, the artillery and what did we find, Jews and women. Moreover the Government is half full of Jews. And the Russian people are with Lenin," exclaimed the Cossacks.

Sineguba replied, "Lenin's whole gang are Jews and you saw some Jews here. Well, there are Jews and Jews. And you miserable Cossacks, you brats and cowards are leaving women and children behind and running off."

The Bolsheviks launched the insurrection on October 24 by the Julian Calendar, and November 6 by the Gregorian Calendar. Life in the capital was not seriously disturbed. Schools and government offices closed earlier than usual. However, most of the shops, theaters, and movie houses remained open.

Late on the night of October 24, the Reds moved. They occupied railway terminals, bridges, the state bank, the telephone exchange, the Central Post Office, and other public buildings.

Kerensky left the Winter Palace the next morning, between ten A.M. and eleven A.M., October 25 (or November 7). At 6:00 P.M. that same day, the besiegers of the Palace called on the Provisional Government to surrender. At 9:00 P.M., the *Aurora* cruiser fired one blank shell, followed by rifle fire from both sides. At 11:00 P.M. cannon fire erupted from the Peter and Paul Fortress, as the Bolsheviks lobbed shells onto the palace. At around midnight, the final assault took place. Thirteen ministers were arrested in the Malachite Chamber at 1:50 A.M. on October 26, (November 8). At 2:10 A.M. a telegram was sent to Smolny Institute, which was serving as Communist Party Headquarters, stating that the Winter Palace was in Red hands. Six men of the Pavlovsky group had been killed.

In less than 48 hours, says W. Bruce Lincoln in his book, *Red Terror,* the Bolsheviks drove Kerensky from power, seized control of Petrograd, issued decrees on land and peace, and established Russia's first government of the people's commissars. The whole insurrection could have been completed in 6 hours, he adds, "had it not been for the ludicrous incompetence of the insurgents themselves, which made it take an extra 15."

True, the Bolsheviks finally seized the Winter Palace. But the planning and the direction came from the Smolny Institute, which we have already visited.

The legendary storming of the Winter Palace, where Kerensky's cabinet held its final session, was more like a routine house arrest, since most of the forces defending the palace had already left for home before the assault began. The only real damage to the imperial residence in the whole affair was a chipped cornice and a battered window on the third floor.

The anniversary of the Bolshevik Revolution was celebrated on November 7, or October 25 in the old-style calendar; hence it was called the "Great October Revolution," and in the USSR, the celebration extended through November 8, the date the Bolshevik-led soldiers actually occupied the Winter Palace, in the early hours of the morning.

For a while, there was still hope of some semblance of democracy. The elections took place in November 1917. They were the first and last fully free elections in the entire history of Russia, until the fall of Communism about 70 years later.

Jewish voters apparently cast the majority of their votes for the Zionist groups.

The Bolshevik party finished second, with about 25 percent of the vote, far behind the Socialist Revolutionary Party, according to David Remnick.

The long-awaited Constituent Assembly opened in January 1918 in Petrograd. A 17-hour session was held on January 15 and 16. At 4:00 A.M., an anarchist, a blue-eyed sailor named Zhelesniakov, mounted the tribune and, tapping Chernov on the shoulder, said "I invite all those present to leave the hall. The guard is tired." The meeting was ended. The Assembly never met again. Denied reentry, the delegates never came back. Thus did Lenin and his cohorts kill parliamentary democracy in Russia.

By the end of 1917, Russia had already sunk into a morass. The German-Russian treaty at Brest Litovsk removed 1.3 million square miles of territory and a population of 62 million, as well as Bessarabia, from Russian sovereignty. Many Jews joined the Red Army as a means of survival, according to Lindemann. The Bolsheviks needed breathing space. A special peace with Germany would give them that time to consolidate their power base, restore the economy, and build a new Revolutionary Army. For the Jewish historian Dubnow, the Revolution was a catastrophe. It devastated not only Russia itself, but also the "dominant center of Jewry."

As we have seen, the Winter Palace once served as the home of the tsars. After the old regime was dethroned in 1917, all the buildings were turned into this famous museum, the Hermitage.

During World War II, guides took groups of soldiers going to the front and showed them the empty frames in the museum, which had names of the paintings they had once held. These treasures have survived fire and flood, Bolsheviks and Nazis, evacuation to Moscow in 1917 and evacuation to Sverdlovsk in 1941, as well as the post-Communist financial crises.

More Sites

Palace Square. You must walk through this masterpiece of architecture known as Palace Square, bounded on the north

The author's wife, Riva Frank, at the entrance to the cruiser Aurora, which fired the single shot that signaled the Bolsheviks to attack the Winter Palace. The ship is now a museum. (Photo credit: Ben G. Frank)

by the Winter Palace and on the south by the crescent-shaped General Staff Headquarters, construction of which was completed in 1829. The facades of the Headquarters form two arcs centering on the Winter Palace, and are joined by a magnificent arch of triumph. The arch was decorated by sculptors S. S. Pimenov and V. I. Deniut-Malinovsky with coats of arms, martial figures, and a victory chariot symbolizing the victory of the Russian people in the Patriotic War of 1812.

The Triumphal Column weighs 600 tons. Raised in 1832, it is taller than the Vendome Column in Paris. A walk through this magnificent promenade gives one a fine opportunity to contemplate Russia, its architecture, and its history. Also, the best way to enter Nevsky Prospekt is to walk through the expanse of the Palace Square.

The Alexander Column, located in Palace Square, was erected in 1832 as a sign of peace in Europe after the defeat of Napoleon. In the center of the square is the huge column commemorating Alexander I and his victory. The chariot, drawn by six horses and located on top of the arch, is also the work of Denuit-Malinovsky and Pimenov. The buildings and the architecture are the work of Carlo Rossi. The superb structure and vast open space highlight the column, which is the world's tallest war monument. The column stands upon a pedestal of bronze and is about 150 feet high. On the pedestal, which is made from Turkish cannon, is the inscription: "To Alexander I, Grateful Russia."

In 1941, the Germans thought they had their domination plans figured out. In his book *The 900 Days: The Siege of Leningrad,* Harrison E. Salisbury tells us that "the Nazi troops would march in triumph through Palace Square, column after column past the General Staff building, past the Winter Palace. There, it was anticipated, the happy Führer would review his victorious armies. Needless to say, the event was postponed many times and never happened."

Aurora. You will see this famous ship often as you drive in and around St. Petersburg. It lies in dock in this city of the Revolution. During the October Revolution, the sailors on board fired a blank round to signal the storming of the Winter Palace.

While it looks like a toy compared to today's nuclear-powered cruisers, the ship, now a museum, became the naval hero of the Revolution. The ship brought about the surrender of the Kerensky supporters who were holding out within the Palace. **Finland Station.** Various writers have described how a short man emerged from a train here and climbed onto the top of an armored car: Lenin was the man emerging from the train, and some have described that arrival as a disaster for the nation. Some have said he was greeted wildly at the station on his return from Switzerland via Germany in that famous sealed train, on April 16, 1917. Here he spoke to the throngs of Bolsheviks. At 11:10 P.M., April 3, the train rolled into Petrograd's Finland Station. Included in Lenin's first words were "The people need peace. The people need bread and the people need land," according to author and journalist Harrison E. Salisbury in *Black Night, White Snow.* Salisbury adds, "The glove was hurled down. No compromise. No armistice." The end of the war was Lenin's theme. He had come to see the fall of the new regime. The Bolsheviks had to seize power immediately. Still, he was opposed in Petrograd by Kamenev, Zinoviev, and Stalin, who took more moderate views, although Lenin won out in the end.

Jewish Community

Judaism is beginning anew in Russia. About one hundred thousand Jews now call St. Petersburg their home. There are synagogues, a Jewish community center, Hillel house, kosher restaurants, Hebrew day schools. Is this London? Paris? New York? It could be any of them, but it is St. Petersburg, where there are at least five Jewish day schools, six kindergartens, six Sunday schools, two Jewish universities, two Lubavitch schools, one Israeli school, and one family school.

Obviously the Jewish institutions are not your American suburban or city Jewish Community Center, or YMHA. Remember, the Jewish community in St. Petersburg or any Russian city has just been reborn. As some would put it, "It is only a 10-year-old child."

More than 25 percent of the population is elderly. Many of the young people have gone to Israel or the U.S. Most are not religious. Most know very little about Judaism. But there will be a Jewish community, because this is their country. "If America and Israel help, we will not lose them," Rabbi Menachem Mendel Pewzner of the Choral Synagogue said in an interview. Pewzner notes that large crowds attend services on major holidays. Sometimes the crowds are as large as 1,500 people. This is a city that boasts such Jewish organizations as B'nai Akiva and Maccabi sports. The Israel Center also has a youth club.

By the end of 1997, emigration from St. Petersburg seemed to have ended, though it could quickly start up again, if the economy gets worse and anti-Semitism continues to rise. Here again, the Jews in the big cities are staying put, but the Jews from the smaller towns and villages are emigrating to Israel, Germany, and other destinations.

The biggest problem for rabbis here is intermarriage.

The St. Petersburg Jewish Community is said to be better organized than Moscow, for example, because life for Jews entering professions and certain careers was once more difficult and the community pulled closer together. Undoubtedly Jewish professionals and businesspersons function better in the new capitalist environment than they did in the stifling Communist bureaucracy.

Ami, Jewish newspaper, Rubinsteina Street 3, No. 50. Tel: (7-812) 113-38-89, (7-812) 311-64-40, Fax: (7-812) 314-51-17. Located at the Jewish Community Center, *Ami,* or "my people," serves the community well. One of the editors, Yakov Zukerman, is reported to have said, "It is my duty to stay as long as there are any Jews here, helping to give them back the culture and religion that was taken from them."

Jewish Sites

Choral Synagogue, Lermontovsky Street 2. Tel: (7-812) 113-62-09 (office). The telephone number for the small synagogue is: (7-812) 114-00-78.

If you travel on a cruise ship to St. Petersburg and you have

This is the entrance to the Choral Synagogue, in St. Petersburg. (Photo credit: Manny Charach)

one or two Jewish sites to go to, ask a guide to take you to the
Choral Synagogue on Lermontovsky Street No 2. Some say the
Choral Synagogue was so named because young boys sang here.
This 1,200-seat domed structure, constructed in the Moorish
style, is open day and most of the night, especially in the white
nights of summer. Considered one of the most beautiful, well-
preserved synagogues in Europe, this is the second-largest
congregation in Europe, after the Dohany Synagogue in
Budapest. The Soviets used this wonderful building as a showplace before 1991.

Before you enter, stop at the gate of this house of worship.
Walk slowly into the front courtyard of the synagogue. Two
thoughts will help illustrate for you the struggle of Jews in this
country since the Bolshevik Revolution of 1917.

For the first thought, do not go immediately into this house
of worship. Do an about-face. Look slightly to your right, across
the street. You will see a modern building. Once, in that very
same building, KGB cameras filmed each visitor entering the
synagogue. Oh, don't worry. Today the building is still there,
but the cameras are gone.

The second thought that must remain with you is that during those terrible 900 days of the brutal siege of Leningrad by
the Germans in World War II, when gasps of starving men,
women, and children resounded in this city by the Neva, dying
Jews dragged themselves or were conveyed by sled to this courtyard where they would die. They wanted to be near God and
Judaism. By this act, they signified that though they might pass
away, Judaism would not.

Prayers are often held in what is called the "small synagogue." If you come with a private guide, ask him or her to
speak to an official of the synagogue to show you various rooms
and the sanctuary.

Morning services are at 9:00 A.M. *Shabbat* services are at 10:00
A.M. Here, Georgian Jews make a separate *minyan*. Also, if you
are interested, arrangements can be made for kosher food at
(7-812) 113-62-09.

The synagogue has tour guides available. It is best to call

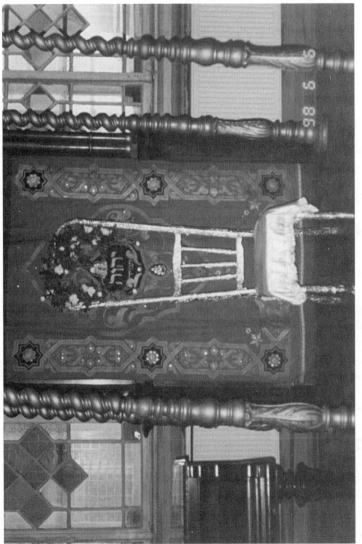

This is the bride's chair in the wedding chapel of the Choral Synagogue. (Photo credit: Manny Charach)

ahead of time. But if you cannot phone, or if you have your own private guide, just take a taxi and introduce yourself.

If your Russian guide is unfamiliar with the synagogue, you may want to ask him or her to fetch the *shamos* (sexton) or an officer of the synagogue.

The massive front door of the synagogue may be locked, so enter on the left side of the building. The Lubavitch rabbi feels this synagogue is a center of *yiddishkeit*, or Jewish culture. It contains a synagogue, a yeshiva, a day care center, a *mikva*, a kosher kitchen, and a ceremonial wedding hall. In this interesting wedding room, located in the synagogue, you can observe a beautiful *chupah*, or Jewish wedding canopy, that graces the floorspace. The room also serves as a reception area. Make sure you see this hall.

Also, for some interesting religious items, including calendars, you can stop off at the gift shop. A Russian Jewish calendar is also offered for sale, as well as a Russian Jewish magazine, called *L'Chaim*.

Rabbi Menachem Mendel Pewzner is the spiritual leader of the synagogue. A Lubavitch Chassid, this Orthodox rabbi is from Brooklyn. Many of the rabbis of Russian Jewish synagogues spout Brooklyn accents. They are "Lubavitch *rebbes*," and can be found throughout Russia and Ukraine. Rabbi Pewzner, for instance, is a native of Crown Heights, in Brooklyn.

Rabbi Pewzner is very proud of the work of Lubavitch. In St. Petersburg, his organization sponsors two Jewish kindergartens, two Jewish schools, a soup kitchen, and a summer camp. He also knows of the tradition that is part of this house of prayer.

The first members of the synagogue were Jews who had fought long and hard to obtain a synagogue in spite of tsarist restrictions and even expulsions.

In 1802, a group of Jews leased a plot of land in the Volkov Cemetery for Jewish burials. They believed that they had established a permanent community. However, when Nicholas I came to power in 1825, he ordered the 370 Jews in the city expelled.

By the middle of the nineteenth century, Jewish merchants, professors, and craftsmen had obtained permission to come to the capital, and many settled there. But they needed a permit

Rabbi Menachem Mendel Pewzner, formerly of Crown Heights, Brooklyn, is now spiritual leader of the Choral Synagogue. (Photo credit: Ben G. Frank)

Shown here is the sanctuary of the Choral Synagogue. (Photo credit: Manny Charach)

Here, British tourists view an exhibition in the main hall of the Choral Synagogue. (Photo credit: Ben G. Frank)

to stay even for six weeks. For example, "rights of residence" were granted to a number of physicians, including the tsar's dentist and the midwife of the royal court. Police hunts for Jews occurred often. Anyone found living in the city without a permit could be drafted into the army, according to the *Encyclopedia Judaica*.

Alexander II, the reforming tsar, liberalized the regulations for some wealthy Jewish merchants and financiers such as Guenzburg, Polyakov, Varshavski, Friedland, and Rosenthal. Jewish physicians, lawyers, and scientists also gained access to the city.

Unlike their co-religionists in the Pale of Settlement, where everyone spoke Yiddish, only 55 percent of the Jews in the capital spoke that language, according to Beizer.

In the 1860s and 1870s, St. Petersburg served as the center for Russian Jewry, especially for the Lithuanian Jewish community. And even though St. Petersburg had excellent Yiddish and Hebrew periodicals, it remained predominantly a Russian-language center. "These periodicals were produced in the capital for political reasons, and not because it was the best or most logical place for them," wrote Sh'marya Levin in his book, *The Arena*.

By 1874 the government had finally granted the community permission to build the Choral Synagogue.

Like all synagogues in Russia, this one went through more than its share of difficulties in its century of existence. First of all, negotiations to build a synagogue started in 1859, but the building was only opened in 1893, when 20,000 Jews lived in the city. Delayed openings, pogroms, the Revolution, harassment by Communists, living through the siege, KGB suppression—all these events are part of the soul of this congregation.

The synagogue's neighbors complained. They argued that the neighborhood would be "filled with Jews and the values of their property would drop," according to Beizer. At the synagogue's completion in 1893, the total cost added up to five hundred thousand golden rubles, most of which was donated by members such as Baron Horace Guenzburg and the Polyakov family of railroad builders and bankers. Samuel Polyakov (1837-1885), was one of the most important railroad builders in

Russia. He initiated the foundation of the ORT (Organization for Rehabilitation through Training).

Only two years earlier, in 1891, Jews had faced expulsion. The Choral Synagogue has existed during times of tremendous change and turmoil, including visits by famous non-Russian Jews amidst government oppression.

Two important Jewish leaders came to Russia and visited St. Petersburg. Moses Montefiore (1784-1885), one of the world Jewish leaders of the nineteenth century, the founder of the London banking house of Montefiore Brothers, and the founder of the first insurance society in England, visited St. Petersburg in the nineteenth century. He appealed for improved conditions for Russian Jews. Montefiore came again in 1872, on the occasion of the celebrations to mark the bicentennial of Peter the Great. Great crowds welcomed him. Author Mikhail Beizer says that when the great philanthropist asked for rights to be granted to Jews, he was told, "They will receive them when they become something like you." Montefiore obtained nothing of substance.

Theodor Herzl, the founder of modern Zionism, also visited in August 1903 and met with Minister of Interior Viacheslav K. von Plehve. Initially, von Plehve liked the idea of Zionism, as long as it meant emigration of Jews out of Russia. Herzl called on the Russians to use their influence with the Turkish Ottoman government to help establish Jewish colonies in Palestine. According to Beizer, von Plehve went so far as to assure Herzl that what would suit the Russian government best would be the creation of an independent Jewish state, capable of absorbing several million Jews. The independent Jewish nation would arrive on the world scene 45 years later, but it would take nearly a century until another million Russian Jews arrived in the Holy Land. At the Choral Synagogue, the leaders and members were quite angry, as Herzl did not visit there.

By 1914, the number of Jewish residents in St. Petersburg had reached 35,000, or 1.8 percent of the city's citizens. Then came World War I, the Revolution, and later the Second World War, all of which we shall discuss as we visit various sites around the city.

By the end of the 1920s, Stalin had cemented his power.

Meet a few of the students and their teacher at St. Petersburg's School No. 522, a Russian state school, which is housed with Jewish students in an Orthodox Jewish school where meals are kosher, Shabbat is observed, and prayers are held by the students in Grades 1 through 9. The Hebrew sign says "A Good and Sweet New Year." (Photo credit: Ben G. Frank)

On the wall of the kitchen of School No. 522 in St. Petersburg, you will notice words for the Hebrew blessing over bread, transliterated into Russian. (Photo credit: Ben G. Frank)

These Russian Jewish students learn about the Sabbath in School No. 522 in St. Petersburg. (Photo credit: Ben G. Frank)

These are the words in Russian for the Hebrew blessing over bread. (Photo credit: Ben G. Frank)

Organized Jewish life was suppressed in Leningrad and throughout the USSR. During the Soviet period, it was difficult indeed for Jews, including members of the Choral Synagogue. One could be imprisoned for contact with Israelis. One synagogue rabbi spent time in a forced labor camp until Stalin died. From 1962 to 1964, baking matza in the Leningrad synagogue was forbidden, and several Jews were arrested for illegally baking the unleavened bread. On and on went the harassment.

In 1962, 25 Jewish youths were arrested for dancing in the street on the Jewish holiday of Simchat Torah. More were arrested in 1964. The next year, the Soviet police put up barriers so Jews could not dance at all.

One incident which gathered world attention occurred when a group of seven young Jews, most of them from Riga, as well as two non-Jews, were tried in Leningrad in December 1970 for allegedly planning to hijack a Soviet plane in order to land abroad and ultimately to reach Israel. They were called the "Leningrad 7." Two were sentenced to death and the others to prison terms of 4 to 15 years. Protests in the West were instrumental in getting the death sentences reduced to 15 years hard labor. Through all the changes and oppression, the Choral Synagogue remained a symbol of the undying Jewish faith.

Chabad-Lubavitch Movement Headquarters, Lermontovsky Prospekt 2. Tel: (7-812) 114-00-78.

Chabad Kindergarten, Bolotnaya Street 3. Tel: (7-812) 247-65-55.

Chabad Day School, Kharchenko Street 5. Tel: (7-812) 245-35-89.

Yeshiva "Tomhei Tmimim" Lubavitch, Lermontovsky Prospekt 2. Tel: (7-812) 113-62-09. Here, about 15 students study Jewish law, Torah, and Hebrew, as well as religion classes.

Machon "Chaya Mushka," Lermontovsky Prospekt 2. Tel: (7-812) 113-62-09. This is a religious education establishment for girls.

Migdal Or (Jewish school, gymnasium), Fontanka 112. Tel: (7-812) 316-76-01. This is a school for boys. A soup kitchen is located at the boys' school. **The girls' division** is located at Voronezhskaya Street 33.

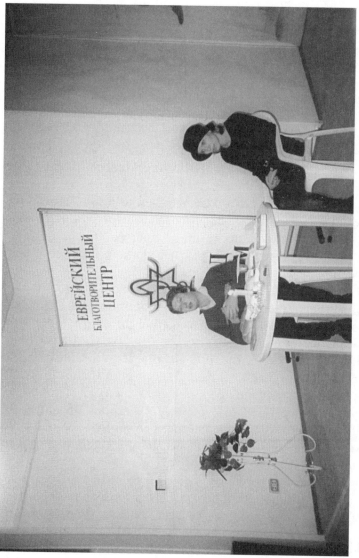

Shown here is a talk on celebrating the Sabbath in the Hesed Avraham Welfare Center, in St. Petersburg. (Photo credit: Ben G. Frank)

Jerusalem Day School, Dachniy Prospekt 34/2. Tel: (7-812) 254-36-23, or (7-812) 156-86-37. There are 270 pupils at this school.

Chabad Day School, Dobrolyubova Prospekt 13. Tel: (7-812) 233-88-01.

Sunday School Club "Beit," Shpalenaya Street 52 H. Tel: (7-812) 224-73-51.

Sunday School "Lamed," Moscow Prospekt 174A. Tel: (7-812) 298-57-15.

Adain Lo (Network of Children's Kindergartens and Sunday Schools), Director Eugenia Lvova; home, Seveniy Prospekt 73 Lod., 1, No. 129. Tel: (7-812) 553-01-66. In several kindergartens, children study Jewish history, Hebrew, Torah, and general educational subjects.

Kharchenko School No 522, Karchenko 5, St. Petersburg, 194100. Tel: (7-812) 245-45-53 and (7-812) 245-07-11. A Russian state school. These children, unlike their parents and grandparents, don't worry about practicing their religion. I was moved by a teacher who told me that when she was a young girl, her grandmother would watch that she did not go into the study of her grandparents' apartment. She was kept out because her grandfather was praying and the grandmother did not want her granddaughter to see this solitary Jewish man praying fervently, since the little girl might go outside and tell other children in Stalin's Russia that her grandfather prayed.

The school also maintains a kosher kitchen. The "meals-on-wheels" program is part of the task of the school. Blessings are transliterated into the Russian language, so that the children can recite them as they begin to eat their wholesome meals; it may be the best meal they receive all day in depressed Russia. A soup kitchen functions and kosher meals are available here for the community. Nothing is fancy. *Shabbat* is observed. Prayers are held by the students in the first through ninth grades. The program teaches the children Halachic Judaism.

Jewish Community Center, Rubinshteina Street 3, No. 50. Tel: (7-812) 113-38-89. Visit the Jewish community center near Nevsky Prospekt. It is in a courtyard, so it may be difficult to find. Unlike the large community center buildings in the U.S., this one is located in an apartment. There is no large synagogue, no Olympic-size pool, no sauna, no large banquet hall. There are several meeting rooms with newspapers, magazines, and books. In one room a picture of Ezer Weizmann, president of Israel, graces the wall. Alexander Frenkel opened the center in 1995. The library needs books and albums on Jewish life, he says. Videos are often shown and concerts are held. Russian Jews have a future here, he maintains.

Hesed Avraham Welfare Center, Bolshoy Sampsonievsky 45. Tel/Fax: (7-812) 327-58-58; 327-13-52. Tel: (7-812) 327-13-53 or 327-13-54. Founded in 1993, with substantial help from the American Jewish Joint Distribution Committee, the center began with only 20 volunteers. Today it has more than 30 workers and 650 volunteers and serves 40,000 Jews.

"It is a shame," said one elderly lady, "we were only allowed to practice our religion when we were very young and very old." Her words tell the story of Russian Jews, for they know very little about Jewish religion, customs, or history. Every Jewish institution in Russia is an outpost of Jewish education.

Generally, in the Jewish Diaspora, grandparents teach their grandchildren, and pass on to the younger generation Jewish customs, traditions, and values. Not in Russia and Ukraine. Here it is the young people who teach Judaism, as witnessed by the young man and the beautiful singer. At Hesed, concerts are offered on Sundays. All holidays are celebrated. A wonderful *Oneg Shabbat* occurs every Friday afternoon in the clubhouse, and the director declares visitors are welcome. But do call ahead.

Hesed represents a social service concept developed by JDC in response to the multifaceted needs of elderly and physically handicapped Jews in the former Soviet Union. The Hesed model, developed first in St. Petersburg in 1993, is a multifunctional service center that provides both outreach and in-house services through paid professionals and volunteers. These services include home care, medical equipment, medical consultations, meals-on-wheels, food packages, club activities, holiday celebrations, and cultural gatherings.

Medicine is scarce in Russia, and so are wheelchairs. But here a senior of Hesed can borrow a wheelchair, crutches, and

Photos of Russian Jewish veterans of World War II hang on the wall of the Center of Jewish Arts and Crafts in St. Petersburg. Half a million Jewish men and women fought in the Soviet Army in the war. (Photo credit: Ben G. Frank)

other rehabilitation equipment. In addition, there are hearing aids, talking books for the blind, and meals-on-wheels, which assures daily delivery of hot meals to seniors along 12 different routes. There are also haircuts, for hairdressers visit people, and nurses visit homes.

About 45,000 Jews are served by Hesed Avraham. Approximately 1,000 clients are in a "home care" program. Three hundred social workers are involved in this work alone. Meals-on-wheels covers 510 people each day along 12 different routes. Nearly 5,000 seniors receive winter clothes each year.

The JDC negotiated $18 to $20 million to pay for services to the elderly from the Claims Conference, an international consortium representing claims against the German government, to be paid to survivors and the State of Israel from the proceeds of Jewish estates seized during the war. These funds serve St. Petersburg, as well as Moscow, Ukraine, and Belarus.

Hesed Avraham is housed in a building constructed in the 1930s. Once the Rovesnik café/nightclub thrived here. Leonid Kolton is director.

Hillel, Bolshoy Sampsonievsky 45. (7-812) 275-54-41. Fax: (7-812) 560-23-14. Founded in 1995, Hillel is sponsored by the Foundation for Jewish Campus Life, in partnership with the American Jewish Joint Distribution Committee and the Charles and Lynn Schusterman Family Foundation.

If you are between the ages of 17 and 35, and are visiting or working in St. Petersburg, you might want to contact and visit Hillel. Here you will find young people; about 300 students belong to this group. There are disco and guitar lessons, Israeli folk dancing, and yes, an English-speaking lunch. There is also an arts studio, Israeli folk dancing, a community service program, an economics club, and a newspaper. Holidays and Sabbath programs are offered to these young adults. The vast majority of members are single and in their twenties and thirties. People meet and even marry here. Performances, special excursions, socials, and Jewish tradition round out the program.

Of course, Hillel did not exist in Russia before the fall of Communism in 1991. In 1993, JDC and Hillel International, in conjunction with the Charles and Lynn Schusterman Family Foundation, developed the idea to reach out to college-age students in the former Soviet Union and set up organizations modeled after groups developed by Hillel in the U.S. and around the world. The first Hillel was opened in Moscow at the end of 1994, followed shortly thereafter by ones in St. Petersburg and Kiev. Later came branches in the cities of Minsk and Kharkov.

St. Petersburg Hillel not only serves Jewish university students in that city, but also in the northwest region of Russia. Hillel has centers in Moscow, St. Petersburg, Kiev, Kishinev, Minsk, Yekaterinburg, Kharkov, Lvov, and Tbilisi. More than six hundred students belong to the organization.

Here, students are provided with resources, guidance, and opportunity "to create a vibrant Jewish life for themselves and the Jewish communities in which they live." Often Jewish community leaders will help students find a job within the Jewish community and obtain the proper training and contacts to advance their career goals.

Other activities include *kabbalat shabbat* (Sabbath program), a theater studio, a Jewish student career and job network, an Israeli folk dance group, and a discussion group. In addition, an English-speaking club meets twice weekly to discuss various Jewish and non-Jewish, secular and religious questions.

Every Passover, Hillel leaders work on a project. Young people go throughout the former Soviet Union to help Jews far from the big cities. These youths organize and conduct Passover celebrations. Some of these seniors are celebrating their first Seder in over 50 years.

Israel Cultural and Information Center, Inzhenernaya Street 6. Tel: (7-812) 272-04-56; or (7-812) 272-78-87. Fax: (7-812) 210-47-10. The Israel Culture and Information Center sponsors youth clubs. It helps Russians who want to emigrate to Israel do so by granting visas. The Russians know they have a right to emigrate. Concerts, lectures, and an ulpan for groups are part of the program. The Jewish Agency sponsors a special program, Naaleh, to help young people study in Israel. Club Maccabi is active. A university and four Sunday schools function in St. Petersburg, as well as Israel Centers in Kiev,

Odessa, Kishinev, Tashkent, and Moscow. Today, the Israel Center is housed in a building constructed at the end of the nineteenth century.

Center of Jewish Arts and Crafts, Gatchinskaya Street 22, No. 33. Tel: (7-812) 233-57-07. Fax: (7-812) 232-48-44 or (7-812) 279-2882. This is one of the most remarkable places to visit in the former Soviet Union. Imagine in the old days trying to display yarmulkas, candelabras, menorahs, challah covers and paintings with a Jewish theme.

But now, it is possible. Indeed, in an act unheard of in the former Soviet Union, the center has finished the framing of 100 Torah manuscripts that survived the siege of Leningrad. Many exhibitions on Jewish themes also take place here.

The group that runs the center was founded in 1995 by the St. Petersburg Association of Veterans of World War II, with the support of the American Jewish Joint Distribution Committee.

This center is indeed testimony to the unbroken Jewish spirit and strength. The Soviet regime did everything to exterminate Jewish heritage, Jewish roots, and the conception of a Jewish community. Despite all these efforts, they did not succeed. Seniors and young people now come to express Jewish creativity.

The photos of Russian veterans of World War II that hang on the front wall of the arts center are especially moving. The veterans know that there is still salacious talk that Jews did not fight in the Second World War. The photos are one way of showing that half a million Jews fought in the Red Army, especially when the photo captions reveal their personal achievements.

Some veterans come to the center to create arts and crafts items. Grandmothers and children also create artwork here. The center offers courses for seniors and children on Jewish heritage, history, and what they call "applied decorative arts." Fabric painting, embroidery, knitting, glassmaking, woodcarving, plastic arts, and jewelry making are part of the center's program.

American Jewish Joint Distribution Committee, Mokhovaya Street 20, No. 5. Tel: (7-812) 275-20-33 and (7-812) 279-28-82. Fax: (7-812) 275-04-44.

Institute of Communal and Welfare Workers, Mokhovaya Street 20, No. 2. Tel: (7-812) 273-36-54 and (7-812) 273-17-68.

Fax: (7-812) 273-36-54. This institute prepares specialists for work in Jewish communities and organizations of social work. **Jewish Agency,** Izmailovsky Prospekt 9/2, St. Petersburg. Tel: (7-812) 251-18-84. Fax: (7-812) 251-32-17. **Russian Jewish Congress,** Moika Embankment 97. Tel: (7-812) 311-82-84. **Jewish Women's Club,** Fontanka 46. Tel: (7-812) 113-38-89. **Ash-Ha-Torah,** Ephimova St. 47, Gkv. Tel: (7-812) 257-03-66. Hours are from Monday to Thursday, 12:00 P.M. to 3:00 p.m. A group of 40 students delivers lectures on Judaism and organizes seminars on Judaism for young people in the former Soviet Union and Israel.

Halom (Society for Studying Jewish Languages), Ryleeva Street 29-31. Tel: (7-812) 275-61-04. Fax: (7-812) 275-61-03. Thousands have studied Hebrew at this institution, which has a number of ulpanim throughout the city.

Jewish Charity Fund, "Eva," Moyka Embankment 60. Tel: (7-812) 210-65-08.

Maccabi Sports Club, Tverskaya Street 8. Tel/Fax: (7-812) 271-68-73.

Association of Petersburg Artists, "Tsaya," Lermontovsky Prospekt 8, No. 110. Tel: (7-812) 114-45-07. This group of artists holds meetings and exhibitions.

The Guenzburg Family Home, Konnogvardeisky Boulevard 17. This building once belonged to the man who was probably the richest and most famous Jew in St. Petersburg, Baron Horace Yevselevitch Guenzburg. The facade to this structure is breathtaking.

For 40 years Baron Guenzburg was the acknowledged leader of the Jewish community in St. Petersburg, and throughout Russia. He gave most of the money for the synagogue here. The barons of the Guenzburg family, as well as other rich Jews, were considered spokespersons of pre-Revolution Russian Jewry. The Guenzburg family easily occupied the first place in Russian Jewry. Guenzburg was a *shtadlan,* a "court Jew," a notable, who, because of his wealth, influenced non-Jews. Some "court Jews" presumed to speak for the Jewish community, without consulting its wishes.

The baron donated money, including bribes, to placate the

bureaucracy, and of course, to plead and petition. He became his father's assistant. In 1859, together with his father, he founded the banking house of I. E. Guenzburg in St. Petersburg, which became the first modern bank in Russia. A patron of the arts and a super philanthropist, he gathered "the best writers, scientists and artists of St. Petersburg to his house," writes Beizer. Between 1868 and 1872, Guenzburg was consul of Hesse-Darmstadt, and there the archduke elevated him and later his father to the rank and title of "baron."

Born in 1833, he died in St. Petersburg in 1909. Because his parents spent most of their lives in Paris, he was buried in that city, next to his father. "This request was, to a significant degree, the result of the worsening situation of the Jews in Russia toward the end of his life," writes Beizer, adding, "loyalty to the government of the day and to the tsar was for him a sacred principle."

Until the Russian Revolution, the family of the Barons de Guenzburg, grand bankers in Russia and Paris, were prominent in Jewish diplomacy. In tsarist days, they were also among most preeminent philanthropic Jewish families. Because of their situation, they made many representations to the tsar.

St. Petersburg Voluntary Organization of Disabled Jewish War Veterans and Soldiers, Gatchinskaya Street 22, No. 33. Tel: (7-812) 233-57-07. Fax: (7-812) 232-48-44.

Jewish Association of St. Petersburg, Rubinshteina Street 3, No. 50. Tel (7-812) 113-38-89. Fax: (7-812) 311-51-17.

ORT-Guenzburg, Torgoviy Pereulok 2-A, St. Petersburg, 191023. Tel/Fax: (7-812) 315-20-49. Many readers of this volume probably know the ORT (Organization for Rehabilitation through Training) for its fine network of vocational schools. But did you know that ORT was founded in St. Petersburg in 1880? ORT provides work skills for Jewish men and women. Its American affiliate dates to 1927. In Russia, Baron Horace Guenzburg, financier, and Samuel Polyakov, financier and railroad builder, wanted to set up a system to teach handicrafts and agricultural training to young Jews. They wanted to change the occupational and economic structure of the Jewish *shtetl.* The ORT'S early slogans were "From trading and acting as middlemen to craft work and agricultural labor."

The author's wife, Riva Frank, is pictured in front of the museum dedicated to the defense of Leningrad. (Photo credit: Ben G. Frank)

Following World War I, ORT spread its wings throughout Europe. Taught here are computer sciences, high-tech automation, and desktop publishing. ORT also helps adults. "Our main task is to develop technological education for the students of our school and all those who want to acquire the knowledge of information technologies. Modern equipment and skilled teachers at our center are the basis for success," says Vladimir Dribinsky, director of ORT-Guenzburg, in St. Petersburg.

St. Petersburg Jewish University, Kievskaya 18. Tel: (7-812) 316-38-30. This is the office of the St. Petersburg Jewish University. But only a few classes and programs are held here. Students attend courses in various buildings in the city. There is also a fine library here, where old books from many Jewish towns can be found. About 1,300 students attend Jewish university courses in the city.

Piskaryovskoye Cemetery, Nepokorennykh Prospekt. This is the cemetery of the World War II siege of Leningrad. Here in Piskaryovskoye Cemetery lies half the city's population that were living there when the siege began. Nobody knows for sure, but probably more than a million victims of the siege are buried here.

At the end of a long avenue of mass graves, people gather at a granite slab etched with the famous words of the poet Olga Berggolts, "No one is forgotten, nothing is forgotten." This wall monument with those words was dedicated on May 9 (Victory Day), 1960.

There is an eternal flame at Piskaryovskoye for the hundreds of thousands who died from Nazi bombs, physical exhaustion, cold, and starvation.

President Richard Nixon visited here in 1972, and President Bill Clinton came here in 1996.

Preobrazhensky Cemetery, also known as the Transfiguration Cemetery. Part of this cemetery is the old Jewish cemetery, which is located at Alexandrovskoy Fermy Prospekt 66, St. Petersburg.

The official title is the "Cemetery of the Transfiguration." No burials take place there. Now burials take place in another communal nondenominational cemetery. The burial vault of the St. Petersburg branch of the Warshawskis is located here.

Also situated here is the memorial stone of Baron Horace Guenzburg, the leader of Russian Jewry, who was buried in Paris, but was so highly regarded that a monument was set here in his memory. Here lies Vera Klimentievna Slutzkaya (1880-1917), member of the Communist Party of the Soviet Union. A professional revolutionary, she was an active participant in the Bolshevik Revolution. A dentist, she was killed on October 30, 1917, while transporting medical supplies to Red Guard detachments near the town of Pushkin. John Reed, the American writer, mentions her in his book, *Ten Days that Shook the World*. After the Revolution, when many Russian towns changed their name, the town of Pavlovsk became Slutzk. Now it is again Pavlovsk.

At one point in our excursion, we come to a tombstone with names such as "Gelb," who died in Auschwitz, "Yosef Lurie" who died at Stalingrad, and others. Until the 1980s, there was no monument to Holocaust victims. So in 1982, the Jews of Leningrad began coming to the cemetery on Holocaust Memorial Day, to this gravesite tombstone, "as a symbolic memorial to the Six Million." There is a metallic network of wire around this grave that Beizer says "perhaps symbolizes barbed wire fences of the concentration camps."

In the right corner of the cemetery, there are two communal graves. One is for the residents of Leningrad who died in the World War II blockade. It is possible to assume that Jews are buried here.

In 1986, new areas were assigned for Jewish burials, this time in the Kovalevo cemetery, as well as other cemeteries.

National Library of Russia, Sadovaya Street 18. Tel: (7-812) 310-98-50. Once called Saltykov-Schedrin, this is a library of 15,000 books and manuscripts, a large number of which are in Ladino. This public library contains one of the world's oldest and most important collections of Hebrew manuscripts, 40,000 volumes in all. Housed here, for example, is the "Leningrad Codex," part of the Abraham Firkovich collection, where it has been for more than 130 years. Firkovich was a Jewish businessman, and a devoted Karaite (a Jew who follows only the Bible and rejects oral or Talmudic tradition). He traveled widely and collected Hebrew manuscripts. He sold the "Codex" to what was then the St. Petersburg Imperial Library, according to Curt Leviant, writing in the Philadelphia *Jewish Exponent* on January 21, 1999. The Codex, along with the "Aleppo Codex," is one of the sources for the biblical tradition, for the study of Hebrew scriptures, and for providing an accurate text for the reading and writing of the Torah and the other books of the Bible.

The Monument of the 900 Days of the Siege of Leningrad in World War II, Victory Square, St. Petersburg. "There is not a Jewish family here which passed the war without losses," wrote Martin Gilbert. By the eve of the German invasion, 200,000 Jews lived in Leningrad. Many of them died in the siege. "Leningrad is not afraid of death, death is afraid of Leningrad," was a saying that helped keep Leningrad alive. One of the great Russian composers, Shostakovich, said that when he looked back onto the war and Russian life, he saw nothing but corpses. He added "The Jews became a symbol for me."

Look at the monument near the Pulkovskaya Hotel. Even from far away you can see it. Note its massive Soviet-style architecture. Here in Victory Square, it is stark, dark, and overwhelming. You descend into a hall of photos, exhibits, and maps. It is well worth a visit to feel the sacrifice made by this marvelous city on the Neva.

Research shows that more people died in the World War II siege than ever died in a modern-day city—more than 10 times the number who died in Hiroshima, according to author and journalist Harrison E. Salisbury. Suny says that of the nearly 3 million trapped in Leningrad, almost half would be dead by the end of the war. Another 200,000 Russian soldiers died in the German attack on the city. For 900 days, from about August 28, 1941, until January 27, 1944, Leningrad was totally surrounded, starved, strafed, bombarded, blockaded, and cut off by the Germans from the rest of Russia. The daily ration provided less than one-seventh of the calories needed to sustain an average adult.

If you want to really feel what it is like for a city to die, imagine Fifth Avenue in New York City, or Fifth Avenue in Pittsburgh, or the 405 freeway in Los Angeles, with no cars, no buses, and all of the city's vehicles "stand motionless in the snow like frozen dinosaurs." Imagine no light, no electricity.

The Holocaust Memorial, known as the "Monument of Sorrow," is located in Pushkin, Russia, just outside of St. Petersburg. The monument resembles a woman weeping. (Photo credit: Ben G. Frank)

The only people on the street are mostly women dragging sleds down the wide avenues. They are wheeling the dead of the city.

Staying with the people were the poet Anna Akhmatova and the composer Dmitri Shostokovich, who wrote much of the famous *Seventh Symphony,* dedicated to Leningrad, while still in Leningrad, until he was ordered to leave, according to Suny.

The Germans held an eight-mile wide corridor south of Lake Ladoga. This extension of land had sealed off Leningrad from the rest of the Soviet Union since September 1941. Leningraders starved, died, broke down, and froze. If they lived, it was through the "white hell of starvation."

Leningrad was bound to suffer, because the ultimate target of the Germans was Moscow. But the German plan did not call for a direct frontal assault on the Russian capital. "Operation Barbarossa" called for the capture of Leningrad first, and then an attack on Moscow. Most Leningrad residents would not leave. They would be thought of as cowards if they did. For this, the city was to pay dearly. Party Secretary Andrei A. Zhdanov (1896-1948), chief of both the Leningrad City and the Leningrad Regional Party organizations, member of the Military Council of the Leningrad District, secretary of the Central Committee of the Communist Party, and right-hand man of Stalin himself, according to Salisbury, had encouraged people not to leave.

This author was told that at the outset of hostilities, many did not flee because they were assured the enemy would soon be hurled back across the border. Had not the government told Leningraders, and the rest of Russia for that matter, that the Nazi-Soviet pact would guarantee security?

Leningrad would resist to the end. After Marshal Zhukov had won the military battle, the starvation battle came to the fore, for the warehouses were destroyed. While death stalked Leningrad, the Germans stalled. With no electricity, Leningrad resembled an abandoned city. More than 3,200 buildings were destroyed and 7,100 more damaged.

But the Russians built a road over the ice of Lake Ladoga. No other possibility of providing Leningrad with the supplies for survival existed. Build the road or die, they swore. So construct they did; 220 miles long; through swamps, bogs, lakes, and dense timber. On the night of November 22, 1941, the first column of trucks arrived in the city. Thousands had died in building this survival road, this road of life.

Salisbury tells us that "on January 27, 1944, at 8 P.M.—882 days when rail communications were cut—over the sword point of the Admiralty, over the great dome of St. Isaacs, over the broad expanse of Palace Square, over the broken buildings of Pulkovo, the dilapidated machine shops of the Kirov works, the battered battleships still standing on the Neva, roared a shower of golden arrows, a flaming stream of red, white and blue rockets, came the end of the blockade."

Party Secretary Zhdanov was one of the main figures in the early postwar period. He stood as supreme authority next to Stalin on all ideological issues. He also played an important role in the coordination of the activities of Communist parties outside the Soviet Union, writes author Walter Laqueur. He initiated the campaign of a regimentation of the arts that brought "so much misery" to the creative minds of artists, writers, and musicians of the Soviet Union. Later, when Stalin launched the Doctors' Plot, it was said that Zhdanov died because a group of prominent Jewish physicians killed him.

Pushkin, Russia

This municipality, actually a suburb of St. Petersburg, is under the administration of the larger city and can easily be reached by public transportation. According to Beizer, Pushkin stands as one of the oldest places of Jewish settlement near St. Petersburg. Even in 1827, Jewish soldiers lived and settled here, for there were many army barracks in the area, and at the end of their military service, many Jewish soldiers stayed in the town as craftsmen, tailors, and other tradesmen. The town provided them with many opportunities to earn money. The Germans occupied Pushkin in 1941. They gutted and destroyed practically all of the Summer Palace and shot all the Jewish residents.

Catherine's Palace, designed by Domenico Trezzini (1670-1734), is the attraction in Pushkin. Once called Tsarskoye Selo, it is located in a perfect setting, with richly colorful facades and sumptuous rooms. "Golden rooms of light in a forest of gold," is the way one observer put it.

Above all, stroll through the park of Catherine's Palace. The Germans mercilessly destroyed the structure, but the Russians painstakingly put it back, piece by piece.

Holocaust Monument—Monument of Sorrow, Alexander Park, in front of the Alexander Palace. A woman kneels. She weeps for all of the Jewish blood that flowed in this town of Pushkin. Located near the airport in Pushkin is the Holocaust Monument. It was erected in 1991 through the efforts of Russian and American Jews, on the spot where the Nazis killed the Jews of the town of Detskoye Selo in October 1941. Vadim Sidur was the sculptor of the monument, which resembles a woman weeping. It weeps for all of us.

Levashovo, Russia

The figure of 20 million is given as to the number of human beings lost in the Stalin purges. I recall the story of how at night, from the KGB headquarters at Lubyanka, the black limousines of the secret police sped out like spiders. Imagine going to sleep every night with the sound prerecorded in your mind, fearing that the black car will screech to a halt in front of your apartment block in the middle of the night. Car doors will slam. The elevator will start up toward you. Up, up, to your floor. A loud knock on your door, and you will be hustled out into the car, into jail, into a trial or not, into a camp, into a yard or a prison cell, and then the shot in the back of the head. These were the Stalin purges.

Guide. Alla Markova, 212 Stachek Prospekt 212, St. Petersburg, 198262. Tel: 718-236-6037 (in the U.S) In St. Petersburg, for a tour of Jewish and general sites and organizations, one can sign up Alla Markova. A professor, writer, and travel professional, Mrs. Markova knows the Jewish scene in this truly beautiful city, the cradle of Russian scholarship and art, and as we have seen, a city once called a "second Paris." From St. Petersburg, Levashovo can be reached by car or suburban train in about an hour.

Zekher Avoteinu, Jewish Tourist and Research Center, St. Petersburg, 198262. Tel/Fax (7-812) 184-12-48 or (7-812) 553-54-00. Founded by Alla Markova and Oleg Vinogradov, the group conducts research and offers tours on Jewish topics. This organization works with the majority of Jewish organizations in St. Petersburg. The group conducts tours geared for various guests of Jewish groups in St. Petersburg, as well as for any person interested in the Jewish heritage in the city.

Zekher Avoteinu can help the traveler with guided tours, accommodations, and kosher meals. If requested well in advance, they say it is possible to organize kosher or vegetarian food, as well as transfers and transportation. They can cater kosher meals for large groups.

The guided tours provided by the Zekher Avoteinu are really unique. They are based on research and many years' experience of conducting trips to Jewish sites. Tourists can participate in cultural and social events of the local Jewish community. Their program includes both sites of traditional tourism and places of Jewish interest.

Genealogical research, tracing of roots, looking for relatives, documents, tombstones, and taking care of the tombstones of relatives in St. Petersburg is also on the agenda of Zekher Avoteinu.

Suggested Reading

Baron, Salo, *The Russian Jew Under Tsars and Soviets*. New York: The Macmillan Company, 1964.

Beizer, Mikhail, *The Jews of St. Petersburg, Excursions Through a Noble Past*. Philadelphia: An Edward E. Elson Book, The Jewish Publication Society, 1989.

Bryant, Louise, *Mirror of Moscow*. Westport, CT: Hyperion Press, Inc., 1923.

Bryant, Louise, *Six Red Months in Russia*. New York: George H. Doran Company, 1918.

Conquest, Robert, *The Great Terror*. New York: Macmillan, 1973.

Dubnow, Simon M., *History of the Jews in Russia and Poland, From the Earliest Times Until the Present Day, Vols. I, II,* and *III*. Philadelphia: The Jewish Publication Society of America, 1916.

Dubnow, Simon M,. *History of the Jews, From the Congress of Vienna* to the Emergence of Hitler, Vol. V. South Brunswick, NJ, London: Thomas Yoseloff, 1973.

Figes, Orlando, *A People's Tragedy: A History of the Russian Revolution.* New York: Viking, 1997.

Florinsky, Michael T., *Russia.* New York: 2 Vols., Macmillan, 1961.

Hosking, *Russia, People and Empire.* Cambridge, MA: Harvard University Press, 1997.

Hughes, Lindsay, *Russia in the Age of Peter the Great.* New Haven and London: Yale University Press, 1998.

Lawrence, John, *A History of Russia.* New York: New American Library, 1978.

Massie, Robert K. Massie, *Peter the Great.* New Haven and London: Yale University Press, 1991.

Norman, Geraldine, *The Hermitage: The Biography of A Great Museum.* New York: Fromm International Publishing Corporation, 1998.

Pares, Sir Barnard, *A History of Russia.* New York: Alfred A. Knopf, 1968.

Pipes, Richard, *A Concise History of the Russian Revolution.* New York: Alfred Knopf, 1995.

Pipes, Richard, *Russia Under the Bolshevik Regime.* New York: Alfred Knopf, 1994.

Radzinsky, Edvard, *The Last Czar.* New York: Doubleday, 1992.

Ro'i, Yaacov, *Jews and Jewish Life in Russia and the Soviet Union.* Ilford, England: Frank Cass & Co., Ltd.,1995.

Salisbury, Harrison E., *Black Night, White Snow: Russian Revolutions, 1905-1917.* New York: Da Capo, 1981.

Salisbury, Harrison E., *The 900 Days; The Siege of Leningrad.* New York and Evanston, IL: Harper & Row, 1969.

Schwarz, Solomon M., *The Russian Revolution of 1905: the Workers' Movement and the Formation of Bolshevism and Menshevism.* Chicago: University of Chicago, 1967.

Volkogonov, Dmitrii, *Trotsky: The Eternal Revolutionary.* New York: The Free Press, 1996.

Wolfe, Bertram D., *Three Who Made a Revolution: A Biographical History.* New York: The Dial Press, 1964.

Moscow
The Heart of Russia, the Heart of the Jewish Community

They say when Stalin suddenly fell to the floor in the Kremlin on February 28, 1953, suffering from a fatal stroke, he could not speak. His so-called comrades left him prostrate, unable to talk, but able to hear. Actually, we are told, Lavrenti Beria, Soviet secret-police chief, and others refused to call a doctor. (Stalin would die five days later.) If at that very moment we could have flown forward in time to nearly a half-century later, what would the tyrant's reaction have been to the sounds wafting up from the nearby Operetta Theater, at 6 Bol'shaya Dmitrovskaya Street, within easy earshot of the Kremlin, where he lay in agony?

Resounding from that concert hall were the clapping and singing of Jews, Russian Jews, attending a standing-room-only performance of Dudu Fisher, the Israeli concert singer, who was offering up a program of Yiddish, Hebrew, and Israeli songs. Mounted on the stage behind Fisher was a huge Star of David, and stationed, respectively, left and right of the stage were the blue and white Israeli flag and the new Russian flag—three square horizontal bands of white (top), red, and blue.

Two months later, in another theater, the Rossiya Concert Hall, several thousand of these same Moscow Jews gathered for a week-long Jewish Music Festival, which also included a tribute to the memory of the great Yiddish actor and theater director Solomon Mikhoels, who was slain by Stalin and his secret

169

police. We will never know what the dictator's reaction would have been to all this, but we do know that Fisher's musical program would have never occurred even a decade before under Communist rulers.

If the concerts do not show you the convulsive changes in the country since the fall of Communism in 1991, here is the clincher, so to speak. Who would have ever dreamed that a Lubavitch rabbi would have organized a ceremony of lighting the Chanukah menorah, on this holiday, which to Jews represents liberation and freedom from oppression? And to top it off, he called in a Russian army band to perform Hebrew songs in a vast area just off "saintly" and public Red Square. One year the menorah was lit by Moscow Vice Mayor Vladimir Resin, who is Jewish.

Welcome to Moscow, where Russian Jews now can freely visit at least five synagogues, 12 religious groups, several kosher restaurants, nearly a dozen day schools, Jewish colleges and a university, an art center, and many other organizations.

Welcome to Moscow, the home of one-half of the Jewish population of Russia.

Welcome to Moscow, which despite frequent economic crises remains the richest city in the former Soviet Union. Moscow, the heart of Russia, where the tourist can spot advertising billboards spelling out in Russian letters the word "business;" where foreign businesspeople can hear words such as "product marketability," "shares," "stocks," and "bottom line;" and where visitors can be wined and dined in five-star restaurants in this booming entrepot where even small businesses flourish. Indeed, Muscovites live far better than most other Russians in this city, the center of economic activity both personal and corporate, far outstripping St. Petersburg, which in the Soviet era was the more cosmopolitan metropolis.

Moscow boasts the famous Bolshoi Theater, as well as world-renowned museums such as the Pushkin Fine Art Museum, the magnificent Armory Museum, and the Tretyakov Gallery. Moscow also has the Moscow Zoo, Gorky Park, and the Moscow Circus, all highlights of any visit to the city.

As for the more than four hundred churches, perhaps that is why Tolstoy called it the "Asiatic City of countless churches."

This is Moscow. This huge city, with cobblestoned boulevards containing heavy traffic, wide squares, and a statue of Lenin in the middle of the railroad station on the track that runs from St. Petersburg to Moscow. No longer is there a single choice such as the old-fashioned department store G.U.M. Now, a glitzy three-level shopping mall attracts the affluent.

Moscow, it has been said, *is* Russia. Of all the capitals in the world, this one most epitomizes its country's principal features, reflecting its virtues and vices. With its 10 million people, it is so different from any other part of Russia that some call it a state within a state. If you are a New Yorker, you just may feel at home in this city. It is fast paced, for sure. Some even say it is pushier than that city on the Hudson.

Before the economic crunch of 1998, Moscow in the 1990s "throbbed with the expectation and achievement of good fortune," wrote Nicholas Weinstock in the December 27, 1998, *New York Times Magazine.*

"Fueled by fast money, loose morals and a hunger for fresh sensations, Moscow is now the world capital of conspicuous consumption. Is it time for Westerners to brave the fearsomely sharp elbows of the babushki?" was the comment of the *Financial Times,* September 1998.

Much less conspicuous consumption exists since the economic downturn Russia has suffered. But the desire is still there. "Whereas the Soviet elite exploited Siberia's treasure house of natural resources to build tanks and warplanes, the new Russian elite has expropriated a large part of that wealth to spend on satisfying its own consumer desires," declares the *Financial Times.*

Still, Moscow today is almost unrecognizable from what it was in the early 1990s, with more colorful and better window displays, as well as outdoor advertising.

Located four hundred miles southeast of St. Petersburg, Moscow is well situated for buying, selling, and bartering. No longer is it difficult for businesspeople or tourists to move in and out of this post-Communist capital, which is a combination of business New York and government Washington. Street crime is a rarity in the Russian capital.

Once a mere village on the banks of the Moskva River, this

great city, just over 850 years old, contains the depth and soul of Russia.

In the 1990s, Mayor Yuri Luzhkov fostered rapid commercial expansion with active government cooperation. Business now thrives in the capital.

Serge Schmemann, who covered Russia for the *New York Times,* observed, "Like others we may see only the veneer." Sometimes one sees homeless people, as well as lonely people hawking goods at the subways, such as vodka, soap, chickens, meat, clothes, and brushes.

When you are here, remember that in Moscow, a new sign of the free-market status is an automobile. The visitor quickly experiences traffic jams and parking problems and learns, as in some American cities, to leave the car at home or in the hotel parking garage and take public transportation, especially since the Moscow subway stations are so artistically unique and attractive. Statues and paintings adorn subway walls and are a must-see for all travelers. The subway system covers 162 miles in Moscow, and is said to be the busiest subway in the world, and one of the cheapest. It is unusually clean and graffiti free.

Architecturally, St. Petersburg lords its status over Moscow. Stalin almost ruined this city with those eight seven-layer-cake skyscrapers. They look like dead, barn-like factories, wedged into the very heart of the city. There is no style, one observes.

There are comparisons galore between Moscow and St. Petersburg, just as there are differences.

St. Petersburg lives on the money of the people and the peasants. Moscow lives off the money it earns.

In St. Petersburg, the streets are basically straight. In older Moscow, the streets revolve around the Kremlin, and they wind and twist. Thoroughfares form circles.

When author Charles A. Stoddard first saw nineteenth-century Moscow, he said the view was disappointing. "The city is 24 miles around and 9 miles across, and to a stranger it seems only a mass of houses and churches without order or plan."

Even one hundred years ago, he added that Russians saw

Moscow as "the embodiment of all that is grand and sacred and national." That description still fits today.

Moscow was not the first major city of Russia. Kiev, Novgorod, Vladimir, and Suzdal came before this metropolis. Like many world cities, it is difficult to pinpoint the origin of the name "Moscow." A seventeenth-century folk tale has it that one Mosokhi, a descendant of the patriarch Noah, founded the city in Old Testament times, and Moskova was a cross of his name and that of his wife, Kva.

Obviously the name could also be a derivation for the several-hundred-mile-long Moskva River on which Moscow stands, says author Timothy J. Colton.

Another story has it that Prince Yuri Dolgoruki felt that God had put it in his heart to build a city on the site of a village situated on the Moscow River bluff, the very spot where the Kremlin now stands and thus, Moscow was established.

And yet another tale, written in an issue of the *Russian Chronicle,* says that in 1147, Dolgoruki entertained his neighbor Prince Svyatoslav of Novgorod with a "mighty dinner," and in this description, the name of Moscow was mentioned in the *Chronicle* for the first time.

Centuries ago, eastern Slavs began trekking north from Kievan Rus. Having converted to Orthodox Christianity and having lived in the area of Kiev, the first capital of Russia, they now began to stray into the Moscow area in the twelfth century, only this time they stayed to plant roots deep in the soil of Russia.

Historians say that this migration from the steppes, from the lands of the Dnieper basin, became one of the most important forces in the history of Russian civilization. These groups mixed with the Finns, and some claim that this brought about the "Great Russian" branch of Eastern Slavs.

Prince Yuri, the son of Vladimir Monomakh, battled other Russian princes for the throne of Kiev. At the time, the area, now known as Moscow, belonged to the boyar Sepan Kuchka. Prince Yuri, who was Stepan's guest, became very angry with him and ordered him killed. Later he founded Moscow on the very site of Kuchka's lands. He had been impressed by the position of one of the villages situated on a height washed by the Moskva, the very spot where the Kremlin is now situated. There he built the city of Moscow. Prince Yuri was nicknamed Dolgoruki ("Long Handled") because of his conquest of vast Russian lands.

Grand Prince of Moscow Dmitrii Donskoi, who reigned from 1319 to 1389, defeated the Mongols at the battle of Kulikovo near the Don in 1380. This gave Moscow the opportunity to grow stronger and bolder, for Muscovy had shattered the legend of the military invincibility of the Mongols.

By the time Ivan I assumed power, the center of Russian political authority had transferred from Vladimir to Moscow. Ivan I convinced the church to move the seat of the church from Vladimir to well-protected Moscow in 1326. At the same time, he reduced the status of Kiev as the spiritual center, and extended his domain by purchase and violence.

With the fall of Constantinople to the Ottoman Turks in 1453 and the collapse of the Byzantine Empire, Russia became the most powerful Orthodox state. The grand princes of Moscow regarded their capital as the new center of orthodoxy, and saw themselves as the protectors of all Orthodox Christians. The "First Rome" had fallen under the control of the papacy. The "Second Rome," Constantinople, had "succumbed to the abhorrent infidel," the Turks. And thus Moscow became the "Third Rome."

After the end of the Mongol domination in the fifteenth century, this giant city stood as the capital of Mother Russia, until Peter the Great moved the capital to St. Petersburg in 1712. Even so, the city retained the title "Holy Moscow," the second city of the empire, the place to which every tsar returned to be crowned.

Moscow began to rule others because its strength lay in its strategic location in the heart of northern Russia's river routes. Its kremlin, or fort, overlooked the River Moskva. Between the fourteenth and the seventeenth centuries, Moscow rose to dominate other Russian city-states.

Ivan III (Ivan the Great), who held power from 1478 to 1485, enlarged Russian territory. Under Ivan IV, the Terrible, the Dread (1544-84), Moscow's main rivals were crushed,

Kazan and Astrakhan were subdued, and Russia became "a vast, integrated state."

Michael Romanov (1613-45), went to Moscow and triumphantly entered the old Russian capital. He became the first Romanov tsar. His family would rule until 1917, and they felt they owned the whole of Russia, according to Orlando Figes.

The actual moving of the seat of the government from Petrograd to Moscow came on March 10 and 11, 1918, when the Soviet government and Central Committee of the Communist Party, headed by V. I. Lenin, moved from Petrograd to Moscow.

There have been various descriptions of Moscow in the 1930s. While generally giving a favorable report on his trip to Russia in 1937, Lion Feuchtwanger wrote, "the greater part of the population lives herded together in mean and tiny rooms, which in winter are almost airless. Shortcomings make everyday life in Moscow difficult."

Severe winter is a way of life for Russians; perhaps that is why adults embrace summer as if they were children. In December the temperature can dip to -26 degrees Fahrenheit. Russians like to say that they are accustomed to the cold. They have an ability to stand it, they mutter.

A Brief History

Interestingly, the *Encyclopedia Judaica* begins its description of the city by stating that Moscow is the capital of the former Soviet Union and for many ages has been the political, economic, and commercial center of Russia. But, as if with immediate emphasis, it states: "Right up to the end of the 18th century, Jews were forbidden to reside in Moscow, although many Jewish merchants and traders from Poland, Lithuania, and Crimea came as visitors to the city."

Moscow may be slightly more than 850 years old, but Jews have a short history there. They simply were not allowed to live freely in the capital legally until the Communist revolution. Still, a few Jewish doctors, prisoners, advisors of Jewish origin, and converts managed to reside in Moscow. The first Jewish traders came to the Khitai-gorod, a huge open area to the northeast of the Kremlin walls that is often translated as "Chinese City." Probably the words "Khitai-gorod" have a partially Mongol origin and may also mean "central fortress." Completely rebuilt today, the section is located behind the Hotel Rossiya. But author Stoddard said in 1891 that it still preserved its ancient walls and towns.

Stoddard points out that every great city in Russia has a "Gostinnoi-Dvor," or "Stranger's Court," like the bazaars in Cairo and Damascus. "In Moscow," he says, "the bazaar is a little city by itself, opening from the main street of the Khitai-gorod, full of arcades, stalls and shops."

Judaizers

In the late fifteenth century, the religious sect known as the Judaizers was discovered in Russia. Several members of the Russian sect who existed in Novgorod and at the court in Moscow were executed after they were accused of having influenced and initiated the establishment of that group.

When Jews did manage to live in Moscow, some earned a living by working in the flour mills, forests, inns, and taverns. Others were merchants, shopkeepers, hawkers, and craftsmen. The fact that Jews had such occupations bothered Russian merchants in Moscow, as the Jews were competing with them. The businesspeople even went so far as to have Catherine the Great expel these Jews from the city.

Only one hundred years after the French and American revolutions, the Declaration of the Rights of Man, and even after the freeing of the serfs in 1861, Jews were still being expelled and barred from Moscow. In February 1891, Grand Duke Sergei Alexandrovitch, a brother of the tsar, was appointed governor general of Moscow. Blind hatred for Jews ruled his mind.

On March 28, 1891, Passover Eve, in the Jewish year 5651, a law was issued abolishing the right of Jewish craftsmen to reside in Moscow and prohibiting them entry into the city in the future, states the *Encyclopedia Judaica*. About thirty thousand Jews, or two-thirds of the Jewish population, were expelled.

"The police broke into Jewish homes, roused the terrified

Jews out of bed, and hustled them off to the police station,"
says one account.

The tsarist police roundups would continue pretty much up
to World War I. During that war a stream of fleeing Jewish
refugees poured into Moscow.

After the Bolshevik Revolution, Moscow became a Jewish
center. The Hebrew printing press flourished; large yeshivas
drew hundreds of Jews into Moscow. Restrictions were lifted.
Habimah, the Jewish theater company, performed An-sky's
famous play *The Dybbuk* in Moscow. After Moscow became the
capital of the Soviet Union, the Jewish population rapidly
increased to 28,000 in 1920; to 131,000 in 1936; and to about
400,000 by 1946.

"Zionists and religious Jews quickly came to regard
Communist rule as a grim continuation of the repressive
regime of the tsars. Indeed, many Jews believed themselves
worse off under the Communists than they had been under
the cruelest of the tsars," according to Potok.

Because Moscow served as the capital and a "window to the
Soviet Union," representations of world Jewry and Israel until
1967 followed the destinies of Moscow's Jews more than those
in other cities. Moscow Jews were somehow able to meet with
Jews from outside the Soviet Union, according to the
Encyclopedia Judaica.

In 1959, about two hundred-forty thousand Jews, or 4.7 percent of the total population, registered in the municipality of
Moscow. But some say that a half-million Jews actually
remained in the capital, because if they could get away with it,
many Jews would say that they were of Russian nationality, and
not registered Jews.

Notable Jews

Ilya Ehrenburg. Born 1891 in Kiev, of an engineering family,
he died in 1967 in Moscow. He joined the Bolsheviks in 1908,
when, under threat of prison, he emigrated to Paris, where he
composed his first poems. He returned to Russia in July 1917.
From 1921 to 1924, Ehrenburg worked as a journalist in Berlin,

where he wrote his first novel. Later, in 1940, he started writing his well-known novel, *The Fall of Paris*. His war journalism, especially for the Red Army paper *Red Star*, was extremely popular in the USSR and abroad, according to Kathy Porter and Mark Jones, in *Moscow in World War II*.

At the end of 1943, Ehrenburg and Vasily Grossman began compiling a collection of Holocaust survivors' tales and details of Nazi murder, which they gave the working title, *The Black Book*. They decided to collect diaries, private letters, and stories of potential victims and witnesses "who had somehow managed to escape the total destruction of all Jews carried out by the Hitlerites in occupied Soviet territory," write authors John Gerrard and Carol Gerrard.

Stalin saved Ehrenburg from certain death or imprisonment, because the dictator needed him as an ambassador to the European left. Had he not gone to Spain during that country's civil war?

Ehrenburg's reputation in the Jewish world was sullied when he published a front-page article in *Pravda* in 1948, in which he attacked Israel and Jews who saw Israel as their homeland. Ehrenburg wrote that Jews should build socialist societies and not emigrate to the Jewish state, according to Wasserstein. He felt Russian Jews should not maintain relationships with Jews in other lands, and helped launch the official Soviet anti-Zionist attack that was to go on until Communism fell in 1991.

But it was this same Ehrenburg who told the world that the Nazi attack on the Soviet Union reminded him of his Jewish origin, that his mother's name was Hannah, and that he took pride in being a Jew. He poured out hatred for the Germans. "Let us kill . . . There is nothing jollier for us than German corpses," he is said to have remarked.

Sites

Pushkin Square. In Pushkin Square in December 1965, according to Potok, about two hundred people assembled near the statue of the poet Pushkin and unfurled placards with the words "Respect The Soviet Constitution." This was the first human-rights action with placards in Soviet history. Two Russian writers were arrested in that demonstration, and then sentenced to hard labor. Others were arrested on January 17-19, 1967. On January 22, 1967, a group of people demonstrated in Pushkin Square demanding freedom for those arrested. Police broke up the demonstration, and a number of demonstrators were arrested and tried. At the Central Telegraph Building, the dissidents practiced silent indoor demonstrations.

On August 21, 1968, the day of the Soviet invasion of Czechoslovakia, friends of a writer on trial, Anatoly Marchenko, heard about the invasion of Russian troops into Prague and decided to hold a demonstration in Red Square the following Sunday. The demonstrators were beaten up, arrested, tried, and sentenced.

The Former KGB Building, now called the Federal Security Service Building, Lubyanka Square. This is the infamous KGB building on Lubyanka Square where many dissidents and Jewish activists were interrogated. Many thousands of Russians and Russian Jews languished in this building, in which KGB agents tried to suppress the struggle for Soviet Jewry that began in the 1960s.

The Lubyanka, once a large business building, has been called the "house of silence," noted Theodore Plievier in his book, *Berlin.*

Lubyanka Square was once called Dzerzhinsky Square, after the first head of the Soviet Secret Police, Felix Dzerzhinsky. Dzerzhinsky was the first head of the "Extraordinary Commission to Combat Counter-Revolutionary Sabotage and Speculation," the dreaded "Cheka." "From that time on, the political police became a fundamental reality of Soviet life," says the noted Russian historian Nicholas V. Riasanovsky, in *A History of Russia.*

By the way, missing from the front of the former KGB headquarters is the statue of Dzerzhinsky, which was pulled down by demonstrators in August 1991.

As one walks or drives by Lubyanka Square, in the center of

Moscow, one usually thinks of the thousands upon thousands who were incarcerated in this dungeon as it existed before the fall of Communism. Of course, the memory of the thousands who never came out of Lubyanka will live forever, too.

As I walked by Lubyanka, I thought of the best-known Jewish fighter for political and human rights in the Communist era, Anatoly (Natan) B. Sharansky, who was actually taken to Lefortovo Prison, not Lubyanka.

Sharansky became an important figure for the Soviet Jewry cause. He had represented the Jewish emigration movement in the unofficial Helsinki Monitoring Group, where he successfully fought for the movement's recognition as part of the Human Rights agenda. Throughout his ordeal, including a one-hundred-day hunger strike, during which time he was force-fed, he moved the Soviet Jewish issue onto the tables of East-West diplomacy and kept public interest in it alive. He was Russian Jewry's most famous activist.

Sharansky, of course, was not alone. The names of those who worked for the same goals as Sharansky live on—Zalmanson, Slepak, Nudel, Dymshits, Kuznetsov, and hundreds of other "Prisoners of Zion."

Sharansky was in his late twenties when he was arrested for treason and espionage; a short, balding, feisty scientist and computer specialist who knew very little about Judaism. He has been described as bright and witty. Anti-Semitism and the Six-Day War turned him into an activist. He applied for an exit visa in the spring of 1973, and was refused.

He married his wife Avital in 1974, and she left Russia a few hours after their wedding day, as her exit visa was about to expire. She would play a large part in keeping up international pressure to free her husband.

His impressive speech when his sentence was handed down included the moving Jewish declaration recited on Passover, "Next Year in Jerusalem," which certainly moved the author, as well as millions of others at the time. Tried in July 1978, Sharansky was sentenced to 3 years in solitary confinement and 10 years in a labor camp. In 1977, he had been thrown into Lefortovo Prison, where he remained incarcerated for 10 months, often in an isolation cell.

"Prisoners of Zion" demanded freedom to leave for Israel. Columnist Si Frumkin wrote in the *Heritage Southwest Jewish Press* of November 20, 1998, that the Soviet government had to face an "open and unafraid resistance." A few Jews were allowed to leave; others were imprisoned and exiled. They persisted. "Let My People Go" was their motto. They knew they were not abandoned, and this often gave them strength to avoid mental breakdown and public recantations. Still, many went to prison to serve long sentences, and many were sent into exile.

Sharansky was finally released in an East-West prisoner exchange on February 11, 1986. The Russian authorities exonerated him in 1992.

In Israel, Sharansky founded a new Russian emigrant party. His party won seven seats in the Knesset. In Prime Minister Benjamin Netanyahu's coalition government in the late 1990s, he became minister of trade and industry.

Ironically, in January 1997, 11 years after he was expelled, Israeli Minister Sharansky was an honored guest in Moscow to promote Israeli Russian trade. He even visited the prison cell in Lefortovo Prison where he was jailed when he was arrested in 1977.

Sharansky, as noted, was not the only refusenik. Vladimir and Maria Slepak had applied for exit visas in 1970, were refused, and stood at the center of the Jewish emigration movement, according to Potok. In June 1978, they found themselves locked in their Moscow apartment by KGB agents. "Let us go to our son in Israel," read their makeshift placard that they hung outside on their balcony. KGB agents broke down the door and the two were arrested. Vladimir spent five years in exile in Siberia, a culmination of nine years as an "enemy of the people," which showcased the Soviet Union's refusal to permit full Jewish emigration.

Western Jews had always been concerned about their brothers and sisters in the former Soviet Union. True, in the 1930s and early 1940s, many believed the Russians had put forth an anti-Nazi stance and had tried to eradicate anti-Semitism. "It was only in 1948, with the first indication of official anti-Semitism in the USSR and East Europe (the Prague trials) that interest in the problems began to revive," relates the *Encyclopedia Judaica*.

But it was because of the "Black Years of Stalin," the Doctors' Plot, and other events, including repression and execution, that Israelis, American and European Jews, and others began telling the world that Jews were being suppressed in Soviet Russia. Two eyewitness accounts helped publicize the oppression and galvanize public opinion. Ben Ami (Arieh L. Eliav)'s *Between Hammer and Sickle,* and Elie Wiesel's *Jews of Silence,* which appeared in several languages and editions.

During the 1960s, the problem of Soviet Jewry, the discrimination against Jews in matters of language, education, and religion; the persecution of individual Jews for such things as economic crimes or Jewish communal activity; the denial to Jews of the right of emigration, particularly to Israel; and the reunification of shattered families became major issues in world Jewish and international discussion, according to the *Encyclopedia Judaica.*

Almost every Jewish organization, Zionist and non-Zionist, raised the problem of saving Soviet Jewry as one of the utmost importance to the Jewish people, second only to the existence and security of Israel. Intellectuals on the left, Jews, and non-Jews held special conferences to investigate the facts and issue appeals to the Soviet government.

Conferences all over the world—Paris in 1960, New York in 1963, and Brussels in 1971—and the establishment of the National Jewish Conference on Soviet Jewry encompassed all the major Jewish organizations in the U.S. Mass rallies, press conferences, meetings in the White House and State Department, discussions, vigils outside the United Nations, and synagogue demonstrations all caused the situation of Jews in the Soviet Union to be reported in the world press.

In Russia, the Six-Day War and the mass gathering of Jewish youth on Simchat Torah at synagogues in Moscow, Leningrad, and Kiev kept up the pressure to free Soviet Jews.

All over the world, Israelis had played a leading role in arousing Jewish awareness of the plight of Soviet Jews.

During the Six-Day War, many refuseniks began to study Hebrew in private groups. Others protested publicly against the refusals to grant them exit permits for Israel, and their protests spread.

By the late 1970s the rescue of Soviet Jewry had moved to the top of the agenda of world Jewry. Nevertheless, in the early 1980s, Soviet Jews still found themselves in a hopeless situation. Their social status continued to decline, anti-Semitism prevented them from fully assimilating, almost all expressions of Jewish life were banned, and at the same time permission to emigrate was denied. Jews were still "slaves in a slave society," as Professor Mikhail Zand, an activist, once stated at a press conference covered by the author. A renewal of Jewish cultural activity that was illegal and centered around the refuseniks began to filter down to the masses of Jews in the USSR.

Public concern about Soviet treatment of dissidents and restriction on Jewish emigration led to the Jackson-Vanik amendment, which linked improvement in trade relations to Soviet emigration policy. As one Soviet Jew from Odessa told me, "I was traded for grain."

For many years, we will be debating what opened the gates of Russian Jewish emigration. Many think American Jews and President Ronald Reagan forced the Russians to allow refuseniks to emigrate, because the Soviets needed trade and technology from the U.S. Gorbachev claims that *perestroika* gave the Jews the chance to leave for Israel. Whatever the reason, Russian Jews can now emigrate freely.

Sparrow Hills. For a great view of Moscow, travel up to Sparrow Hills. If the weather is nice, you can see from four to six miles. This is probably the best panoramic view in the city. It was from this height that Napoleon first saw Moscow after his long and weary march. "At last, the famous city, it was high time," he said, according to author Charles A. Stoddard. The Sparrow Hills were known as the Lenin Hills from 1924 to 1991, but like the names of so many other places in Russia, the name has reverted back to the pre-Communist-era "Sparrow Hills."

For four years I went down the walk at the University of Pittsburgh. Little did I know I would be seeing a similar structure at the University of Moscow. At the Lenin [Sparrow] Hills, writes B. Z. Goldberg, "Moscow University towers over the entire city." "It's a monstrosity," some say. Yet it was modeled on the towering Cathedral of Learning at the University of Pittsburgh.

Many important dignitaries have stood on Sparrow Hills admiring the vista below. On September 14, 1812, Napoleon entered Moscow. For days his advance guard had chanted "Moscow, Moscow, Moscow." From Sparrow Hills, Napoleon observed the vast city through field glasses, admiring Moscow's thousand churches and monasteries, each with glittering golden domes flashing in the bright sunlight. Moscow in 1812 was described as a city of glittering domes, pointed spires, and cupolas.

The city also served as a large arsenal and provisions depot. But now Moscow was deserted. Never before had a conquering force marched into a completely deserted city, according to Leonard Cooper, author of *Many Roads to Moscow: Three Historic Invasions.*

Nobody came out to meet the conqueror as was the custom. General Mikhail I. Kutuzov, commander of the Russian army, the "old fox of the North," as Napoleon had named him, pulled out of Moscow to save the army for another day and another engagement. Kutuzov would never wage a great battle against the French. According to *Napoleon in Russia,* by Alan Warwick Palmer, Kutuzov said "Moscow will be the sponge that will suck him [Napoleon] dry," and it did just that! After entering the city, the French sought the easy life. Instead they soon found a city in flames.

The great fire of Moscow burned for four days and destroyed three-quarters of the city, according to Palmer. There is some doubt over how the fire started, but historians indicate the Russians probably ignited the flames. As flames enveloped the city, Napoleon is said to have remarked "a demon inspires these people." As Tolstoy said, "the beast is mortally wounded." The French also felt a thing no Westerner among them had yet known—the winter advancing from out of Asia, from the frozen steppes, to annihilate a beaten enemy.

Napoleon stood at Poklonny Hill and gazed at the panorama of the city before him. He also saw Moscow from the Petrovsky Zamok (Peter's Palace). The palace is a site to see in and of itself. "Unbelievable and beautiful," is the way Galina Ryltsova, guide and historian of Moscow, puts it regarding this palace.

She notes that that building today is owned by the Military Academy and is named after Marshal Georgi K. Zhukov.

Palmer says that over a half-million Frenchmen failed to return from Russia. "General Winter," "General Famine," the partisan sniping attacks, and the attacks by Kutuzov's forces harassed the French commander all the way to Paris, more than one thousand miles. Only fifty thousand of six hundred thousand French soldiers made it home. The French army had "melted away."

According to historian Sir Barnard Pares, the Russians denounced Napoleon as a renegade who had sold himself to the Jews and claimed to be the Messiah.

Russia crushed Napoleon. The battle at Waterloo was only the last act in a drama. With the French emperor's defeat, Russia became a major player on the international scene.

Red Square. I like to stand in Red Square at the first sign of darkness. The stillness of the night prevents intrusion. There is no fear. One conjures up the sights and sounds of Russian history, much of which took place here—the walls of the Kremlin, Lenin's tomb, the shining Red Star still waving high over the Kremlin, too expensive to remove in these dire economic times, so the government leaves it there. There is the balcony above Lenin's tomb where many a Cold War photo showed Soviet leaders lined up in a rogue's gallery, perhaps mouthing what Communist ruler Nikita S. Khrushchev once said in Cold War phraseology, "We will bury you." We ranked those Communist leaders in importance by where exactly they stood in relation to the leader.

Here, too, in Red Square, stands the well-known, magnificent, sixteenth-century Cathedral of St. Basil, built in the reign of Ivan the Terrible by the Russian architects Barma and Pastrik to commemorate the conquest of Kazan.

Sometimes, large groups turned out here for ghoulish purposes. In 1937, about two hundred thousand poured into Red Square to hear the verdict of one of the Stalin purge trials. The temperature was 27 degrees below zero.

By the way, on November 7, 1941, Stalin reviewed the Red Army from Lenin's mausoleum in the traditional celebration of the "Great October Socialist Revolution." The Germans had planned to be in Red Square on that very day, the twenty-fourth anniversary of the Bolshevik Revolution. Stalin ordered the parade as usual. The soldiers stood before the Kremlin and then marched straight off to the front, says Kathy Porter.

Only about fifty miles away, the Germans were moving at a quick pace toward the capital; indeed, they were at the gates of Moscow. The skies were dotted with barrage balloons and patrolled by fighter planes. The streets were littered with anti-tank obstacles, and German guns and troops were active.

Stalin, who rarely spoke in public, did so that day. Destroy the "German robber hordes," he told the troops. He then reverted to citing the "patriotic emotions of mother Russia," or as he stated, "May you be inspired in war by the spirit of our heroic ancestors." Cited were Aleksandr Nevski, Dmitrii Donskoi, Kuzma, Minin and Pozharsky, Prince Dimitrii, Aleksandr Suvorov, and Mikhail Kutuzov. "Our task now is to destroy every German, to the very last man, who has come to occupy our country. Death to the German invaders!" declared Stalin.

Throughout the war and afterwards, the Communist Party continued to celebrate the day, marking it with the military parade past Lenin's Mausoleum in Red Square, with huge banners proclaiming Soviet achievements and armed might. Serge Schmemann of the *New York Times* said the day was the "premier feast of Soviet Communism." Actually it was a two-day holiday. November 8 was also a day off.

In the 1990s President Boris Yeltsin issued a decree renaming the holiday, "Day of National Reconciliation and Agreement," but now it is only celebrated for one day.

Kremlin. Remember Moscow *is* the Kremlin, the seat of power. The Kremlin is a city within a city. And the Russian author Mouravieff, according to Stoddard, compared Rome to Moscow. "Rome," he said, "is interesting because it reminds him of Moscow," but then, he says, "Rome is Moscow without the Kremlin."

Stoddard, who wrote about his travels throughout Russia, compared the Kremlin to what the Acropolis was to Athens. "The Prince lived in the palaces of the Kremlin, surrounded by his family and courtiers, the superior clergy of the nation and the principle nobles," he writes.

Historian George Kennan said a kremlin (or *"kreml,"* in Russian) was a walled enclosure with towers at the corners. Serving as a stronghold, it "differs from a castle or fortress in that it generally encloses a larger area, and contains a number of buildings, such as churches, palaces, treasuries, etc., which are merely protected by it." Of course, there were kremlins in other cities.

In 1156 the wooden Kremlin (citadel) was built in Moscow by Yuri Dolgoruki, prince of Suzdal. In the thirteenth century, it became an important trading town of the northeast.

Speaking of the Kremlin and tsars, Nicholas II, who had not yet married, had an affair with a Jewess. This tsar, wrote Edvard Radzinsky in his book, *The Last Tsar*, had become embroiled with a ballet dancer named Mathilde Kschessinska. He met her on a walk, and a romance sprung up. His father sent her away, along with her entire household, and the Jewess was never seen in the capital again.

Kremlin Wall, Burial Place of Stalin and other Communists. At the Twenty-second Party Congress in 1956, Nikita S. Krushchev departed from the prepared scenario and launched into a vehement attack on Stalin's crimes. The Congress then voted to remove Stalin's body from the Lenin Mausoleum; it was buried beside the Kremlin wall, beneath a stone and a bust of the tyrant. After the fall of Communism, Stalin's statues came down in many places across the Soviet Union, and his name disappeared from institutions and cities. However, to fully understand the significance of Stalin's burial place, of the fact that one of cruelest dictators in history is buried in this spot, one must look at the story of Stalin.

Stalin

Historian Martin Malia claims Stalin "was the only member of Lenin's Politburo who came from the people." His father was an alcoholic, a village cobbler who became a worker in a shoe factory. His mother was an illiterate, pious peasant. His uncompleted education in a seminary of the Orthodox Church gave him the equipment to become a well-read auto-didact in Russian, though not in European literature. He had also absorbed a thorough grounding in Marxist ideology.

In his book, *The Soviet Tragedy: A History of Socialism in Russia, 1917-1991*, Malia argues that Leninism and Stalinism had to be tried out somewhere, but it was Russia's bad luck that it was tried out there first. And it was her supreme bad luck that it was actually carried out by so bad a man as Stalin, a misfortune that was compounded by his longevity.

Stalin became secretary-general of the Communist Party in 1922. Lenin died two years later, and Trotsky was banished in 1927. In effect, Stalin seized power and justified his actions by saying he was the sole and rightful heir to Lenin, since he had been appointed secretary-general by Lenin. But, as writer Richard Lourie noted, toward the end of his life Lenin sought Stalin's removal as secretary-general. Lenin might have saved millions of lives had he succeeded.

By 1928, Stalin had emerged the clear victor in the power struggle that had broken out in the Party after the death of Lenin. He had eliminated Trotsky, Kamenev, and Zinoviev as rivals, and intimidated all the rest. He was ready to assert his power.

Stalin would rule the Soviet Union for almost a quarter of a century, from 1929 to his death at the age of 73 in 1953. For most of those years, he ruled as an unconstrained autocrat. Historian Walter Laqueur says, "Stalin concentrated more power in his hands than any ruler in modern history, and he had been deified like the pharaohs of ancient Egypt." Like Lenin, Stalin did not believe that the Jews were a nation. In fact, in 1913, he said that they were not a nation, since unlike the Ukrainians or Armenians, they did not inhabit a particular historic territory.

Under Stalin, anti-Nazi feelings and warnings were kept out of the press, as were descriptions of German atrocities in Nazi-occupied countries. No mention was made of the Third Reich's anti-Jewish measures or the tremendous sufferings by the Jews of both Poland and Germany, according to author Fran Markowitz. Because of this, Jews did not feel really threatened.

Referring to the late 1920s and 1930s, Michael Scammell,

author of *Solzhenitsyn: A Biography,* points out that "Stalin established the most complete police state the world had yet known. But this development was masked not only from the outside world but also from the bulk of the population of the Soviet Union itself, let alone from its young people."

In Sovietologist Cohen's words, Stalin believed he could "squeeze everybody and everything, into the state's mailed fist."

There has been much debate as to whether Stalin inherited Lenin's philosophy full-force or created the cruelty itself. Robert Service, historian, wrote "Lenin's ideas on violence, dictatorship, terror, centralism, hierarchy and leadership were integral to Stalin's thinking." The Cheka, the forced labor camps, the one-party state, the mono-ideological mass media, the legalized administrative arbitrariness, the prohibition of free and popular elections, the ban in internal party dissent—not one of these had to be invented by Stalin, according to Service.

According to historian Norman Cantor, author of *The Sacred Chain: The History of the Jews,* when Stalin gained control over the Communist Party and the Soviet government in the late 1920s, Jews should have seen this as warning, but they treated it as an ideological struggle, a political one, not an ethnic one.

After he turned against the Ukrainians with his catastrophic famine policy, Stalin turned against the Jews between the years of 1936-39, and then 1948 to 1953, an era that we shall soon explore.

No one has managed to calculate the exact number of deaths under Stalin. Some estimates suggest 20 million, which is probably a conservative figure. Many, like Sovietologist and author Stephen Cohen, declare that Stalinism created a Holocaust greater than Hitler's. We know about death camps Kolyma and Magadan in the Gulag, the chain of prison and labor camps and remote areas of exile, stretching across thousands of miles, because of the books of the noted writer Aleksandr I. Solzhenitsyn.

The historian Dmitrii Volkogonov tells us in a biography of Stalin that he had talked to "hundreds of people who knew Stalin personally and concluded that for this man, cruelty was quite simply an inalienable attribute of his being."

Stalin was a strong leader during World War II. During the

war, Stalin wrote: "Our cause is just, the enemy will be smashed, victory will be ours." But he had almost doomed Russia to slaughter because before World War II he had not taken precautions to defend the USSR, for fear of provoking Hitler, says Malia.

The evidence indicates that Stalin, Zhdanov and the others received the intelligence that a war was in the offing, but consistently misinterpreted it, regarding it as a provocation. The situation was less immediately pressing, and this fit into Stalin's concept of an attack by Germany not earlier than autumn 1941 or spring of 1942, writes Salisbury.

In truth, the Soviet Union was unprepared for Germany's invasion of June 22, 1941.

The evidence is overwhelming that the Nazi attack came as a total surprise and shock to Stalin, according to Salisbury. At most he believed Hitler was trying to blackmail him. Stalin did not believe the Germans would breach the Nazi-Soviet pact, according to Erickson. That pact would guarantee the country against attack, the government had told the people.

Historian John Lawrence, who served as a European intelligence officer and organizer for the BBC in World War II, said, "That was obvious even to the present writer, who did not have access to captured and secret information that yes, the Germans were planning to attack Russia." Stalin concluded a pact with Hitler, which enabled the Third Reich first to smash Poland and divide its territory with the USSR, and then to turn against France and the Low Countries and menace Britain. "The Molotov-Ribbentrop pact furthered the influence of Nazi anti-Jewish propaganda," writes Gennadi Kostyrchenko "The effect of the August 1939 Pact was to free Hitler from a war on two fronts like the one that had defeated Imperial Germany, and this alone made possible Hitler's stunning expansion over the whole continent during the next two years," says Malia, adding "the bad gamble of the Molotov-Ribbentrop Pact must be counted as the first of Stalin's errors leading to near defeat, even worse than was his conduct of operations in 1941." Deals with the devil never pay off.

The year 1937 would go down in Russian history as synonymous with Stalin's unchecked terror against his own people.

Volkogonov says that "tens of millions of people were seized. 23,000 NKVD officials were arrested in 1937-38 alone." Most of those interrogated informed on others in order to survive. Suspicion turned people into scoundrels. The best estimates indicate that between 1937 and 1938, 1 million people were executed and 2 million died in labor camps, says Robert Conquest, author.

One of the ironies of history, points out Karel van Het Reve, editor and author, "is that while the Soviet authorities were jailing and killing completely innocent people by the hundreds of thousands, year after year, under Stalin, many Soviet intellectuals sincerely believed the victims to be guilty."

Between 1918 and 1953, famous writers, for instance, were shot for being murderers, counterrevolutionaries, conspirators, terrorists, traitors, spies, and "fascist dogs."

Commenting on another explanation of Stalin's terror, Abraham Brumberg, citing a book by Vadim Z. Rogovin entitled *1937*, writes in the *Times Literary Supplement*, of December 11, 1998, that Stalinist terror reached its height in 1937 and would swallow millions of victims. This act "was not, as much of the received wisdom holds, the product of a warped mind, not the result of Stalin's paranoia, not something so irrational as to beggar description or understanding, but the brilliantly executed plot of a man determined to obliterate every last vestige of opposition, real or potential, and to promote new cadres of men and women with no ties to the generation of the Old Bolsheviks, ruthless, unshaken in their belief that they were advancing the cause of 'socialism,' no matter what the price, and utterly faithful to the Leader." In other words, Stalin crushed millions of people just to achieve his political objectives.

Thus, just as many a tyrant before him, Stalin waged political wars. He made war against Russian culture. Many Russian literati met a terrible fate.

He also waged war against the Jews; albeit subtle, not always physical, but war it certainly was. Stalin got his lessons in anti-Semitism when he was a small child, but began to show this anti-Semitism strongly at the Moscow show trials in the late 1930s.

Still, the Soviet Union retained a reputation through the 1930s as the least anti-Semitic of the great powers. According to

Sovietologist Brumberg, while Stalin destroyed Jewish leaders and intellectuals in the first years of his power, anti-Semitism was not a "significant component of his policies. After all, other nationalities, too, suffered from accusations of 'bourgeois nationalism.'" What is true, however, is that Stalin personally harbored poisonous anti-Jewish prejudices (not altogether surprising in the light of his early social milieu). He was not averse to exploiting anti-Semitic sentiments in his struggle against his opponents, and was responsible for turning the secret police largely into a band of anti-Semitic thugs. (KGB interrogations were often accompanied by anti-Jewish invective.)

We can see traces of this later anti-Semitism as early as 1907, when he wrote, in the small underground paper he then controlled at Baku, that somebody among the Bolsheviks said jokingly that since the Mensheviks were the faction of the Jews, and the Bolsheviks that of the native Russians, it would be a good thing to have a pogrom in the Party, according to his daughter Svetlana Alliluyeva.

However, both his son and daughter married Jews, although he once cursed his daughter for dating a Jewish man.

Stalin saw enemies everywhere, not just among the Jews. Nevertheless, many of his enemies and virtually all of his major enemies were Jews, especially Trotsky.

However, true politician that he was, Stalin also spoke out from time to time against anti-Semitism.

Vasily Grossman, in *Black Book*, cites the words of Stalin written in response to a request from the JTA in America in the 1930s, in which Stalin says that anti-Semitism is "the most dangerous vestige of cannibalism." He added that anti-Semitism was severely prosecuted as a phenomenon deeply antithetical to the Soviet system. Active anti-Semites, were, in accordance with Soviet law, executed in the USSR, according to this account.

The new round of purges in Eastern Europe, the "Doctors' Plot," the murder of Jewish intellectuals—all of this awoke fears that Stalin was somehow taking a page from Hitler's book, says Lindemann.

In 1948, a sustained anti-cosmopolitan campaign was orchestrated by Zhdanov, with Stalin's obvious approval. The key words were "cosmopolitanism" and "rootlessness." All Yiddish schools, newspapers, theaters, and Jewish institutions, as well as synagogues (except in Birobidzhan), were closed. The Jewish Anti-Fascist Committee was disbanded and its newspaper confiscated. Then Mikhoels, the great Jewish actor, was murdered under suspicious circumstances. Writers Markish, Fefer, Bergelson, and P. Kahanovich (who was known as "Der Nister") were also executed. The Jewish writers shot in August 1952 were accused of the political offense of wishing to set up a secessionist state in the Crimea, a charge very faintly linked with reality. A proposal had indeed arisen in the Jewish Anti-Fascist Committee after the war to resettle Jews in the then-desolate peninsula.

In those years, anti-Semitism became virtually an open Party policy. It threatened the very survival of the Jewish communities in the Soviet Union. "Like a poisonous weed, anti-Semitism found its natural breeding ground in the fetid atmosphere of the Stalinist hothouse," declares Blumberg.

Stalin was annoyed at the admiration Russian Jews displayed toward the Zionist movement. He was especially peeved at the warm welcome given to Golda Meir, the first Israeli ambassador to Moscow, and was outraged at the friendliness that high-ranking people such as Molotov's wife, Polina Zhemchuzhina, showed Mrs. Meir. Zhemchuzhina was arrested in 1949; Molotov fell into disgrace.

Not a single Yiddish book was published in the USSR between 1949 and 1958. Yiddish radio broadcasts in Russia ceased. The Jews had become, in Elie Wiesel's words, "the Jews of silence." The Jews had also become a "security risk." The percentage of Jews in the Central Committee dropped drastically. In 1952, it fell to 3 percent, and in 1956, to 2 percent.

The Prague trial can be seen as the forerunner of the Doctors' Plot, for the charge of political murder by doctors was common to each.

The Doctors' Plot

The attack against the Jews known as the Doctors' Plot started in November 1952, when Stalin ordered the arrest of his personal physician, A. N. Inogradov. Arrested, too, were others on the medical staff in the Kremlin hospital-clinic that serviced

the ruling class of the Soviet Union. According to Potok, leading physicians in the Soviet Union, all of them Jews, were
accused with plotting the murder of top Soviet government
officers, including Zhdanov, whose death, it was claimed, was a
medical murder.

On January 13, 1953, *Pravda* told its readers that a "group of
saboteur-doctors" were arrested. Six of them were Jews. "They
were reported to be 'connected with the international Jewish
bourgeois nationalist organization, 'Joint,' established by
American intelligence for the alleged purpose of providing material aid to Jews in other countries,'" said Ronald Grigor Suny.

The Doctors' Plot case was set in motion by a police
informer named Dr. Lydia Timashuk. No sooner had the doctors been tortured to obtain confessions, when a letter "edited
by Stalin," calling for the deportation of all Jews eastward was
circulated in Moscow among prominent Jews. Under threat of
arrest or worse, many signed the document, though a few,
including novelist and journalist Ilya Ehrenburg, refused to
sign, according to Suny.

The plan consisted of deporting all persons of Jewish origin
to the Arctic region or some other remote area of the Soviet
Union, notes Walter Laqueur, author.

"Stalin intended to turn the trial of the doctors into a show
trial to end all show trials, and then to start banishing thousands of Jews to forced labor in Siberia and to physical annihilation," said Ben Ami, in *Between Hammer and Sickle*.

While all this was going on, a bomb exploded at the Soviet
legation in Tel Aviv on February 12, 1952, and the Russians
broke off diplomatic relations with Israel.

Stalin did not want to divide the Jews into good and bad. He
probably intended to punish all Jews. By trying the doctors
first, Stalin would be preparing the way to exile the Jews.

According to rumor, March 5 was the day on which the Jews
would be loaded onto trucks, and the great purge would follow, but Stalin died on March 5.

Without question, the doctors would have been paraded in
a show trial and put to death had Stalin not died. Historian
Radzinsky says that in Siberia and Kazakhstan, people still

point out "the remains of the flimsy wooden huts, without heating, in which hundreds of thousands of Jews were meant to live, or rather to die."

On April 4, 1953, the Doctors' Plot was formally declared to have been based on fraudulent testimony extracted from the accused by the use of impermissible means of investigation strictly forbidden under Soviet law, i.e., by torture. The surviving victims were freed and their torturers arrested. Dr. Timashuk, whose denunciations of her colleagues had launched the affair, was deprived of the Order of Lenin she had earlier been awarded.

After Stalin's death the Soviet regime would launch a new campaign substituting the word "Zionists" for "Jews." This way the Communists avoided charges of being anti-Semitic. But for Jews the changes in wording meant little.

Historian Omer Bartov says "seen in terms of regimes, both Hitler and Stalin were vicious, homicidal tyrants." He was commenting on the book *Judgment a Moscou,* which states that the Communists murdered more people than the Nazis.

Amazingly, there are still those in Russia who admire Stalin. Some raise their glasses on March 5 and toast the "great leader who made the Motherland strong." They only see that under him the Soviet Union modernized, defeated Germany, became a world power, and then a superpower by the 1970s. In March 1988, Nina Andreeva, for instance, published a letter in Russian newspapers demanding the rehabilitation of Stalin's reputation and "implied that the country's woes after the October Revolution had been chiefly the fault of the Jewish element in the party's leadership composition," according to Robert Service.

For Jews, Stalin turned out to be both "Haman and Hitler." However, when he died, a million people stood in line to view his body, and at least four hundred died in a stampede to see his body.

His iron grip marked the Soviet era for half of the Communist rule. Many curse him as the "greatest criminal our country has known. After all, Stalin destroyed more people than all the wars in history," according to Rodzinsky.

Other Sites

Lenin Mausoleum, Red Square. Don't fret, dear traveler. Long lines no longer weave in and around Red Square to visit the Lenin Mausoleum. It has been on the tourists' must-see list since 1924. Actually, within six days of Lenin's death, on January 21, 1924, the Soviets put up a temporary wooden mausoleum in Red Square to hold the embalmed corpse. The permanent monument of red granite, constructed in 1929-1930, was designed by architect Aleksei Shchusev. Aldo Buzzi, in his book, *Journey to the Land of the Flies,* writes that Shchusev "perhaps had in mind the Kaaba, the gray kube [*sic*] in the courtyard of the Great Mosque in Mecca, around which Muslim pilgrims walk seven times." He points out that during the war, Lenin's body was evacuated to Kuibyshev, the ancient Samara. When Stalin died, Lenin had "to cohabit with Stalin." Later, Stalin was removed and buried in the Kremlin Wall. "The mausoleum reminds me of a time when we were proud and strong. It is a symbol of all the good things embodied by the former Soviet Union. If they close the mausoleum there would be absolutely nothing to do in Red Square," said a Muscovite. Others believe Lenin should be buried in St. Petersburg next to his mother.

Most historians say Lenin's radicalism stemmed from his brother being hanged by tsarist authorities in 1887. His brother was part of a revolutionary group that attempted to assassinate Tsar Alexander III. This punishment was instrumental in shaping the character of the future leader of the Revolution.

Born in 1870, in the provincial town of Simbirsk, Lenin's real name was Vladimir Ulyanov. When he entered revolutionary politics, Lenin became his pseudonym. Ironically, his later bitter enemy Kerensky, head of the Provisional Government in 1917, was also born in Simbirsk. The son of a provincial school inspector, Lenin's background was a mixture of Jewish, German, and Kalmyk, as well as Russian elements.

Historian Orlando Figes says that Maria Alexandrovna, Lenin's mother, was the daughter of Alexander Blank, a baptized Jew who rose to become a wealthy doctor and landowner

The author is shown in front of the Lenin Mausoleum. The Cyrillic letters spell out the name "Lenin." (Photo credit: Ben G. Frank)

in Kazan. Alexander Blank was the son of Moishe Blank, a Jewish merchant from Volhynia who had married a Swedish woman by the name of Anna Ostedt. Lenin's ancestry was always hidden by the Soviet authorities, despite an appeal by Anna Ulyanov, who, in a letter to Stalin in 1932, suggested that this fact could be used to combat anti-Semitism.

In no uncertain terms, Stalin told her to never breathe a single word about Lenin's Jewishness. Indeed, Lenin had approved the decree of the July 1918 Council of People's Commissars condemning anti-Semitism as "fatal to the interests of workers." He thought that the Jews should and would assimilate, according to Potok.

Lenin rejected the idea of a Jewish nationality. It ran counter to the interests of the Jewish proletariat, he argued, for it fostered among them, directly or indirectly, a spirit hostile to assimilation. He regarded Jews rather as a caste, whose isolation in Russia resulted from the tsarist government's discriminatory policies.

Lenin gave Stalin the task of further developing the Communist position on the issue of nationalities.

Stalin believed that barriers between peoples would disappear, and he reiterated that Jews did not constitute a nation, they did not have a land, they did not qualify for the program of determination, and should therefore work toward immediate amalgamation with the peoples of the regions in which they lived. He felt that Jews should continue assimilating.

Journalist and author Harrison E. Salisbury, who covered Russia for many years, believed that Lenin also was the only one at first to back the idea of the October coup in 1917. Lenin's associates opposed him and thought him violently mistaken; but he single-handedly overcame their opposition and was prepared to go to any lengths (including conspiring against his own party) to achieve his goal.

On August 30, 1918, Lenin was seriously wounded by revolver shots from the gun of a young Jewish woman, Fanya Kaplan. A member of the Socialist Revolutionary Party, she was 28 years old, and her parents had emigrated to America. Fanya claimed she acted on her own, because she felt Lenin had betrayed the Revolution. After a speedy investigation, she was executed on September 3, 1918 by the Cheka. Her remains were destroyed. "Red terror is not an empty phrase," her Red executioner is supposed to have intoned.

Ironically, on the same day Lenin was shot, Moisei Uritsky, a Jewish Bolshevik, was assassinated in Petrograd. While Fanya Kaplan failed in her assassination attempt, it still changed the course of history, as Lenin never really recovered and went into a deep decline. He had a stroke in the spring of 1922 and died on January 21, 1924. After he died, long lines formed up at the House of Unions for citizens to pay their respects to the Bolshevik leader, who was 53 when he passed away. He was succeeded by a triumvirate consisting of Stalin, Kamenev, and Zinoviev. The latter two, of course, were Jews.

Despite the publication in 1997 of an uncompromising Lenin biography by Dmitri Volkogonov, a Russian historian, as well as other such books, and despite the knowledge among many that Lenin bequeathed to Stalin the instrument of terror, a naive view lingers in Russia that Lenin was a democrat whose plans were twisted by Stalin into a murderous dictatorship.

Lenin is still a legend in Russia; his body, as we have seen, is still in a place of honor and statues of him all over Russia have not been removed. One reason for this admiration is that with the economy in shambles, there is a certain nostalgia for the certainties of Communism and disappointment in the much-heralded free-market capitalism. As a guide told this writer, "After all, Lenin is a part of our history."

"The Communists would have liked to believe that Lenin was a man drawn into revolutionary activity by the execution of his brother and driven by a selfless desire to improve the lot of working people," writes Steven Merritt Miner, author of *Between Churchill and Stalin.* But Robert Conquest quotes Mikhail Gorbachev as saying "cruelty was the main problem with Lenin."

Robert Daniels notes that Lenin felt no scruples taking 12 million marks back from Germany with him when he returned to Russia. Documents from secret German archives recently revealed that the Bolsheviks continued to receive German money even after the Bolshevik Revolution, according to Edvard Radzinsky.

"It seems clear that the basic elements of the Stalinist regime—the one-party state, the system of terror and the cult of their personality—were all in place by 1924," the year of Lenin's death, writes Orlando Figes.

The Mall, Manezh Square. The new mall is called Okhotny Ryad, which in English means "Hunter's Row." The glittering new Manezh shopping center was built under the walls of the Kremlin, at a cost of about $350 million. Located in the commercial heart of Moscow, it features a three-story marble atrium with an indoor fountain, and is planned to eventually hold 26 restaurants and 86 shops, as well as travel agencies and banks. It opened in January 1998.

The Jews of Moscow

How does one measure Jewish life in Moscow? Being a relatively new community, it will take a long time to develop institutions and find leadership.

But meanwhile there is activity and growth and functioning facilities, and in a community which has been devoid of development or continuous Jewish education, this is a good beginning.

There are five synagogue buildings, 12 religious congregations, a Hillel house and organization meeting halls, several kosher restaurants, an art gallery, many clubs, Jewish community centers, a Holocaust Museum, a Jewish art center, many groups for young adults, five Jewish cemeteries, and three yeshivas. Jewish Moscow comprises at least 250,000 Jews, but the figure could be as high as 350,000, or, as Chabad Rabbi Berel Lazar and others estimate, a half-million Jews may reside in this capital.

The holidays, of course, attract large numbers of Jews. A concert hall was rented for one such large gathering.

Seven Jewish day schools serve more than 1,100 students. These schools are full-time state schools providing tuition-free education. In addition to the general curriculum, Jewish day schools teach Hebrew, Jewish tradition, history, and English.

These are the famous white pillars of the Moscow Choral Synagogue. (Photo credit: Ben G. Frank)

Moscow kindergartens have become centers of Jewish culture, a cohesive force in the community, and a positive gathering place for Jewish families. Teachers distribute newsletters and hold holiday celebrations.

By 1999, the Russian Jewish Congress was playing a very formidable role in the community.

Moscow Jewry is very well-organized. As in other Russian Jewish communities, new organizations sprout up every day.

The JDC helped organize a Moscow Welfare Committee, which oversees welfare activities. It is a very representative body and allocates funds four times a year.

One of the huge problems facing Moscow Jews today is that many senior citizens are lonely; their children have made aliyah to Israel or moved to America. The government's welfare program is crippled. As the JDC has noted, "thousands of senior citizen Jews can not make ends meet."

Synagogues

Moscow Choral Synagogue, Spasoglinishchevsky Peroulok (Archipova Street), Moscow, 101000. Tel: (7-095) 923-47-88. If there is time to visit only a few Jewish sites in Moscow, naturally one stop would have to be the Moscow Choral Synagogue, the oldest Jewish institutional building in Moscow. Until 1991, it served as the symbol of Jewish resistance to Communist forces in denying Russian Jews their right of religion. Basically, it serves as one of the headquarters of Moscow Jewry.

While the street name of the synagogue, as you note, is now "Spasoglinishchevsky," many still refer to the street as "Archipova Street."

If ever there was a story to show what Jewish courage was needed to keep Judaism alive, it is symbolized in this house of worship.

The Choral Synagogue, which served as a magnet for Jewish activities during the Soviet era, is one of the most beautiful synagogues in the world.

The chief rabbi of Russia is Adolf Shayevitsh. His office is at the Choral Synagogue.

Rabbi Pinchas Goldschmidt, chief rabbi of Moscow and

Rabbi Pinchas Goldschmidt, chief rabbi of Moscow, is pictured here. (Photo credit: Ben G. Frank)

president of the Rabbinical Court of the Union of Jewish Communities in the CIS, is available to help the traveler. (Tel: 7-095-923-4788, Fax: 7-095-956-73-40.) People in his office do speak English. Daily services are at 8:30 A.M. in the morning and *Mincha* and *Maariv* services, depending on sunset in the winter. In the summer, *Mincha* is usually around 7:30 P.M. and the time for *Maariv* services depends upon sunset.

For travelers who walk to synagogue on *Shabbat,* one can stop at the Kempinsky, Savoy, Metropole, or Rossiya hotels. The Moscow Choral Synagogue can provide kosher food to these hotels. Contact Rabbi Goldschmidt, or his office, regarding kosher food.

The synagogue contains a library and a mikva, in addition to separate services for Ashkenazic Jews, and prayer services for those Jews from Bukharia and the Caucasus, all in the same building.

Many young people in the congregation speak English. Jewish leaders in Moscow often help American Jewish businesspeople locate the right partners for a business venture.

Life has been anything but normal for this synagogue that survived the tsars, the Cossacks, the Whites and the Reds, Stalin and Hitler, the purges, and the Communist plots. In Stalin's time, despite harassment by police, thousands of Soviet Jews would gather outside the synagogue on high holidays, especially Simchat Torah. Natan Sharansky first met his wife, Avital, outside the synagogue in the early 1970s.

One of the most historic encounters ever to take place at this house of worship was the Sabbath visit, in 1948, of Ambassador Golda Meir, who later became prime minister of Israel. Thousands of Soviet Jews spontaneously came out to meet her. Golda, as she was affectionately called, was the first Israeli Ambassador to the USSR, and when the Jews saw her they burst out singing "Hatikvah," the anthem of the Zionist movement and the national anthem of Israel. The cry, "The people of Israel live," echoed through the air.

"Within seconds they had surrounded me, almost lifting me bodily, almost crushing me, saying my name over and over again," wrote Golda, adding, "that women in the women's gallery would come over to me, touch my hand, stroke and even kiss my dress."

Golda wrote that "Jews were expressing their joy . . . and their need to participate in the miracle of the establishment of the Jewish state, and I was the symbol of the state for them." She was right.

"Our Golda," "Shalom Goldele," "Long life and good health," "Happy New Year," people shouted. "Such an ocean of life overwhelmed me that I could hardly breathe. I came close to fainting," she is reported to have said. Her words to the crowd were: "Thank you for still being Jews," a dangerous thing to say in Stalin's kingdom.

The mere presence of an Israeli diplomatic mission with an Israeli flag in the center of Moscow was a constant stimulus to Jewish and pro-Israel sentiments among the Jews of Moscow, according to the *Encyclopedia Judaica.*

The Six-Day War and the rupture of diplomatic relations with Israel in June 1967 put an end to even limited gatherings and cultural events between the Soviet Union and Israel. But Moscow Jewish youth would go on to express pro-Israel feelings. They would gather at the synagogue and stage collective protests against the refusal to grant them exit permits.

Some naive Jews even went so far as to petition the authorities to let them join the Israel Defense Forces as gunners, tank drivers, sailors, and pilots, according to Ben Ami. Soviet authorities would now have to extinguish the Jew's cultural and national feelings "with freezing water," it was said in Communist circles at the time.

In visiting the Moscow Choral Synagogue and other synagogues, should you arrive without an appointment, you might ask that the *shamos* (sexton) or other officials explain various aspects of the synagogue. They might show you numerous Torah scrolls behind the ark, an emotional sight to see, because these Torahs came from Russian synagogues that were destroyed during World War II.

The Moscow Choral Synagogue had the dubious honor of being constructed in the same year that the Russians wanted to expel the Jews from the city. This very synagogue, with its huge white pillars that provide strength to hold up the building, and the splendid cupola with the Star of David, was almost demolished by the government, those "Hamans of Moscow," as Jewish historian Simon M. Dubnow described them.

The Jews were forced to worship in cramped quarters in private homes. There were 14 *minyanim* (Jewish prayer groups). But on Passover, the governor general ordered 9 of them closed. Still, several thousand Jews prayed in five homes, because they had to pray in secret, as did the Marranos in Spain. These worshippers were called the "Marranos of Moscow."

In October 1897, the government ordered the synagogue's school of one hundred children to be closed down. Children could go to school, it was maintained, but they had to attend Russian schools. Authorities threatened that unless the synagogue was converted to a hospital or other charitable institute within two months, it would be sold at auction. The congregation was renovated, and the struggle over the building continued for eight years. Then Grand Duke Sergei Alexandrovitch, the governor general who wanted to close down the house of worship, was assassinated, and the synagogue that had been condemned to death was at last restored to life.

Today, the Choral Synagogue is looking ahead to a brighter future. A $2 million expansion is planned, as well as a $10 million Jewish community center, directly across the street from the Moscow Choral Synagogue. Four buildings, including a gym and small pool, will be included. It probably will not be completed until well into the twenty-first century.

Chabad. There are about 30 Chabad rabbis in the former Soviet Union. Chabad comes across as a high-profile group with many synagogues, yeshivas, schools, and study groups.

Marina Roscha Synagogue, 2 Vysheslavtzev Peroulok 5-A. Tel: (7-095) 289-23-25 or (7-095) 289-94-23. E-mail: lazar@glasnet.ru. The first thing you have to know about this synagogue is that during the Stalin years and afterward, it was an underground synagogue, and a most impressive site. Located in a large Jewish neighborhood, this is the headquarters of Rabbi Berel Lazar. Rabbi Lazar leads this Lubavitch synagogue and is chairman of the Rabbinical Alliance of the Commonwealth of

This is the sign for the Marina Roscha Synagogue, a Lubavitch synagogue in Moscow.
(Photo credit: Ben G. Frank)

Independent States. A native of Italy whose his wife is from Pittsburgh, Pennsylvania, Rabbi Lazar believes that despite attacks and economic downturn, Russia eventually will be one of the strongest Jewish communities in the world.

During the Soviet years, Marina Roscha Synagogue was the only synagogue not under the control of the KGB and thus, in the words of Rabbi Lazar, "it became the center of underground *yiddishkeit.*" The original building, founded in 1926, was probably the most active underground synagogue in Russia. When public worship was illegal, it was considered a symbol of resistance to Soviet-endorsed anti-Semitism and religious oppression.

In post-Communist Russia, the synagogue stands as a bastion of Jewish determination to practice Judaism in the face of belligerent attacks. Since the fall of Communism in 1991, it has withstood three acts of terrorism—an arson fire and two bomb blasts. The Moscow city government allocated $60,000 to rebuild the synagogue.

Moscow Jewish Community Center, 2 Vysheslavtzev Peroulok, 5-A. Tel: (7-095) 218-00-01. Fax: (7-095) 219-97-07. The new Jewish Community Center of Moscow was scheduled to open in the fall of 1999. It is designed to house a large synagogue, two mikvas, a hall for large gatherings and weddings, a restaurant, an auditorium, sports facilities (including a gym and training rooms), a library, offices, and classrooms. The new multi-million-dollar, seven-story Jewish community center will cover 70,000 square feet. In the fall of 1998, more than 5,000 people gathered at the then-unfinished center for a dedication.

Visitors can tour the facility and, if they desire, can make arrangements for kosher food.

Chabad Lubavitch Synagogue, also known as Bolshaya Bronnaya, Bolshaya Bronnaya Street 6. Tel: (7-095) 202-73-70, (7-095) 291-64-83, and (7-095) 202-45-30. This synagogue was opened in the beginning of the twentieth century, and is sometimes referred to as the Polyakov Synagogue, after the railway magnates, the Polyakovs. Closed down in the 1917 revolution, it served during the Soviet era as a "House of Culture," or club. More than 3,000 people are involved with this synagogue, which is also considered a Jewish community center. Jewish holidays are widely attended, and a library and book shop that includes religious items are part of the synagogue. Among its many activities is food distribution. The center can deliver more than 100 meals to people who cannot leave their home. One of its main activities is to help war veterans of Jewish origin.

Rabbi Isaak Kogan is the spiritual leader of this congregation. It is said that the Lubavitch rebbe himself assigned Rabbi Kogan to Moscow to help build the Jewish community in this city.

Darchei Shalom, Novoviadykinsky Pereulok 2. Tel/Fax: (7-095) 903-07-82. Fax: (7-095) 903-22-18. A Lubavitch congregation located in the Otradnoye district, this building was dedicated in early 1998.

Congregation of Progressive Judaism (also known as Progressive Synagogue or Hineini Novo), Ryazanskaya Street 26. Tel: (7-095) 261-16-73. This synagogue occupies the former House of Culture of Car Manufacturers. If you have difficulties reaching Zinovy Kogan at the congregation, contact him or his secretary at his office at the Choral Synagogue by telephone at (7-095) 924-24-24 or by fax at (7-095) 956-75-40. Zinovy's home number is (7-095) 918-26-96. Zinovy is not a rabbi, but he is head of Hineini. His office is located in the Choral Synagogue administration office, on Bol'shoi Spasoglinishchevsky Pereulok 10. Services are at 6:00 P.M. Friday evening and also at 11:00 A.M. Saturday morning and 4:00 P.M. Saturday evening. Youth and club activities are held Sunday nights. Check with the synagogue for a complete schedule.

This synagogue is a member of the World Union of Progressive Judaism.

Zinovy Kogan had the distinction of saying Kaddish (the mourner's prayer) at the moving burial service of the one Jewish boy who was part of the group of three students killed in the attempted putsch of 1991. Zinovy explained in an interview that the secular service was held on a Saturday. Even though Jews do not normally bury their dead on Saturday, the Sabbath, Zinovy felt he had to attend and recalled that he walked to the Russian memorial program. No one could believe that a Jewish leader or representative would ever participate in a Russian ceremony of such magnitude as the burial service of the three. Zinovy is proud of how his synagogue started, although Jews do not need a synagogue building to hold a prayer service. According to Orthodox Jewish law, 10 men are required to make a *minyan*, or a prayer group. The first gathering of this group was held in a park surrounded by trees. Zinovy thought a few friends would join him, but about a hundred people showed up, all under the watchful eye of the KGB. For the second service, Zinovy gave out his home address as the site of the service. The turnout swelled.

Jews from various foreign embassies have attended services here. From the very beginning, the ladies refused to sit in a separate section, he said. Zinovy is convinced that in the future, the rabbis in Russia will be natives of Russia.

For the high holidays the group holds services in the House of Culture in Moscow. About two thousand people usually attend.

In an interview, Kogan stated that since the economic collapse in 1998, it has become difficult for many of his fellow congregants, in that people have less to eat. Repairs to many buildings and institutions have been postponed. Nevertheless, the congregation is more united than ever. He praised JDC for sending parcels to Hineini. "It gives us hope that we know we are not left alone," he said.

Vostryakovo Cemetery, Ozermaya Street 49. (7-095) 437-47-00. This is the only cemetery in Moscow that has a Jewish section for burial.

Restaurants

King David Club of the Moscow Central Synagogue, Bolshoi Spasoglinishchevsky Peroulok 6, door code 77. Tel: (7-095) 925-46-01. Fax: (7-095) 924-42-43. E-mail: ail@ail.msk.ru. Nothing is fancy here, since this clean restaurant is literally a dining room in an apartment building several doors up from the synagogue. It serves strictly kosher food.

The Karmel Restaurant in Moscow was kosher at one point, it was reported. At press time it is not kosher. It serves dishes with Jewish-style cooking. (Photo credit: Ben G. Frank)

NaMonmartre, Vetoshnyi Peroulok 9, 5th floor. Tel: (7-095) 725-4797. Located in the French Gallery Mall near Red Square, this restaurant is glatt kosher, under the supervision of Rabbi Berel Lazar, chairman of the Rabbinical Alliance of the CIS. The restaurant seats about 40 people. It is open Sunday through Thursday, from noon to midnight. It is closed Friday and Saturday. A wide variety of meats, such as lamb and steak, are offered in this dining room. Kosher wines are listed on the menu. Prices range from $12 to $15 for lunch and from $20 to $25 for dinner.

Kosher Facility, Bolshaya Nakitskaya Street 9-3. Tel: (7-095) 229-87-96. Open every day except Friday and Saturday from 11:00 A.M. until 10:00 P.M.

Karmel Restaurant, Tverskaya Yamskaya A-7. Tel: (7-095) 200-57-63. Tel/Fax: (7-095) 250-11-80. At press time, this restaurant was not designated kosher, although some consider it kosher style. The upscale, gourmet restaurant serves gefilte fish, chickpeas, breast of veal, matza, dumplings, and challah, all at New York prices, so meals can be expensive. Metro: Makovskaya, Beloruskaya subway. Call ahead to make a reservation.

Institutes, Schools, Clubs, and Museums

Hillel, Bobrov Pereulok No. 2, Apt. 50.Tel: (7-095) 923-74-59. E-mail hillel@glasnet.ru. The director is Zhenya Michalyova, a former instructor in drama and culture at the Jewish University in Moscow. The facility is open from Sunday to Friday, but not on *Shabbat.* This is a fine place to meet young adults. A plethora of activities geared to students is a highlight of this well-attended Moscow Jewish institution. It is a relaxed meeting place, and is home to more than 200 members, who participate in clubs, programs, teas, theater, and film groups. Lectures and talks on Jewish life plus English-speaking clubs can also be found here. On Friday evenings at 8:00 P.M., Hillel hosts a weekly program that at times includes a talk by an outside speaker. Young professionals also belong to this organization.

Seminars acquaint students with Jewish rituals. One by-product of the founding of Hillel is that Hillel parents are becoming unwitting members of the Jewish community. They want to know what their young people are doing at group activities, so Hillel in Moscow started a "Parents' Club." For many of the parents, Hillel provides a chance for parents to meet and talk about what it means for their children to be so involved in Jewish life and compare it with their own experiences as children, when it was forbidden to practice Judaism.

The truth is that were it not for Hillel, it is doubtful that these students would be involved with any organized Jewish activity, especially in cities like St. Petersburg and Moscow, where aliyah among this age group is not large.

Here, too, as in other major cities, students can be found who are willing to travel to the former Soviet Union towns and cities to conduct Passover Seders.

Moscow Hillel was the first such institution in the former Soviet Union. It was founded in 1994 with the cooperation of JDC, Hillel International, and the Charles and Lynn Schusterman Family Foundation.

Special Rosh Hashanah and Yom Kippur services are held here. In 1998, more than 1,300 young Jews attended a holiday service organized by the Moscow Hillel and the American Jewish Joint Distribution Committee at the local Radisson Hotel. The event that year was the largest turnout in the history of Hillel, which serves Jewish students at universities and colleges in Moscow.

It is important to note that students in Russia are becoming the activists in the Jewish community.

MEOD Jewish Community Center. (MEOD is a Russian acronym which stands for "Moscow Jewish Community House.") This center is on the premises of the Jewish Theater "Shalom," Varshavskoye Shosse 71. Tel: (7-095) 110-86-11. Fax: (7-095) 119-90-60. About 1,200 people attend a multitude of activities here, including a woman's club, a literary club, *Shabbat* program for families, and events for senior citizens. Former ghetto prisoners and pensioners have their own club. One of the Moscow Jewish community's largest libraries is located in MEOD. In October 1998, MEOD and the library organized a Jewish Community Book Festival. The Russians are a literary people; the country has one of the highest literacy rates in the world, higher than the U.S., we were told. The Intelligentsia Club holds its sessions in the building. MEOD also publishes a newspaper called *Nash Dom,* which is read by a large percentage of the community. The meals-on-wheels program is also based here. The center also houses the Moscow Jewish Association of Former Prisoners of Nazi Concentration Camps and Ghettos. The Vaad (Conference of Jewish Organizations and Committees) maintains its offices here, too.

Social clubs for senior citizens meet at MEOD. The building also serves as a focal point for distribution of clothes. A Sheket (Hebrew for "quiet") Club for the deaf also has its headquarters here.

In 1995, Shalom Theater offered space to MEOD on the ground floor of the structure. The JDC and the Russian Jewish Congress came to the rescue with financial aid. Today 70 percent of the MEOD's operating budget comes from the JDC.

As this is the home of the Jewish Theater, many tourists are also attracted here, although this is not the theater where the great Jewish actor and director Solomon Mikhoels (1896-1948) played to large audiences. The present Shalom Theater was founded by Mikhoels' students, who work to keep the traditions of his theater alive. (Mikhoels' old theater is now called the Moscow Theater of Drama and is located on Malaya Bronnaya Street 4. Tel: (7-095) 290-40-93.)

This Yiddish theater is no newcomer to the Jews of Moscow. Even in tsarist times, the Jewish Theater functioned so well that for a time the Russian government attempted to stifle its development, especially from 1883 to 1905, after which the theater was allowed to put on Yiddish productions.

As noted above, the Jewish Theater was named after Solomon Mikhoels, who was head of the Moscow State Jewish Theater and chairman of the Jewish Anti-Fascist Committee, which was founded during World War II. He first attracted attention while performing in Sholom Aleichem's *Agents,* and *Tevye.* One of his most memorable performances was as King Lear in 1935. As chairman of the Jewish Anti-Fascist Committee (JAFC), he appealed to "our Jewish brethren" in the West to help the Soviet war effort against Nazi Germany. He and Itzik Fefer, both later murdered by Stalin, traveled on behalf of the JAFC to the U.S., Canada, Mexico, and England, where they were enthusiastically received by the Jewish community. After the war, Stalin gave orders to construct a case against the JAFC. Mikhoels stood in his way, for he had become too popular, according to historian Edvard Radzinsky. Mikhoels' death has been surrounded by legend. But the one story that seems to be close to the mark says that on the night of January 13, 1948, Solomon Mikhoels was invited by the secret police to a social gathering. They sent a car to his hotel and took him out of town to a dacha belonging to L.F. Tsanava, minister of state security of the Belarussian Republic. The story goes that he was killed there, and that his body was then taken to an unfrequented back street in the city, laid in the road, and ran over with a truck, writes Radzinsky.

Mikhoels, like Kirov and others, was murdered at Stalin's command. Stalin gave Mikhoels a state funeral in the building of the Moscow Jewish Theater, which he would soon close. Thousands paid their final respects to this great Jewish actor.

The killing of Mikhoels was the beginning of Stalin's open "war against the Jews." With Mikhoels dead, Stalin went after the Jewish Anti-Fascist Committee. Designed chiefly to influence Jewish opinion outside the Soviet Union, JAFC was not established "to safeguard Jewish interests or help the Allies as a whole win the war." Its main purpose was "to enlist support for the Soviet Union in particular," which meant the spreading of Soviet propaganda, writes Solomon Schwarz in *The Jews in the Soviet Union*. Thus, we see the JAFC was not set up to supply relief aid to Jews on Soviet soil, nor to raise money for the Red Army (it only raised $2 to $3 million in the U.S.), but to dispatch propaganda material abroad. "The Soviet leader intended to use the JAFC as a master key to American wealth," writes Gennadi Kostyrchenko. But fund-raising campaigns were an excellent means for spreading Soviet propaganda, and had the additional advantage of paying the way of the JAFC, Schwarz adds.

According to novelist Chaim Potok, "It was the only Jewish

institution in the entire Soviet Union officially recognized by
the Soviet government." Members included the writer Ilya
Ehrenburg, the Yiddish poet Itzik Fefer, the Central Committee
member Solomon Lozovsky, and the actor Solomon Mikhoels,
who was its chairman.

Members of the JAFC traveled throughout the U.S. They
talked about ties to Russia. They told of the heroic role being
played by Jews in the Red Army.

The Jewish Anti-Fascist Committee attempted to continue
with its activities even after the war, until it was brutally liqui-
dated by Stalin in 1948-49 as a first step in the total liquidation
of organized Jewish life during the "Black Years." Most of its
leading members were arrested and executed in 1952, according to the *Encyclopedia Judaica*. Stalin detested the spirited
activities of Mikhoels as head of the JAFC, and his self-
assumed position as leader of the Jews.

All who had suffered during World War II, including Jews,
wanted to believe that their suffering had not been in vain. But
it was not to be. The Communists outlined the plot against
Jewish intellectuals. In 1944, in a memo to Stalin, Solomon
Lozovsky had suggested the setting-up of a "Jewish Autonomous
Republic" in the Crimea in the place of the failed Birobidzhan,
says Potok. "Stalin had taken careful note of the work of the
Jewish Anti-Fascist Committee and its inner discussions which
he had approved in April 1942." The frame-up would claim that
the U.S. sought to develop a potential "fifth column" within the
Soviet Union. It was the Joint Distribution Committee which
maneuvered the visit of the Jewish Anti-Fascist Committee,
charged the Stalin regime, adding that in its World War II visit
to New York, Mikhoels and Itzik Fefer met with leaders of the
JDC and the Americans made known their desire for a secret
base in the Crimean peninsula, to be occupied the moment a
war between the U.S. and the USSR broke out. The JDC was to
get the base, which was to take the place of Birobidzhan. The
same frame-up apparatus was used for the second plot, the
Doctors' Plot. Solomon Mikhoels was supposed to have recruited
his relative, the noted physician Dr. Vofsi, to inveigle fellow medical specialists, who treated top Soviet leaders, in a plot to poison
them. It was a nightmare indeed.

Murdered were Itzik Fefer, Peretz Markish, Pinchas Kahanovich ("Der Nister" or "the Hidden One"), Tabreant Goldshtein, Leib Kvitko, and David Bergelson. Many others were taken to Lubyanka Prison and shot. According to Potok, the total was 25 Jewish writers and public figures. All were charged with being spies, Zionists, and traitors.

While we should remember all of them, let us make note of a few:

David Bergelson (1884-1952). Bergelson was an important Jewish writer following in the footsteps of Mendele Mocher Sforim, I. L. Peretz, and Sholom Aleichem. Born into a Chassidic family in Ukraine, Bergelson worked as an ardent communist. He was active in the Jewish Anti-Fascist Committee. Arrested by Stalin, he was shot on August 12, 1952, his sixty-eighth birthday. He was subsequently "rehabilitated" (had his social status restored) and his works published.

Peretz Markish (1895-1952). This Yiddish-language poet, novelist, and playwright was born in Volhynia Province, Ukraine. He was the youngest member of the "Kiev Lyric Triumvirate," which consisted of himself, David Hofstein, and Leib Kvitko. His novels were full of praise for Stalin and communism. In 1939 Markish was awarded the "Order of Lenin." A very prolific writer, especially in World War II, he expressed hatred of the enemy, applauded great Soviet patriotism, and voiced sorrow at the extermination of the Jews. Despite his "Ode to Stalin," Markish was also executed on August 12, 1952. After Stalin's death, Markish was also "rehabilitated."

Itzik Fefer (1900-1952), was a Soviet Jewish poet whose life was also snuffed out. An active and devoted member of the Communist Party, he was prominent in Soviet Jewish literary circles. While he wrote a well-known poem, "Stalin," he also penned the poem "I Am a Jew," during World War II. He was a lieutenant colonel in the Red Army and, along with Mikhoels, had visited the U.S. with the Jewish Anti-Fascist Committee. Like Markish and Bergelson, he was also executed on August 12, 1952, and later "rehabilitated."

Chabad Community Center, Myasnitskaya Street 40. Tel: (7-095) 923-01-85. The center provides a full range of activities, including *Shabbat* programs, youth clubs, and educational projects. The center also holds Hebrew language and computer courses, as well as teaching programs and classes in Jewish tradition.

Israel Cultural Center, Nikoloyamskaya Street 51. Tel: (7-095) 911-27-80 and (7-095) 912-87-18. Fax: (7-095) 230-65-26. This center sponsors discussion groups, dances, and, twice a year, camps for young people. The emphasis here is on youth movements.

Jewish Arts Center, Nizhne Taganskaya Square, Moscow, 109172. Tel/Fax: (7-095) 912-04-70. The projects of this arts center are a Jewish arts school, a cantorial art academy (including a male choir of cantorial art academy), a Jewish youth club, a dance group, and a jazz band.

Museum of Modern Jewish Art, Pervomajskaya 26. Tel: (7-095) 163-93-93. Here, Alexander Feldstein has created a museum in two rooms in an apartment, and not a fancy apartment at that. Its only occupants are Feldstein and his wife and daughter. "This art is the history of our country," he told the author in an interview. Most of the art was produced by artists after World War II.

Important Russian Jewish artists in the twentieth century include Natan Altman, Leon Bakst, Isaak Brodsky, Marc Chagall, Leonid Pasternak, Yehuda Pen, and Isaac Levitan.

Shown here in this apartment museum is an excellent collection of paintings, drawings, prints, and decorative art. Pictured are portraits of Jewish authors and actors, images of Jewish life in small towns, illustrations of famous works by Yiddish writers, Biblical scenes, sketches of stages and costumes and set ideas from the Moscow Jewish Theater, as well as avant-garde paintings from artists who admired the aesthetic beauty of the Hebrew alphabet. Some of the modern Jewish artists are Zaruade, Molovkaya, Kaplan, Axelrod, and Inger.

"Soviet Jewish culture of the prewar period is better known. Very few are aware that it continued to exist even when most of the artists were forced to go underground," says Feldstein, referring to the post-war period. Despite censorship and the watchful eyes of the state security forces, Russian Jewish artists still painted Jewish themes.

From the Stalin to the Brezhnev era, Feldstein collected the works of Jewish artists and painters. Wonderful Jewish art from all over Russia and Ukraine survives because of him. Prices of the art range from $20 to $2,000. Torah covers from as far back as the eighteenth century are on view here. Above all, sign the guest book. Also, call first to make sure Mr. Feldstein is on the premises.

Macabi Sports Club, Pervaya Tverskaya-Yamskaya 11, Apt. 101. Tel/Fax: (7-095) 250-48-71.

Schools

State Jewish National School, No. 1311, Leninsky Prospekt 97-A. Tel: (7-095) 132-32-56. Fax: (7-095) 132-75-39. Actually, this school is called the **Lipman School,** after principal Grigory Lipman, who founded the school in 1991. More than 250 students are enrolled here. Student clubs are active. One activity of the school children is to deliver lunches prepared in the school canteen to seniors.

Chabad Jewish Day School, (known as Achey Tmimim and Beit Rivka), Myansnitskaya Street 40. Tel: (7-095) 923-01-85.

Migdal Ohr Day School, No. 1313, Michurinsky Prospekt 68. Tel: (7-095) 932-25-94 and (7-095) 932-62-62.

Etz Haim, kindergarten, affiliated with the Moscow Choral Synagogue. The boys' school is located at Lomonosovsky Prospekt 18. Tel: (7-095) 939-07-82. The girls' school is located at Sadovo-Chernogryazskaya Street 5/9. Tel: (7-095) 975-38-59.

Etz Haim, Jewish Day School, School No. 1621, Maly Kozlovsky Lane 3. For boys—Tel: (7-095) 924-01-58. For girls—Sadovo 5/9 Chernogryazskaya Street. Tel: (7-095) 975-3859.

Beit Yehudith, Jewish day school for girls, School No. 1330, Klara Tzetkin Street 15 "B." Tel: (7-095) 159-01-69.

The Gahlilit Sunday School, School No. 506, Trofimova Street 13.

The Snunit Sunday School, School No. 347, Schelkovskoye Shosse 58. Tel: (7-095) 468-35-89 (h).

Hineini, 21 Rozhdestvensky Street. This is a progressive Sunday school. Zinovy Kogan is the principal.

Chama Children's Educational Center, School No. 1812, Valdaisky Proezd 20. Tel: (7-095) 457-63-71. Here is a wonderful kindergarten consisting of about 40 children and an elementary school of 85 children. One-third of the school is supported by the Moscow JDC and the Russian Jewish Congress.

Chama Soup Kitchen, Butyrskaya Street 9. Tel: (7-095) 285-46-63/78-74. At 2:00 A.M. one morning, the loud ring of a telephone awoke Greta Elinson. A friend who worked at the Karasky railroad station was aware of the fact that Greta was Jewish. The friend asked Greta if she would take under her care a Jewish woman who was obviously weak and starving, and had collapsed from malnutrition? The answer, of course, was "Yes."

Over and over again, stories such as this surface in Russia. Senior citizens everywhere are generally lonely, but in Russia this is compounded by the fact that many children of Jewish parents have left for Israel. Today, thanks to Director Greta Elinson and her soup kitchens, these senior mothers and fathers can have a hot kosher meal. Most of the Jewish elderly who come for lunch are also members of the Pensioners Club (retired people). The club, sponsored by JDC, has a library, with a television, VCR, and tape recorder and video/audio cassettes, as well as a physical therapy and a lecture room.

According to JDC, more than 250 elderly Jews are provided hot meals at the Chama Soup kitchen on a daily basis. Open from 12 noon to 2:00 P.M., except on the Sabbath, many of the people who come here do not just come for lunch and then leave. They participate in the center's activities before or after their meal. Here one finds educational programs, lectures, and videos on Jewish subjects and Israel. There is a library where one finds programs for Jewish holidays, which are celebrated in the building. Medical services are also offered. Doctors often come to the headquarters to help parents and offer talks on childcare. About fifty meals are delivered to homebound clients. A new meals-on-wheels project has been started with the support of JDC.

Yeshiva Mekor Haim. Once this yeshiva was located in a lovely wooded setting near Moscow. This small synagogue and Judaic studies center started by Rabbi Adin Steinsaltz in Moscow's outskirts was razed by fire in 1996. An electrical malfunction was said to be the cause, but many suspect this did not occur by chance.

Rabbi Steinsaltz is described by some as the spiritual leader of Russian Jewry since 1995. His name became "familiar to Russian Jews in the late 1980s with the beginning of freedom of religion," wrote Lev Krichevsky. Russian translations of books by Steinsaltz were among the first works on Judaism that appeared in the country in the new period of openness instituted by former Soviet leader Mikhail Gorbachev.

The building now being renovated is located at Goncharmaya Naberezhnaya 1, Building 3, Moscow, and is near the Tanganka Metro station. Both the Institute of Judaic Studies and the Yeshiva Mekor Haim will be located here.

Ash HaTorah Educational Institute for Jewish Students, Brestskaya Street 60-6, Room 12.

Pedagogical College for Girls, Voevodina Street 4. Tel:(7-095) 241-63-73.

Technical Educational Complex, Novslobodskaya Street 57. Tel: (7-095) 978-35-84. This is a World ORT school.

Universities

Sefer, Moscow Center for University Teaching of Jewish Civilization, Leninsky Prospekt 32-A, Block B, Room 808, Moscow, 117334. Tel: (7-095)938-57-16. Fax: (7-095) 938-00-70. E-mail: sefer@glas.apc.org; sefer@f108.tower.ras.ru. Few people predicted the end of the Soviet regime, least of all Victoria Motchalova. As mentioned in the quote at the beginning of the chapter on Russia, she went to a séance and spoke to the "ghost." It is worth repeating what happened then. She said to the ghost, "Will I live to see the end of the Soviet regime?" The ghost answered, "Yes." To which, Motchalova recalled, she burst out laughing.

If you are a teacher, you should contact Sefer. Founded in 1994, this group is an independent branch of the International Center for University Studies of Jewish Civilization (Hebrew University of Jerusalem), in cooperation with the American Jewish Joint Distribution Committee. More than 800 members help those who have little or no Jewish educational background.

Scholars and teachers from Tbilisi, Vilnius to Birobidzhan, and throughout the former Soviet Union engage in issues of Jewish studies and teaching. Sefer encourages publication of textbooks prepared by Russian authors. Its members comprise both scholars and independent researchers, as well as university professors and students whose professional activity and scholarly interests are related to various aspects of Jewish civilization. In cooperation with the Russian Academy of Sciences, Sefer has attracted the attention of prominent academics in the former Soviet Union, and has been granted official status under the aegis of the academy.

Dr. Rashid Kaplanov is the academic chair of the center, and Victoria Motchalova is director.

Here again is that amazing thrill of the rebirth of the Jewish people, especially in the area of scholarship.

Ralph Goldman, honorary executive vice president of the American Jewish Joint Distribution Committee, addressed a recent convention of Sefer. Attending were 450 Jewish scholars from throughout the former Soviet Union. Not only is the figure amazing, but also the fact that the convention was held in the Lenin Library. This is yet one more example of the changes in the lives of not only Russian Jewry, but of all Russians. Ninety universities in this huge country teach Jewish studies.

Mr. Goldman disclosed there was one man who, back in the 1960s, saw that the oppressiveness of the Soviet Union would not last. Interviewed in 1960 for the American magazine *Look*, David Ben-Gurion, the first prime minister of Israel, was asked how he envisioned Russia in 25 years. He replied, "The Cold War will be the legacy of the past. The internal pressure of the intelligentsia which incessantly grows in Russia for more freedom, and the pressure of the masses for raising the standard of living, may bring about democratization of the Soviet Union during the next quarter of a century."

Once, these teachers of Sefer dreamed of "freedom of religion," and they have seen this dream come true.

Let us not confuse the lack of democratic traditions, the upheavals throughout its history, or the poor economy and standard of living with the fact Russia is still a very educated, cultural country, currently existing in a free atmosphere. Nearly 99 percent of the Jewish young people go to university in Russia.

In addition, for the first time in more than 1,000 years, the arts are not state controlled. The joke is often told, "If you see a Jew without a violin, he plays the piano." Courses and seminars are sponsored by Sefer. One popular topic is "History of the Jews in Eastern Europe."

Project Judaica is a joint venture of the Russian State University for Humanities (ROGGU), the Jewish Theological Seminary of America, and the YIVO Institute for Jewish Research, Chayanov Street 15, No. 401, Moscow, 125267. Tel: (7-095) 250-64-70. Also at Nikol'skaya Street 15. Tel: (7-095) 928-52-97. E-mail:pichuga@glasnet.ru. Here, pupils receive a diploma from the Russian State University and a certificate from the Jewish Theological Seminary.

Jewish University in Moscow, Mokhovaya Street 9, Suite 329, Moscow, 103009. Tel: (7-095) 203-34-41. E-mail: jewunimali@glas.apc.org, jum@cityline.ru. Jewish University in Moscow, New York office—225 West 34th Street, Suite 2205, New York, NY, 10122. Tel: 212-328-1036. This institute of higher learning was founded in 1991. Several hundred students graduated in its first commencement exercises in 1997. It maintains a four-year program in Judaica, history, and sociology.

Center for Judaica and Jewish Civilization, Mokhovaya Street 11, Office 366, Moscow, 103009. Tel/Fax: (7-095) 203-62-58. E-mail: cjs@iass.msu.ru. Three groups participate in this joint venture—Hebrew University of Jerusalem, the Institute of Asian and African Studies at the Moscow State University, and the Jewish University in Moscow. Directors are Professors Israel Bartal and Arkady Kovelman.

State Jewish Maimonides Academy, Department of Jewish Studies and Languages, Maly Tatarsky Pereulok Bldg. 1. Tel: (7-095) 951-85-42. This institution boasts a number of departments, including math, medicine, philosophy, law, and music. Music and Law departments are located at Sadovnicheskaya 51/45. Tel: (7-095) 951-78-67.

Touro Jewish Academy for the Humanities, Armyansky Pereulok 13. Tel: (7-095) 921-87-03. Fax: (7-095) 921-93-90. E-mail:ovgend@center.chph.ras.ru. The rector here is Dr. Shlomo Gendelman. A four-year course on Judaism is offered.

Organizations

Russian Jewish Congress, c/o Office 835, American Business Centers, Radisson Slavianskaya Hotel, Berezhkovskaya Embankment 2, Moscow, 121059. Tel: (7-095) 941-83-92. Fax: (7-095) 941-83-91. The pinnacle of Jewish organizations is the Russian Jewish Congress (RJC), which has given a national scope to Russian Jewry. This organization is committed to the advancement and continuation of Jewish life in Russia, whether it be financially, culturally, or politically. And it is doing it with 48 branches throughout the former Soviet Union. Its significance lies in the fact that in smaller cities throughout this vast land, the RJC hopes that local officials will see it as a national organization. This, in part, has already been accomplished.

Not only that, but it attempts to gather within its ranks Russian Jewry's top achievers, including businesspeople, artists, sports personalities, lawyers, and doctors.

The organization may have started with budgets of several million, but by the late 1990s the budget had gone up to $10 to $12 million. That amount has been given to Jewish communal institutions in Russia. According to RJC, money from its donors is not tax-deductible. Much of the money is given by Vladimir Goussinsky, a banker who owns the second-largest non-government television network, NTV, as well as the MOST Bank Group. Mr. Goussinsky has said that he and others would like to ensure that the Russian Jewish community eventually meets its own financial needs.

Aleksandr A. Osovtsov has been executive vice president of the RJC since 1996. He was a member of the national Duma, as well as the governing board of the Moscow City Council. Osovtsov has said that the RJC "represents the Russian Jewish community in the Jewish world."

In an interview, Osovtsov outlined the program of the RJC.

First of all, it is to help finance Russian Jewish communal institutions. Second, to offer public support for Jewish education, and psychological and political support so that "we continue Jewish life in Russia." Third, it considers itself the umbrella organization for the Russian Jewish community and it cooperates and works with JDC, the Conference of Presidents of Major American Jewish Organizations, World Jewish Congress, and the Jewish Agency for Israel. Fourth, it sees itself as the political leader of Russian Jewry, and as such it makes representations to the Russian government, national and local. The Congress, for example, has called on the government to "take official measures" against ultra-nationalist neo-fascists suspected in anti-Semitic attacks on Jewish institutions.

In 1999, the Russian Jewish Congress and the Anti-Defamation League of B'nai B'rith joined together in an initiative on Russian anti-Semitism, reported Lawrence Cohler in the *Jewish Week*.

The Russian Jewish Congress supports synagogues, Jewish Community Centers, schools, various day schools, and community projects. One of the projects of the RJC is to put computers into Russian Jewish schools.

Federation of Jewish Communities of the CIS, Vysheslavtzev Pereulok 5-A, 2nd floor, Moscow, 103055. Tel: (7-095) 201-45-23. Fax: (7-095) 281-26-72. E-mail: FJC@ropnet.ru. Web site address: www.FJC.ru. The federation serves as an umbrella organization in more than 300 Jewish communities in the former Soviet Union. It provides religious and welfare aid to various communities and helps them establish synagogues, summer camps, holiday programs, educational institutions, soup kitchens where needed, and Seders. "We are helping build a community infrastructure," said Mendel Goldshmid, director of the group. Mr. Goldshmid added that the federation represents diverse groups. Its various departments include the Rabbinical Department, served by the Rabbinical Alliance of the CIS, as well as educational, humanitarian, anti-defamation, legal, and restitution. Its U.S. office is at 580 Fifth Ave., Suite 800, New York, NY, 10036. Tel: 212-262-3688. Fax: 212-262-2357. E-mail:FJC18@aol.com.

Confederation of Jewish Religious Organizations and

Communities of Russia, Bolshoi Spasoglinishchevsky Pereulok 10, Moscow, 101000. Tel: (7-095) 924-24-24. Fax: (7-095) 956-75-40. E-mail: keriir@chat.ru. This group serves as an umbrella body for most of Russia's synagogues, but does not include Lubavitch. Members include Rabbi Adolph Shayevitsh, Rabbi Pinchas Goldschmidt (Moscow chief rabbi and Choral Synagogue rabbi).

Zinovy Kogan is chairman of the confederation. Among its activities are representations to the government, participation in community dialogues with the Russian Orthodox Church, the publication of Jewish magazines, and setting up a calendar of events and printing translations of Jewish religious books into Russian, including such books as the *Shulchan Arukh* and the Passover *Hagadahs.* Contact Zinovy Kogan for more information on this important group.

World Union of Progressive Judaism, Varshavskoe Shosse 71, Teatr Shalom. Tel: (7-095) 110-78-86.

The Jewish Agency in Russia, Presnensky Val. 36 A, Moscow, 123567. Tel: (7-095)-253-46-57. Fax: (7-095)-253-46-67. The Jewish Agency is located in several dozen Russian cities, including Moscow. In the past, it has transported whole Jewish communities to Israel.

It may be called on to do so again, considering the collapse of the Russian banking system, and the fall of the ruble, which has driven many Jews to think or rethink about moving to Israel.

Aliya in the past few years has been fixed at an average figure of about sixty thousand a year. But as noted elsewhere in this volume, in the long run Jews themselves will decide if they want to live in the Jewish state or stay in Russia.

Not every Jew succeeds in Israel. There are Jews who have returned to Russia because of the difficulties of starting a new life in another country and in another climate. There are Jews from Russia who are afraid to go to Israel because their sons will be called up for army service.

But one out of every seven persons in Israel is a Russian Jew. And Russian Jews have contributed enormously to Israel in the fields of the arts, theater, and music, and in science and engineering. Despite the difficulties, this has been a very successful and vital emigration for Israel. As one high Israeli official put it, "Israelis like aliyah, (emigration), they just don't like *olim*, (emigrants)." That may be the deep truth of both emigrant and citizen adjusting to each other, but if the million-plus Jews in the former Soviet Union would in one day pick themselves up and come to Israel, they would be welcomed with open arms; they know it, so do the Israelis, and so does the world.

At the Jewish Agency, the emphasis is on Hebrew. For so many years, the teaching of Hebrew was prohibited, but today, the Jewish Agency has set up about three hundred ulpanim in the former Soviet Union, of which more than half are in Russia itself. The Jewish Agency (or the Sochnut as it is called in Hebrew), sponsors a program called Naaleh for youngsters 15 to 16 years of age. They then finish their high-school studies in Israel.

The American Jewish Joint Distribution Committee, Novo-Alekseyevskaya 13, Eighth Floor, Moscow, 129626. Tel: (7-095) 286-69-72/69-48/41-49. Fax: (7-502) 935-86-59. JDC is no stranger to saving Russians Jews. Even before the Russian Revolution, the agency prevented Jews from starving in the former Pale of Settlement, which included war-torn Ukraine during the Russian Civil War.

As we have mentioned, the JDC is the major agency serving Jewish communities abroad. It receives its funds mainly from UJA/Federation campaigns. The aim of the JDC is saving Jewish lives, providing enough food so no Jew will go to bed hungry, and the reconstructing of Jewish communal life. In 1998-99, it fed 170,000 Jews in the former Soviet Union.

The Anti-Defamation Committee of the Russian Jewish Congress. This organization deals with issues of anti-Semitism and fascism. It publishes a magazine called *Diagnosis*. The address is the same as that of the Russian Jewish Congress.

Vaad, Confederation of Jewish Communities and Organizations of Russia, Varshavskoye Shosse 71, Moscow, 113556. Mikhail Chlenov is chairman of the Vaad. It helps coordinate various Jewish organizations, offers information, and includes political representations as one of its goals.

Jewish Telegraphic Agency, 38-47 Frunzenskaya Nab., Moscow,

Shown here is the statue of women putting their hands over their children to shield them from the horrors of war. These impressive figures are near the main hall of the Poklonnaya Gora-Memorial Hill Complex in Moscow. (Photo credit: Ben G. Frank)

119270. Tel/Fax: (7-095) 241-09-73. E-mail: lekrich@glasnet.ru.

The Russian State Library (formerly known as the Lenin Library), Vozdvizhekna Street 3. Tel: (7-905) 202-57-90. The Schneerson Library is located here. For more than 70 years, the collection of twelve thousand books and manuscripts collected by five generations of Lubavitch rebbes has been stored here. The books were confiscated by Soviet authorities in the early 1920s and brought to the library. At one time, the Lenin State Library was one of the three largest in the world, with about 20 million items. Still among the largest, it also has the distinction of being the site of the first Moscow Jewish Book Festival, which was held in 1998.

Poklonnaya Gora-Memorial Hill Park Complex (dedicated to the victory of the Soviet Union in the Great Patriotic War). "I lost my father at the front." "I lost my uncle at the front." "I lost my cousin at the front." Over and over again, even today, more than a half-century after the end of World War II, what the Russians call the Great Patriotic War, you hear these words about dear ones lost at the front. There is not a family in all of the former Soviet Union that did not lose someone "at the front."

The war is to this day "a scar that may never heal." On the other hand, it is also a healing force. The nation prides itself on its victory and its "glorious Red Army" that hurled back the German invaders.

"The war became the central moment of Soviet history for generations to come, eclipsing the revolution of 1917 and the 'revolution from above,' of the early 1930s," writes historian Robert Grigor Suny.

Construction of this massive memorial hall and park began in the mid-1980s and was dedicated during the 850th anniversary of the founding of Moscow. It is situated next to the Victory Arch, which was erected in honor of the victory over Napoleon. The complex covers 132 hectares, and is located in a prestigious part of the city. It contains three houses of worship—a Russian Orthodox church, a mosque, and a synagogue, since soldiers in the war practiced different religious faiths.

In 1995, President Bill Clinton was on hand here for the fiftieth anniversary of the end of World War II.

A huge statue of a Red Army soldier greets visitors to Poklonnaya Gora. (Photo credit: Ben G. Frank)

At the Russian Memorial site, outside the main hall, there is little recalling the Jewish contribution to the Soviet Union/Allied victory in World War II, but there is an impressive statue of women putting their hands over the eyes of their children to shield them from the horrors of war. Inscriptions in various languages are written on the back of each statue. One statue has writing in Hebrew and Yiddish.

The museum and park are must-sees. Some call this a memorial monument, others a sacred shrine. Still others come here to pay tribute to the victory of the Russians over what they call the "fascist invaders," the Germans. Some liken it to the Tomb of the Unknown Soldier and Arlington National Cemetery in Arlington, Virginia; others to the battlefield at Gettysburg or the Vietnam Veterans' Memorial Wall, or the statue commemorating the raising of the flag at Iwo Jima.

This memorial hall contains a large-scale military exhibit. Above all, it is the Russian Central Museum of World War II. You can spend a good part of the day studying the exhibits, photos, and displays that highlight the conflict. Outside the museum is a huge obelisk sword of victory.

Enter the Hall of Glory, with the huge statue of the Red Army soldier, signifying victory, a victory won at an enormous price. "Mass murder, deportations, deliberate starvation of prisoners in cages, the burning alive of school children, target practice on civilian hospitals. . . . No man coming fresh to the scene of World War II could stay sane without acquiring a protective veneer of brutalization," wrote miliary historian Alan Clark in *Barbarossa: The Russo-German Conflict, 1941-1945.*

Here, one can view the history of the war through the battles of "Hero Cities," such as Odessa, Smolensk, Tula, Stalingrad, Leningrad, Moscow, Kiev, and Minsk. Photos and information on Soviet generals such as Zhukov, Vassilevsky, Rokossovsky, Konev, Govonov, Malinovsky, and Timoshenko are also displayed.

This monument attracts Russians from all over the nation. Each year, from May 7-12, several million Russians visit this site in honor of their country's role in V-E Day. Victory Day in Russia is celebrated on May 9, the date of the formal German surrender to Marshal Zhukov in Berlin. (Americans celebrate on May 8, the date of Jodl's capitulation to Eisenhower at Rheims, France.)

Preparations for the first victory celebration in Moscow in 1945 took almost two months to set up, as the Soviets wanted to ensure that the Allied generals could all be present. As part of the ceremony, on June 24, Soviet soldiers cast down two hundred Wehrmacht standards. This symbolic act was an allusion to the victory over Napoleon, when French standards were cast at the feet of Alexander I.

During the ceremony Marshal Zhukov, head raised high, gallantly rode across Red Square on a white horse. Stalin wanted the honor for himself, but got thrown from the horse in rehearsal. Zhukov, you see, was a former cavalryman.

The number of Russians killed in the war? We will never know the truth. Most observers say 25 to 32 million soldiers and civilians were killed in World War II. Here while at the Victory Memorial at Poklonnaya Gora, I saw a figure of 32 million Russian victims listed as being killed in the Great Patriotic War. William C. Fuller Jr., of the U.S. Naval War College, claimed that there were another 25 million homeless.

In order to understand the significance this complex has for the Russian people, it is necessary to understand the sacrifices and suffering they went through during the war. We shall now look more deeply at the war's impact on Russia.

The Second World War

On Sunday, June 22, 1941, first light occurred at 3:15 A.M., Moscow time. A train—carrying goods and wheat as cargo— chugged over the Koders Bridge on the Bug River, between Poland and Russia. At the same time, as the driver waved goodbye to Russia, on what would soon be his and the train's last journey, German soldiers approached the bridges all along the Bug River and shot the defenders there. Overhead, Luftwaffe bombers flew across western Russia and the Ukraine, wreaking havoc and confusion at Soviet airports. About 115 armed divisions were heaved across the border; their destination was

Moscow. They would crawl to within 19 miles of the Russian capital.

There will never be another day like June 22, 1941, the date of the German invasion. It was the head-on crash of the two greatest armies, the two most absolute systems, in the world. It was a more momentous day than "the first ponderous heave of August 1914, when all the railway engines in Europe sped the mobilization of troops," says historian Alan Clark, in his book *Barbarossa: The Russo-German Conflict, 1941-1945*. Before it was over much of western Russia would be in flames. Worldwide, 50 to 60 million people, a high proportion of them civilians, would be dead, as compared to 11 million in World War I.

This huge attack force and invasion was called Operation Barbarossa, after Emperor Frederick I (1152-1190), who was known as Barbarossa, or "Redbeard," and was a "legendary figure in German folklore. He symbolized one of the pinnacles of medieval German history, and his mysterious death by drowning during the Third Crusade gave birth to the myth that this great monarch had not died, but was waiting in the bowels of the holy mountain of Kyffhauser, and would emerge some day to lead the German people to victory and to fresh triumphs," according to Leni Yahil in her book, *The Holocaust: The Fate of European Jewry, 1932-1945*.

Hitler believed all of Russia would crumble "as soon as we kick in the door." True, the door was opened, but the house never crumbled.

"The invasion of the Soviet Union was to have been just one more lightning victory, particularly as it was fought against the inferior races of the East," thought Hitler and his generals, especially after their victories in Europe between 1939 and 1941.

"Harsh trials had begun for the Soviet people," wrote Marshal Georgi K. Zhukov in the book, *Soviet Generals Recall World War II*. Historian Pares calls it "The Second Fatherland War."

Three elements have been attributed to the success of Allied victory against Germany: Britain's survival in 1940-41, American supplies, and the Red Army.

German generals wanted to concentrate their forces on the central front leading to Moscow. Hitler knew that Napoleon had taken Moscow, but failed to capture the Russian Army. In order to avoid that same fate, Hitler sent Army Group North toward Leningrad, and another army group toward Kiev. He was eager to snare the Donetz industrial basin and the oil fields of the Caucasus. Politically, the capture of Moscow would have been a great victory, as it would have eliminated an important rail center and crushed Russian morale, according to authors Porter and Jones.

If Hitler had listened to his generals and gone straight for Moscow along the Smolensk-Moscow axis instead of diverting forces to Leningrad and Kiev, "nothing could have saved the capital," according to the Germans. With Moscow gone, the USSR would have been "brain-dead," since more than any capital in the world, Moscow served as the absolute center of government.

Many argue that the move on Leningrad and Ukraine was a fatal mistake. While Kiev was a great victory, the drive for Moscow was interrupted for 78 days, according to Ronald Grigor Suny. In addition, when the Germans finally launched their attack on Moscow, it was already toward fall, past the time when they might have been able to capture the city in the summer sun. Fearful that he was losing momentum in the Caucasus, Hitler stripped Army Group Center of its striking power. Thus, he lost the chance to take Moscow before winter and disrupt the entire Soviet government.

Now in late fall, the "Battle of Moscow" was about to begin. Three million soldiers would fight in this battle, 60 percent of all Soviet ground forces and 38 percent of all German infantry on the Eastern Front.

The Germans had launched what they called "Operation Typhoon." In all, there were three phases of the battle: the first German offensive, from September 30 through October; the second offensive, from November 7 to December 5; and the Russian counteroffensive of December 5 into the spring of 1942.

"Russia is never as strong as she looks and Russia is never as weak as she looks," it has been said, and it bears repeating. But by July 3, 1941, she looked as if she was about to crumble before the Nazi onslaught. German tanks were halfway to Moscow. On July 20, Leningrad and Moscow experienced their first raids. The German Army Group Center advanced almost 250 miles in 18 days, and on July 10, it attacked Smolensk, less than 122 miles from Moscow. The Germans snared huge numbers of prisoners and seized large quantities of tanks and guns. By fall, 2.5 million Russians were already dead. Leningrad was isolated and neutralized, and Ukraine was wide open to the Germans.

Not until October 2 did the Germans launch their attack on Moscow. At first, they advanced almost to the outskirts of the city, and the Soviet government was evacuated to the east.

By mid-October the Russian war effort certainly took a dramatic turn for the worse, as Moscow was seriously threatened. The German advance looked irresistible, and on October 16 the Soviets mobilized all available reserves. That was the day that panic spread throughout the city. Many fled to the east, while the government headed for Kuibyshev.

Stalin is said to have outfitted out a Douglas DC-3 for his escape. Bureaucrats burned offices and files. In the city, Communist Party members cowed and flushed their party cards down the toilet. The Bolshoi Theater and many public buildings were mined. Factories were idle. Numerous Muscovites turned tail in the great panic of October 16-20, according to Timothy Colton in his book *Moscow: Governing the Socialist Metropolis.* Under wartime measures, thousands were detained; hundreds were shot.

In the middle of October, the Moscow Soviet issued orders that all women with children under 14 were to register at evacuation centers and prepare for immediate departure to the east. Moscow was a frontline town.

But as Clark points out, the panic died away. "It was the antithesis of the apathy and resignation that lay behind the French collapse in 1940. Then a people sacrificed their country and institutions for their own personal safety. They could preserve pleasures by refusing to fight." For the Russians, "privation and sacrifice were, and for centuries had been, their habitual condition; and now in the German invader, they had a focus for all their misery and resentment," he adds.

"Every man, woman, and child in the capital was a soldier,"

according to Porter and Jones. This was due to the spirit of this "fiercely patriotic people who over all other concerns, defended their nation, mother Russia."

While Moscow citizens were already prepared to fight to the last drop of their blood, they learned that Stalin had stayed in Moscow. It made a difference. "Stalin is with us," they repeated over and over again. He became the symbolic focus of national unity. It is hard for us to believe, but there is no doubt that during the war, he was really "*Tovarish* [comrade] Stalin." His appeal to the Russian people to defend themselves and to drive out the invaders has been compared to Churchill's renowned speeches during the Blitz in England.

The Russian people rose to defend their capital, and as the Germans neared Moscow, people laid anti-tank obstacles and sandbag barricades along the city's streets.

If you go on an excursion outside of Moscow, remember that in snow and frost, under bombardment and fire, hundreds of thousands of people, most of them women, got up early in the morning and dug into the hard earth with spades, shovels, and crowbars. Their hands carved out trenches and anti-tank ditches. Dressed in black dresses, hair in a bun, no makeup, round faces, Slavic noses and smiles, those women strung 30 miles of barbed wire, and made such an impression that even Zhukov was impressed when he visited the tank ditch construction.

More than half a million civilians took part in constructing fortifications for the city of Moscow, including more than 20 miles of anti-tank ditches.

It is interesting to note that eight hundred thousand women served in the Red Army in World War II. Most were medical workers, but thousands were full-fledged combatants, bomber pilots, tank drivers, snipers, and artillery troops.

Moscow became the intersection of frontline traffic. The trolley buses were running, but on the Leningrad Highway people would soon be fighting and dying.

"Moscow is behind. There is nowhere left to retreat," the poet Sarkov wrote in a memorable poem. Russian opposition stiffened. New Russian formations and new armor were brought into the battle.

The Nazis could see the golden domes of the cathedrals. But the suburbs resisted. Moscow resisted. The defense lines resisted. Zhukov resisted. Still, Moscow was within gunfire range from the front line, and the atmosphere was grim and tense. Bombing raid followed bombing raid. Hospitals filled up. People shivered under a freezing winter.

At this point, Russians could put in the field only ninety thousand men and about 190 tanks to defend Moscow. This handful of tanks and men stood between the Germans and the city.

"There would be no Moscow as we know it if the Great Patriotic War had tilted against the Soviets," writes Colton. No open city here. This city was not to be spared as was Paris, Hitler said. There would be no surrender. The city was to be obliterated and in its place would stand a gigantic reservoir.

The German's "Operation Typhoon" uncoiled so swiftly in 1941 that the Politburo evacuated Lenin's mummy to Tyumen in Siberia. Some shops and buildings were sandbagged and boarded over, the windows blinded with wooden frames or heavy black paper.

It looked like the German advance would never stop.

But helping Russia were "General Winter" and "General Cold."

"Each day that passed brought closer the time when the icy wind now gathering strength over the Aral Sea would sweep down over Siberia, across the steppe through Moscow and onto the battlefield," writes Clark.

"Yet by itself, the impact of the winter would not be enough for an exhausted and outnumbered Red Army to turn the tables on its adversary," Clark continues. The weather was the same for both sides, but the Russian troops were better prepared with their winter gear, and could bear the sub-zero temperatures more easily. The Nazi effort to supply their troops in winter was indeed third-rate, despite so-called German efficiency.

"The ferocious winter, whose severity no European could ever calculate, for which their own soldiers were trained and clothed, and to which they were accustomed since childhood, certainly helped the Russians," writes Clark.

On November 7, 1941, the Germans were only 50 miles from Moscow. At this point, Stalin brought in the 30 reserve divisions of Siberian troops. Soviet intelligence had informed Moscow that Japan would not enter the war and therefore the Russian Asian front could spare the troops. As the Germans crept to within 15 to 20 miles of Moscow, they made one last lunge for the city. According to military historian John Erickson, author of *The Road to Stalingrad: Stalin's War with Germany*, hand-to-hand combat occurred in the suburbs of Moscow.

Soviet units were cramped into their defensive positions in the snow-covered fields and woods (snow was as yet light and thinly spread) or were locked in the spoiling attacks which Zhukov had ordered. "That morning, in the first phase of the final offensive against Moscow, German forces in the northwest surged forward," Erickson writes. The Russians resisted. The Germans reached the city limits. But just after the winter frosts, German tanks ceased to operate in extreme cold.

Red Army infantry divisions and nine armored brigades of General Apanasenko's Far Eastern Front contained some of the finest units of the Red Army. Perhaps at that moment the Germans realized that the war would not be over soon, as Clark has pointed out. The Germans understood that they were few, the Russians many, the territory vast.

On December 2 and 3, the German troops saw the towers of the Kremlin reflecting in the dim, red, setting sun. But on December 4, the German offensive had burned itself out. The blitz had stalled.

Field Marshal von Kluge then threw his 20th Corps into one final, furious, and dangerous bid to seize the shortest route to the Soviet capital, along the Minsk-Moscow Highway. On those days of December 4 and 5, in a deep and terrible freeze, German soldiers screamed in the snow that they could not go on.

As we have noted, the Wehrmacht was never equipped to handle the terribly cold weather that occurred on December 5. On that day, Zhukov launched the counterattack with his Siberian reserves. The attack caught the Germans off-guard. By the end of December, the Red army had advanced between 20 and 40 miles and had liberated Kalinin, Tula, Yelets, and Istra.

Zhukov had saved the capital.

Not every military historian agrees as to the result of the battle. The war did not end here. It would take more than three years for the Russians to drive all the way to Berlin.

Others believe that with the Battle of Moscow lost, the German Wehrmacht forfeited the Battle of Russia. After the Battle of Moscow, and after the American entry into the war on December 7, 1941, the U.S., Britain, and Russia joined in an alliance that the Germans could not withstand. The Battle of Moscow was a crucial hinge on which the outcome of the war turned. There were to be other turning points; Stalingrad was one, the battle of the Kursk salient was another. But the Battle of Moscow was the first engagement that stopped further expansion of German power, it has been said.

Russian losses would mount after Moscow. The Germans captured 3,335,000 Soviet prisoners of war, including Stalin's older son, Yakov, who died in a Nazi camp. "Soviet dead may have numbered 4 million by the end of 1941," according to Suny.

The war was far from over. In fact, Suny points out that until early 1943, most observers were reluctant to predict which side would emerge victorious in the conflict between Germany and the USSR. Only after the "colossal battle" at Stalingrad (August 1942 to February 2, 1943) could one see that Soviet superiority in battle was possible.

Because Stalin coveted Berlin, he had wanted it captured by May 1, 1945 (May Day), an important date in the Communist Party calendar. To make that date and prevent the Americans from getting there first, Marshalls Zhukov and Konev engaged in a race that took a heavy toll in Russian lives. Generally, military people point out that Russians often had little regard for casualties. Authors John Gerrard and Carol Gerrard, for instance, charge that Stalin and his generals wasted enormous numbers of men. Millions of soldiers died in human-wave assaults. Stalin had ordered that the Red Army never retreat. The official order, Number 327, was issued on July 28, 1942, and was entitled "Not one step back." Prisoners would be condemned as traitors to the motherland.

In Berlin, the Reichstag and the Chancellery fell to Marshal Zhukov on May 2, 1945.

On Wednesday, May 9, over Soviet government radio, came the victory announcement. "Attention, this is Moscow. Germany has capitulated. This day, in honor of the victorious Great Patriotic War, is to be a national holiday, a festival of victory." Then followed the "Internationale," and the national anthems of Great Britain, France, and the U.S.

Four years and two days after the German invasion, the Soviet Union staged a triumphant victory parade in Red Square.

As already stated, at the height of the ceremony, Marshal Zhukov, a former cavalryman, rode across Red Square on a white horse. Stalin apparently had wanted the honor for himself, but was thrown off the horse in a rehearsal.

Within a few months of the victory parade, Stalin set out to build a case against Zhukov. The police searched his apartment and dacha. He was charged with "political unreliability" and "moved to an unimportant post," according to Alexander and Alice Nakhimovsky in *Witness to History: The Photographs of Yevgeny Khaldei.*

After Stalin's death, Krushchev brought Zhukov back to the Kremlin. After all, the marshal had helped Krushchev by having Lavrenti Beria tried in secret and then executed. Later, Krushchev apparently felt threatened and started worrying about Zhukov's popularity. In 1957, he forced Zhukov into retirement.

In the state-sponsored publication *History of the War,* produced while Krushchev was in power, Zhukov's leadership is minimized.

In 1972, Zhukov invited the noted photographer Yevgeny Khaldei to his dacha. The marshal asked Khaldei for a copy of the photo Khaldei had taken of him riding on the white horse during the victory celebration in Red Square. While visiting with Zhukov, Khaldei took a portrait shot. It was to be Zhukov's last, according to the Nakhimovskys. (Incidentally, the late Yevgeny Khaldei was the photographer who took the historic photo of Red Army troops hoisting the Soviet flag over the Reichstag in Berlin, as the Russians conquered the capital.)

"The Russian recovery and their winter offensive of 1941 remain one of the most remarkable achievements in military history," writes Clark. The Soviets may have won that battle, but they still were limited in supplies. However, at the end of 1941 and early 1942, the Germans regrouped. By July 1942, Hitler and the Germans were again boasting that the Russians were finished, Clark points out; although, as it has been said, the truth is that there is too much of Russia and too many Russians and that, even if there are many roads to Moscow, there are even more that lead away from it. In effect, the Germans had lost the battle for Russia.

The three elements that have been attributed to the success of Allied victory against Germany—Britain's survival in 1940-41, American supplies, and the Red Army were still in effect.

The Russian front vastly depleted German manpower and firepower, and certainly helped make possible the Allied invasion and eventual victory over the Axis.

In the first six months of the war on the Eastern Front alone, a quarter of a million Germans were killed, and a half-million wounded. The battle for Russia would end in disaster for Germany.

Could the German attack have been blunted? Certainly. The Soviets were warned about a possible invasion. But they thought they could buy peace "by relieving Germany of all anxiety as to a second main front," wrote Pares. The August 1939 Molotov-Ribbentrop pact made World War II "inevitable," he added.

Among the 20 million people who died in the great Stalin terror of 1937-38 was the flower of the Red Army command, including Marshal Mikhail Tukhachevsky, deputy commissar of defense, who had created a modern, efficient Red Army.

We cannot assume that he and others would have stopped the Germans at once. But Marshal Tukhachevsky, Marshal A.I. Yegorov, Marshal V.K. Blucher, Army Commander I.E. Yakir, and Army Commander I.P. Uborevich (Yakir and Uborevich were Jews) were only a few of the able professionals who worked and studied hard. Stalin had every commander of an army corps shot. Almost every division commander had been killed or sent to Siberia, according to Salisbury. The Red Army paid an extremely high price in men because of their deaths.

Some historians believe that Hitler knew he could not defeat England. To end the war, he had to win complete victory on the continent. His real target was Moscow, which was to be attacked only after the fall of Leningrad.

The Red Army was devastated in the first year of the war, with many in the officer corps either killed or captured. This wasn't a retreat; it was a collapse. The Germans had penetrated deep into Russian territory. Intoxicated by their military success, the blitzkrieg swept forward four hundred miles in only four weeks, according to Barton Whaley in his book, *Codeword Barbarossa.* "The bear was dead, but he would not lie down," as Alan Clark put it. By September 1941, at least 2.5 million Russian soldiers had been killed. Even if a Red Army soldier was captured instead of being killed on the field of battle, his life was probably over, as only one in eight would survive German captivity. Clark recalls that Germans were told by their allies that "you always had to kill a Russian twice over; that the Russians had never been beaten, that no man who drew blood there ever left Russia alive."

Not noticed in 1941 was an achievement that was significant regarding the outcome of the war. The Russians dismantled and moved to the east nearly one-quarter of the country's industrial capacity, including government factories. This was reported by none other than Communist Party leader Nikita S. Khrushchev. Far away from German eyes, these plants continued to pour out the tanks and guns and planes desperately needed to feed the front.

On October 16, factories were evacuated and relocated to the Ural Mountains. Western Siberia and central Asia became the country's main arsenal in the autumn of 1941. Mikhail Gorbachev says that between 1941 and 1945, a third of Soviet industry was moved from European Russia to the east. This was one of the reasons for the Allied victory.

Leonard Cooper, author of *Many Roads to Moscow: Three Historic Invasions,* says that war in its basic elements depends on three things—the courage of men, the shape of the ground, and the vagaries of climate. But in Russia, there were more obstacles to an invader—the almost infinite marching distances, the Russian winter, the lack of good roads, and the great dividing obstacle of the Pripet Marshes. Winter played a part, but it was not decisive. Add into that mix the stubborn Russian character, the Russian indifference to suffering and hardship, and the almost mystical courage of the Russian when fighting in defense of his homeland, according to Cooper, and you can sense the victory that was to be.

Still, by the spring of 1942, the Germans had penetrated almost one thousand miles into Russian territory, and were pushing toward Stalingrad. They were "marching on their way to the city, healthy and confident without a shadow of doubt in the inevitability of victory," writes historian Omer Bartov. The Germans thought the war was over.

The story of the German invasion is told in the letters of a German soldier to his parents. "I'll be home in one month," he wrote. "I'll be home for Christmas," was his message in his next letter. Then, "I'll be home in several months." Then, "I'll be home in a year." Then the letters ceased. He may have joined the quarter of a million German dead, or the half-million wounded.

The Russians were fighting for their homeland, which accounted for their tenacity and courage. At Stalingrad alone, from October 1942 to February 1943, the Red Army lost a half-million men, more than the U.S. lost on all fronts in World War II.

"Of the 13.6 million Germans killed, wounded, missing or made prisoner during World War II, 10 million of them met their fate on the Eastern Front. The Soviets lost between 7 and 8 million soldiers, compared to 405,000 for the U.S. and 375,000 for Great Britain, and about 19 million civilians," according to Suny.

"The Soviet Union suffered $128 billion in damage; 1,700 towns and 70,000 villages were destroyed; 25 million people were made homeless; 31,000 industrial enterprises were destroyed; along with 65,000 kilometers of railroad track, 17 million cattle, 27 million sheep and goats, and 20 million pigs were slaughtered," according to Suny.

During the Second World War, some 5.7 million Russian soldiers fell into German hands. Of these, about 3.3 million died in captivity, according to historian Omer Bartov.

Although the Soviet Union emerged from the war as a military superpower, it took decades to recover from the human tragedy and economic disaster of the German occupation, according to Bartov in *Confronting the Nazi Past, New Debates on Modern German History*.

At the end of the war, the USSR was ravaged, "but at the same time, the principal victor over fascism and an ally of the

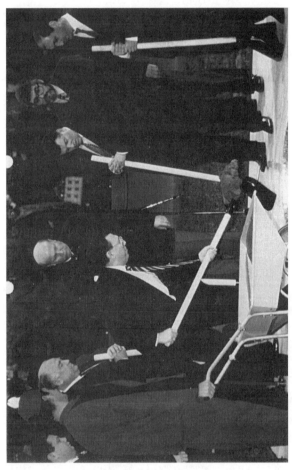

Groundbreaking ceremonies of the Holocaust Memorial Synagogue and Museum, at Poklonnaya Gora Memorial Hill Park Complex, were conducted in 1996. Shown, from left to right, are: then-Prime Minister of Russia Victor Chernomyrdin, President of the Russian Jewish Congress Vladimir Goussinsky, Deputy Mayor of Moscow Sancev, Vice President of the Russian Jewish Congress Boris Hait, and Vice President of the Russian Jewish Congress Vitaly Malkin. Second from right, without shovel, is Executive Vice President of Russian Jewish Congress Alexander Osovtsov.

most powerful states on the globe," says Suny. He also cites British historian John Erickson, who, in his work *The Road to Stalingrad: Stalin's War with Germany,* wrote: "Whatever the scale of measurement, the decisive role in defeating the 'Fascist Bloc' was played by the Soviet Union."

The USSR had not only stopped the Germans from taking over Russia, but stood as the strongest military power in Europe. It reoccupied the three Baltic states that it had seized in 1940; it annexed most of East Prussia; it took land from Finland and acquired the sub-Carpathian region from Czechoslovakia and Bessarabia and parts of the Bukovina from Rumania; and it reoccupied the eastern part of Poland. "Poland was compensated by large stretches of formerly German areas up to the Oder Neisse Line," notes Walter Laqueur in his book *Europe in Our Time.* "At the end of the war, Stalin extended the borders of the USSR and promoted the cause of communism."

All Eastern Europe and the Balkans, with the exception of Greece, Albania, and Yugoslavia, was now occupied by the Russians.

More Sites

Holocaust Memorial Synagogue and Museum in Memory of Jews Who Perished in 1941-1945, The Memorial Hill Park Complex of the Great Patriotic War, Poklonnaya Gora, in Ploshchad Pobedy (Victory Square), on the Ally (Avenue) of Memory 3E. Tel: (7-095) 149-19-07, (7-095) 148-08-87. Fax: (7-095) 148-19-07. "Having a Jewish Holocaust Synagogue and Museum at this prestigious location is an amazing achievement of the highest level for the Russian Jewish community," said Michael Steiner, director of JDC Moscow. "All official guests to Russia, kings and queens, presidents and prime ministers from all countries of the world, visit the Poklonnaya Gora, which is known as Memorial Hill Park. And now, they will visit the Jewish Holocaust Museum and Synagogue as well. The effect of this event in elevating the status of the Russian Jewish Community cannot be over-emphasized. The Russians and Jews shared the Great Patriotic War. Since the Communist regime never talked of the Jewish role in the War, it is important to Russians to know that Jews died in the conflagration," added Steiner.

The dedication, said Steiner, was the first acknowledgment of a partnership between the Russians and the Jews regarding the war, and a partnership in building the new Russia.

On September 2, 1998, President Boris Yeltsin dedicated the 32,275-square-foot, three-story building. Prominent Russian and Israeli architects Moshe Zarchi and Frank Meisler created the concept for the memorial complex. The complex includes a synagogue and exhibits emphasizing the Holocaust and the role of Russian Jews in the war. A rim of black stone wraps around the top of the house of worship. The cost of the entire project was between $15 to $17 million, which was donated by the Russian Jewish Congress in memory of Holocaust victims and the two hundred thousand Jewish soldiers killed in action in the Red Army in the battle against the Nazis. About five hundred thousand Jews served in the Red Army in World War II.

Moscow Mayor Yuri Luzhkov, Russian and world Jewish leaders, and other officials, including several U. S. senators, were on hand for the dedication of the synagogue. President Yeltsin paid tribute to the hundreds of thousands of Soviet Jews who perished in that war. At the end of his speech, he bowed his head in memory of Jewish victims of the war and Nazi genocide.

At the dedication, Mayor Luzhkov presented the new synagogue with a nineteenth-century Torah scroll. It was under the mayor's initiative that the municipality gave the Jewish community the land to build a memorial synagogue. The cornerstone of the synagogue had been set in the presence of then-Russian Prime Minister Victor Chernomyrdyn, who, it was reported at the time, attended the Jewish event and finished his speech with the Hebrew word *shalom* (peace).

Government instructions required the building to be a synagogue. The synagogue has a pyramidal shape and it contains pews. A lower level has been established for exhibits and a women's gallery. Documents, photographs, and objects related to the Holocaust are displayed along the walls of the round hall.

A crude homemade Chanukah lamp reminds one of the Soviet religious persecution and stands in contrast to the elegant religious items produced in the Russian Empire before the Communist takeover.

Services are scheduled to be held about nine times a year, including Rosh Hashanah and Yom Kippur. Sabbath evening services are held every Friday at 5:00 P.M. and on Saturday mornings. The services are led by Zonovy Kogan and are conducted in the liberal tradition. Prayers are also held on Jewish holidays. Services are not held every day. However, each day at noon the Jewish prayer for the dead is recited by a Khazar person. The Holocaust Museum and Synagogue are open Tuesday, Wednesday, and Thursday from 11:00 A.M. till 5:00 P.M., and there are tours on Sunday. But it is a good idea to call ahead and check on the schedule. The guides generally do not speak English, so if you do not speak Russian, it is wise to have a local English-speaking person with you, both for the Holocaust Museum and for the main Memorial Complex and Museum. Please remember that the main Memorial Complex and Museum are open every day from 10:00 A.M. to 5:00 P.M., except Mondays and the last Thursday of every month.

Most Russians do not know about Jews and the Jewish role in the war, as this information was suppressed by the Communists. As Zvi Gitelman points out in *The Holocaust in the Soviet Union,* "It remains true that the overall thrust of the Soviet literature was to assign the Holocaust far less significance than has been given in the West."

Much of the panorama of recent Russian Jewish history can be seen here. For instance, the medals of L.S. Polyakov that commemorate his work in industry and finance, as well as his activities as patron of the arts in the late nineteenth and early twentieth centuries, are on view here. Important religious items such as menorahs, candelabras, Torah scrolls, and Torah covers can also be observed. This is an educational institution, too. Among the many documents on display are the Decree of the Supreme Soviet that awarded the Order of Lenin to Dr. Lidya Timashuk, who provoked Stalin's Doctors' Plot, as well as Communist papers revoking citizenship from Russian Jews who wanted to move to Israel. Soviet documents that prohibited production of Jewish and religious and cultural items in the USSR are shown. Since the Russian Empire is the land of the *shtetl,* a wonderful display of *shtetl* life can be observed in the museum, including a painting by Marc Chagall. The museum notes that the world of the *shtetl* perished in the conflagration that was the Holocaust.

In the section dealing specifically with the Holocaust, there is much testimony. One can view documents on the administration of the Germans in the occupied territory, the Nazi's mass killing of the Jews, and examples of fascist propaganda, as well as religious items that survived the ghettos. Visitors to the Holocaust Museum in Washington may have noticed or known about a medal commemorating the exploits of Masha Bruskina. She was a student at a Minsk Jewish school, and a prisoner in that city. She helped to transport wounded Soviet officers to the partisans, as well as carrying out other brave deeds. When she was captured, she was 17 years old. She was then pubicly hanged. She became a hero of the Soviet Union, but the Soviets never acknowledged that she was Jewish.

In the museum one can see photos of Jewish resistance fighters. Righteous Gentiles in Russia and Ukraine who saved Jews in those lands during World War II are also honored.

The Jewish Holocaust Museum and Synagogue was developed in partnership between the American Jewish Joint Distribution Committee and the Russian Jewish Congress. It houses original documents and materials relating to the Holocaust in Russia. It also hosts educational programs and commemorations to Holocaust victims and utilizes interactive media to make the material as accessible as possible to various age groups, said the JDC.

Jewish losses in the war were proportionately four times higher than those of the population as a whole.

In 1939, the Jews numbered more than 3 million in the USSR, with about one-half of that figure living in Ukraine, according to Jewish historian Lucy S. Dawidowicz.

Jewish losses in the pre-1939 borders of the USSR during the Holocaust are put at about 1.5 million. Approximately two hundred thousand Jews died in combat, according to Jewish historian Zvi Gitelman in *The Holocaust in the Soviet Union.*

What hurt the Jewish community in the western part of the

The statue of Marshal Georgi Konstantinovich Zhukov, supreme commander of Soviet armed forces in World War II, is located in Manezh Square. (Photo credit: Ben G. Frank)

Soviet Union was that even after the war began, Stalin and his government never specifically warned the Jews about the Nazi onslaught. The government certainly knew that Jews were being murdered within the first hours of the invasion and that no Jew would ever get out alive if caught by the Germans.

Many Jews in the Red Army had "Russified" their names. But it is still possible to pick out hundreds of Jews who were crucial to the defense of the motherland. Jews did make a difference in the outcome. Major General L.M. Dovator, the brilliant Jewish commander of the 2nd Guards Cavalry Corps, was just one who stood out.

Of the eighty-six thousand Soviet partisans, twenty thousand were Jews. Some Jews formed their own partisan detachments. In small groups, they sought to protect those Jews who had escaped the German net and found refuge in remote areas. Some of these partisans were Misha Gildenman, known as "Uncle Misha," who commanded a group of Jewish partisans; Abner Kova, in Vilna; Moshe Uritsky; Hersh Gurevich; Tobias Bielski; Leyb Woliak; and Dr. Ezekiel Atlas. Their names will live on in the history of the war.

The highest Soviet state military decoration, the Hero of the Soviet Union, was awarded to 121 Jews.

The overwhelming majority of Soviet Jews lived in regions that were quickly occupied by the Germans. Indeed, they were at a disadvantage, for throughout the period before the war itself, readers of the Soviet press had been kept in the dark regarding the Nazi attacks on Jews. Stalin's neutrality "blinded" Soviet Jews to the mortal dangers facing them if an attack came. Thus, many of them stayed put and perished.

Historian Martin Gilbert says that once Germany invaded, the majority of Jewish inhabitants seized by the Germans were killed immediately, for the German invasion of Russia was in reality the start of the Holocaust. Following their invasion of Russia in June 1941, the Germans in effect conquered the whole of the former Jewish Pale of Settlement.

The Germans, according to historian Omer Bartov, "embraced the idea that the war was a defense of civilization against Jewish/Bolshevik barbarism, a war of racial survival to be waged at all costs." The average German soldier sank to a primitive level of existence under the extreme weather. The fighting was savage. The Germans massacred prisoners mercilessly and wiped out villages suspected of aiding partisans. Nazism also denounced the people of the east. The Russians were seen from the start as "Jewish Bolsheviks," "*untermenschen*," and Mongol hordes, according to Bartov.

During the war in Russia, Germany's process of dehumanization of the enemy was probably more successful than in any other war in modern history. The Russians, Slavs, Jews, Mongols, "all had lost any relationship to the human race," wrote Bartov. "Thus the Russians and Jews were not to be treated according to any accepted rules of military conduct, as they had lost their right to such a treatment both by their racial and cultural inferiority and by the historical role they had played against Germany," he goes on to say.

New York Times writer Richard Bernstein defined the Holocaust as "history's greatest single act of evil." In December 1941, the first deportations of Jews from western Poland and Ukraine to the death camps took place. By the summer of 1943, a million Jews in western Russia and the Baltic states had been murdered, wrote Jewish historian Martin Gilbert in the *Times Literary Supplement* on June 7, 1996.

Statue of Marshal Georgi Konstantinovich Zhukov, supreme commander of Soviet forces, Battle of Moscow, Manezh Square, near the Central Historic Museum. While here, gaze at the striking statue of Marshal Zhukov. When he took command of the Russian army at the gates of Moscow, his nation stood at the edge of defeat. He is perhaps the greatest Russian general who ever lived, a four-time hero of the Soviet Union. Zhukov was not an ideologue. He had fought in World War I and joined the Red Army in 1918. He rose quickly through the ranks and was considered a hard-driving, no-nonsense commander, with a total disregard for casualties. He won his spurs, so to speak, during the Russo-Japanese conflict on the Mongolian border in the late 1930s. Today in Russia, his reputation remains intact, according to authors Porter and Jones.

This Finnair jet is part of the fleet that flies five times a week from New York to Helsinki to St. Petersburg and five times a week from New York to Helsinki to Moscow. Helsinki is a leading East-West gateway. Flight time from New York to Helsinki is 7 hours and 55 minutes, and flight time from Helsinki to St. Petersburg is 1 hour and 6 minutes. If you travel on a Finnair flight to Helsinki you can reserve an air taxi to continue a journey to any of the more than 300 destinations in the former Soviet Union. In the 1950s, Finnair was the first western carrier to fly to Moscow, and later to St. Petersburg and Murmansk. (Photo credit: Finnair)

In choosing the hero to be honored here, one Russian journalist explained, the government could not very well honor Stalin, or Molotov, or even Khrushchev. Zhukov was the only one who was "clean."

You can still see the tank roadblock in Moscow's Leningradskoe Shosse, one of the suburban points reached by the Germans in their drive on Moscow, a drive that Zhukov's forces stopped.

Galina Ryltsova, Moscow Tour Guide. Tel: (7-095) 713-01-29. Fax: (7-095) 327-52-54. (The fax beeps automatically after a greeting in Russian.) This lady, Galina Ryltsova, is a wonderful tour guide. Her tours include: **Moscow Synagogue Tour.** This tour features a visit to the Moscow Choral Synagogue and the synagogue at the Poklonnaya Gora Memorial Complex; **Moscow Orientation Program,** which is designed for first-time visitors to Moscow who would like to shop in city markets and not the exclusive tourist stores. This combination sightseeing tour includes do's and don'ts on how to shop, drive, use public transportation, telephone, and how to handle everyday needs while in the capital; **Moscow Sightseeing Tour,** a three-hour tour introducing the traveler to the capital; **Red Square,** which includes a two-hour look at the most picturesque square in Russia, including visits to St. Basil's Cathedral; **Kremlin and Armory Museum,** which lets the traveler tour the Kremlin and then visit the armory's collection of gold, silver, jewelry, and Fabergé Easter eggs. This tour runs three to four hours; **Kremlin Cathedrals,** during which Galina also talks about the personal lives of the tsars; **The Diamond Treasury,** a one-hour tour of one of the world's largest and most memorable treasure chambers; **The Tretyakov Art Gallery,** where one will see a large collection of Russian art. This is a two- or three-hour tour; **The Novodevichy Convent and Cemetery,** a two-hour tour of the historical convent and cemetery that is the resting place for many famous Russian artists, musicians, actors, scientists, and former Soviet military leaders, cosmonauts, and politicians; **Kolominskoe,** a unique oasis in the center of Moscow, a summer residence of the tsars dating back from the time of Ivan the Terrible. This is a two-hour tour;

Moscow Metro features the beauty of the Moscow subway, which is considered one of the most beautiful in the world and was founded in the 1930s. Galina also offers tours to towns such as Vladimir and Suzdal, as well as a visit to a typical Russian family. **Isram World of Travel,** 630 Third Avenue, New York, NY, 10017. Tel: 1-800-223-7460. This is a U.S. travel group that provides tours to Russia and Ukraine. Morris Schuster, managing director of Central and Eastern European as well as Jewish heritage tours, knows the wonders of Russia, including St. Petersburg, Moscow, Kiev, Novgorod, and Russian waterway cruises.

All Ways International, 225 West Thirty-fourth Street, New York, NY, 10122. Tel: 212-947-0505. Fax: 212-947-7197. Web site: www.awintl.com. E-mail: allways@awintl.com. This travel agency specializes in Jewish heritage tours to Russia and Ukraine for groups, business travelers, families, and individuals. Tours cover Russia and Ukraine in 13 days and include Kiev, Jewish *shtetls,* memorials, Moscow, and St. Petersburg, as well as meetings with Jewish leaders. Tours can be expanded to include Odessa, Minsk, Vilna, Riga, Lvov, and Tashkent.

The Russian Travel Bureau, Inc., 225 East Forty-fourth Street, New York, NY. Tel: 1-800-847-1800, 212-986-1500. Fax: 212-490-1650. This company, an American company, has been in business for 30 years and conducts general tours to such cities as Kiev, St. Petersburg, Moscow, Vladimir, and Novgorod. It can customize an individual tour, as well as a Jewish heritage tour.

Suggested Reading:

Baron, Salo, *The Russian Jew under Tsars and Soviets.* New York: The Macmillan Company, 1994.

Cantor, Norman F., *The Sacred Chain: The History of the Jews.* New York: HarperCollins, 1994.

Clark, Alan, *Barbarossa: The Russo-German Conflict, 1941-1945.* New York: Morrow, 1965.

Colton, Timothy J., *Moscow: Governing the Socialist Metropolis.* Cambridge, MA, London, England, The Belknap Press of Harvard University Press, 1955.

Conquest, Robert, *The Great Terror.* New York: The Macmillan Company, 1973.

Cooper, Leonard, *Many Roads to Moscow: Three Historic Invasions.* New York: Coward, McCann, 1968.

Dobroszycki, Lucjan, and Gurok, Jeffrey S., *The Holocaust in the Soviet Union.* Armonk, NY, London: M.E. Sharpe, 1993.

Erickson, John, *The Road to Stalingrad, Stalin's War with Germany, Vol. I.* New York: Harper & Row, Publishers, 1975.

Figes, Orlando, *A People's Tragedy: A History of the Russian Revolution.* New York: Viking, 1997.

Florinsky, Michael T., *Russia,* 2 Vols. New York: The Macmillan Company, 1961.

Freeze, Gregory L., editor, *Russia: A History.* New York, Oxford: Oxford University Press, 1997.

Gerrard, John and Gerrard, Carol, *The Bones of Berdichev: The Life and Fate of Vasily Grossman.* New York: Free Press, 1996.

Gilbert, Martin, *Holocaust Journey: Traveling in Search of the Past.* New York: Columbia University Press, 1997.

Goodman, Susan Tumarkin, *Russian Jewish Artists in a Century of Change, 1890-1990.* Munich, New York: Prestel-Verlag, 1995.

Hosking, *Russia, People and Empire.* Cambridge, MA.: Harvard University Press, 1997.

Khaldei, Yevgeny, *Witness to History, The Photographs of Yevgeny Khaldei, Biographical Essay by Alexander and Alice Nakhimovsky.* New York: Aperture, 1998.

Meltzer, Milton, *World of Our Fathers, The Jews of Eastern Europe.* New York: Dell Publishing Co., Inc., 1974.

Palmer, Alan Warwick, *Napoleon in Russia.* New York: Simon & Schuster, 1967.

Pipes, Richard, *The Unknown Lenin: From the Secret Archive.* New Haven: Yale University Press, 1996.

Porter, Kathy and Jones, Mark, *Moscow in World War II.* London: Chatt and Windus, 1987

Potok, Chaim, *The Gates of November: Chronicles of the Slepak Family.* New York: Alfred A. Knopf, 1996.

Radzinsky, Edvard, *The Last Czar.* New York: Doubleday, 1992.

Riasanovsky, Nicholas V., *A History of Russia,* Fifth Edition. New York, Oxford: Oxford University Press, 1993.

Ripp, Victor, *From Moscow to Main St., Among the Russian Emigres.* New York: Little, Brown and Company, 1984.

Salisbury, Harrison E., *Black Night, White Snow: Russian Revolutions, 1905-1917.* New York: Da Capo, 1981.

Scammell, Michael, *Solzhenitsyn: A Biography.* New York: Norton, 1984.

Schwarz, Solomon M., *The Russian Revolution of 1905, the Worker's Movement and the Formation of Bolshevism and Menshevism.* Chicago: University of Chicago, 1967.

Schwarz, Solomon M., *The Jews in the Soviet Union.* Syracuse, NY: Syracuse University Press, 1951.

Service, Robert, *A History of 20th Century Russia.* Cambridge, MA: Harvard University Press, 1998.

Sharansky, Natan, *Fear No Evil.* New York: Random House, 1988.

Suny, Ronald Grigor, *The Soviet Experiment, Russia, the USSR and the Successor States.* New York, Oxford: Oxford University Press, 1998.

Vaksberg, Arkady, *Stalin Against the Jews.* New York: Alfred A. Knopf, 1994.

Vitukin, Igor, editor, *Soviet Generals Recall World War II.* New York: Sphinx Press, Inc., 1981.

Whaley, Barton, *Codeword Barbarossa.* Cambridge, MA: The MIT Press, 1973.

Wiesel, Elie, *The Jews of Silence, A Personal Report on Soviet Jewry.* New York: Schocken Books, 1987.

Yahil, Leni, *The Holocaust: The Fate of European Jewry, 1932-1945.* New York: Oxford University Press, 1990.

Moldova

Here we are in Moldova, formerly Moldovia, also once known as Bessarabia, a country of 4.5 million inhabitants, 65 percent of whom are Rumanian.

Moldova is a nation that is landlocked. It lies west of the Carpathian mountains and between the Prut and Dniestr Rivers. Once a part of the Soviet Union, it is sandwiched between Rumania and Ukraine. Its two main areas are the provinces of Bessarabia and Transnistria. Bessarabia was part of the Pale of Settlement in tsarist times. After World War I, Rumania acquired Bessarabia and held it until 1940, when the Russians, with German acquiescence, grabbed the province. But one year later, Rumania allied itself with Nazi Germany, seized Bessarabia, and moved into Ukraine. At the end of World War II, Russia retook the area and also extended Communist domination over Rumania and other Eastern European countries.

Indeed, "the history of the Republic of Moldova is the history of two different regions that have been joined into one country, but not into one nation: Bessarabia and Transnistria," according to authors William E. Crowther and Helen Fedor in *Belarus and Moldova: Country Studies.* Its history has been shaped by the many foreigners who either passed through or settled here—Greeks, Turks, Tartars, officials of the Russian Empire, Germans, and Ukrainians. Moldova also shares much

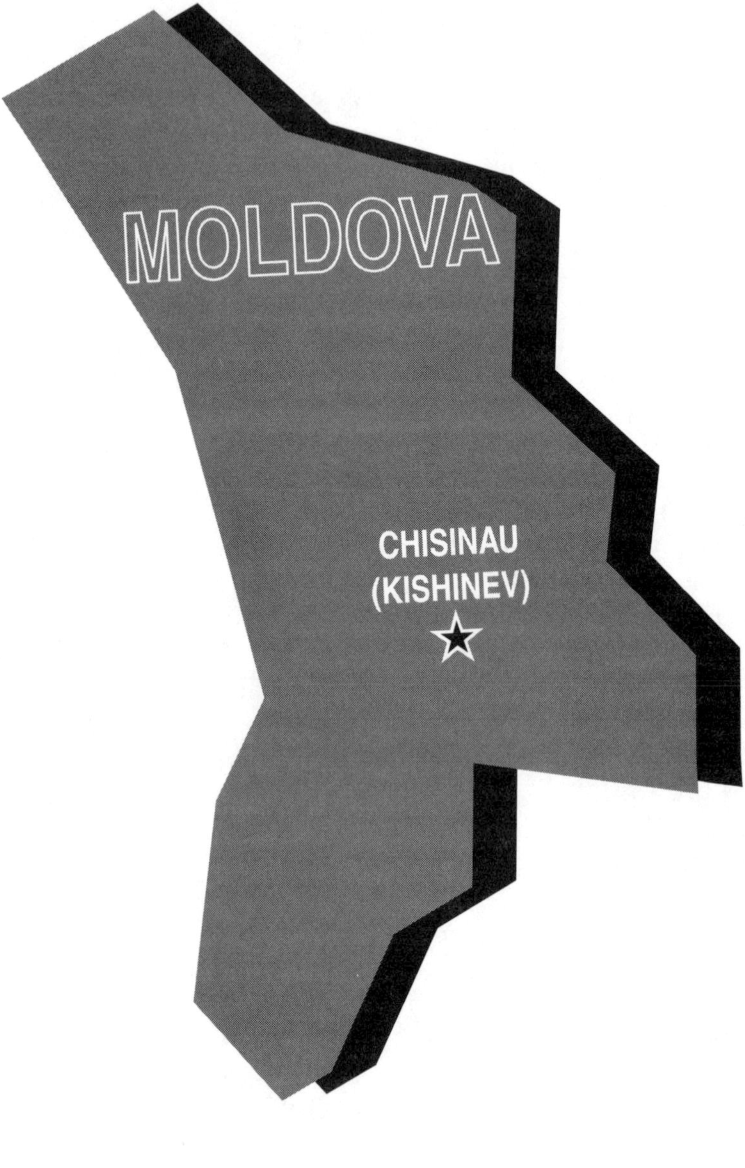

MOLDOVA

CHISINAU
(KISHINEV)
⭐

of the history of Rumania. "Each group has left its own legacy, sometimes cultural and sometimes political, and always unwelcome," note Crowther and Fedor. The ability of the country to make it into the twenty-first century depends in large part on how the ethnic groups manage to get along and how long they can keep out the next group of foreigners that attempts to take over the nation that broke from the USSR and achieved independence on August 27, 1991, the same general time that Ukraine and other republics became free.

Moldovans speak Moldovan, a dialect of Rumanian. The Russian language is also retained here, certainly by the ethnic Russians who constitute 13 percent of the population, as well as many others, including Ukrainians, Gagauz, Bulgarians, and Jews.

In some ways Moldova resembles its neighbor, Ukraine. The former, too, possesses rich, black soil in more than three-fourths of its territory. In fact, Moldova so excels in agricultural production that I was told that Odessans can travel a few hours from their Black Sea port to various cities and towns in Moldova to buy fruits and vegetables. But because of deep economic difficulties in this newly independent country and in Ukraine, people may not have the money to buy such produce.

Like many of the former Soviet republics, Moldova faces serious problems because it, too, relies on the former Soviet Union, which, with its own dire struggle to keep afloat economically, is in no position to help anyone.

A Brief History

Jews lived in what we now call the Moldova area, including Bessarabia, for centuries before the partitions of Poland in the eighteenth century. But it was not until Russia obtained Kishinev in 1818 that Jews came to this city in large numbers. From a population of 10,509 Jews in 1847, the Jewish population grew to about fifty thousand in 1897, according to the *Encyclopedia Judaica*.

Many today know the name Kishinev in a negative sense because of the pogroms that took place here, especially the one that broke out during Easter Sunday, April 6, 1903, a date that we shall soon examine when we stop at the Monument of the Victims of Kishinev Pogrom of 1903.

World War I shattered the community, as it was located in the battle areas. As we have seen, after the war, Moldova in essence reverted to Rumania, which ruled the land from 1918 to 1940. In its 22 years of rule, Rumania did little to calm the tensions between the Jews and their neighbors.

When the German-Russian agreement gave the green light to the Reds to take over Bessarabia in 1940, the Communists immediately moved to close Jewish institutions, as well as the Zionist movement, which was outlawed. Although Jews were considered a religious group in the West, they were a nationality under Russian government rules, even though, in an obvious contradiction, the Communists suppressed Judaism as a religion.

Jews were not spared when the Germans invaded in World War II; the massacres began immediately. Of the 65,000 Jews in Kishinev in 1941, 53,000 perished during the Holocaust, according to the *Encyclopedia Judaica*. By 1959, the Russian census reported 42,934 Jews, and in 1970 the Jewish population was estimated at about 60,000.

Chisinau (Kishinev)

Be careful, dear reader. If you go to recent books on Moldova or look for the city of Kishinev on very recent maps, you may not be able to locate the city immediately. You will hunt and hunt until eventually you find the name of the capital and largest city listed as Chisinau. In the Moldovan language, a dialect of Rumanian, Chisinau is the name of the city many know and still refer to as Kishinev. For the sake of continuity, in the rest of this chapter, the city will be referred to as Kishinev.

This tree-lined city with broad avenues has a number of good hotels, including Cosmos and Intourist.

Twenty-five thousand Jews live in Kishinev. Unlike Russia or Ukraine, the Jews in Kishinev were under Communist rule from 1940-41 and again after 1945, not for 70 years, as in the Soviet Union. Despite Soviet repression of religious practices, Jews in

Moldova managed to hold on to their religious identity, so much so that there are several Jewish newspapers in the country.

The government not only created the Department of Jewish Studies at the state university in Kishinev, but also called for the opening of a Jewish high school and has introduced Judaica classes in high schools in several cities.

Jewish Sites

Monument to the Victims of Kishinev Pogrom in 1903, Calea Esilor Street. Of all the pogroms that rocked tsarist Russia, the one in Kishinev in 1903 is one of the most infamous. It aroused a great outcry throughout the world. Many countries protested to the tsar regarding the murder of Jews.

This pogrom "differed from the pogroms of the eighties (1880s) in that this time the rioters concentrated on murder, rape and torture," says historian Shmuel Ettinger in *A History of the Jewish People*.

At the time of the pogrom, the population was about 50,000 Jews, an equal number of Moldovans, and about 10,000 ethnic Russians, according to Lindemann. In the pogrom, 49 Jews were killed, 500 injured, and 1500 homes and shops were vandalized in this city that at the time was the capital of Bessarabia.

Among the troublemakers who stirred up the pogrom was an anti-Semitic journalist, Pavolachi Krushevan, who conducted a "scurrilous campaign against the Jews," writes Lindemann. Ettinger reiterates what others have said: "The government of Nicholas II chose to fan anti-Semitic sentiment among the masses as a means of creating a political weapon." He adds that the tsarist regime started "to finance the publication of anti-Jewish newspapers," particularly Krushevan's newspaper, which spouted anti-Jewish hatred.

"Agents of the Ministry of the Interior and high Russian officials of the Bessarabian administration were involved in its [the pogrom's] preparation, evidently with the backing of the Minister of the Interior, von Plehve," says the *Encyclopedia Judaica*.

The agitation of Krushevan's newspaper and other reactionary forces had its effect. It was the usual blood libel and false murder rumors spread about Jews around the arrival of Easter, which often coincides with the celebration of Passover. The situation in the town was explosive, and soon after, the body of a Christian child was found. Moreover, a woman patient committed suicide in a Jewish hospital The mob became violent, and the soldiers who could have put down the riots stood by. (It was later proven that the child was murdered by his relatives and that the suicide was not connected with Jews.)

As stated earlier, the pogrom started on Sunday, April 6, 1903, Easter Sunday, and the seventh day of Passover. Rioters fell upon Jewish houses and stores. The cry of "Death to the Zhyds!" rang through the streets, according to historian Simon Dubnow. The mob "marched around smashing the windows of Jewish homes and stores and attacking any Jews they came across, in an eerie prelude to the Nazi Kristallnacht of November 1938," noted John and Carol Gerrard in *The Bones of Berdichev: The Life and Fate of Vasily Grossman.*

Sh'marya Levin, in his book *The Arena,* stated that the collapse of the Russian government began with the Kishinev pogrom. The pogrom showed what he called the "ghastly rottenness" which had entered the government. Did not the disastrous defeat of Russia in its war with Japan occur the following year?

Jewish historian Ettinger notes that von Plehve was "believed to be directly responsible for the bloodshed in Kishinev." Some time after the Kishinev pogrom, von Plehve was assassinated and Krushevan was shot. The latter survived.

The great Hebrew poet Chaim Nachman Bialik took the Jews in Kishinev to task for not fighting back, for being ineffective. Bialik said Jews reacted with "trembling knees" to the rioters and cowered before them, according to Lindemann. Bialik's poem about the pogrom was called "In the Town of Death."

Ettinger points out that after Kishinev, the "mood" of the Jews changed. "It was brought home to them cruelly and unequivocally that they could not rely on the authorities even for simple physical protection," he added. From here on, Jews would attempt to protect themselves, but would still face many difficulties, as now the tsarist police would disarm not the perpetrators, but the Jews.

Another result of the pogrom was that it spurred aliyah to Palestine, as these young, idealistic pioneers of the Second Aliyah were "shocked by the helplessness of the Russian Jewish community in the face of the Kishinev pogroms," according to Ettinger. He adds that a few years later thousands more Jews emigrated to Palestine, after they saw the hopes of the first Russian Revolution of 1905 shattered by the government's crackdown of liberal forces and the increase of iron rule in the country.

Other Jewish Sites

Kishinev Synagogue, Habat Liubavic 8, 2012 Chisinau. Contact Rabbi Zalman-Leib Abelsky. Tel: (372-2) 541-023 or 541-052. Fax: (372-2) 226-131.

A number of Jewish institutions are located at Diordita Street 4. Among these are: **Association of Jewish Organizations and Communities of Moldova,** Diorditsa Street 4. Tel: (372-2) 243-203, 225-557. Fax: (372-2) 243-203. The contact here is Semyon Shoihet. **The Jewish Cultural Society of Kishinev.** Tel/Fax: (372-2) 243-203. The contact here is Moisey Lemster. **Jewish Library/Jewish Community Center.** Tel: (372-2) 225-557. Tel/Fax: (372-2) 213-337. The library is named after Y. Manger. The contact here is Anna Batsmanova.

Hesed Yehuda, Jewish Welfare Center, Teilor Street 6. Tel: (372-2) 764-967, Tel/Fax: (372-2) 564-108. The contact here is Lev Gineizor.

Institute of Social and Communal Workers, Aleco Rosso Street 1, Twelfth Floor. Tel: (372-2) 438-458 and 438-420. Fax: (372-2) 438-400. The contact here is Ilya Vaiselbuch.

Schools and Universities

State University of Moldova, Mateevici 60, MD 2009. Tel/Fax: (372-2) 240-655. Forty-four Jewish students were registered here in 1999 for courses in Hebrew and Yiddish, ancient Jewish literature, Jewish history, history of the Jews of Moldova, Yiddish literature, and how to teach Hebrew and Yiddish.

Professor Yacov Kopansky, who is head of the Department of History and Culture of the Moldavian Jews, can be reached at the **Institute of Inter-Ethnic Research of the Academy of Science,** Bul. Stefan cel Mare 1, 2002. Tel: (372-2) 260-456, and 263-083.

Jewish Day School No. 15, Chabad Lubavitch, Independentei Street 5/2. Tel: (372-2) 775-994. The contact here is Sofia Shkolnik.

Jewish Day School No. 22, Romana Street 14. Tel: (372-2) 243-444.

Jewish Kindergarten No. 68, Chabad Lubavitch. Dima Street 11/4. Tel: (372-2) 440-142 or 441-110.

Organizations and Institutions

JDC Office, Alecu Russo Street 1, Twelfth Floor. Tel: (372-2) 445-202, 438-420, or 438-389. Fax: (372-2) 438-400. The contact is Yigal Kotler.

Israel Consulate, Tighina Street 12. Tel: (372-2) 245-587. Fax: (372-2) 544-280. Also located in this office is the **Israel Cultural Center.** Tel: (372-2) 544-282. Fax: (372-2) 544-280.

Jewish Agency, Pushkin Street 24. Tel: (372-2) 223-305 or 221-981. Fax: (372-2) 228-158.

Suggested Reading

Ben-Sasson, H.H., editor, *A History of the Jewish People.* Cambridge, MA: Harvard University Press, 1976.

Fedore, Helen, editor, *Belarus and Moldova: Country Studies.* Washington, DC: Federal Research Division, Library of Congress, 1995.

Gerrard, John, and Gerrard, Carol, *The Bones of Berdichev: The Life and Fate of Vasily Grossman.* New York: The Free Press, 1996.

Lindemann, Albert S., *Esau's Tears: Modern Anti-Semitism and the Rise of the Jews.* New York: Cambridge University Press, 1997.

Ukraine:
The Land of the *Shtetl*

Ukraine, with its three hundred to four hundred thousand Jews, has one of the largest Jewish communities outside of Israel. Only the U.S., France, Great Britain, and Russia have a larger Jewish population.

That should not startle us, even though many believe that this country is so far away mentally and physically. The pre-Communist Empire once contained the largest cultural and spiritual center of Jewish life. And that center was Ukraine. Even after World War I, more than half of the Jewish community of the Soviet Union resided in Ukraine.

From these towns and cities in Ukraine came the leaders of the Zionist movement: Golda Meir, an Israeli prime minister, born in Kiev; Ber Borochov, a founder and philosopher of Socialist Zionism, born in Zolotonosha; Itzhak Ben Zvi, second president of Israel, from Poltava; and Ze'ev Vladimir Jabotinsky, founder of the Zionist Revisionist movement, born in Odessa.

From the Ukrainian cities of Kiev and Odessa and other municipalities came the great Jewish writers Mendele Mokher Seforim, Sholom Aleichem, Chaim Nachman Bialik, Isaac Babel, and Vasily Grossman, just to name a few.

What type of land was this that gave birth to such wonderful, talented people? Often called the "breadbasket of Europe," Ukraine is the land of the "famous Russian black earth" that

"lies deeper than a plow can reach." If the Ukraine ever becomes well organized, this country could feed not only the former Russian Empire, but also much of East-Central Europe. In many ways, the Ukraine startles the visitor. Flowers unfold before your eyes in a "gold and green sea on which millions of flowers of different colors sparkle," wrote Nikolai Gogol. "Meadows as beautiful as the Elysian Fields . . . domestic and wild birds and animals are so plentiful that it makes one think that this is the birthplace of Ceres and Diana," said a sixteenth-century document describing Ukraine. The authors of the document wrote the country was a "Promised Land, a land of 'rivers of milk and honey.'" Whoever has been to Ukraine "can never leave her because she attracts men as the magnet attracts iron," according to W.E.D. Allen's *The Ukraine, A History.* The above was written, of course, before the industrial age, but even today if you travel outside the cities and towns to the countryside, "it is a beautiful universe."

Roots

The ancestors of millions of American Jews sailed to the "Land of the Free" at the turn of the century because the U.S. was the one land, more than any other in history, which had given Jews religious freedom, opportunity, and equality before the law.

To most American Jews, the word "roots" means Eastern Europe, especially the pre-1917 Russian Empire, including Russia, Belarus (or White Russia), but especially Ukraine.

The ancestors of many American Jews emigrated from the Volhynia or Podolia *gubernia* (provinces) in Ukraine. This area was also the "first arena" of the Chassidim. The group's founder, Israel Ba'al Shem Tov, and his followers, were from these provinces, according to the *Encyclopedia Judaica.*

Most American Jews rely heavily on legends, stories, and folktales. And while fire and war obliterated some records, the fall of Communism has made it easier to access old records. In some cases, the story of each person in those papers would tell the story of Jews in Ukraine. Perhaps one reason that our forebears did not reveal much of Ukraine in many cases was that this was the land of the pogroms, which they most likely wanted to forget. Ukraine had been seared into Jewish historical memory as synonymous with "suffering." Estimates claim that more Jews were killed here—in the range of hundreds of thousands during the 300-year period before the Bolshevik Revolution of 1917—than anywhere else in the world. Between 1919 and 1920, during the Russian Civil War alone, more than 1,200 pogroms were counted, with more than 150,000 reported deaths, according to Orlando Figes.

Ukraine became an independent country in 1991. Early in their history, the Muscovites had taken it upon themselves to be called "Great Russians," and they and others called Ukrainians "Little Russians." No longer. Today, the new nation proudly waves its own flag, boasts its own president and prime minister, assigns its own ambassadors to foreign lands, issues its own passport and visa requirements, and raises its own army and navy.

Ukraine is bound on the north by Belarus and Russia; on the east by Russia; on the south by the Black Sea and the Sea of Azov; on the southwest by Romania and Moldova; and on the west by Hungary, Slovakia, and Poland. Under the Soviets, Ukraine was called the Ukrainian Soviet Socialist Republic of the Union of Soviet Socialist Republics (USSR). Now a founding member of the present Commonwealth of Independent States (CIS), Ukraine has always had its own seat in the United Nations.

Ukraine, with its 233,089 square miles of area, is the size of France and Denmark combined, twice the size of Arizona, and the third largest of the former Soviet republics. In 1999, it was estimated that 52.1 million people lived in this, the second-largest country in Europe. Only Russia, its eastern neighbor, is larger. Kiev is its largest city (2,616,000), followed by Kharkov (1,618,000), Odessa (1,106,000), and Lvov (798,000). This land is made up of about 73 percent Ukrainians and 22 percent Russians. They live side by side with Belarussians, Moldovans, Hungarians, Bulgarians, Poles, Crimean Tartars, and, of course, Jews. Most of the Tartars were forcibly transported to Central Asia in 1944 for "anti-Soviet activities during World War II."

Partly because of Russification, the Russian language is still spoken in the big cities, but Ukrainian, a Slavic language close to Russian, is gaining acceptance. The Orthodox Church is the main religion, while there are Baptists and a number of sects, as well as Jews. The Uniate Church (Greek Catholic) remains predominant in western Ukraine. The western Ukrainians maintain historical ties to the West, ties that go back to the Hapsburg Empire.

Parts of Ukraine have often been in dispute. For example, even now, the status of the Crimean Peninsula, inhabited largely by ethnic Russians, is troublesome. To mark the three-hundredth anniversary of the union between Russia and Ukraine, the Crimea was the birthday gift of Nikita Khrushchev, who handed it over to Ukraine in 1954 as a symbol of the friendship and solidarity between the two peoples, according to writer and editor Michael Mandelbaum.

The Crimea, which has no border with Russia, is ruled today by Ukraine, even though about 70 percent of the present Crimean population is Russian. Called the Crimea Autonomous Republic, it has been elevated from an oblast (province) to an autonomous status, with the right to form its own government. While the threat of conflict between Russia and Ukraine over the Crimea has diminished greatly in the last few years, many Russian leaders want it back, observes David Remnick, editor of the *New Yorker* and author of several books on Russia.

Before the breakup of the USSR, this highly industrialized country, possessing vast mineral resources, once produced nearly half of the former Soviet Union's iron ore and 40 percent of its pig iron. Huge deposits of coal, manganese, bauxite, titanium, and salt are all here in the Donets Basin area. Coal and nuclear fission are the leading sources of energy, with each accounting for roughly 30 percent of Ukraine's domestic energy production.

Democracy is functioning and developing here, including the advent of free parliamentary elections. Civil liberties are preserved, such as freedom of speech and freedom of religion and assembly, although government pressure is often brought to bear against newspapers. Regarding civil rights, it has been reported also "that police, prisons and the court system are still basically Soviet, with many abuses," such as corruption and inefficiency. The *New York Times* and other publications have said that Ukraine remains saddled with "Soviet-era bureaucrats and Soviet ways." Other problems appearing on the political screen tend to be holdovers from the Soviet regime.

Still, as Michael Wines wrote in the *New York Times,* the country also boasts "something no other former Soviet state has: a second freely elected President. If it is poor, Ukraine is also stable, democratic and—for the moment at least—insistent on remaining sovereign."

Yet, it is reported that the legal and court system remains under the Soviet structure and needs to be revised. The constitution of 1996 was written to allow a transitional period until the year 2001. Parliament can at that time adopt a new legal system. A presidential election was set for October 1999.

But today the economy is highly dependent on the former Soviet republics for oil and natural gas. It is this reliance that most Ukrainians are trying to alter, both economically and politically, while some say that there should be closer political and economic ties with Russia.

Ukraine has tried to bind itself with Europe because it suspects Moscow's long-term intentions. Ukraine's foreign policy appears to balance "gradual but steady integration into Europe's political and economic structures with constructive, friendly relations with Russia," say authors John Edward Mroz and Oleksandr Pavlink.

NATO and the U.S.

Strategically placed between an expanding NATO and a resentful Russia, Ukraine has even been labeled "Eastern Little Poland."

The independence of Ukraine has fundamentally altered the status of other Central and East European countries. Now the latter find themselves separated from Russia by Ukraine. In any analysis of Eastern Europe, a new iron curtain in the East most likely will be impossible if Ukraine enjoys a positive relationship with both the West and Russia. That is why Ukraine is extremely important to the U.S., to the extent that for the most part of the 1990s the Ukrainian economy was propped up by the U.S. and the International Monetary Fund. Surprising to many, Ukraine is the third-largest recipient of U.S. aid after Israel and Egypt. Recognizing the geopolitical importance of Ukraine as a buffer between Russia and NATO's Central European states, the U.S. provides about $225 million in aid to Ukraine, with approximately $100 million going to Russia. The U.S. sees Ukraine as containing vast natural resources, a large population, and potential economic power, or put another way, a "small superpower."

Meanwhile, perhaps wisely, Ukraine conducts a balancing act between East and West. Still, in 1999 it welcomed the eastward expansion of NATO, and hoped that the addition of Poland, Hungary, and the Czech Republic into NATO would contribute to the "further promotion of the ideals of democracy and liberty on our continent."

A Brief History

Until it became independent in 1991, parts of Ukraine were ruled by an array of East European powers, including Poland, Lithuania, Poland-Lithuania, Austria, Czechoslovakia, Rumania, and of course, Russia. Its borders were as "flexible as its political fortune."

Only at the end of the eighteenth century, writes historian Bertram D. Wolfe, "with the defeat of the Turks, the partition of Poland, and the dissolution of the free Cossack settlements, did Moscovy's power expand securely through the Ukraine to the shores of the Black Sea."

Interestingly, Ukraine may have a history that is more than two thousand years old, but it only got its name, "Ukraine," in the eighteenth century. During the period from March 1917 to August 1920, Ukraine established a National Council (the Rada), which in January 1918 proclaimed the separation of Ukraine from Russia, but the parting never stuck. In August 1920, during the Civil War, the Red Army conquered Ukraine from the Whites and returned the country to Russia.

While it may not have been an independent state before 1991, thousands of years before the beginning of written history, various tribes roamed this fertile area, according to W.E.D. Allen. In 1500 B.C., nomadic herders settled in the region. They were followed by the Armenians, Scythians, Greeks, Sarmatians, Germanic tribes, and Huns.

During the 800s, Slavic civilization arrived on the scene, when an east Slavic state was established in Kiev. We know it as Kievan Rus, and we shall hear more about this when we visit Kiev itself. But for now, let us note for the record that in 988, Vladimir, grand prince of Kiev from 980 to 1015, chose Orthodox Christianity as the area's, and subsequently Russia's, religion. Not only did Rus sprout its roots in Kiev, but it also settled its citizens along other points on the river route between the Black and Baltic Seas. In 1240, Batu Khan, grandson of Genghis Khan, leveled the city on the Dnieper, a city that would decline when the Crusades opened the eastern Mediterranean to Christian shipping.

Polish Influence

Lithuania-Poland had annexed Kiev in 1320, and the Jews were granted certain rights ensuring their safety and prosperity. Some Jews collected taxes, and a few amassed fortunes.

The dynastic union of Poland and Lithuania in 1386 opened up the Ukraine to Polish expansionism, and the relationship between Poland and Ukraine has been difficult ever since. But then again everyone, including the Poles, the Ukrainian nobility, and certainly the Russians, would treat Ukraine as a colony. When the Poles moved further east into Ukraine they subjected the peasants to local lords and agents, and the latter often were Jews. In 1569, Ukraine found itself only under Polish rule, rather than that of Polish-Lithuanian control.

But the Poles could not control Ukraine. From 1624 to 1638, Cossacks and peasants rebelled and only with difficulty did the Poles put down the uprising, according to historian Nicholas V. Riasanovsky, in *A History of Russia*.

In 1648, the Zaporozhian Cossacks, led by Bohdan Chmielnicki (whom we shall soon meet), supported the peasantry, and in alliance with the Crimean Tartars inflicted a crushing defeat upon the army of King Jan Casimir of Poland. Some call it the Ukrainian War of Independence. As we shall see, it was a catastrophe for the Jews.

Chmielnicki signed the Peace of Zborov in 1649. Realizing his inability to win a victory over Poland, Chmielnicki then appealed to Tsar Alexis, asking him to take Ukraine under his protection. In this, the tsar saw his chance to regain Kievan Rus. As history has shown, one should never ask the Russian bear for protection. Chmielnicki wanted an autonomous duchy, but he never got it. In January 1654, the Cossacks took an oath of allegiance to the tsar at the signing of the Treaty of Pereyaslav.

There is much debate on the significance of that treaty, whereby the Ukrainians swore loyalty to the tsar. "It would seem that contrary to the opinion of many Ukrainian historians the new arrangement represented unconditional Ukrainian acceptance of the authority of Moscow," according to Riasanovsky.

But the Ukrainians, he adds, have a point in their complaints against the Russians, a group that "eventually abrogated entirely the considerable autonomy granted to the Ukrainians after they had sworn allegiance to the Muscovite Tsar, and which imposed or helped to impose upon them many heavy burdens and restrictions, including serfdom and measures meant to arrest development of Ukrainian literary language and culture."

Ukraine was divided between Poland and Russia in 1667. Poland gained control of lands west of the Dnieper River, while Ukrainian lands east of the Dnieper had self-rule, but came under Russian protection.

By 1764, Russia had abolished Ukrainian self-rule, and in the 1790s, she took control of all of Ukraine, except Galicia, which Austria ruled from 1772 until 1918.

After a few years of separation, in 1918-20, Ukraine became one of the four original republics of the USSR in 1922.

Famine

Ukrainians certainly suffered under the Russian Empire and Russian Communist rule. For instance, the 1932-33 famine— man-made mass starvation brought about by Stalinist collectivization of agriculture—was part of Stalin's plan to totally reconstruct Soviet society through rapid industrialization, points out historian Barbara Green.

The population of many villages starved to death. "Thousands of peasants who left villages in search of bread lay dead at the railway stations." Vasily Grossman, a great Russian Jewish writer, tells us that when the Kiev Odessa Express came past they would kneel there and cry "bread, bread. They would lift up their horribly starving children for passengers to see. And sometimes people would throw them pieces of bread and other scraps." Scholars have concluded that the number of people who died exceeded 7 million.

"Kulak" became the name applied first to rich, then to moderately well-off, and eventually to almost all independent peasants who showed hostility to collectivization, as well as to innocent persons who were so-called "kulak-minded." "Kulak" is also the Russian word for "fist." Stalin was determined to liquidate the kulaks as a class.

"In the end," writes Michael Scammell, author of *Solzhenitsyn: A Biography,* "it made little difference, for all who opposed the collectivization in any way were herded off to Siberia, either to swell the growing numbers in the labor camps, or simply to be let loose in the Arctic tundra to fend for themselves or die." It was all kept quiet. As many people would starve to death in this famine as fell on all fronts and in all countries in World War I.

Meanwhile Jews certainly were part of Ukrainian history. They settled in villages and towns when permitted.

Jewish Arrival in Ukraine

How did Jews get to Ukraine?

In the sixteenth century, Jews moved in large numbers into

Ukraine because of improved conditions. The Poles owned much Ukrainian land, but did not live there. They leased their sprawling estates to Jews, who were considered commercial bourgeoisie. Since the Jews were lessees of the Polish nobles, the Ukrainian townsmen became jealous of these "unbelieving Jews who administered the estates of the Polish nobles."

The Polish-owned complexes consisted of a single estate or a whole region, according to the *Encyclopedia Judaica.* In both Podolia and Volhynia, Jews collected custom duties and taxes on export and import trade. They returned immense profits to the absentee Polish and Lithuanian landlords.

As a reward for their stewardship, the Jews were allowed to corner the liquor trade in rural Poland and Ukraine. "They possessed retail liquor licenses as well as long-term leases on taverns," writes Norman Cantor in his book *The Sacred Chain: The History of the Jews.* When a Polish or Ukrainian peasant wanted his necessary shot of vodka, he had to buy it from the Jewish tavern owners, whose markup in this monopoly situation was indeed lucrative, adds Cantor. In 1804, Alexander I forbade Jews to continue in the liquor trade.

Ukrainian hatred against Jews was nurtured by the increase of the Jewish population in the country, and by their economic position. Later, when Jews leaned toward the Russian language and culture, they incurred the anger of Ukrainian intellectuals, who regarded this as collaboration with the Muscovite Russian government.

But for Jews, cultural life and social life prospered. At the close of the sixteenth century, there were about forty-five thousand Jews in Western Ukraine and up to at least one hundred and fifty thousand by 1648, the year of the Chmielnicki massacre.

Everything fell apart in the middle of the seventeenth century, according to Jewish historian Lucy S. Dawidowicz. Violence flared up in 1648, during the reign of John Casimir II, with the uprising of the Zaporozhian Cossacks, who were led by Bohdan Chmielnicki. This revolt, as we have seen, went on for 10 years. As part of a sideshow for the Cossacks, as one history professor told me, Jews were slaughtered by the thousands.

Chmielnicki hit hard at Jewish life in Volhynia, for instance. This province, one of the most densely populated regions of Jews in Ukraine and Russia, was a region in northwestern Ukraine, which has been part Russia, part Lithuania, part the Polish-Lithuania state, and later the USSR. Situated in the upper reaches of the Bug River, a tributary of the Vistula and the Pripet Rivers, as well as a tributary of the Dnieper, Volhynia was a center of Jewish culture, and its golden era lasted from the annexation to the Polish crown in 1569 to the massacres of 1648, according to the *Encyclopedia Judaica.*

Chassidism grew at an enormous rate in Volhynia and Podolia. Jacob Joseph, one of the most prominent disciples and followers of the tradition of the Ba'al Shem Tov, lived in Polonnoye. The leader and successor of the Ba'al Shem Tov, Dov Baer, lived in Mezhirech and Rovno, and Levi Isaac resided in Berdichev.

As noted, another important province of Jewish settlement was Podolia, located in southwest Ukraine. The Russians took this region, then located in southeast Poland, in the partition of Poland in 1793. The history of the Jews in the region was largely dominated by its position as a border territory between Poland-Lithuania and the Ottoman Empire. It was actually ruled by the Ottomans and in 1772, the area where one-third of the Jews lived was annexed by Austria and became an integral part of Galicia.

By 1881, there were nearly a half-million Jews in Podolia. But after the pogroms and the restrictive May Laws, thousands of Jews emigrated south to the "New Russian Lands" in Bessarabia or overseas to the U.S. and western Europe.

The *Encyclopedia Judaica* says 88 Jewish communities with more than 1,000 Jews each existed in Podolia in 1897, including Kamenets-Podolski, Balta, Mogilev, Vinnitsa, Proskurov, Tulchin, Bershad, Medzibozh, Chmielnik, Bar, Bogopol, Krivoye, Ozero, and Nemirov.

That same year, the occupational structure of the Jewish population of Ukraine consisted of 43.3.percent commerce, 32.2 percent crafts and industry, 2.9 percent agriculture, 3.7 percent communications, 7.3 percent private services, 5.8 percent public services, and 4.8 percent of no permanent occupation.

Shtetl

Two million Jews lived in Ukraine and the southern lands of "New Russia" by the end of the nineteenth century. According to the census of 1897, the Jewish population amounted to 41 percent in the towns of Volhynia and Podolia. Most lived in what we now call the *shtetl,* the little towns made famous by such writers as Sholom Aleichem and others.

Here is one description of the *shtetl* by Sholom Aleichem: "From a distance it looks like a loaf of bread thickly studded with poppy seeds. Some of these houses are built on the slope of a hill and the rest are huddled together at the base, one on top of the other, like the gravestones in an ancient cemetery; big streets, little streets, back streets, alleys . . . a tiny place, stuck away in a forgotten corner, far from the great world and . . . all its bleak tumble-down little houses, huddled together without yards, without streets, without fences, like gravestones in an old cemetery . . . a small cottage with small windows and brightly painted shutters surrounded by a garden full of bright yellow sunflowers that carried themselves as proudly as lilies or roses."

As Jews moved out of the *shtetl* and into towns and cities, especially after the 1917 Revolution, many assimilated into Russian culture, often not of their own free will, but because the practice of Judaism was being curtailed. For a while it was permissible to participate in the revival of Yiddish, but Hebrew was barred.

Another great writer who described the *shtetl* was Sholem Asch, a contemporary of Sholom Aleichem, Peretz, and Bialik. Sholom Asch not only wrote about the *shtetl,* he romanticized those little Jewish towns in most of his Yiddish stories. Scholarship on the *shtetl* continues, and a recent contribution to this study is the 1998 volume, *There Once Was a World: A Nine-Hundred-Year Chronicle of the Shtetl of Eishyshok,* by Dr. Yaffa Eliach.

The Civil War

The entire population of Ukraine, including Jews, suffered terribly during the Russian Civil War. This was another link in the chain whereby Russia has been scarred nearly to extinction by violence, wrote George Steiner. The Civil War between the Bolsheviks and the Whites that broke out in 1918 was no exception. And again the Jews were caught in the middle.

"The whole of Russia was awash with blood," wrote Scammell. "A Russian graveyard," was the way General Denikin described the Civil War. Sheer carnage made it one of the most violent in recorded history.

The south of Russia was "drowning in horror," added George Steiner, in the *New York Times Book Review,* of March 1, 1998. "All Russia was ablaze," wrote Alexei Tolstoy in his Civil War novel *The Road to Calvary.*

According to various sources, between 10 and 25 million people died from the White and Red terror, famine, and disease of 1918-1920.

The precise number of Jews killed by pogroms in the Civil War will never be known, says Figes. "The most important document to emerge from the Russian archives in recent years, a 1920 report of an investigation by the Jewish organizations in Soviet Russia, talks of more than 150,000 reported deaths and up to 300,000 victims, including the wounded and the dead."

Not since the Cossack uprising against Poland in the middle of the seventeenth century was the slaughter of Jews conducted on so vast a scale, mostly from Whites and guerrilla bands.

At the same time, because of "the virulent attacks on Jews, particularly in Ukraine, and because of the high visibility of Jews among the Bolsheviks, many Jews joined the Soviet cause," historian Suny points out.

Peter Ephross wrote in *Congress Monthly* that "while historical evidence has long pointed to the anti-Bolshevik White Army as responsible for the pogroms, more recent evidence has indicated that the Red Army was responsible for some of these actions as well."

The Reds also committed atrocities, though this practice was said by some to have been stopped by Trotsky, who headed the Red Army during the Civil War. Generally, the Soviets attempted to stop anti-Semitism and the resulting pogroms whenever they could, but it is doubtful if the population listened or obeyed them.

"During the Civil War, anti-Semitism was so rife among

Russians of all ages, parties, classes and nationalities as virtually to border on national psychosis. Reinforcing the traditional picture of the Jews promulgated by church and state for a thousand years was the fact of their sudden appearance in the army and government throughout Russia," writes Potok, in *The Gates of November: Chronicles of the Slepak Family.*

The Ukrainian peasant soldiers hated the Jews, who were perceived only as traders, innkeepers, and moneylenders.

White propaganda portrayed the Bolshevik regime as a Jewish conspiracy and spread the myth that all its major leaders (apart from Lenin) were Jews. Jews were blamed for the murder of the tsar, a charge that incidentally has yet to be buried.

The Whites were led by General Anton I. Denikin, and the counterrevolutionaries were headed by Admiral Alexander V. Kolchak and General Peter N. Wrangel.

Added to the fray were a group of Ukrainian nationalists commanded by the bandit Simon Petlyura (1879-1926). Thousands of Jews were killed by these hoodlums. Among Jews, Petlyura would acquire a reputation second only to Adolf Hitler.

When Denikin nearly conquered the entire Ukraine in the summer of 1919, the Jews felt deeply threatened. Petlyura was a leader of the Ukrainian Social Democratic Party and was prominent in several of the anti-Bolshevik regimes in Ukraine that rapidly replaced one another from 1917 to 1920. This categorization of "leader" is too kind, for he was a murderer of Jews, a *pogromchik*. He committed 40 percent of anti-Jewish atrocities during the Civil War, according to Suny.

I had heard about Petlyura from a Brazilian Jew who had fled the pogroms. "Petlyura was just one more Jew-hater following in the footsteps of Chmielnicki," it has been said.

After the Red Army defeated the Poles, the fortunes of the Petlyuraists fell and most of them escaped abroad, according to W.E.D. Allen. Petlyura, like so many figures of the Russian Revolution, retired to Paris, where some years later he was shot while on the Boulevard St. Michel. The shot was fired by a young Jew named Sholem Schwartzbrod, who stated at his trial that he was taking vengeance on Petlyura for the pogroms committed by the Petlyuraists. He was acquitted.

All the armies claimed to be fighting for justice, but, as one

Jew told Isaac Babel, the great Jewish writer, all of them pillaged just the same. Babel himself traveled with Semyon Budyonny's Red Army cavalry through the doomed cities and *shtetls* of western Ukraine and eastern Poland, including Dubno, Chelm, Belz, and Zamosc. These were "the scenes of Jewish pogroms and twenty-odd years later the scene of Jewish obliteration at the hands of the Nazis."

The Russians faced external enemies, too, during this period. White armies, including British and American units, landed at Murmansk as well as Archangel. Japanese and U.S. troops came ashore in Vladivostok. The Allies wanted to defeat the Bolsheviks so Russia would keep fighting in World War I and keep Germany and the Central Powers at bay. French troops landed in Odessa, where they joined German troops in Ukraine, although they were still at war with each other. Even so, by the end of the 1920, the Bolsheviks appeared victorious, and the counterrevolution collapsed.

When the Civil War ended in 1921, Soviets controlled Ukraine, and the Soviet Union finally reached some sense of stability. After the secession of Poland, Finland, and the Baltic States, and the inclusion of Ukraine, its western frontiers became clearly defined and lasted until the outbreak of the Second World War, according to Baron.

With the end of the Revolution and Civil War, Jews faced difficulties finding work, since they were often religious schoolteachers, clergy, and businesspeople, occupations not exactly praised by Communist authorities. Jewish youths, on the other hand, flocked to schools of higher learning and technical institutes. In 1897, Jews made up nearly 10 percent of the student population. By 1926, they held 16 percent of the seats in medicine.

"In the early years [of Communist rule] it seemed to many, not only among the Communists in Russia but also in Jewish groups abroad closely following events in the Soviet State, that the triumph of the Revolution had put an end once and for all" to anti-Semitism, according to Solomon M. Schwarz, author. But he adds in his book, *The Jews in the Soviet Union,* "anti-Semitism reappeared widely in the mid-1920s."

Lubavitch

In 1939, Rabbi Levi Zalman Schneerson (1878-1944), father of the late Lubavitcher Rebbe Menachem Mendel Schneerson, was dismissed from his post of chief rabbi of Dnepropetrovsk, Ukraine for distributing matza to needy Jews and for receiving the unleavened bread from a foreign Jewish community. For anti-Soviet crimes, he was sentenced to exile in central Asia, where he died in 1944.

Another Chabad rebbe, Rabbi Joseph Isaac Schneerson (1880-1950), who led Chabad from 1920 to 1950, and was the predecessor and father-in-law of the last Chabad Rebbe, "demanded that his followers teach Judaism under the Stalinist regime." He sent hundreds of chassidim to the Soviet Union to create underground *yeshivot*. He was arrested four times and was the one who moved Lubavitch to the U.S., according to Jewish historian Dr. Yaffa Eliach.

The first Menachem Mendel Schneerson (1789-1866), the Tzemach Tzedek, lived in early nineteenth-century Russia. The forebear of his twentieth-century namesake purchased a large tract of land in the Minsk province, in the Pale of Settlement, where Jews could settle free.

As time went on, even with reduction of anti-Semitism under the Communists, two decades of the Soviet regime would prove that Ukrainian anti-Semitism was not eradicated. Not only that, it would also show that during World War II, large parts of the Ukrainian population "wholeheartedly collaborated with the Nazis in exterminating the Jews in occupied Ukraine," states the *Encyclopedia Judaica*.

World War II

When the Nazis marched into Ukraine in 1941, the local Ukrainian nationalists hoped that an autonomous or independent Ukrainian Republic would be set up under German protection. The Germans instead brutalized the civilian population.

"If Hitler had treated the Russians with a little humanity or a little consideration, he might have had many more on his side, particularly in the Ukraine," notes John Lawrence.

Jews who did not get out from Ukraine and White Russia before the invading Germans perished in the ditches and ravines. It would take until November 6, 1943 for Kiev to be retaken, and almost another year until the entire Ukraine was free of German troops.

A fact that is not too well known is that a civil war took place at the end of World War II. "The Ukrainian Insurgent Army, a force of about 40,000 soldiers, fought both Germany and the Soviet Union for Ukrainian independence. It continued fighting Soviets until the early 1950s," says the *World Book Encyclopedia.*

About nine hundred thousand Jewish lives, or 60 percent of the Jewish people, were lost in Ukraine during the Holocaust, according to Dawidowicz.

The Ukraine SSR became a charter member of the United Nations in 1945.

Under Krushchev, the traditional hatred of Jews in the Ukraine was again shown with the approval by the government of the anti-Semitic book, *Judaism Without Embellishment.* The book appeared in 1963, under the auspices of the Ukrainian Academy of Sciences.

According to the census of 1959, underestimated to be sure, Jews were concentrated in the towns of Kiev (153,000), Odessa (106,000), Kharkov (84,000), Dnepropetrovsk (52,000), Czernowitz (36,500), Lvov (24,000), and Donetsk (21,000).

Ukraine has always seemed to be flashing news alerts before the world. Sixty-five miles northwest of Kiev, there are four reactors at the Chernobyl Nuclear Power Plant. On April 26, 1986, part of this station exploded, killing several people and spreading radioactive waste over a large area. The Soviet leadership was slow to react and reveal the full implications of the worst nuclear disaster to date.

Mike Edwards wrote about the disaster site in *From the Field, a Collection of Writings from National Geographic.* "Today, an estimated 180 tons of uranium fuel remains in the rubble, scattered or fused with melted concrete and steel. Ten tons of radioactive dust coats everything."

"A saga of technical incompetence and irresponsibility, of bureaucratic sloth, mendacity and plain contempt for human life, the Chernobyl affair epitomized everything that was wrong with the Soviet Union," wrote Anna Reid in her book *Borderland: A Journey Through the History of Ukraine.*

The World Health Organization estimates that 4.9 million people in the Ukraine, Belarus, and Russia were affected by the accident at Chernobyl. But the consequences, though obviously tragic in some aspects, remain unclear, says Edwards. According to rumors circulating in Kiev, as many as 10,000 Ukrainians have died from various ailments somehow connected with the accident.

Above it all, the Ukrainian longing for independence remained consistent. Ukrainian nationalism never quite died. The Russian Communists, as well as the earlier tsars, tried to suppress it. While Ukrainians possessed so-called "younger brother" status, their nationalists were the most prominent group in the 1950s gulag.

Independence At Last

On August 24, 1991, after centuries of foreign domination, which at times included suppression of its language, the Ukrainian Supreme Soviet, on behalf of the second-largest country in Europe, declared the independence of the nation of Ukraine. About 90 percent of the people would vote for independence.

The economic situation in Ukraine reflects 70 years of Communist management. Since independence, the Ukrainian standard of living has plummeted. Its turn to privatization and reforms are small indeed, even when compared to Russia. Unlike Poland, Ukraine has not implemented the structural reforms necessary to be successful. Heavy industry is still in state hands. Corruption and organized crime exists here, too. Since 1991, it appears that Ukraine's tilt toward the West causes anxiety in the minds of Russians, according to Sherman W. Ganett, writing in *The New Russian Foreign Policy*. What must also be on the mind of some Russians is their perception that "Ukraine has been the most anti-Russia of the newly independent states of the former Soviet Union and a role model for other former Soviet republics in their attempt to distance themselves from Moscow," according to an article in the *Financial Times* of January 7, 1998.

In February 1994, Ukraine joined the Partnership for Peace program of NATO, in a plan designed to promote military cooperation between NATO and non-NATO members.

The real danger in Europe at the turn of the century is that Russia will try once again to regain Ukraine, which has a weak economy and a sizable, restless Russian minority. But for now, at least, Russia, burdened by its own economic depression, does not appear to want to get involved in a fight with one of its neighbors. Both Russia and Ukraine realize that, despite serious disagreements, they should maintain a stable relationship. In May 1997, the two finally signed a Black Sea Fleet treaty and a Russian-Ukrainian Friendship treaty.

After the economic collapse in Russia, I often asked how the Ukrainians were faring. A Ukrainian travel person said, "You cannot fall when you are lying down."

With the fall of Communism, anti-Semitism in Ukraine stabilized. The Ukrainian government doesn't really want difficulties with the U.S. government, from which it receives much aid, as we have noted. Thus, it makes sure that there is no harm done to Jews, was one Kievan professor's assessment of the situation.

A new page of Jewish history is now being written in the post-Communist age. Some feel that with the aging population, the aliyah to Israel, and the movement of young people to lucrative positions in Europe and Germany, that Jews may not be here much longer. But don't count on it. Too many pundits have written off Jewish communities by saying a community is dead, and yet those very same communities are thriving today.

Suggested Reading:

Aleichem, Sholom, *In the Storm*. New York: G.P. Putnam's Sons, 1984.

Allen, W. E. D., *The Ukraine, A History*. New York: Russell & Russell, Inc., 1993.

Ascherson, Neal, *Black Sea*. New York: Hill and Wang, 1995.

Baron, Salo, *The Russian Jew under Tsars and Soviets*. New York: The Macmillan Company, 1994.

Bartov, Omer, *The Eastern Front, 1941-45, German Troops and the Barbarisation of Warfare*. New York: St. Martin's Press, 1986.

Bartov, Omer, *Hitler's Army: Soldiers, Nazis, & War in the Third Reich*. New York, Oxford: Oxford University Press, 1991.

Ben-Ami, (Arie L. Eliav), *Between Hammer and Sickle*. Philadelphia: Jewish Publication Society, 1967.

Cantor, Norman F., *The Sacred Chain: The History of the Jews*. New York: HarperCollins, 1994.

Clark, Alan, *Barbarossa: The Russo-German Conflict, 1941-1945*. New York: Morrow, 1965.

Conquest, Robert, *The Great Terror*. New York: Macmillan, 1973.

Dawidowicz, Lucy S., *The War Against the Jews: 1933-1945*. New York: Holt, Rhinehart & Winston, 1975.

Dubnow, Simon M., *History of the Jews in Russia and Poland, From the Earliest Times Until the Present Day, Vols. I, II, and III*. Philadelphia: The Jewish Publication Society of America, 1916.

Dubnow, Simon M., *History of the Jews, From the Congress of Vienna to the Emergence of Hitler, Vol. V*. South Brunswick, NJ, London: Thomas Yoseloff, 1973.

Ehrenburg, Ilya and Grossman, Vasily, *The Black Book, The Ruthless Murder of Jews by German-Fascist Invaders Throughout the Temporaily-Occupied Regions of the Soviet Union and the Death Camps of Poland During the War of 1941-1945*. New York: Holocaust Library, 1980.

Erickson, John, *The Road to Stalingrad, Stalin's War with Germany, Vol. I*, New York: Harper & Row, Publishers, 1975.

Figes, Orlando, *A People's Tragedy: A History of the Russian Revolution*. New York: Viking, 1997.

Florinsky, Michael T., *Russia,* 2 Vols. New York: Macmillan, 1961.

Gilbert, Martin, *Holocaust Journey, Traveling in Search of the Past.* New York: Columbia University Press, 1997.

Gilbert, Martin, *The Jews of Russia, Their History in Maps and Photographs.* London: first published by the National Council for Soviet Jewry of the United Kingdom and Ireland, 1976.

Gittleman, Sol, *From Shtetl to Suburbia, The Family in Jewish Literary Imagination.* Boston: Beacon Press, 1978.

Hamm, Michael F., *Kiev: A Portrait, 1800-1917.* Princeton, NJ: Princeton University Press, 1993.

Kuznetsov, Anatolii, *Babi Yar: The Long-Suppressed Version of the Complete and Uncensored Text of the Great Russian Novel of World War II.* New York: Pocket Books, 1971.

Levitats, Isaac, *The Jewish Community in Russia, 1772-1884.*

Lindemann, Albert S., *Esau's Tears: Modern Anti-Semitism and the Rise of The Jews.* New York: Cambridge University Press, 1997.

Malcanson, Scott I., *Borderlands: Nation and Empire.* Boston: Faber and Faber, 1994.

Mandelbaum, Michael, *The New Russian Foreign Policy.* New York: Council on Foreign Relations, 1998.

Milner-Gulland, Robin, with Nikolai Dejevsky, *Cultural Atlas of Russia and the Soviet Union.* New York, Oxford: Facts on File, 1989.

Pares, Sir Barnard, *A History of Russia.* New York: Alfred A. Knopf, 1968.

Reid, Anna, *Borderland: A Journey Through the History of Ukraine.* London: Weidenfeld & Nicolson, 1997.

Riasanovsky, Nicholas V., *A History of Russia, Fifth Edition.* New York, Oxford: Oxford University Press, 1993.

Ripp, Victor, *From Moscow to Main St., Among the Russian Emigres.* New York: Little, Brown and Company, 1984.

Scammell, Michael, *Solzhenitsyn: A Biography.* New York: Norton, 1984.

Schwarz, Solomon M., *The Russian Revolution of 1905, the Worker's Movement and the Formation of Bolshevism and Menshevism.* Chicago: University of Chicago, 1967.

Shabad, Theodore, *Geography of the USSR, A Regional Survey.* New York: Columbia University Press, 1951.

Tolstoy, Alexei, *Road to Calvary.* New York: Alfred A. Knopf, 1946.

Vernadsky, George, *Ancient Russia.* New Haven: Yale University Press, 1943.

Vernadsky, George, *A History of Russia.* New Haven and London: Yale University Press, 1961.

Wolfe, Bertram D., *Three Who Made a Revolution, A Biographical History.* New York: The Dial Press, 1964.

Kiev:
The Mother of All Russian Cities

On the lips of every Red Army soldier, even in the rubble of war-torn Stalingrad, were the words, "All roads lead to Kiev." The city had been captured by the Germans in September 1941. When Russian troops saluted an officer or greeted a Party member, they repeated their oath, "All roads lead to Kiev." Over and over again, they stated this phrase, until, after enormous sacrifice, their army reclaimed this Ukrainian city in November 1943.

For Jews, too, all roads may have led to Kiev, but too many barriers stood in the way.

On the lips of my late aunt Ann Frank, for example, who lived in a small Ukrainian town called Tomashpil, were the words, "Oh, if only to live in Kiev." There was just one problem. She was Jewish, and to reside in that city, Jews needed a special permit, special talents, and just plain special connections.

Sholom Aleichem, the renowned Jewish author and story-teller, wrote similar words about Jews traveling to Kiev. He called it "Yehupets" (the big city) as opposed to the *shtetl* (a small town). "You get there in the morning," he wrote. "You slip away at night and you're in a panic all day because if you're caught and served a *prokhodnoyo*, that is, an expulsion order, you're right back where you started from." One needed, he stressed, a *pravozshitelestvo*, that is, a residence permit. This segregation kept the Jewish presence in Kiev to about one percent, says

Lindemann. Aleichem fled Kiev, that "crazy commercial city," after the 1905 pogrom.

Yet, despite all the pogroms and barriers, some Jews, especially professionals and merchants, were able to obtain permission to live in Kiev, even though at the turn of the century, it remained a place where the police "hunted down" Jews without permits as if they were "homeless dogs." The Jewish historian Simon M. Dubnow described the operation as a "search and seize mission." Each policeman received 1,500 rubles for every Jew he picked up. Indeed, the Jews had to "ante up" the bounty money, or as Dubnow put it, the "condemned were forced to pay the hangman for the rope."

Author Michael Hamm, author of *Kiev: A Portrait, 1800-1917*, argues that despite the roundups and expulsions, a substantial Jewish community "had taken root in Kiev."

After the fall of the tsar, Jews could settle in any section of the city. But as history unfolded, Jewish residents, except for a short time in the 1920s and the first half of the 1930s, would never really relax in dangerous Kiev. If the pogroms, or the Civil War, or the First World War atrocities did not cost a Jew his life, the Nazi hordes and the death that came at the bottom of a pit in Babi Yar, in the bowels of Kiev, would finish him off. Later, more difficulty descended: the Second World War, the "Stalinist fury," and the struggle of the refuseniks to emigrate to Israel were all still to come. Finally, in 1991, freedom and independence came to the Ukraine. Jews were able to pray openly as Jews. They could belong to a Jewish organization. They did not have to follow the laws of the oppressive Union of Soviet Socialist Republics. They could, if they desired, emigrate to Israel.

The City

Once again, we are in a city of our fathers and mothers, our grandfathers and grandmothers. Today, expressing Judaism in Kiev is not restricted or off-limits. This city, which encompasses three hundred square miles and about three million people, stood as the third largest in the former Soviet Union.

The "Mother Russia" statue overlooks the city of Kiev and the Dnieper River. (Photo credit: Rozaline Kleyman)

Welcome to Kiev, the "mother of all Russian cities," or the "Jerusalem of Russia," because of its many churches. Once the very heart of Russia and literally the first capital of its huge neighbor to the north, Kiev at one time was called "Rus," or "Rossiya," which we know as Russia. The latter never let Ukraine forget that its umbilical cord was still connected.

As it is said, if Moscow is the heart of Russia, and St. Petersburg is its head, then Kiev is its mother. Greeting tourists and welcoming visitors, Kiev is neither monstrous nor monotonous.

Entering Kiev, your plane touches down to a relatively spotless airport. Your preconceived notions quickly melt away as you spy a surprisingly livable city. For sometime during your stay in this capital, which lies on the Dnieper River, in the middle of a rich agricultural and industrial region, you will say to yourself or to fellow travelers, as others have repeated before you, "This really is a pretty, hilly city with a lot of green parks and attractive boulevards. It was not ruined by that 'Bolshevik-Stalinist wedding-cake architecture.'" It flaunts its broad streets, fine old buildings, and beautiful churches. It may not evoke the hustle and bustle of Moscow, nor the splendor of Peter the Great's architecture and planning, but it still could return to its status as one of the most attractive cities of Europe, a prestige it flaunted when it stood at the crossroads of Europe and Asia, when caravans carrying spices and silks from the Orient intersected with the traffic that moved from the Baltic to the Black Sea.

You will want to visit most of the historical and architectural monuments in the city. Among these are the **Cathedral of St. Sophia,** completed in 1037 and reconstructed in the seventeenth century. Its interior is decorated with frescoes and mosaics. Despite having certain modifications made to it in the eighteenth century, this cathedral remains one of the finest and most beautiful examples of early Russian-Byzantine ecclesiastical architecture. This cathedral is sometimes called the "Church of All Churches." It stands in Bohdan Chmielnicki Square, where there is a statue of Chmielnicki, on whom we shall comment later. Close by is the baroque church of **St. Andrews,** designed by Bartolomeo Rastrelli and built in the mid-eighteenth century.

Tourists take the funicular Poshtova Ploscha *into St. Michaels, St. Sophia, St. Andrews, and the Chmielnicki Statue.* (Photo credit: Rozaline Kleyman)

You will certainly want to walk down the steep Andreyevskaya Spoosk, as this wide avenue leads past row upon row of souvenir stands, down to the river and into Podol, once one of the main Jewish neighborhoods. Some of the sidewalk merchants here are Jewish. I met several.

The Kievo Pecherskaya Larvra Monastery (Monastery of the Caves) is the main tourist spot. This is a "place of pilgrimage for many centuries," writes A. Anatoli Kuznetsov. The monastery is one of the most famous and important monasteries in Russian history. Here the monk Nestor wrote the earliest surviving primary writings of early Russian history. Much of the monastery, built during the eleventh century, was destroyed during World War II. While now a museum, it is still used as a monastery.

A visit to the **Tomb of the Unknown Soldier** is a somber visit, indeed. Besides the untold suffering and deaths of millions in Kiev and Ukraine, it is witness to the fact that 85 percent of the center of the city was demolished in the Second World War.

A jewel of the crown, Kiev, from about the ninth century to the thirteenth century, was one of Europe's greatest centers of commerce and culture, the center of political power in Russia. We are told by historian George Vernadsky that the prosperity of the Kievan state was based on trade and commerce. Kiev was about "as civilized as Western Europe," and often compared to Paris.

Today, at the beginning of the twenty-first century, life in this commercial crossroads and busy port still carries it forward as a central location on the Dnieper River, the same spot that first attracted the Rabbanites, the Karaites, the Jews, and the transient merchants of many groups from both east and west. Here rode the tribes of the Scythians, the Goths and their herds, the Huns, the Khazars (who conquered Russia when it was situated along the Dnieper), and the Tartar hordes.

Meander through Kiev's streets. Stroll through its inviting parks and famous main boulevards, such as the Khreshchatik. Visit its colleges, universities, research institutes, museums, and theaters. Hike through the seven wooded hills above the west bank of the Dnieper River. Here, grassy areas cover most of the west bank river slopes and form a delightful seven-mile "nature strip." Kiev is not called the "green city" for nothing.

This is a scene from along the main avenue of Kiev, the Khreshchatik. (Photo credit: Rozaline Kleyman)

Stop off at the modern, covered Bessarabska market. Lazar Brodsky left 500,000 rubles when he died in 1904 so that meats, fish, and vegetables could be kept fresh here, according to Hamm.

Wherever you walk, remember Russia itself began here in Kiev. This city, which was once Russia's chief city and ruling center, plays a pivotal part in the long saga of Russian and Ukrainian history. All expansion north and south began from here. When Kiev declined, Moscow, or Muscovy, rose to dominate all the Russian city-states.

A Brief History

The first Slavic groups lived in Kiev as early as the fifth century. As legend has it, the city itself was founded by a Slavic prince, one "Kiy," and his family. This mythical personage had settled in the hills on the right bank of the Dnieper.

The people of Kiev were ruled by three brothers and a sister. All of the brothers, including Kiy, settled on a nearby hill.

Later, another east Slavic group made their way to the great watershed of the river and teamed up with Kiy, the progenitor of today's Russians, Ukrainians, and Belarussians.

Historian Sir Barnard Pares points out that Prince Kiy's people were called the "Polyane," or people of the plain. What makes this period fascinating as it regards Jewish history is that located east of Prince Kiy's group were a people of Turkish origins, the Khazars, who practiced Judaism, and whom we shall meet up with later.

While Kiev was being settled, between 860 and 862, the people of Novgorod invited a Viking prince named Rurik to rule their city. Tradition says Rurik had established himself at Novgorod on the river Volkhov in 862, according to John Lawrence, in his *History of Russia*. While the story of Rurik is partly a romantic legend, there is an element of truth in his tale. He did become the prince of Novgorod. The Vikings, or "Varangians," as they were called, had the job of defending the frontiers and "it was the performance of this all-important duty that probably led to the shifting of the center of the future

Russian state from Novgorod to Kiev," according to historian Michael T. Florinsky. Kiev would become Rurik's base.

Since both Kiev and Novgorod were united by a system of waterways, the Vikings realized that from Kiev, they could control all traffic moving down toward the Black Sea, toward the Byzantine colony of Kherson, and toward the sea route to the Don River and the Khazar Empire.

An additional factor that brought the Vikings and other groups from Novgorod to Kiev was the Arab seizure of both the southern Mediterranean and Spain. This Arab intrusion undermined the commercial traffic between Western Europe and the Orient. In search of alternative trade routes, the Vikings began their exploration of the Russian riverways. As we have seen, they finally succeeded in opening a new way from the Baltic to the Black Sea and Caspian region, via Kiev.

Between the ninth and thirteenth centuries, the east Slavic tribes, together with the neighboring principalities, coalesced into the Christian state of Kievan Rus. It was ruled by the dynasty of Rurik, whom we shall meet as we visit various sites in Kiev. All rulers of Russia claimed they were descendants of Rurik.

Oleg must be credited with laying the cornerstone for what became the vast Russian Empire, for it was he who subdued rivals by bringing about the unification of Kiev and Novgorod into the principality of Kievan Rus. He also encouraged movement along the trade route that connected the Vikings with the Greeks, according to Patricia Herlihy, in *Odessa: A History, 1794-1914*. Thus, the circle was completed and Kiev became the political and geographical "pivot of the Russian state."

The next major development occurred when Rurik's descendent, Svyatoslav—who reigned from 964 to 973—broke the power of the Khazars.

Enter Vladimir, who seized Kiev in 980 and ruled it until 1015. In 988, he converted to Christianity and the city entered the world stage. According to legend, representatives from the world's religions were invited to present arguments on the value of their religion for Vladimir and his people.

So Jews from Khazaria were invited to visit Vladimir to try to advance arguments on why he should convert to Judaism. He rejected the Jewish arguments, according to Salo Baron in his *The Russian Jew Under Tsars and Soviets*, primarily because the Jewish spokesman had purportedly replied to his question of where the Jews lived by saying, "We do not (live in Jerusalem) for the Lord was wroth with our forefathers, and scattered us all over the earth for our sins, while our land was given away to the Christians." Thereupon Vladimir exclaimed, "How then dare you teach others when you yourselves are rejected by God and scattered? If God loved you, you would not be dispersed in strange lands. Do you intend to inflict the same misfortune on me?"

"Vladimir's triumphs over competing rulers and neighboring powers established him as the sole ruler of the East Slav tribes, and gave his heirs a monopoly over the right to succeed him," notes Janet Martin, in *Russia: A History*. Vladimir hoped to make Christianity the state religion. He introduced Christianity to other areas of Russia and the city on the Dnieper was soon called the "City of Churches," in a country that was to be predominantly a Slav nation.

The Russian choice of Greek Orthodoxy is fateful for Jews. Novelist Chaim Potok says that when Orthodoxy arrived from Byzantium, it brought a new hatred for the Jew that lasted for centuries, on into Muscovy and for centuries among the Romanovs.

Kiev's increased business activity brought with it an increase in its population, "The expansion of Kiev's commercial and craft activity was accompanied by an increase in its population," points out writer Janet Martin. "By the end of the twelfth century between 36,000 and 50,000 persons—princes, soldiers, clergy, merchants, artisans, unskilled workers, and slaves—resided in the city. Kiev, the political capital of Kievan Rus, had become the ecclesiastical, commercial, and artisanal center of the realm as well," she added.

Kiev's geographical position, its greatest asset in the ninth and tenth centuries proved its undoing two hundred years later, adds Florinsky, as tribe after tribe flew across the flat Asian steppe and attached this "stronghold of Eastern Slavic Christianity."

In 1169, Prince Andrew attacked and conquered Kiev and proclaimed the city of Vladimir, five hundred miles northeast of Kiev, as the new capital. It would be only a matter of time before the center of Russia moved to Moscow.

In Kiev, Jews "stood astride the cradle of ancient Russia," and watched the rise of Muscovite Russia. Indeed, ancient Russian sources mention "the Gate of the Jews," in Kiev. Kiev's Jewish community would grow in both size and influence. It was a community that functioned quite well in 986. Historian George Vernadsky also tells us that Jews served as a "link between the German and Czech commerce and the Russian."

Actually, it has been 20 centuries since a small group of Jews established a Jewish colony on the shores of the Black Sea, according to historian Simon M. Dubnow. Jewish settlements included the Transcaucasus, the Crimea (from at least the fifth century), and certainly Khazaria, where the rulers converted to Judaism in 741.

The Khazars

Here we must pause to discuss and meet the Khazars, a nomadic people of Turkic descent who held the Black Sea steppes in the eighth and ninth centuries.

Talk about Jews in Russia and someone, somewhere, will immediately exclaim excitedly, "The Khazars!" At the peak of their power, the Khazars played a crucial role in shaping the destinies of medieval and eventually modern Europe, says writer Arthur Koestler, in *The Thirteenth Tribe: The Khazar Empire and its Heritage.* The point is that the Khazars converted to Judaism en masse. They in turn were conquered by the Russians and absorbed into their environment, meaning, therefore, that the Jews were certainly found among the early Russians.

Some observers point out that when Charlemagne was crowned Emperor of the West, the eastern confines of Europe, between the Caucasus and the Volga, were ruled by a Jewish state known as the Khazar Empire. There are also references in ancient Russian literature to the Khazars as Jews. Warriors were referred to as the "Zhidovin."

Who were the Khazars before they converted to Judaism? Author Milorad Pavic tells us in the *Dictionary of the Khazars,* that the Khazars are to be portrayed as "an autonomous and powerful tribe, a warlike and nomadic people who appeared from the East at an unknown date, and who, from the seventh to the tenth century, settled in the land between the Caspian and the Black Seas, where the great Eastern powers of the period confronted each other."

Khazaria acted as a buffer that protected Byzantium against invasions by the lusty barbarian tribesmen of the northern steppes—Bulgars, Magyars, Pechenegs, and later the Vikings and the Russians. The Khazan armies also effectively blocked early Arab invasions. This prevented the Muslim conquest of Eastern Europe.

Florinsky notes that "while preserving the nomadic mode of life, the Khazars were interested in trade, an interest that may be partly explained by the considerable influx of Arabs and Jews in their midst." Arab geographers noted that the "Khazars use the Hebrew script."

Many Jews from Greece, Asia Minor, Persia, and Mesopotamia found refuge in Khazaria.

The influence of the Jews had to be sufficiently strong to induce the Khazar ruler and many of the chieftains to embrace Judaism. Khazars, as we have seen, converted to Judaism in 740.

Significantly, since Judaism was not normally a proselytizing faith, this is one example of a Jewish state a thousand miles away from Palestine.

Jews did not totally disappear, even after the Khazars lost their imperial power and came under Russian and Tartar domination. Their populace was absorbed into the world of Kievan Rus.

The Khazar state never really recovered from the shattered series of blows dealt it by the Kievan Prince Svyatoslav, who in 965 gobbled up the Khazar Empire like an apple, without even dismounting from his horse, according to legend.

Interestingly, some historians believe that the Khazar tribes migrated to Russia and Poland and other areas of Eastern Europe, where, in the last few centuries, Jews have concentrated in large numbers. In his book, *The Thirteenth Tribe,* Arthur Koestler proposes that the Khazars are the ancestors of the world's surviving Jews. He conjectures that a substantial part— perhaps the majority of Eastern Jews and hence of world

Jewry—might be of Khazar and not of Semitic origin. His theory is that if this is so, it could be that Jewish ancestors came to Russia and Poland, not from the Jordan, but from the Volga; not from Canaan but from the Caucasus, once believed to be the cradle of the Aryan race; and that generally Jews are more closely related to the Hun, Uigur, and Magyar tribes than to the seed of Abraham, Isaac, and Jacob. If that is the case, then the term anti-Semitism is "void of meaning."

Be that as it may, we know that Jews lived and traded in southern Russia and that a Jewish presence was there before the year 1000.

Benjamin of Tudela

Our favorite medieval Jewish traveler, Benjamin of Tudela, met Russian merchants as he traveled through the Near and Middle East from 1160 to 1173. When he was in Constantinople, he wrote that he met traders from Russia who came to the metropolis from across the Black Sea, which he called the Sea of Russia, and said was guarded by the Empire of Russia. In the twelfth century, one of the city gates in Kiev was known as the "Jewish Gate," evidence that Jews occupied the section of the city close to it.

During the twelfth century, there is mention of Rabbi Moses of Kiev, who "corresponded with rabbenu Jacob Meir Tam R in the West and with the Gaon Samuel b. Ali in Baghdad," according to the *Encyclopedia Judaica*. At that time the Jews of Kiev communicated with their co-religionists in Babylon and Western Europe on religious questions.

Rabbi Petachia of Ratisbon traveled east about a decade after Benjamin of Tudela, along the route from Prague to Poland to Kiev, and for 6 days he explored the Dnieper River. It took him 16 days to travel through Ukraine, which he described as level. "The inhabitants," he wrote, "live in tents; they are far sighted and have beautiful eyes because they eat no salt and live among fragrant plants."

He did not find Jews in Ukraine, he explained, but he did locate Karaites, a Jewish religious sect, who would reach the Baltic by A.D. 1250 and the Crimea by A.D. 1500. They told him they had never heard of the Talmud. Actually, the Karaites "categorically rejected the Talmud and its homiletic methods as a burden that should no longer be borne and as human invention, coming from those who deceived the people through the force of tradition and their own institutional powers," according to *A History of the Jewish People*. They decried the resulting elimination of direct and individual contact between the Jews and the Torah and the fact that the people were led to follow the "evil shepherds."

Destroyed in 1240 by the Mongols, Kiev would never completely recover the splendor or magnificence it had enjoyed earlier.

Still, by the year 1540, Kiev was beginning to come to life again. About twenty thousand inhabitants lived and worked in the city and frequented six Orthodox churches. In the lower part of the city, along the bank of the Dnieper, a mixed population of artisans and tradesmen, including Poles, Germans, Jews, and Armenians lived in a section called "Podol." A stone castle commanded the upper part of the town.

The year 1569 is crucial in Ukrainian history. In that year, the Poles took over the rule of Ukraine and the area began to prosper.

The Poles sponsored Jewish settlement in Kiev, a fact that caused tension with the merchants and burghers of Kiev. "Jewish trade and settlement rights remained precarious in Kiev and the city's Jewish community almost certainly remained small," notes Hamm.

Over the years, those who had settled along the western borders with Lithuania and Poland became known as the White Russians. The descendants of the "White Russians" lived in Belarus. Those who moved south and settled in Ukraine became known as "Little Russians." Those who settled in the northwest around Moscow were the "Great Russians," according to authors James P. Duffy and Vincent L. Ricci in *Czars: Russia's Rulers for More Than One Thousand Years*. Russia itself, as we have seen, got a foothold in Ukraine in 1654 and took Kiev.

A reestablished Jewish community was set up in 1793, when the city became the economic and commercial center of the southwest region of Russia. By the turn of the nineteenth century, Kiev was being absorbed into the Russian Empire, according to Hamm.

Jews were generally barred from living in Kiev for the next hundred years, unless of course they could procure a special pass. Although Jews could not live in the city itself, they could settle down in Kiev Province.

But in 1861 two suburbs, Lybid and Podol, were assigned to Jews who were entitled to reside in Kiev, says the *Encyclopedia Judaica*. Tsar Alexander II (1855-1881), opened Kiev to Jewish settlement, and the community grew. These new citizens were wealthy craftsmen and merchants, industrialists, employees, and members of free professions. For the next 50 years, Jews were often oppressed, harangued, or killed in their homes in the surrounding countryside. As we have seen, those who did live in the city often feared for their lives.

With the toppling of the tsar in 1917, Jews became free, and thousands flocked to the cities. In that year, too, Ukraine opted for separation, and it was even protected by the German army for about a year. After the Russian Revolution, Kiev was overrun by refugees from the Bolshevik north. "The city had an atmosphere of frenzied excitement, with everyone living as if there was no tomorrow," it was said. In the ensuing Civil War, Kiev itself was occupied 12 times. Occupying forces included the Ukrainian Nationals, the Germans, the Poles, the Whites, the Ukrainians again, the Soviets, the Polish occupation, and finally, the Ukrainian Soviets on June 2, 1920.

After the February 1917 revolution, all residence restrictions were abolished, says the *Encyclopedia Judaica*. But then came the Civil War and the guerrilla gangster Simon Petlyura, an opponent of the Bolsheviks. His forces indiscriminately killed Jews. White armies committed "pillage, rape, and murder of Jews," which lasted until his volunteers were driven out by the Red Army in December 1919. Anti-Semitic agitation was widespread on both sides, with Red Army units also running riot. Pogroms erupted with slogans such as "Beat the Yids."

In December and January, the Red Army occupied Nikolaev and Kherson. On February 7, 1920, Odessa fell, and that

A synagogue in Kiev is shown as it appeared around 1920. (Photo credit: The American Jewish Joint Distribution Committee)

meant the end of the Civil War. The Whites fled across the border into Rumania and Poland, where they were disarmed, says W.E.D. Allen.

In 1920, under the Polish leader Jozef Pilsudski (1867-1935), the Poles marched into a ravished Ukraine. They were beaten back to the gates of Warsaw by the Russian general Mikhail Tukhachevsky(1893-1937). But the tide turned again and this time, the Russians retreated until peace finally came in the form of the Peace of Riga. Poland received large chunks of Ukrainian territory, large parts of Volhynia, and Podolia, including half the area of White Russia, according to Allen.

After the Communists came to power, Kiev became a major center of officially fostered Yiddish culture. The state set up a public school system in which the Yiddish language was used, although for indoctrination. Flourishing were institutes of higher learning and education, such as a Department for Jewish Culture at the Ukrainian Academy of Sciences, which was formed in 1926. In 1930, this facility became the Institute of Proletarian Jewish Culture, under the direction of Joseph Liberberg. Yiddish poets were prolific. Among those active in this period in Kiev were writers Peretz Markish, David Hofstein, and Leib Kvitko.

In 1922, Ukraine became one of the four original republics of the Soviet Union and was named the Ukrainian Soviet Socialist Republic. In 1934, Kiev was chosen as the capital of the republic. As rulers, both the tsars and Communist Russia pushed "Russification." The Stalinist regime favored Russian culture over Ukrainian, and pressured Ukrainians to speak Russian. Nearly all the important posts in Ukraine were filled by Russians, who ruled the country like colonial masters, says Figes. Still, the nationalist ideal of an independent Ukraine was never completely crushed.

Millions of Ukrainians, the majority in farms and rural areas, died from starvation after Soviet authorities forcibly took food from their fields in 1932 and 1933.

By 1941, Kiev was home to about one hundred and sixty thousand Jews. Jews had moved up the social ladder; they had become engineers, government officials, academicians, and

The statue of Bohdan Chmielnicki, in Chmielnicki Square, Kiev, one of history's chief murderers of Jews, is shown here. (Photo credit: Ben G. Frank)

professionals. But we must remember that about fifty thousand Kievan Jews lost their lives during the Holocaust.

In World War II, the Germans surrounded Kiev. After the great Battle of Kiev, the city fell on September 19, 1941. More than 600,000 Red Army soldiers were captured in the Kiev area. Authors John Gerrard and Carol Gerrard claim 400,000 Russian troops were killed in "the biggest military defeat in recorded history." Hitler called it "the greatest battle in history." Stalin had made an unwise decision that Kiev was to be held at all costs.

As for prisoners, it is estimated that only 3 percent of Russian prisoners would eventually reach their homes. They were deliberately starved by the Germans. Their camps were ravaged by typhus. They were pushed beyond endurance in forced labor gangs. Brutal medical experiments were conducted on their bodies.

After Kiev was captured, said the Germans, "all we need is one more attack, the house will cave in, and we can winter in Moscow." The result, of course, was different.

When Kiev fell to the Germans on September 19, 1941, after a fierce 80-day battle, it marked the end of Kiev Jewry. About 60,000 Jews out of 160,000 failed to escape the Nazis. It is estimated that most of that 60,000 were slaughtered by Einsatzgruppen C. Sonderkommando 4A, commanded by Col. Paul Bobel, who was under orders to exterminate the city's Jews.

A new German policy was enacted in occupied USSR—the systematic destruction of entire Jewish communities, writes Martin Gilbert in his book *The Holocaust*. No Jew was to be left alive. "Within five weeks of the German invasion of Russia on June 22, 1941, the number of Jews killed exceeded the total number murdered in the previous eight years of Nazi rule," Gilbert adds.

Statue of Bohdan Chmielnicki, Chmielnicki Square, Kiev. Most Jews do not know the name Chmielnicki. During the Communist era, Jewish students in the USSR knew the name, but did not know that he was the worst murderer of Jews before Hitler.

To Jews, he was a butcher, one of the most sinister oppressors of the Jews of all time. He was the initiator of the terrible massacres that began in 1648. One-third of the Ukrainian Jewish community was slain by Chmielnicki and his Cossacks in 1648. The *Encyclopedia Judaica* says that more than 100,000 Jews were murdered by the time the terror ended, about 10 years later. Most of the Jewish communities in Ukraine were destroyed. Some put the figure of Jews killed at 200,000; others at 500,000. Chmielnicki's hatred and jealousy of Poland was vented on the Jews, or as one Ukrainian Jewish history professor put it, the death of the Jews was a "side-product." He was bent on eradicating the Jews from the Ukraine, according to the *Encyclopedia Judaica.*

The destruction that Chmielnicki caused has been "etched like acid" into Jewish historical consciousness. Yet, his statue appears in the main public square of the capital of Ukraine. To the Ukrainians, who often stand and admire his statue, he is a hero. Ukrainian nationalists see him as a symbol of the awakening of the Ukrainian people. These nationalists insist "Polish magnates and their Jewish stewards" were oppressing them, and Roman Catholics were discriminating against the Ukrainian Orthodox Church. At the same time, some Ukrainian nationalists say this "hetman," or leader of the Cossacks, sold out to the Russians.

Russian nationalists view Chmielnicki as a government patriot who "led Ukraine out of Polish bondage," into "the welcoming arms of Moscow," says author Anna Reid. This of course eventually brought about the unification of Ukraine with Russia. But Chmielnicki needed more support, and to get Moscow on his side against Poland, he took a unilateral vow of loyalty to the tsar in Pereyaslav in January 1654. Russian and Soviet historians subsequently portrayed his oath as a merger of Ukraine with Muscovy, even a "reunification" of Muscovy with Kievan Rus. By contrast, Ukrainian historiography depicts this oath as "the beginning of an independent 'hetman state,' which lasted until the time of Catherine the Great," according to Hans Joachim Torke, in his chapter in *Russia: A History.* By the eighteenth century, as we have seen, Russia had incorporated Ukraine.

Author Anna Reid asks what possibly could have induced this socially respectable, middle-aged figure to start a rebellion that would kill hundreds of thousands of people? Could it have been a personal grudge?

Chmielnicki had a feud with a local neighbor who had kidnapped the woman he planned to marry. Having failed to win redress from the local courts or the Senate in Warsaw, in January 1648, the infuriated Chmielnicki fled to the *sich,* a large Cossack reservation, where he succeeded in persuading the Zaporozhian Cossacks to rise under his leadership, notes Anna Reid.

Calling for war on the Polish gentry, he employed slaughter, arson, rape, and pillaging. Landlords, Catholic and Uniate priests, and especially Jews, were hunted down and blinded, burned, decapitated, and even "sawn between boards," historians tell us.

With all his native ability, Chmielnicki was but "an eminent savage," writes historian W.E.D. Allen. Florinsky questions whether he deserved the imposing equestrian statue erected to him in Kiev and the aura of national hero, "defender of Orthodoxy," and empire builder that surrounds his name in the writings of patriotically minded Russian historians. He lived and died an adventurer and soldier of fortune. He set himself apart from the other leaders of Zaporozhe "chiefly by his vast ambition, tireless energy, and a certain quality of romantic imagination often stimulated by an excessive use of alcohol. In this respect, he was a true Cossack," says Florinsky.

The Cossacks saw the Jews as not only the despised tax collectors, but also non-believers. As agents of the Polish nobility, Jews incurred the hatred of the serfs. Gogol, in his work *Taras Bulba,* has the Cossacks comment on what they call "the disgraceful domination of the Jews on Christian soil." To this day, the word "Cossack" is anathema to Jews.

Some say the Cossacks even originated with the Khazars. The word "Cossack," borrowed from the Tartars and first recorded in 1444, was of Turkic origin, and connoted a person who was "free" in the sense of being outside the community. As a privileged class, they were presumed to have a large stake in the tsarist regime. Indeed, during the revolution, Cossack regions were the last to submit to Bolshevik rule. They were given land and absolved from all taxes, in exchange for being forever "on call" by the tsar. In both war and in peace, they were the prae-torian guard for the tsars.

The Jewish Community

"We are not a dying, old community, we are developing," said a Ukrainian Jewish leader. He was right. Just as we have seen in St. Petersburg and Moscow, the miracle of Jewish revival is tak-ing place here in Kiev. We shall visit institutions that did not exist even a few years ago.

The Ukrainian Jewish community is not as organized as the Russian one. Each city, such as Kiev, Odessa, and Dnepropetrovsk, has its own structure of cultural and welfare associations.

As we have noted in other cities and from all we have read, seen, heard, and learned about the Jewish people's past in tsarist and Communist Russia, it is a miracle to see Jewish life thriving once again, even in the Ukrainian capital. This is just one of the rewards for the Jewish traveler to Kiev.

About 80,000 Jews live in Kiev, out of approximately 300,000 to 400,000 residing in Ukraine. The numbers often vary, because there are no accurate figures.

Any travel guide on Jewish Russia and Ukraine must point out that at the beginning of the twenty-first century, a large part of the Ukrainian population is going through dire eco-nomic times. It is as if one traveled to a land lodged in a deep depression, such as the Great Depression of the 1930s.

Travelers may not see the hardship because of limited time and because visitors usually reach out to the tourist sites that do not show poverty. But it will not take the visitor long to real-ize that Russians and Ukrainians, Jews included, often face malnutrition, lack of heat and running water, blackouts and brownouts, and serious shortages of proper medicine.

Even in so-called middle-class families, Kievians often bake their own bread, partake of soups for dinner, and have little meat in the family menu, not just because of health reasons, but because of high prices.

The main problem is that for the last decade Ukraine and Russia have gone through economic crisis after economic crisis as they moved to a market economy. The safety net of communism, whatever its minimums, was lost, and the older generation, living on fixed incomes, suffered the most. At the end of 1997, for instance, about 30 to 40 percent of the Jewish community are qualified pensioners, subsisting on $25 a month, and it takes about $35 to exist. Often people are forced to choose between medicine and food. That is why meals-on-wheels, soup kitchens that are called *stolovaya* and are located in welfare centers, and synagogues are so crucial to Jewish survival.

Such hardship is also why Jewish men and women in Kiev, and throughout the entire Ukraine, benefit from a large number of helpful and varied programs sponsored by the American Jewish Joint Distribution Committee and other charitable organizations.

In Kiev, as throughout Russia and Ukraine, and other lands in the former Soviet Union, the "Joint" (Joint Distribution Committee) works through local Jewish organizations, schools, and cultural groups to support the development of programs to meet the needs of the local Jewish community.

Without this aid, Jews would be in a terrible predicament. For instance, unlike other countries, here in Kiev, as in other cities of the former Soviet Union, a large number of young Jewish men and women have departed for other lands, especially Israel. Their parents are often left without support from their own children.

Many Ukrainian Jews themselves praise Hesed Avot, that wonderful building where Jews can obtain a hot meal, medicine, and even a haircut or a wheelchair, the last incidentally very hard to come by in Ukraine or Russia. We shall soon visit Hesed Avot welfare center, which also has a large outreach program, including meals-on-wheels.

Besides stopping at the synagogues and the Babi Yar memorial, it is this author's opinion that travelers should also stop in at Hesed Avot to see the results of their local American Jewish community's contributions, to see for themselves how money raised in the U.S is truly helping these Jews in the former Soviet Union during difficult times.

Needless to say, these organizations help with not only material needs, but with spiritual matters. At Hesed Avot and at synagogues, there are activities for seniors, concerts, prayer

The Podol Synagogue in Kiev is shown here. (Photo credit: Ben G. Frank)

services and lectures, discussion groups, classes, and *Oneg Shabbat* and *Shabbat* services.

The hard times will not affect the tourist. Hotels are comfortable and adequate and making progress. Restaurants are well stocked. You can tour Kiev at a reasonable price. The Jewish sites are inspiring, and meeting Ukrainian Jews is a rewarding experience. As has been said before, "brains and heart" characterize Russian and Ukrainian Jews.

Jewish Sites in Kiev

Nearly 30 years ago, a Jewish tour guide listed six sites to visit in all of Kiev. One was a Jewish cemetery; another was the Babi Yar monument, the site of the murder of Jews by the Germans in 1941. Two synagogues were also listed, one of which had been turned into a puppet theater by the Communists.

In 1922, there were 97 synagogues in the city, of which 55 were in the Podol district. Of course, hundreds of prayer halls thrived in an invigorating Jewish atmosphere. In 1945, a single synagogue remained; the rest had been closed down by the Communists. Today there are at least 3 functioning synagogue buildings.

So, our first stop should be in that famous section called the Podol, where Jews have been active in business and politics. Podol was once described as an area composed of a pattern of rectangular streets, including the old merchants' trading exchange and the House of Contracts, which was built in 1817. This is an interesting neighborhood, and should be seen by every traveler.

Synagogues

Podol Synagogue, Shcekavitzkaya Street, Kiev. Tel/Fax: (380-44) 463-70-87 or (380-44) 463-70-88. This is the headquarters of the Kiev City Jewish Community (Kehilla) and the Kiev Jewish Religious Congregation. The synagogue also serves as the home of the Union of Jewish Religious Congregations of Ukraine. When you stand outside the Podol Synagogue, you are observing one of the oldest centers of Jewish religious life

in Kiev. Gabriel Yaakov Rosenberg was its founder and bene-
factor. This is also the one synagogue that withstood one hundred years of riots, roundups, police hunts, wars (in World War
II, the Germans turned it into a stable), death squads, occupations, restrictions, and closures, and is still here and functioning. It could fly a banner any day that would say, "The Jewish
people live."

Rabbi David Bleich, an American, is chief rabbi of Ukraine.
He is a *shaliach* (messenger) of the Stoliner rebbe, and arrived
in Kiev in 1989. Rabbi Bleich has been described as unusually
effective. He has been in Kiev for more than six years and he is
indeed charismatic and flexible and as one writer noted, "He
is in Kiev for the long haul."

Access to the synagogue is not difficult, since many trolley
buses stop there. The metro stop is Kontractovaya Ploshad.
The nearest hotel is the Domus Hotel, while the Impressa
Hotel is a 10- to 12-minute walk. A little further, but also with-
in walking distance, are the Kreshchatik Hotel and the
Dniepro Hotel.

This house of worship, built in 1896, was put under constant
surveillance by the KGB. Rarely was it left off the watch list; in
fact, it was observed more than any other synagogue in any
other city. Yiddish folklore concerts and shows were almost
completely banned.

In the 1960s, this main synagogue of Kiev resembled a "sad-
looking two-story structure." During the Stalin period, a few
dozen old Jews prayed in the basement. Perhaps a few more
hundred worshippers attended Sabbath services. "They don't
talk; someone might be listening," observed Ben-Ami, who also
recalled being in the synagogue during one Yom Kippur. He
found thousands, probably tens of thousands of people,
jammed together at the entrance and in the alley. "They
arrived singly or in pairs, but not in groups," he wrote, adding,
"the people in the street did not speak to each other; that's
how frightened they were." When Kievan Jews tried to hold a
minyan in a private house, they were closed down, and the
house's owners were punished. From 1960 to 1966, even the
baking of matza was prohibited.

In the 1970s, the main synagogue was the only functioning

A Kievan Jew is shown in front of the Podol Synagogue in Kiev. (Photo credit: Ben G. Frank)

house of worship in all of Kiev. This did not stop several thousand Jews from attending services in the synagogue on the high holidays. In the 1970s and 1980s, there were only about 60 synagogues in the USSR. The Communists always kept a few Russian and Ukrainian synagogues open for show.

Today, the synagogue is in contact with 62 Jewish communities in Ukraine.

Tourists can contact Rabbi Bleich regarding kosher food. Kosher meals can be served to individuals or to groups. This congregation has a kosher kitchen that prepares food for the soup kitchen, or *stolovaya*. About fifty people come to the facility each day. The synagogue supports a mikva (one for men and a separate one for women) and a matza factory. On the Sabbath, meals are prepared for youths that come to spend the day at the synagogue.

Services are held each morning at 8:30 A.M. and each evening for *Mincha* and *Maariv,* depending on the time of day. On Saturday morning, prayers commence at 9:00 A.M.

Jewish Preservation Society, Shekavitzkaya Street 29. Tel/Fax (380-44) 463-70-87 or (380-44) 463-70-88. E-mail: Jul@jpcu.freenet. kiev. ua. Founded in 1993 at the initiative of Rabbi David Bleich, the society can help you trace your roots. Some requests can be done quickly, while others will take time, the society has indicated. During the last several years, the society has successfully conducted more than 50 investigations. The group works with professional historians and archivists, and has compiled a complete database listing all cemeteries in Ukraine, as well as their condition. It also helps search archives for those seeking to locate the roots of their family. The group collects information on what was formerly Jewish property, as well as other Jewish sites, including synagogues, schools, hospitals, cemeteries, and mass burial sites throughout Ukraine.

Seeking Your Roots

Seeking one's roots is a long, arduous task; however, it can be most rewarding, if you are prepared to put in the time, as it is not true that all records and documents were destroyed by · the Germans.

The first people to contact are members of your own family. You can play reporter or detective and interview every person that may know something about your family members. You would be surprised what can turn up in an interview. Search out all living members. Contact the New York Public Library, the Mormon Church, and above all obtain a book called **From Generation to Generation: How to Trace Your Jewish Genealogy and Family History,** by Arthur Kurzweil.

Another valuable book to consult is Miriam Weiner's **Jewish Roots in Poland: Pages from the Past and Archival Inventories.** This book lists places where birth, death, and civil records might be found, town by town and archive by archive, going back to the 1700s. This valuable volume deals with Poland and former Polish areas of Belarus and Ukraine.

Tours by the Jewish Preservation Society of Ukraine

The society sponsors individual and group tours, some of which include trips to various Jewish towns in Galicia, a special Sholom Aleichem tour through the Kiev, Vinnitsa, and Chmelnitsky provinces. There is also a Sholom Aleichem city tour. Transportation, guide-translators, and hotel reservations can be provided.

A travel agency in Kiev that can help you book tours is **Dominanta,** Krasnoarmeyskaya Street 66, Room 3. Tel: (380-44) 227-40-05. Fax: (380-44) 265-19-89. Make sure you ask for Director Larisa Krivoviaz. She is familiar with Jewish organizations and can reach out to various Jewish groups for you.

Central Synagogue, (also called Brodsky Synagogue), Shota Rustaveli Street 13. Tel: (380-44) 246-60-64 and (380-44) 246-60-65. Tel/Fax: (380-44) 225-00-69. **Headquarters of the Chabad Religious Community,** Tel: (380-44) 225-00-69. Forty years ago, a Jewish travel writer noted that Kiev's "Great Synagogue still stands, but it is a puppet theater." Well, in the late 1990s, the puppet theater finally moved out. In fact, the Jewish community donated funds, at least $100,000, to cover expenses for the move, so the management of the theater would not think Jewish groups appropriated it without taking into consideration their situation, too. The synagogue was

Shown here is a photo of the Central Synagogue of Kiev. (Photo credit: Ben G. Frank)

once called the Brodsky Synagogue, since two brothers named Brodsky, who owned 90 percent of the sugar industry in Russia, contributed to the building fund.

Lazar Brodsky (1848-1904), who was known as "the sugar king of the south," was one of the city's greatest philanthropists, and helped finance this synagogue. He owned three homes in Kiev, and had major financial interests in Kiev's tram network and other public services. He served on the city council until Jews were excluded in 1894, according to Hamm.

Construction began in 1897 and the building officially opened in 1898. After the Revolution, the synagogue was turned into a Jewish club and Jewish theater. The Communists closed the synagogue in 1926. In the 1950s, the building became the puppet theater the travel writer mentioned. It is still sometimes called "the synagogue that was a puppet theater." Vladimir Rabinovich, president of the All-Ukrainian Jewish Congress, renovated the building and donated funds for its operation. Today Chabad Lubavitch is helping to organize the activities in the synagogue.

There is always a *minyan* in this synagogue, and prayers are held three times daily. *Shabbat* morning services are at 10:00 A.M. During the week, 8:30 A.M. is the time for morning services; time for evening services depends, again, on sunset.

The weekly prayers are held in one of the congregation's smaller rooms. The large hall can seat up to 500 persons. Large groups come to the synagogue at Passover and Purim, when an extensive program is usually presented.

Synagogue officials say that if they are notified ahead of time, they can obtain kosher food for any visitor and have it dispatched to the hotel. One can also eat at the institution's soup kitchen, where about one hundred persons partake of a hot kosher meal every day.

Educational youth programs help young people learn Hebrew. The synagogue also sponsors a summer camp.

Rabbi Moshe Azman, originally from St. Petersburg, is a graduate of the Chabad movement in Israel. He says each big city in Ukraine has a Chabad (Lubavitch) unit. Rabbi Azman is vice president of the Kiev Jewish Community and chief rabbi of

Rabbi Moshe Azman (left) presents Israeli Minister of Trade Natan Sharansky a draw-ing of the Central Synagogue in Kiev, which was once known as the Brodsky Synagogue. (Photo credit: Central Synagogue of Kiev)

the Central Synagogue. Garik Liogvinsky is program manager of the Kiev Jewish Community.

Rabbi Azman pointed out that the synagogue and officers can help Americans visiting in Ukraine or doing business in this city or throughout the country. The rabbi said Ukrainian Jewish leaders can give travelers information on reliable security people, directions, and help with bringing together businesspersons. If one wants to be within walking distance of the Central Synagogue, one can stay at the Kievskaya, Rus, or Ukraine hotels.

Hatikva-Reform Congregation, Yarasloval Street 7, near the Golden Gate Metro and the Opera, in the center of the city. For information, call the home of Rabbi Alexander Duchovny. Tel: (380-44) 213-1313; or the president of the congregation, Boris Kutik, at (380-44) 547-0695. Rabbi Duchovny speaks English. As the former spiritual leader of this congregation told me in an interview, "This is the only *shul* in town that does not have a *mechitza.*" (A *mechitza* is a physical separation between men and women, such as a curtain or balcony. In Reform congregations, men and women sit together.) Services are held Friday at 7:00 P.M., or at 7:30 P.M. in the summer. On Saturday afternoon at 5:00, a weekly Torah portion is read. *Havdalah* follows.

The synagogue is sponsored by the World Union of Progressive Judaism, the international branch of the American Reform Judaism movement.

According to Rabbi David Wilfond, there are more than 56 Progressive congregations (as the Reform movement is known here) in the former Soviet Union, and 21 registered congregations in Ukraine. Few of them have synagogue buildings or Torah scrolls.

Rabbi Wilfond spent two years in the Ukrainian capital leading the congregation there. At the time, he was the only Reform movement rabbi in the former Soviet Union. By the summer of 1999, he felt that the level of anti-Semitism there was less than that of Russia, and he attributed this to the media's vigilance in keeping hate talk and slogans off the air.

Rabbi Wilfond's successor, Rabbi Duchovny, born in Kiev, is the first Ukrainian rabbi to be trained at the Leo Baeck Rabbinical College in London and return to his homeland.

Here, a young man studies in the small prayer hall of the Central Synagogue in Kiev.
(Photo credit: Central Synagogue of Kiev)

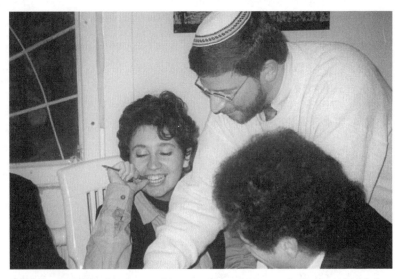

Rabbi David Wilfond is shown with some of his students at the Institute for Modern Jewish Studies, which is sponsored by the World Union for Progressive Judaism.
(Photo credit: Ben G. Frank)

Until the summer of 1999, the **Institute for Modern Jewish Studies** was located in Kiev. Sponsored by the World Union for Progressive Judaism, it was scheduled to move to Moscow in 1999. In 1998, 37 representatives of the World Union of Progressive Judaism, the Union of American Hebrew Congregations, the National Federation of Temple Brotherhoods, and Women of Reform Judaism attended a graduation ceremony at the institute.

Golda Meir Courtyard, Basseynye Street, No. 5. This is not the original house that "Golda," as she was affectionately called, inhabited. That house was destroyed. This is the spot where Golda grew up until she and her family emigrated to America. From the U.S., she then emigrated to Palestine and went on to become prime minister of Israel.

Schools

Two Jewish day schools in Kiev are sponsored by Rabbi Bleich and his organization. They are: **Kiev Jewish School for Boys,** Makevskaya 9, No. 299. Tel: (380-44) 430-67-14; **Kiev Jewish School for Girls,** No. 299, Timoshenko Street, 2B, 254205, Kiev. Tel: (380-44) 410-46-07. Fax: (380-44) 418-75-85.

Kiev Jewish School for Boys, No. 128, Raisy Okipnoy 6, 253167, Kiev. Tel: (380-44) 295-02-06. Fax: (380-44) 419-63-83. Classes here are held in a government school.

Simcha School, Kibalchicha 3. Sponsored by Chabad.

Kindergartens of the Reform Movement, Gorkava Street 168, Gorkava Neighborhood, Kiev; and O Teligi 25/29, Seretz Neighborhood, Kiev.

Jewish Pedagogical Center of Jewish Education, Artima Street 52A, Corp. 2, Kiev, 252053. Tel: (380-44) 211-94-76 and (380-44) 211-16-89.

International Solomon University, Goloseevskaya Street 12, Kiev, 252039. Tel: (380-44) 265-16-53, 265-28-05, 265-16-75, and 265-16-50. The Jewish University in Kiev is located here. Courses include Hebrew language study, Jewish history, history of Israel, and a special department of Judaic studies.

Iosif Akselrud, director of Hillel in Kiev, right, greets Asaph Jagendorf, formerly with the JDC in Kiev. (Photo credit: Ben G. Frank)

Shown here is a meeting in Kiev of Hillel directors from throughout the former Soviet Union. Starting at the head of the table and going clockwise are: Misha Levin, director of St. Petersburg Hillel; Galina Tenenbaum, director of Moldova Hillel; Zhenya Zelotnik, director of Minsk Hillel; Yan Yankovsky, director of Urals Regional Hillel; and Ina Bdyakovich, director of Kharkov Hillel. (Photo credit: Sarai Brachman Shoup)

Organizations

All-Ukrainian Jewish Congress, Mechnikova Street 14/1, 25203, Kiev. Tel: (380-44) 225-71-20. Fax: (380-44) 225-10-67.

The Jewish Foundation of Ukraine, Institutskaya Street 19B, Kiev, 252021. Tel: (380-44) 293-84-37 and (380-44) 265-45-16.

Vaad (also known as the Association of Jewish Public Organizations and Communities of Ukraine), Kurskaya Street 6, Kiev, 252049. Tel: (380-44) 276-12-14, (380-44) 276-74-21, and (380-44) 265-45-16. Tel/Fax: (380-44) 293-84-37.

B'nai B'rith of Kiev, Artema Street 52 A, Kiev. Tel: (380-44) 263-89-13. Fax: (380-44) 295-96-04.

Magen Avot, Mezhigorskaya 24, Apt. 11, Kiev. Tel: (380-44) 416-09-10. Fax: (380-44) 271-71-44.

Jewish Council of Ukraine, Nemanskaya 7, Kiev, 252103. Tel: (380-44) 296-39-61, (380-44) 295-65-93. Fax: (380-44) 295-96-04. The Jewish Cultural Society is also located here.

Kiev Jewish City Library, Sretenskaya Street 4/13, Kiev, 254025. Tel: (380-44) 212-39-18.

TV Program *Yahad,* Kreshchatik Street 26, Kiev, 252001. Tel: (380-44) 441-82-23 and (380-44) 220-43-01.

Hillel House, Dimitrova Street 6, Apt. 25, PO Box 131, Kiev. Tel/Fax: (380-44) 220-64-36. E-mail: hillel@hillel.kiev.ua. "Come to our organization and at least once a week you'll feel yourself a real Jew." That is one motto of this active group. Founded in May 1996, this organization was originally set up in the Student's Club of the International Solomon University, the first Jewish university in Ukraine. Now part of Hillel International, this local Hillel sponsors many activities, including a club for Jewish history and culture. Many students belong to the Intellectual Club. Hillel also publishes a newspaper.

Students put on shows and musicals. Filmmaking is very popular in Russia and Ukraine, and Hillel helps young people produce movies. *Shabbat* and Jewish holidays are celebrated, candles are lit, and the blessing over wine is recited. Students help out at Hesed Avot, the welfare center. Since students want to fulfill their motto of helping others, they often travel to the small Ukrainian cities to conduct Passover Seders.

Several weddings have already taken place in Hillel.

Iosif Akselrud, the director, can be contacted as a source for information regarding activities. Friday night, at 6:00 P.M., is a fine time to attend. Do call ahead.

Hesed Avot Welfare Center, Ul. Piterskaya 4A, Kiev. Tel/ Fax: (380-44) 242-68-80. Tel: (380-44) 241-03-02 and (380-44) 241-03-03. Direct line to director's office:(380-44) 241-07-48. Standing in this fine building, with a picture of Sholom Aleichem gracing its walls, I talked with a Jewish veteran of World War II. While we talked, he caressed a book entitled *The Family Mashber,* by the great Russian Jewish writer, Pinchas Kahganovich, or "Der Nister" (1884-1950). Although born in Berdichev, "Der Nister" lived here in Kiev and is famous for his novel, which has been described as perhaps "the single great- est achievement of Soviet Yiddish prose." By the way, "Der Nister" in Yiddish means the "Hidden One."

This aged Red Army veteran and I both knew that Der Nister and many other Jewish writers were victims of the Stalin purges. Their names will live.

That this former Jewish soldier and I were standing and talk- ing in a Jewish library (established with the support of the Jewish community of Chicago) in a Jewish welfare building in Kiev was extraordinary, considering the 70 years of Communist rule. Actually, many individual American Jews have helped erect this and other institutions that daily aid hundreds of Jews in Kiev, through the support of the American Jewish Joint Distribution Committee. Reports indicate that this center, which covers about three thousand square meters, serves about fourteen thousand needy Kievan Jews.

The establishment of the Hesed Avot Welfare Center was made possible with the help of a $1.5 million grant from the Conference on Jewish Material Claims Against Germany, in 1996. Since then the JDC finances have gone a long way to keep Jewry alive physically, mentally, and spiritually.

On a visit to this wonderful institution, a second home for hundreds of Kievan Jews, I discovered that this is not only a welfare center, but also a community center, a place for intel- lectual stimulation for people, a place of comradeship. It is open from 9:00 A.M. to 5:00 P.M., Monday to Friday.

In this photo of the library of Hesed Avot Welfare Center in Kiev, note the picture of the writer, Sholom Aleichem, on the bookshelf. The writer lived in Kiev, which, in his writings, he called "Yehupetz." (Photo credit: Ben G. Frank)

Some of the seniors are shown at a meeting in Hesed Avot Welfare Center in Kiev. (Photo credit: Ben G. Frank)

The Haifa Restaurant is located near the Podol Synagogue in Kiev. At press time, this restaurant was not kosher, though at one point it was considered kosher. (Photo credit: Ben G. Frank)

Administration personnel may be there on Sundays. For a visit, it is best to make an appointment. Several hundred volunteers come here each day and give of their expertise. About three hundred home-care workers make personal visits, and 6,500 food packages are given to the most needy each year. Many Jewish doctors have emigrated, so doctors are in short supply in Kiev. (There is a scarcity of medicine in Ukraine and Russia; so remember, take your own medication and even some bandages, antibiotics, and other basic supplies.)

At Hesed Avot, watches are fixed, clocks are repaired, haircuts are given to those men in need, and a beauty salon cuts and coifs the hair of elderly women. Each day, many come to the *stolovaya* to eat and participate in an *Oneg Shabbat,* club dancing, and lectures.

Jewish Agency for Israel (commonly called the Sochnut), Kosiora 24. Tel: (380-44) 274-80-35 and (380-44) 274-69-31. Fax: (380-44) 274-80-26.

Israel Embassy in the Ukraine, Boulevard Lesya Ukrainka 34. Tel: (380-44) 295-69-25 and (380-44) 295-65-96.

Israel Cultural Information Center, also located at the Israel Embassy. Tel: (380-44) 295-68-36 and (380-44) 295-48-66.

Restaurants

Haifa Restaurant, Konstantinovskaya Street 57. Tel: (380-44) 417-25-12. As you drive down this boulevard, you will see right before you the Hebrew letters spelling "HAIFA." Yes, its name is from the famous Israeli port city on the Mediterranean. This establishment has been kosher, and it has been non-kosher. At press time we were informed that it is not kosher. But the traveler should check as he or she sees fit. It is not far from the Podol Synagogue.

Kosher Soup Kitchen, Podol Synagogue, Shekavitskaya 29, Kiev, 254071. Kosher food is available at this synagogue, but arrangements must be made beforehand. Call the synagogue, which can also arrange to have kosher food delivered to your hotel. Tel: (380-44) 463-70-87.

Kosher Product Shops

Shop, Semen Skliarenko Street 1.

Premiera, Khmelnytskiy Street 23, opposite the Opera House. Tel: (380-44) 225-62-85 or (380-44) 462-04-61.

Lileya, Khreshchatik 5, next door to the Dnipro Hotel.

Other Sites

Sholom Aleichem Statue, near Basseynye Street, which is located near the market, on Boulevard Lesya Ukrainka; **Sholom Aleichem House,** Krasnoarmieskaya Street 5. His real name was Sholom Rabinovitz. We call him Sholom Aleichem. His very appellation, "Sholom Aleichem," is a greeting meaning "peace be unto you," which is offered to a stranger coming from a distance. But, according to the *Encyclopedia Judaica,* Sholom Aleichem developed the idea of his amusing pen name (which again, is something like "How do you do," in meaning and usage) into a comic persona, that of a vagrant or traveler who is given to practical jokes. And boy, did he do a lot of traveling. "You'll find me on the road nearly eleven months of the year," wrote Sholom Aleichem.

More than any other Jewish writer, Sholom Aleichem wrote about Jewishness "as if it were a gift, a marvel, an unending theme of wonder and delight." He was immensely popular, even beyond the Yiddish-speaking public.

If any Jewish writer ever wrote about the *pintele* or "typical Jew," Sholom Aleichem did, and he wrote about it in Russian, Yiddish, and Hebrew.

His topic was three million neglected *shtetl* Jews. He made this sphere his very own. Curt Leviant, who selected and translated Sholom Aleichem's *Old Country Tales,* called him "the watchman of Jewish provincial life."

Born near Kiev in 1859, in a small town called Pereyaslav in Ukraine, Aleichem received a traditional Hebrew and secular education. He served as a crown rabbi (employed by the regime to record births and deaths). Later he served as a publisher, stockbroker, and businessman, but his first love was writing. He

The statue of the great Jewish writer, Sholom Aleichem, near Basseynye Street is shown here. (Photo credit: Rozaline Kleyman)

literally rode the trains, roaming between Odessa and his fictional cities Yehupets and Kasrilevke. Later destinations were London and New York, where he went about obtaining stories, talking to people, and watching them.

One of the worst pogroms that he experienced took place in Kiev. The authorities stood aside, it was reported. From October 1 to October 5, 1905, Cossack soldiers went around the city, breaking into Jewish homes, demanding money, raping, and killing. "Medieval terror in the streets," was one description of the soldiers' actions. Sholom Aleichem's daughter wrote in her book, *In the Storm,* that there were "three terrible days and nights during which we were unable to sleep or eat, walking in silence and fear. The rage of hate and evil finally subsided and it was safe to return to our apartment." Having taken refuge with his family, Aleichem departed Russia, only to return for brief visits.

Sholom Aleichem met the great Hebrew poet Chaim Nachman Bialik in Odessa for the first time, although they had heard of each other before. Both were delegates to the 1907 Zionist Congress at The Hague and were attending a conference of Hebraists.

Aleichem died at age 57 in the Bronx on May 13, 1916. "He was very superstitious of the number 13, so we call it 12½ of May," said Bel Kaufman, his granddaughter and the author of the best-selling novel, *Up the Down Staircase.* According to the newspaper *Jewish Week,* ever since Aleichem's death, family and friends of the great Yiddish writer have gathered together on May 13, on his *yahrzeit* (anniversary of his death) as he requested, to read his will and hear one or two merry stories. In 1997, at the Brotherhood Synagogue in Gramercy Park in New York City, the tradition was passed from his grandchildren to his great-grandchildren.

On the day of his funeral, most of his Jewish friends from the greater New York area stopped work. Hundreds of thousands escorted him to a last resting place, says the *Encyclopedia Judaica.*

Site of the courtyard building where the Beilis Trial was held, Saint Sophia Square, near the statue of Bohdan Chmielnicki. The victim's name was Mendel Beilis, a humble unknown Jew and a worker in a brick factory. He soon became a front-page story the world over, the center of an international media event.

One beautiful spring day in 1911, some children found the corpse of a schoolboy hidden in a deep cave overlooking the western districts of Kiev. The child, identified as Andrei Yustshinsky, was a thirteen-year-old pupil at the Sofia Ecclesiastical College. There were 47 stab wounds in his head, neck, and torso. The boy's clothing was caked with dried blood. Nearby the child were his school cap and some notebooks.

After the discovery of the child's body, the Black Hundreds and other anti-Semitic groups would make him a saint. They leveled the ancient accusation from the Middle Ages that the Jewish religion prescribes the use of Christian blood during the ritual of the Passover service. At the turn of the century, the blood-libel had become one of the keystones of the Russian government's policies to arouse hatred against the Jews.

Following on the heels of the infamous Dreyfus trial of 1897 in Paris, the 1913 Russian charges shocked the world because it was yet another ritual murder trial of a Jew. The anti-Semitic groups also used the infamous *Protocols of the Elders of Zion,* a "scurrilous document that poisoned the minds of millions of people and was to be distributed by anti-Semites throughout the world," writes historian Leni Yahil. It was composed at the end of the nineteenth century in France, at the instigation of the Russian secret police. The *Protocols* are a fictional account of the proceedings of an allegedly secret Jewish organization that was planning to take over and rule the world. The original purpose of this "document" was to aid the struggle against the liberal forces in Russia, but it had little effect in that context, writes Yahil. "The *Protocols* would be used again during the Russian Revolution, this time by the White Army in an attempt to invoke anti-Semitism as part of its war against the Red Army." With the defeat of their army, the White Army officers brought the *Protocols* to Germany, where they were distributed and would later find their way into bed with Nazi ideology.

For two years, the Beilis case "provided the pabulum" for a wild anti-Semitic campaign that was carried on among the upper classes, the workers, the newspapers, and even the Duma. The government knew the real murderers had been discovered, rounded up, and interrogated. Some of them confessed. The prosecution's case actually collapsed in the courtroom, exposing bribery, intimidation, and corruption, often to the laughter of the larger audiences, according to Lindemann. Author Mikhail Beizer notes that after the trial itself, Nicholas II decorated those who had taken part in the investigation against Beilis, in the indictment, and in the trial. When the real story was told through documents in 1917, it was learned that the minister of justice and the tsar himself had both acknowledged Beilis's innocence long before he came to trial. But they continued to prosecute the Jew so they could prove the Jewish cult of ritual murder was a fact, according to Figes.

Opera House. Known as one of the finest opera houses in Ukraine, this building attracts large numbers of tourists. The Opera House, which during Communist days was named after German revolutionary Karl Liebknecht, faces Korolenko Street, just off the main shopping center. In September 1911, in a performance of Rimsky-Korsakov's *The Legend of the Tsar Sultan,* given at the Opera House, Prime Minister Stolypin, who supported the Russian monarchy and suppressed the Revolution, was seated in the stalls. Tsar Nicholas II was stationed in the imperial box. During an intermission, a young man in evening dress approached the prime minister, pulled out a Browning pistol, and apparently fired two shots. Five days later, Stolypin was dead.

Lindemann says Bogrov, the assassin, was a Jewish anarchist who was also employed as a police spy and double agent. Dubnow writes in Vol. III of his *History of the Jews in Russia and Poland* that Bogrov "proved to be the son of a lawyer who was of Jewish extraction, though he had long before turned his back upon his people." "Bogrov was a renegade Jew," not acting as a Jew at all, says author D. M. Thomas, biographer. A pogrom was averted only because the government was afraid it would mar Nicholas's visit, and "the authorities made it known that the Tsar was not in favor of riots," says Simon M. Dubnow. According to Geoffrey Hosking, author of *Russia, People and Empire,* Stolypin "intended to extend full civil rights to the Jews."

Babi Yar Monument, Melnikova Street at Olena Tolega Bus Station. Nearly every day, you can see non-Jewish couples who have just married visit a statue of the founders of the city— their ancestors, if you will. Many Jewish couples also make their "after-marriage stop ceremony" at Babi Yar; they, too, want to be close to their forebears, who perished here at the hands of the Germans.

Take Bus No. 16 or a taxi. Everyone knows the location of Babi Yar. If you see the large television-radio antenna, you know you have arrived at the right spot.

And if the memorial before you is in the form of a menorah (a symbolic candelabrum that was modeled after the one in the Temple in Jerusalem), then you are standing at what is called by many the "Jewish Memorial" to Jews murdered here in Babi Yar, as opposed to the "old Soviet memorial," which has no outward Jewish memorial symbol, other than Yiddish words that do not mention that Jews died here.

The menorah monument, which was sculptured by Yuri Paskevich, is located in a cul-de-sac and sits on a stepped pedestal. A Babi Yar committee is raising money to build a memorial complex on the site. The complex will include a museum and archive dedicated to all the Ukrainian Jews killed in World War II.

To visit the Jewish memorial, get on the path alongside the television station. It will take you straight up to the menorah memorial. The road follows the actual final mile of the Jewish victims.

For a half-century, the Soviets purposely shut out any memory of the disaster. For example, Elie Wiesel told an interviewer in 1991 that when he went to the neighborhood around Babi Yar in 1965, no one wanted to show him the site of the dreadful scene. "No one would tell me where it was. It was as though it hadn't happened."

Tourists were discouraged from coming here, yet refuseniks, activists, and travelers from abroad still came to the ravine. Their presence was felt, and many did protest, even in the 1960s when it was still dangerous to do so.

Only in 1991, when the menorah memorial was erected for the fiftieth anniversary of the tragedy of Babi Yar, did the

Here, the author is shown in front of what is considered the Jewish memorial to the thousands of Jews killed by the Germans at Babi Yar, Kiev. (Photo credit: Ben G. Frank)

Ukrainian government dedicate and recognize the spot as the area where Jews were killed and buried. When it was dedicated, delegations from Israel, Europe, and the U.S., as well as top officials from Ukraine, attended, including Ukrainian President Leonid Kravchuk, who apologized for those Ukrainians who cooperated with the Germans in the roundup of Jews.

The Ukrainians are like other people; when it comes to directions, you have to be specific. When you wish to visit the Jewish site, the "menorah," you must make it clear that you want to see the Jewish memorial. Unless you do so, everyone will direct you to the huge Soviet memorial. Actually, you should see both monuments.

But wherever you stand, even today, you would never know an unfathomable, incomprehensible, human slaughter took place here. Senior citizens stroll near the forest with its deep ravines. Young children roller-skate. Adults exercise their dogs. Mothers steer baby carriages. Most not only don't remember, most don't even know what went on here.

It is said that it is so quiet that some people stand here and "listen for the voices of the dead."

As you face the menorah, glance slightly to the left and down the yonder ravine. That is the direction where the mass murder took place.

After the Six-Day War, Babi Yar became a rallying cry for Soviet Jews as well as a day of remembrance. Jews came not only to recite the Kaddish (the Jewish prayer for the dead), but also to express their Jewish identity. Their protests once even halted a plan to build a soccer bowl on the Babi Yar site.

The German einsatzgruppen reached the city between September 19 and September 25, 1941. On September 22, Russian soldiers set off two explosions. The second one destroyed the German headquarters and a large part of the city center. About twenty-five thousand people were left homeless. In retaliation, on September 28, the German authorities demanded resettlement of the Jews and "called on them to assemble on the next day, September 29 for transfer."

This killing occurred in the last week of September 1941,

during the Days of Awe, the 10 days of Repentance, the days between Rosh Hashanah and Yom Kippur.

Posters were plastered on all the walls of Kiev. One could not miss them. They stated: "All the Jews of Kiev and the vicinity are to appear on Monday, September 29, 1941, at 8:00 A.M. on the corner of Meenkovskaya and Dukhtorovskaya, near the cemeteries. They are to bring their documents, money, other valuables and warm clothes, linen etc. Any Jew found disobeying these orders will be shot. Citizens breaking into flats left by Jews and taking possession of their belongings will be shot." For Jews, the derogatory word, *Zhid*, or "dirty Jew" was used, and not the usual *evrei*, which simply means "Jew."

The more than 30,000 people who assembled did not suspect that anything wrong was going to happen. They thought they were being resettled. Instead, they were taken to the forest and were slaughtered over the course of two days.

According to the German report, "there were no incidents." The report emphasizes that "thanks to the outstandingly efficient organization," up to the last moment the Jews felt that they were being taken to their new homes. The local population, it is further reported, believed the story and was gratified by it.

Only afterward did the truth emerge. The Germans boasted of having solved the housing problem by evacuating a suitable number of apartments, an act made possible by exterminating approximately 35,000 Jews, according to Yahil.

The official report of the SS unit in charge of the mass extermination stated that 33,771 Jews were murdered in Babi Yar on September 29 and 30, 1941. By November 3, 1941, the Germans had gone on to kill at least 80,000 Jews. In all, Babi Yar was the scene of one of the bloodiest and most notorious of all slaughters of Jews in the Holocaust.

As you stand at the site, you remember scenes you have read about in literature. The suitcases and small bundles of food that each person was allowed to bring were put neatly into piles. Rounded up like sheep, Jewish men and women were lined up along the edge of pits, 60 yards long and 8 feet deep, and shot rank after rank, the still-living trampling on the bodies of the dead. The Germans then tried to soak the area with petrol and burn the bodies, according to author and journalist Edward Crankshaw.

A watchman later recalled how Ukrainian policemen "formed a corridor and drove the panic-stricken people towards the huge glade," where there were "sticks, swearing, and dogs who were tearing the people's bodies," according to historian Martin Gilbert.

The area was bounded by barbed wire, so as to prevent escape. Hundreds of Germans, aided by the Ukrainian militia, blocked off any escape route.

At the mouth of the ravine, Jews found themselves on the narrow ground above the precipice, 20 to 25 meters in height; on the opposite side there were the German machine guns. The killed, wounded, the half-alive fell down and were smashed there. Then the next hundred were brought, and everything repeated again. The policemen took the children by the legs and threw them alive down the Yar.

Vitaley Korotich, who as a child lived in German-occupied Kiev, says Nazis destroyed 200,000 Jews in the ravine. "Every week they transported a truckload of children's shoes from Babi Yar. I don't know who needed this footwear, but imagine how many children had to be killed to fill up a truckload of children's shoes."

People in the city knew about the slaughter, but no one spoke about what happened. A. Anatoli wrote in his book, *Babi Yar,* that "for the first time, I realized what was happening; from Babi Yar came quite distinctly the sound of regular bursts of machine gun fire, ta-ta-ta-ta-ta. People were being fooled . . . . All the baggage, the bundles and cases were being put into a pile on the left, and all the foodstuff on the right."

The reader would do well to read A. Anatoli Kuznetsov's powerful documentary novel *Babi Yar.* Dr. William Corey, writing in *The Holocaust in the Soviet Union,* says Kuznetsov shows that some Ukrainians welcomed the Nazis, some collaborated in the mass killings, and many "had passively accepted German rule, striving in every way possible to survive."

In his novel *The Storm*, Ilya Ehrenburg describes a scene at Babi Yar when a German soldier grabbed a baby from its mother's arms and flung the child over the edge of the ravine. The mother shrieked and shouted at the Germans, saying, "Osya will come, the Red Army will come. You shall pay for everything, you beasts." Thus was Babi Yar.

Before the fall of Communism in Ukraine in 1991, every September 29 Jews have led a peaceful demonstration to Babi Yar, even risking harassment and arrest by the KGB. Today, participants do not worry about the police, or the KGB, or that the demonstration is unofficial. Now Jews openly honor the memory of those who perished there.

Before the Germans arrived in Kiev in 1941, many of the 175,000 Jews who lived in Kiev had managed to leave the city. "Most of the victims were the old, the sick, and women and children who had been left behind," according to Yahil. "Before the German occupation, 175,000 Jews had lived in the city; thus the Holocaust victims accounted for the loss of only part of the Jewish community, which had comprised both local residents and refugees. A large percentage of these Jews had escaped before the Germans arrived.

Yahil also says that many Jews escaped death at the hands of the Nazis because the evacuation of Ukranian workers, along with their factories, was better organized. But it should be made clear that a large number of Jews were saved not because the Soviets made a special effort to save Jews, but strictly as a "function of political and military policy."

Yet it would take a Russian, a non-Jew, to bring the world's attention not only to what went on here, but also to the hypocrisy of the Communist regime, which refused to acknowledge publicly that Jews were killed at the ravine. His words from 1961 still ring true: "No monument stands over Babi Yar." He also said, "he is each old man here shot dead; he is every child here shot dead." The poet's name was Yevgeny Yevtushenko, who defied the regime when so many meekly played along. Born in 1937, Yevtushenko denounced anti-Semitism in the famous poem, "Babi Yar."

The poem denounced not only the Nazi mass murder of Jews in Ukraine but also the Stalinist terror regime. Surprisingly, Yevtushenko was not jailed, killed, or sent to Siberia. But he was verbally abused by top Communist leader Nikita S. Khrushchev in *Pravda*.

Yevtushenko was the most popular Soviet poet of the late 1950s and early 1960s. "I love my country and my people. I am a modest successor to the great tradition of Russian literature of such writers as Pushkin, Tolstoy, Dostoevsky," he once said.

Yevtushenko's protest against anti-Semitism in the USSR was set to music in Dmitrii Shostakovich's *Thirteenth Symphony*.

One in three of the inhabitants of Kiev were killed during the occupation. But if one adds to this figure the number of those who died from hunger, or who failed to return from Germany and so forth, then it appears that every second person must have perished.

The other monument, the Soviet memorial, was erected in 1974, a decade after Yevtushenko went public. Of this monument, many agree with Dr. William Korey, who wrote that there is nothing to "even remotely suggest the Jewish agony at Babi Yar."

Although Jews were the principal victims of the massacre, the Yiddish inscription on the stone makes no mention of Jews. This so-called Russian memorial, in the form of an obelisk, was belatedly raised in a spot not actually on the area of the massacre. The text says, "Here in 1941-43, 100,000 citizens of city of Kiev and POW's were shot by the German fascists occupation." The statue is in the form of a resistance fighter. It is a huge monument surrounded by a ditch. The Communist officials built it a half-mile to a mile from the ravine where the killings took place, and in the process, bulldozed Kiev's main Jewish cemetery.

Actually, some say the Soviet monument marks the location where the Nazis later tried to conceal evidence of the massacre by burning many of the corpses in a huge pile.

Babi Yar itself also became a symbol against anti-Semitism. Going there made a political statement. Presidents Bush and

Here, the author is pictured in front of the Soviet monument at Babi Yar. The monument was erected in 1974. (Photo credit: Ben G. Frank)

Clinton have been among the visitors who have stopped to remember, and every traveler to Kiev will probably want to stop at Babi Yar.

Suggested Reading

Aberbach, David, *Realism, Caricature and Bias, the Fiction of Mendele Mocher Sefarim.* The Littman Library of Jewish Civilization, 1993.

Adler, Elkan Nathan, *Jewish Travellers, A Treasury of Travelogues from 9 Centuries.* New York: Hermon Press, 1966.

Aleichem, Sholom, *Selected Stories of Sholom Aleichem, with an introduction by Alfred Kazin.* New York: Modern Library, 1956.

Allen, W.E.D., *The Ukraine, A History.* New York: Russell & Russell, Inc., 1993.

Baron, Salo, *The Russian Jew under Tsars and Soviets.* New York: The Macmillan Company, 1964.

Bartov, Omer, *The Eastern Front, 1941-45, German Troops and the Barbarisation of Warfare.* New York: St. Martin's Press, 1986.

Bartov, Omer, *Hitler's Army: Soldiers, Nazis, & War in the Third Reich.* New York, Oxford: Oxford University Press, 1991.

Ben-Ami, (Arie L. Eliav), *Between Hammer and Sickle.* Philadelphia, PA: Jewish Publication Society, 1967.

Ben-Sasson, H.H., *A History of the Jewish People.* Cambridge, MA: Harvard University Press, 1976.

Clark, Alan, *Barbarossa: The Russo-German Conflict, 1941-1945.* New York: Morrow, 1965.

Conquest, Robert, *The Great Terror.* New York: Macmillan, 1973.

Dobroszycki, Lucjan and Gurock, Jeffrey S., editors, *The Holocaust in the Soviet Union: Studies and Sources on the Destruction of the Jews in the Nazi-Occupied Territories of the USSR, 1945-1945.* Armonk, NY, London: M.E. Sharpe, 1993.

Dubnow, S. M., *History of the Jews in Russia and Poland, From the Earliest Times Until the Present Day, Vols. I and II.* Philadelphia: The Jewish Publication Society of America, 1916.

Dubnow, S.M., *History of the Jews, From the Congress of Vienna to the Emergence of Hitler, Vol. V.* South Brunswick, London, New York: Thomas Yoseloff, 1973.

Duffy, James P. and Ricci, Vincent L., *The Czars: Russia's Rulers for More Than One Thousand Years*. New York: Facts on File, 1995.

Ehrenburg, Ilya, *The Storm*. New York: G. P. Putnam's Sons, 1984.

Eliach, Yaffa, *There Once Was A World, A Nine-Hundred-Year Chronicle of the Shtetl of Eishyshok*. Boston, New York: Little, Brown and Company, 1998.

Erickson, John, *The Road to Stalingrad, Stalin's War with Germany, Vol. I*. New York: Harper & Row, Publishers, 1975.

Feshbach, Murray and Friendly, Alfred, *Ecocide in the USSR: Health and Nature Under Siege*. New York: Basic Books, a division of HarperCollins Publishers, 1992.

Figes, Orlando, *A People's Tragedy: A History of the Russian Revolution*. New York: Viking, 1997.

Florinsky, Michael T., *Russia, 2 Vols*. New York: Macmillan, 1961.

Freeze, Gregory L., editor, *Russia, A History*. Oxford, New York: Oxford University Press, 1997.

Gerrard, John and Gerrard, Carol, *The Bones of Berdichev: The Life and Times of Vasily Grossman*. New York: Free Press, 1996.

Gogol, Nikolai, *Taras Bulba*. New York, London: Everyman's Library, Dutton, 1962.

Hamm, Michael F., *Kiev: A Portrait, 1800-1917*. Princeton, N.J.: Princeton University Press, 1993.

Korey, William, *Russian Anti-Semitism, Pamyat and the Demonology of Zionism*. Switzerland: Harwood Academic Publishers, 1995.

Kostyrchenko, Gennadi V., *Out of the Red Shadows: Anti-Semitism in Stalin's Russia*. Amherst, NY: Prometheus Books, 1995.

Kurzweil, Arthur, *From Generation to Generation: How to Trace Your Jewish Genealogy and Family History*. New York: HarperCollins Publishers, 1994.

Malcanson, Scott L., *Borderlands: Nation and Empire*. Boston: Faber and Faber, 1994.

Markowitz, Fran, *A Community In Spite of Itself: Soviet Jewish Emigres in New York*. Washington and London: Smithsonian Institution Press, 1993.

Milner-Gulland, Robin, with Dejevsky, Nikolai, *Cultural Atlas of Russia and the Soviet Union*. Oxford, New York: Facts on File, 1989.

Pares, Sir Barnard, *A History of Russia.* New York: Alfred A Knopf, 1968.

Pavic, Milorad, *Dictionary of the Khazars.* New York: Alfred A. Knopf, 1988.

Pipes, Richard, *The Unknown Lenin: From the Secret Archive.* New Haven: Yale University Press, 1996.

Potok, Chaim, *The Gates of November: Chronicles of the Slepak Family.* New York: Alfred A. Knopf, 1996.

Reid, Anna, *Borderland: A Journey Through the History of Ukraine.* London: Weidenfield & Nicholson, 1997.

Riasanovsky, Nicholas V., *A History of Russia, Fifth Edition.* Oxford, New York: Oxford University Press, 1993.

Shabad, Theodore, *Geography of the USSR, A Regional Survey.* New York: Columbia University Press, 1951.

Suny, Ronald Grigor, *The Soviet Experiment, Russia, the USSR, and the Successor States.* New York, Oxford: Oxford University Press, 1998.

Tager, Alexander B., *The Decay of Czarism, the Beilis Trial, a Contribution to the History of the Political Reaction During the Last Years of Russian Czarism.* Philadelphia: The Jewish Publication Society of America, 1935.

Tolstoy, Alexei, *Road to Calvary.* New York: Alfred A. Knopf, 1996.

Vernadsky, George, *Ancient Russia.* New Haven: Yale University Press, 1951.

Vernadsky, George, *A History of Russia.* New Haven and London: Yale University Press, 1961.

Wiesel, Elie, *The Jews of Silence: A Personal Report on Soviet Jewry.* New York: Schocken Books, 1987.

Wolfe, Bertram D., *Three Who Made a Revolution, A Biographical History.* New York: The Dial Press, 1964.

Yahil, Leni, *The Holocaust: The Fate of European Jewry, 1932-1945.* New York, Oxford: Oxford University Press, 1990.

ZHITOMIR:
Jewish Life is Reborn

Once, this was a flourishing Jewish community here. Once, there were 40 synagogues. Now, there is one serving about five thousand Jews.

This is Zhitomir, one hundred miles west of Kiev. A city of 100,000 residents, the town has a synagogue, a Hesed, and a kindergarten. Zhitomir also once stood as the administrative capital of Volhynia Province, which in the nineteenth century contained hundreds of thousands of Jews.

Once, the city was one of the largest *shtetls* in the Ukraine. In 1897, it reported 30,748 Jews, who formed 46.6 percent of the total population.

Once, it had a new rabbinical school established by the Maskilim, the enlightenment people. But it never measured up to the other yeshivas in the Russian Empire, and the students could not obtain legitimate rabbinical posts. Many of them used the school as a steppingstone to the university. The rabbinical school failed, and was ultimately converted into a teaching seminary.

A Jewish technical school opened in Zhitomir in 1862. After nearly 23 years of training young people, it also was closed down by the government in 1884, on the grounds that the artisans it trained "exploited the Russian population." Or put another way, "it gave the Jews economic superiority over the Christians."

In 1905, Zhitomir also had a pogrom, which was planned by the police in conjunction with the notorious Black Hundreds, according to Milton Meltzer in his *World of Our Fathers: The Jews of Eastern Europe.* This time, newly formed Jewish defense units put up a fight, but the police interfered and stopped them. Fifteen Jews were killed and nearly one hundred wounded in the three-day attack, according to Jewish historian Simon M. Dubnow. In the Civil War, hundreds of Jews lost their lives at the hands of Petlyura, the Ukrainian Army, and Polish soldiers. But the Jewish community survived, and by 1926, some thirty thousand Jews lived in the city.

Zhitomir was temporary Ukrainian headquarters of the German Sixth Army and the SS in World War II. It was the site of rest and recuperation for front-line German units, and also the murder of the Jewish population, according to authors John and Carol Gerrard. Ukrainians rounded up and positioned the Jews for murder at the Zhitomir massacre. When the war broke out in 1939, thousands of refugees flocked to this city on the Teterev River. When Hitler attacked Russia in June 1941, even thousands more poured into this municipality. The total number of people slaughtered by the Einsatzgruppen at Zhitomir, including POWs, was forty-three thousand. There is little doubt that the German army also assisted in the murder, according to Leni Yahil.

Zhitomir is about an hour and a half west of Kiev. Situated in a rich agricultural area at the junction of four railroads, it is an industrial and transportation center. While it maintains large furniture factories, it is considered a cultural and educational center.

Founded in the ninth century and part of Kievan Rus, it was sacked by the Tartars in 1240. The Lithuanians took over in the fifteenth century, and by 1569, the town had become part of Poland. In 1793, the Russians annexed Zhitomir.

Actually, until 1792, Jews were not allowed to legally live in Zhitomir. In 1789, 882 Jews resided there and compounded one-third of the total population, according to the *Encyclopedia Judaica.* Like so many of their co-religionists in Ukraine, they were innkeepers, merchants, and craftsmen.

When the Communists took over in 1917, Jewish life quickly disintegrated, only to be reborn again in the last decade of the twentieth century, when the Soviet state collapsed.

Jewish Sites in Zhitomir

Synagogue, Malaya Berdichevskaya 7. Tel: (380-412) 226-608. Contact: Rabbi Shlomo Wilhelm.

Hesed Shlomo, Malaya Berdichevskaya 7. Tel/Fax: (380-412) 208-616. Contact: Director Daniel Kleiman.

Chabad Lubavitch, Chehova 57. Tel: (380-412) 251-793. Contact: Stepanskaya Anna Arkadievna.

The Jewish Agency, Vostochnaya 68. Tel: (380-412) 374-772. Contact: Mihail Moiseev.

Cemetery, Malaya Berdichevskaya 7. Tel: (380-412) 226-608. Contact Shribman Grigiriy Moiseevitch.

The Jewish Center, Borodiya 12-B. Tel: (380-412) 363-450. Contact Evgeniya Gilgur.

Suggested Reading

Bartov, Omer, *The Eastern Front, 1941-45, German Troops and the Barbarisation of Warfare.* New York: St. Martin's Press, 1986.

Bartov, Omer, *Hitler's Army: Soldiers, Nazis, & War in the Third Reich.* New York, Oxford: Oxford University Press, 1991.

Eliach, Yaffa, *There Once Was A World, A Nine-Hundred-Year Chronicle of the Shtetl of Eishyshok.* Boston, New York, London: Little, Brown and Company, 1998.

Reid, Anna, *Borderland: A Journey Through the History of Ukraine.* London: Weidenfeld & Nicolson, 1997.

Shabad, Theodore, *Geography of the USSR, A Regional Survey.* New York: Columbia University Press, 1951.

Berdichev:
The Jerusalem of Volhynia

Welcome to Berdichev, which epitomizes the typical Jewish community. This city, 115 miles southwest of Kiev, is the "Jerusalem of the historic region Volhynia gubernia."

This city was the home of noted scholars and rabbis, including Rabbi Levi Isaac Ben Berdichev. Berdichev once had 80 synagogues and *battei midrash* (houses of prayer and study). Known for its training of cantors, Berdichev dispatched the new singers of Jewish prayer to hundreds of municipalities in Ukraine and beyond.

This city, one of the largest centers of the Bund, was the birthplace of the great Russian Jewish writer Vasily Grossman, and was commented upon and written about by other great Jewish writers, including Mendele Mokher Seforim, Sholom Aleichem, and Der Nister.

Berdichev ranked as the second-largest Jewish community in Russia in 1861. Nearly one-half of the city was Jewish. At the beginning of World War I, there were more than thirty thousand Jews in Berdichev. Today, there are about eight hundred Jews.

This city was also the scene of a German massacre of about twenty thousand Jews on September 15, 1941.

Rabbi Levi Isaac Ben Berdichev

For a quarter of a century, Rabbi Levi Isaac Ben Berdichev (1740-1810), lived here. In an interview, Dr. Yaffa Eliach, author of *There Once Was A World*, said that Rabbi Levi Isaac has been described as "*Zaddek*, rabbi, one of the most famous personalities in the third generation of the Chassidic movement. He was one of the most loveable figures in Chassidism, because he was a defender of people."

Levi Isaac served as rabbi in this wonderful Jewish town where he "won great renown as rabbi, Chassidic leader and scholar. Even his opponents, the *mitnaggedim*, admitted he was a noted Torah scholar," said the *Encyclopedia Judaica*.

As a young man, he had become acquainted with the Chassidim of Israel b. Eliezer Ba'al Shem Tov. He became a student of Dov Baer, the maggid of Mezhirech. Levi Isaac went on to become the founder of Chassidism in central Poland. In his teachings, Levi Isaac stressed the element of joy in Chassidism, devotion to God, and the necessity of fervent prayer. He won thousands over to the Chassidic movement and was a popular hero in Jewish poetry and fiction, in both Hebrew and Yiddish.

Vasily Grossman

In *The Bones of Berdichev: The Life and Fate of Vasily Grossman*, Grossman says, "I was born on December 12, 1905 in the town of Berdichev in Ukraine. My father, Semyon Osipovich Grossman was a chemical engineer." Grossman was the author of the great Russian novels *Life and Fate* and *Forever Flowing*, the writing of which "put him on a par with the greatest Russian writers of this century," according to historian Orlando Figes in the *Times Literary Supplement*, December 6, 1996.

Communist Party boss Suslov predicted that *Life and Fate* would not be printed for 300 years; it was published in 1980. *Life and Fate*, like that of Solzhenitsyn's *One Day in the Life of Ivan Denisovich*, deeply affected Soviet society.

Grossman studied at Kiev's modern high school in 1914. He spent the war years as a correspondent of the military newspaper *Red Star*. His experiences of collectivization, terror, and war, including the Battle of Stalingrad and the Holocaust in Ukraine, taught him that there was no real difference between Stalinism and the Nazi occupation. His belief was reinforced by

Stalin's anti-Semitic policies. Grossman wrote about the Holocaust on Soviet soil, and his essays are included in *The Black Book,* co-authored with Ilya Ehrenburg. Grossman also became famous throughout the USSR for his vivid accounts of the Battle of Stalingrad.

Jewish Sites in Berdichev

Synagogue, Sverdlova 8. Tel/Fax: (380-4143) 20-222. Contact: Rabbi Slomo Breier.

Hesed, Sverdlova 8. Tel/Fax: (380-4143) 20-222. Contact: Coordinator Koval Anna.

The Jewish Agency, Sverdlova 17/2, Apt. 38. Tel: (380-4143) 20-854. Contact: Igor Vaiderman.

Yeshiva, Sverdlova 8. Tel/Fax: (380-4143) 20-222. Contact: Rabbi Slomo Breier.

Cemetery, Sverdlova 8. Tel/Fax: (380-4143) 20-222. Contact: Rabbi Slomo Breier.

Jewish Center and Sunday School, K. Libhnehta 30, Apt. 2. Tel: (380-4143) 22-278. Contact: Ella Vanshelboim.

Reform Congregation, Novoivanovskaya 3, Apt. 4. Tel: (380-4143) 32-517. Contact: Felix Doctor.

Suggested Reading:

Bartov, Omer, *The Eastern Front, 1941-45, German Troops and the Barbarisation of Warfare.* New York: St. Martin's Press, 1986.

Bartov, Omer, *Hitler's Army: Soldiers, Nazis, and War in the Third Reich.* New York, Oxford: Oxford University Press, 1991.

Eliach, Yaffa, *There Once Was A World, A Nine-Hundred-Year Chronicle of the Shtetl of Eishyshok.* Boston, New York, London: Little, Brown and Company, 1998.

Gerrard, John, and Gerrard, Carol, *The Bones of Berdichev: The Life and Times of Vasily Grossman.* New York: Free Press, 1996.

Reid, Anna, *Borderland: A Journey Through the History of Ukraine.* London: Weidenfeld & Nicolson, 1997.

Shabad, Theodore, *Geography of the USSR, A Regional Survey.* New York: Columbia University Press, 1951.

Kharkov:
"Industrial Hub"

Kharkov stands as one of the major cities of Ukraine, and is second in size only to Kiev. Unusual for Ukraine, this large metropolis of 1.6 million citizens was not built along the banks of a river. Kharkov was originally founded as a strong point along the southern frontier against the Crimean Turks. There are about fifty thousand Jews in Kharkov. The largest rail center in the former Soviet Union, Kharkov sits on the railroad network that runs from the Donets Basin to Moscow. Eight major rail lines converge here.

Located in an industrial center, Kharkov contains one of the world's largest farm truck factories. Today, a large research and development establishment supports its industrial basis.

Jewish Sites in Kharkov

The Central Synagogue of Kharkov, Pushkinskaya Street 12, Kharkov, 310003. Tel/Fax: (380-572) 12-65-26. Fax: (380-572) 45-21-40. E-mail: chabad@kharkov.com. Rabbi Moshe Moskovitz is chief rabbi. There is also a mikva in the synagogue.

Hillel, Kharkov Jewish Day School, 34 Chernishevsky Street, No. 170. Tel/Fax: (380-572) 43-19-81.

The Joint Distribution Committee, Krasnoshkolnaya Embankment 34, Kharkov, 310125. Tel/Fax: (380-572) 28-26-46 and (380-572) 28-26-47.

The Jewish Agency for Israel is also located at 12 Pushkinskaya Street, Kharkov. Tel: (380-572) 40-16-87. Fax: (380-572) 47-02-82.

Israel Cultural Center, 5R Klochkovskaya Street 159, Kharkov, 310141. Tel/Fax: (380-572) 43-91-81.

The Orthodox Union, Sumskaya Street 45, Kharkov, 310000. Tel/Fax: (380-572) 14-03-01 and (380-572) 40-83-78.

Or Avner Jewish Day School, Chabad, Gostello Street 13. Tel/Fax: (380-572) 43-19-81.

Day School, Chabad, Otakara Yarosha Street No. 140-7A. Tel/Fax: (380-572) 32-10-37.

International Solomon University, Eastern-Ukrainian Branch, "ISU-Kharkov," Chichibarbina Street 11. Tel: (380-572) 21-94-94. E-mail: bsoelkin@kharkov.ua

Suggested Reading:

Reid, Anna, *Borderland: A Journey Through the History of Ukraine.* London: Weidenfeld & Nicolson, 1997.

Shabad, Theodore, *Geography of the USSR, A Regional Survey.* New York: Columbia University Press, 1951.

LVOV:
Once It was Called Lemberg

In Russian, it is Lvov.

In Polish, it is Lwow.

In German, it is Lemberg.

In Ukrainian, it is Lviv.

And Jews have lived here in this city under every name, every occupier.

The *Encyclopedia Judaica* tells us that "it is thought that the first Jews arrived from Byzantium and the southeast." Jews from Germany and Bohemia came to this crossroads of trade routes in 1340, and the town took on an Ashkenazi character. Today, 850,000 persons call Lvov their home.

Lvov is just about forty miles from Poland and is considered one of the most European-looking cities. The largest city of the western Ukraine, with over a half-million citizens, it is an important rail hub, industrial area, and transit center. Historically, Jews were involved in trade between the East and West. The wholesale trade was their prime occupation. They also "leased estates, operated brandy distilleries and breweries, acted as customs and tax agents, and loaned money to the nobility and the king."

Visitors find Lvov attractive. It is built on a radial street pattern and is noted for its many parks and tree-lined squares. Founded by Prince Danil of Galicia around 1250 as his capital and named for his son, Lev, the fortress that became a city was

located at the crossroads between Kiev and Western Europe, and between the Black Sea and the Baltic.

According to Theodore Shabad, editor of *Soviet Geography,* "Lvov passed to Poland in 1340, Austria in 1772, back to a restored Poland after World War I, and to the USSR in 1939."

For those centuries, the eastern half of the country was ruled by Russia, and the western half by the Poles and Austrians. Today, Lvov is part of independent Ukraine and is a hotbed of Ukrainian nationalism.

Lvov suffered during the Chmielnicki massacres that occurred between 1648 and 1655, and during the eighteenth century the importance of the Lvov community declined.

From 1772 to 1914, the Jewish population of Lvov rose from 18,302 in 1800, to 26,694 in 1869, and 57,000 (28 percent of the total population) in 1910. The 1820 census showed that 55 percent of the Jews engaged in commerce (the majority as shopkeepers and retail traders), and 24 percent in crafts, according to the *Encyclopedia Judaica.*

This was a center of the Haskalah (Enlightenment) and in 1844, a Reform temple was opened. The assimilationist intelligentsia circle of Lvov identified themselves with German culture.

World War I (1914-1918) and the dislocation of thousands along the region's borders with Russia, including the pogroms, made this urban area a "city in conflict."

During the period of an independent Poland (1918-1939), Lvov, then part of that country, was the third-largest city in Poland and one of its most important centers.

In September 1939, Nazi Germany and Stalin's Russia divided Poland, and Lvov became part of Soviet Ukraine. But when Hitler turned on Russia, the Germans took Lvov, in July 1941. The city then had a Jewish population of about 150,000.

"The local Ukrainian population welcomed the German troops," says the *Encyclopedia Judaica.* Jewish historian Leni Yahil cites Lvov as an example of the collaboration of the Ukrainians with the Nazis. Tens of thousands of Polish Jews had fled here after the Germans and Russians invaded Poland in 1939. Two years later, Germany moved across the border toward Moscow, and 160,000 refugees somehow found their way to Lvov. The nationalist Ukrainians eagerly awaited the Germans, convinced that together with the eastern Ukraine, they would now be able to establish an independent Ukraine.

The Nazis urged the Ukrainians to conduct pogroms against the Jews. Charges were leveled against the Jews for allegedly having committed atrocities against Ukrainians during the Russian occupation. Moreover, Anna Reid relates in her book *Borderland: A Journey Through the History of Ukraine,* how one massacre, dubbed the "Petlyuria action," was held in revenge for the assassination of the bandit Petlyuria—killer of Jews in the Russian Civil War—who had been gunned down in the streets of Paris by Sholem Schwartzbrod 25 years previously.

Jews would suffer here. Many were deported to and executed at the Belzec concentration camp. Although imprisoned in a ghetto in June 1943, Jews still resisted the Nazis.

Apart from a few Jews in labor camps, Lvov and the environs were made *judenrein,* or "clear of Jews." No longer. The Jews have returned to this city. Seven thousand Jews live here.

Jewish Sites in Lvov

Synagogue, Miknovskih 3. Tel: (380-322) 330-524 (secretary). Tel/Fax: (380-322) 333-535. Contact: Rabbi Bold.

Jewish Cultural Society, Ugolnaya 3. Tel/Fax: (380-322) 729-843. Contact: Chairman Parhomovskiy Arkadiy Semenovich.

Hesed Arye, Ugolnaya 3. Tel/Fax: (380-322) 970-734. Contact: Director Kolomisev Leonid Vladimirovich.

Day School, Pasechnaya 64-A. Tel: (380-322) 229-219. Contact: Director Boris Mirkin.

Kindergarten, Pasechnaya 64-A. Tel: (380-322) 229-219. Contact: Director Boris Mirkin.

The Jewish Agency, Grigorovicha 3, Apt. 4. Tel: (380-322) 727-631, (380-322) 726-512. Contact: Boris Mihtuk.

The Jewish Center, Sholom Aleichem 12. Tel: (380-322) 627-368. Contact: Mirsky Rudolf Yakovlevitch.

Hillel, Ivan Fedorov 29. Tel: (380-322) 227-490. Contact: Selunina Irina Iosifovna.

Suggested Reading

Eliach, Yaffa, *There Once Was A World, A Nine-Hundred-Year Chronicle of the Shtetl of Eishyshok*. Boston, New York, London: Little, Brown and Company, 1998.

Reid, Anna, *Borderland: A Journey Through the History of Ukraine*. London: Weidenfeld & Nicolson, 1997.

Shabad, Theodore, *Geography of the USSR, A Regional Survey*. New York: Columbia University Press, 1951.

ODESSA:
"By the Sea, By the Sea"

If your parents or grandparents hailed from Odessa, a visit to this city located nearly 300 miles south of Kiev and 19 miles north of the mouth of the River Dniester is a must. Of the major cities of contemporary Europe, Odessa, founded in 1794, is among the youngest.

Odessa still retains some of its old flavor. Outdoor cafés and bustling casinos also dot its landscape. There is no bleakness here.

This was once a vibrant center of Jewish culture and a great intellectual center of Russian Jewry. On the eve of World War I, a third of the city's population were Jewish and spoke Yiddish.

A must is a stroll up or down the Potemkin Steps, or Odessa Steps, as they are often called. These steps are as sacred a site to the people of Russia as Runnymede and Yorktown are to the British and Americans. The steps are some 25 yards wide and are made of 12 flights of 20 steps each, or 240 steps in all. Each flight is broken by a broader step some 25 feet deep. Massive blocks of granite along each side act as a boundary, separating the steps from the steeply sloping garden below the Nikolaevsky Boulevard. As you walk these steps, you, too, may recall the story or epic film by Sergei Eisenstein regarding the Cossack murder of innocent people that occurred on or near the steps. Odessa citizens and workers were slaughtered by soldiers of the tsar in the riots of June 1905. "This was the nightmare scene which every worker peasant in the land had learned to fear from childhood . . . slashing whips, the saber cuts, synchronized volleys of rifle fire or the thunder of hooves. It was the very stuff of Tsarist tyranny," wrote Richard Hough in his book, *The Potemkin Mutiny.*

Houge was commenting on the epic film scene on the steps in the movie *The Battleship Potemkin,* directed by Sergei Eisenstein (1898-1948). The *Potemkin* was the battleship that had been named after Catherine the Great's favorite minister, Gregori A. Potemkin. Potemkin deceived Catherine about the state of rural Russia by setting up what became known as "Potemkin villages," and which were composed of empty stucco shells that only appeared to be part of a prosperous village.

Eisenstein was Russia's most famous movie director in his day. He filmed the movie in Odessa, much of it on the steps and in the harbor. Actually, Robert Leiter, writing in the May 20, 1999 issue of the Philadelphia *Jewish Exponent,* cites Ronald Bergon's new book, *Sergei Eisenstein: A Life in Combat,* as stating that there was no massacre on the Odessa Steps. Bergon claims Eisenstein made up a great deal of the film.

The actual *Potemkin* mutiny occurred on June 14, 1905. The sailors on the *Potemkin* brought the ship bearing the Red flag and not the normal Russian naval insignia to Odessa Harbor. They thought their mutiny would spread to the rest of the Black Sea fleet. It did not.

In Odessa, workers who had been on strike joined with the sailors in mourning a comrade, Gregori Vakulinchuk, a sailor who had been shot on the ship. Thousands of persons gathered in the harbor around the bier of the martyred sailor and placed wreaths on it. Troops were sent to stop the huge crowd and, while moving down the steps, they fired wildly into the gathering. Two thousand people were killed and three thousand wounded in the massacre, according to Figes.

After the killings, the *Potemkin* pulled out of Odessa and docked in Costanza, Rumania. The ship was exchanged for the "safe refuge" of the sailors, Figes adds.

Eisenstein also had difficulties with Stalin over his two-part film, *Ivan the Terrible (1944-45),* an allegory of Stalin, and had to go through all the right motions to survive under Stalin and the Soviet state. Eisenstein came from a German Jewish family and, though baptized, was "never really permitted to forget about his Jewish background." The Communists "viciously reminded him of it," notes Leiter. Yet he also stood up for Soviet Jews.

"Eisenstein would die from a massive heart attack after his fiftieth birthday, his life as an artist having been severely compromised," adds Leiter.

Statue of Richelieu, the Potemkin Steps. At the top of the steps is the statue of Duc de Richelieu. The statue is dwarfish, smaller than life size. Richelieu, a French aristocrat and the first governor of Odessa, watched over Odessa with paternal care. He spent his fortune freely to the same end—and endowed Odessa with a sound prosperity. He built this noble stairway with money from his own funds.

Here, one can walk along Primorski Boulevard to the Opera House (one of the most beautiful in all of Europe), gaze at the statue of Pushkin at the town hall, or take an excursion to Arkadia.

Visitors all come away with the feeling that this city has spice to it, a touch of the Riviera. It is a true melting pot of Ukrainians, Russians, Greeks, Turks, and of course, Jews.

This is above all a trader city. Even during the Communist era, an underground economy and business flourished here. During the day, men and women would work at dull jobs, but at night some became jewelers working in their illegal workshops.

"All southern Russian Jewry stood under the influence of Odessa," wrote Sh'marya Levin in his book, *The Arena.* Odessa meant freedom, and people were lured here by the possibility of escape from the restrictive Pale of Settlement.

Here great Jewish writers held court. Indeed my grandfather, a cantor, on his way to the synagogue, could have passed the writer Mendele Mokher Seforim.

Some of the greatest names of Zionist and Hebrew literature came from Odessa and its environment—Ze'ev Vladimir Jabotinsky, Joseph Trumpeldor, Chaim Nachman Bialik, and Saul Tchernichowsky. Young Hebrew poets thrived here, until the Communist Revolution ended it all. From here came the

The famous Potemkin Steps in Odessa are shown here. (Photo credit: Scott Richman)

calls of M. L. Lilienblum to revive the land of Israel. Headquartered in the city was "The Odessa Committee," officially called the "Society for the Support of Agricultural Workers and Craftsmen in Syria and Palestine," the only legally authorized institution for the Zionist movement in Russia between 1890 and 1917.

Odessa opened the gates to Palestine. Boats from Odessa took the future citizens of Israel across the Black Sea to Turkey, on their way to the land of Israel.

Odessa went up with a rush. In 1795, two thousand settlers lived in town. By 1814, it counted thirty-five thousand citizens, says Neal Ascherson, author of *Black Sea*. It soon blossomed into a commercial and industrial center for southern Russia.

Rising from a modest seaport to a city of international importance, it offered Jewish residents a range of opportunities rarely encountered in the Pale of Settlement, according to Steven J. Zipperstein, author of *The Jews of Odessa, A Cultural History, 1794-1881*.

The Jewish population of Odessa also rose rapidly. In the late nineteenth and first half of the twentieth century, Odessa ranked as the largest Jewish community after Warsaw. In 1939, New York counted 2,085,000 Jews, or 28 percent of its population; Moscow had 400,000, or 10 percent; Warsaw, 365,000, or 28.8 percent; and Odessa had 180,000 Jews, or 29.8 percent of its population, the tenth-largest Jewish-inhabited city at that time. Odessa's population is today about 1,115,000, including 45,000 to 50,000 Jews.

Whenever I would tell a Russian or Ukrainian that my mother was from Odessa, they would smile. I found Odessans have a good sense of humor. Russians often laugh about Odessa. They make fun of the way people speak the language. It's natural Jewish humor, with a Jewish intonation.

In Jewish folklore, Odessa became synonymous with disbelief, sinfulness, and frivolity, says Jewish historian Lucy S. Dawidowicz. It also was known as a city that threw off tradition. This situation was expressed by the popular Jewish saying, "The fire of hell burns around Odessa up to a distance of ten parasangs." It was a center of the Haskalah (enlightenment) movement that enveloped large segments of the Jewish population. Actually, until the Maskilim, or people of the enlightenment, arrived on the scene, the Hebrew language was only used in prayers, and Yiddish was the daily means of expression. The Maskilim popularized Hebrew.

The terms for this city are probably romanticized, but Odessa has been labeled "Right Bank Paris," and "Little Paris," and yes, even "Little Vienna" and "Mother Odessa." A popular song known as "Odessa Mamma" typifies the city. After all, "the Odessans were good-looking people, mostly with round black eyes," wrote author Edmund Wilson in *Red, Black, Blond, and Olive: Studies in Four Civilizations.*

Trotsky, the revolutionary who lived here, said Paris was like Odessa, only Odessa was better. Actually, it has been said this capital of the south resembles a French cathedral town, with its wide boulevards, rather than a provincial Russian city. It also reminds visitors of Naples and Genoa. While at the turn of the twenty-first century, the city finds itself somewhat run-down, with potholes, buildings in need of repair, and needing a good paint job, one still can observe the splendor of its architecture.

Odessa sits on a promontory that rises to a height of almost 200 feet above the Pontine plain. This location makes for a great view. Odessa was a port thrown up hastily on a barren shore to bring "New Russia" into the capitalist age. Foreigners built Odessa and ran it for the Russian Empire. The architects were Italian, and many of the shipping businesses were owned by Greeks. The suppliers who sent wheat to this port were Polish, according to Ascherson. Interestingly, as we have mentioned, the first governor was a French aristocrat, the Duc de Richelieu.

Odessa, this southern window to Europe, has also been compared to Marseilles, the port on the southern coast of France. "Our port was notorious for smuggling goods into the country and smuggling people out of the country," reflected Abraham T'homi in his book, *Between Darkness & Dawn: A Saga of the Hehalutz.*

Walk along the Nikolaevsky Boulevard, located high above

the harbor. It offers a great view. In the old days, the upper class strolled along this boulevard, as well as around Odessa's green-shrouded squares and wide streets. The spires, minarets, and cupolas of the university and cathedrals, and the town hall and city library are all beautiful to see.

A Brief History

How did Odessa get its name?

The Russians had captured a Tartar fortress on the Black Sea, 20 miles north of the mouth of the Dniester. Called Yeni Dunai (New World), it was located beside the town of Khadzhybey. Six years later would be renamed Odessa.

Catherine the Great is supposed to have picked the name. Like the province named Kherson, Odessa boasted strong Greek connotations. It was named after the ancient Greek settlement Odessos, located east of Khadzhybey, on the left bank of the Tylihul Lagoon. Instead of "Odessos," Catherine changed the name to Odessa, in the feminine gender. A Greek name would attract Greek merchants and settlers to the new foundation, she figured. She was correct.

When Pushkin arrived in this relatively civilized city in 1823, he found a city populated with an opera house, French restaurants, and bookstores. Pushkin obviously loved Odessa, as he wrote some of his greatest poetry here.

The government needed settlers for the area, and encouraged Jews to settle in the fertile northern shores of the Black Sea. Odessa's original Jewish settlers were much like their non-Jewish counterparts—rugged, young, generally unmarried males, similar to the itinerant Jewish merchants and laborers who had worked in the southern steppe area for centuries.

According to Bertram D. Wolfe, the tsarist government offered state lands in the so-called "New Russia," the sparsely settled Ukrainian provinces of Kherson and Ekaterinoslav, for Jewish agricultural colonization. Later the land would be taken away, but while it lasted, this use of this land was a release from economic strangulation in the Pale of Settlement.

Odessa's Jewish population tripled from 17,000 in 1834 to nearly 52,000, out of a total population of 193,000 in 1873.

Jews rapidly began to supplant the Greeks in the export trade, and by 1875, more than 60 percent of the city's commercial firms were in Jewish hands. During this period, Odessa became the foremost port of entry for Asian goods bound for European markets. Goods were transported across Persia by land to Turkey, shipped to Odessa, and then sent by river or road through Brody and Leipzig to the northwest, and in particular to England.

Pogroms

But the tranquility was not to last. As the city's economy burgeoned, so did the hate and jealousy. In 1821, the first modern Russian pogrom occurred in Odessa, and was probably instigated mainly by Greek merchants. Jewish shops were trashed in the pogrom.

Fifty years later, on May 27, 1871, another major pogrom erupted in Odessa. Within four days, 6 people were killed and 21 wounded, and 863 houses and 552 businesses were damaged or destroyed. Not a single Jewish street or neighborhood was left unnoticed, according to Jewish historian Steven J. Zipperstein.

While each pogrom had its own local characteristics, there were several general principles behind every one. Alfred Kazan, author and critic, says Jews were constantly harassed by the tsarist government and were surrounded by peasants who were usually anti-Semitic and could easily be goaded, with the help of encouragement from the government itself and a lot of vodka, into beginning pogroms.

Simon M. Dubnow insists that "in many localities the pogroms were deliberately permitted or even directly engineered by the police." And according to Hosking, in his book, *Russia, People and Empire,* local policemen and officials "were often at their wit's end, not certain any longer where authority lay." They claimed they had insufficient forces to deal with large-scale disorders. On the other hand, says Hosking, "some officials directly encouraged anti-Semitic violence, but this was never the agreed policy of the government."

In his *History of the Jews,* Simon M. Dubnow backs up his view on the pogroms by telling us that "Surreptitious emissaries from St. Petersburg appeared in the southern Russian cities, (Odessa, Elisavetgrad, Kiev) in the month of March, to carry on secret negotiations with the chiefs of police, concerning a probable outburst of the people's indignation against Jews." These emissaries hinted that it would be undesirable for the police to oppose the people.

That the pogroms were prepared and organized is evident from the fact that they erupted simultaneously in many localities in southern Russia, and were executed according to the same pattern everywhere. The action of the rabble was uniform, and the lack of action of the authorities was likewise uniform, Dubnow asserts.

Moreover, some say the pogroms were needed by the government to act as a safety valve for the revolutionary restlessness of the Russian people.

According to historian Michael T. Florinsky, "these bloody anti-Jewish outbreaks which occurred in more than 100 localities would probably have been impossible without the connivance and, in some cases, the instigation of the police."

The government blamed the Jews for the growing revolutionary movement, by painting them as Jewish conspirators and at the same time turning the grievances of the Russian peasants and working class from the government onto the Jews.

"We must not forget," wrote Tsar Alexander III in 1890 in the margin of a report depicting the plight of Russian Jewry, "that it was the Jews who crucified our Lord and spilled his precious blood." Every official knew that the tsar despised Jews and "was not likely to be distressed by physical attacks on them," according to Abraham Ascher.

According to W.E.D. Allen, it was unjust to accuse the imperial government of being accomplice and instigator of the mobs. There is no question, however, that there was state-supported anti-Semitism, including acts by many of the top officials of the tsar. Leading the attack against the Jews was Konstantin Pobedonostsev (1827-1907), "the Torquemada of the nineteenth century." He and Viacheslav Konstantinovich von Plehve, minister of interior from 1902 to 1904, were "inveterate Jew haters," wrote Florinsky. Sh'marya Levin called Pobedonostsev "an evil genius," and the "reactionary inquisitor." Pobedonostsev was a former professor of civil law at the University of Moscow, and chief procurator of the Holy Synod. He dragged Russia from disaster to disaster.

Regarding Jews, von Plehve is supposed to have declared, "We shall make your position in Russia so unbearable that the Jews will leave the country to the last man."

The period of 1905-1907 has been aptly called the First Russian Revolution. Actually, as Ascher notes, "the agitation against the government began in the autumn of 1904, when middle class liberals, appalled by Russia's defeats in the war against Japan, launched a campaign for political reform." The trouble reached its climax with the march of Father Gapon to the Winter Palace. The killing of some 130 peaceful marchers triggered a period of unrest that culminated in a general strike in October 1905, "which literally paralyzed the government," according to Ascher. The tsar and his officials issued the October Manifesto, which agreed to reforms. But "pogroms against the Jews suddenly and unexpectedly erupted into a mass movement of brute force," according to Ascher. "All told, according to the most reliable estimates, 690 anti-Jewish pogroms occurred in those six weeks, primarily in the southwestern provinces, where 876 people were killed and about 8,000 injured." The Jews lost property estimated in the millions of rubles.

No other town or city in the Russian Empire was to suffer such disaster and bloodshed in the whole series of pogroms and riots that occurred in Russia in 1905 as Odessa. During the Odessa pogrom, which lasted four days, more than 500 persons were killed and 1,500 Jewish homes and businesses were broken up, according to M. A. Novemeysky, in *My Siberian Life*.

Civil War

A dozen years later, the tsar fell. Eight months later, the Kerensky Government was overthrown by the Bolsheviks, and Russia was hurled into a civil war between the Reds and the

Whites. The French, the British, and the Greeks sided with the Whites. Odessa and the Crimea became a White sphere of influence.

At the same time, the Association of Jewish Combatants was formed here. It consisted of former officers and soldiers of the Russian army. The association's existence has been cited in explaining why no pogroms occurred in Odessa throughout the Civil War period, according to the *Encyclopedia Judaica.*

During that bloody conflict, Odessa changed hands more than once. General Anton Ivanovich Denikin (1872-1947), led the anti-Bolshevik forces from 1918 to 1920. There was a flourishing black market. All lived "on top of the world," until the end, which came when the Communists took over. The city soon fell in stature.

A Small Dunkirk

Alongside Leningrad, Moscow, and Stalingrad, Odessa ranks as a "hero city" of World War II. Between August 5 and October 16, 1941, German and Rumanian troops and artillery battered away at this Black Sea port. For 72 days the city defended itself, a fact that is remarkable in view of German air superiority. Not only did the Russians stand up to the siege, but they were also able to evacuate about three hundred fifty thousand civilians, (about one-half the population), as well as about two hundred thousand tons of industrial equipment.

The evacuation was one of the most daring in the history of World War II. Historians call it "a small Dunkirk," after the French port where, in World War II, the British rescued their army from the continent by transporting it across the English Channel via military ships and civilian fishing boats. Before they left, Red Army engineers blew up important objectives, toppled cranes into the harbor, and dynamited port installations. They destroyed coastal batteries and military defenses. Instead of 20 days, the evacuation was accomplished in one night. "At 05.10 hours on 16 October, the last transport set course for Sevastopol," wrote historian John Erickson.

"The Town of the Hanged"

"The town of the hanged" was the name Vera Inber, noted writer, gave to Odessa. The Germans and the Rumanians occupied the city and spared no effort to transform the port into a Rumanian outpost. Anyone who drove around the city after October 16, 1941 could see Jews hanging from the lampposts. The city was described as a dungeon, "washed with blood, festooned with gallows."

That very day, October 16, Sonderkommando 11b, together with an operational division of the Rumanian Intelligence Service, slaughtered over eight thousand residents, most of them Jews.

Innocent people were herded into outdoor camps in Berezovka, Bogdanovka, and Domanevka, all located near the Bug River. Many were left in the cold for days; women and children froze to death. One young boy wrote: "each letter of these names should be 'burned into our brains,' never to be forgotten." Innocent people were destroyed simply because they were Jews.

But the worst tragedy occurred on October 22, when partisans blew up the Rumanian headquarters building, once the headquarters of the NKVD (Soviet secret police). Several dozen Rumanian soldiers and officers died. Ion Antonescu ordered two hundred Communists executed for each officer who had been killed, as well as one hundred for each soldier. Every Communist was to be picked up, as well as one member of every Jewish family.

In an unimaginable scene, on the very next day, nineteen thousand Jews were herded into a square down at the harbor. Gasoline was poured over them and they were burned to death.

In another incident that took place that week, the Rumanians assembled another twenty thousand Jews. They were then taken to the village of Dalnik, where some were shot and others other shut in warehouses that were set on fire. Following this massacre, as well as later killings, many Jews were sent from Odessa to their death in the camps of Bogdanovka and Domanevka, as well as Akhmetchetka, in the Golta Region.

"The Jews who died in the first days of the occupation were the fortunate ones," said one observer.

Here is the memorial to the Odessa Jews who were marched by the Nazis from this point in the Moldavanka section of Odessa, to the death camp known as Bogdanovka. (Photo Credit: Scott Richman)

On April 10, 1944, Odessa was liberated by the Red Army. According to the report of the authorities, nearly one hundred thousand Jews had been killed in the city.

After the war, Jews came home to Odessa. By 1959, 102,000 were living in the city. Odessa became one of the largest Jewish centers of the Soviet Union. Until 1956, Israeli vessels docked in the harbor. Usually Israeli sailors fanned out and met Russian Jews.

Notable Jews

As you walk the streets of Odessa, you cannot help but recall some of the great Jewish and Zionist leaders who lived or spent time here: Chaim Nachman Bialik, Vladimir Zev Jabotinsky, Joseph Trumpeldor, and that revolutionary, Leon Trotsky, whom we met in St. Petersburg. Here are just a few more notable Jews who were associated with Odessa.

Isaac Babel (1894-1940). If you want to understand Odessa, you will want to read Babel, who is considered one of the greatest prose writers of the Soviet period. He was the first Jewish writer to enter Russian literature as a Russian writer, and many of his Russian stories were written about the Jews of Odessa. Babel belongs on the list of the greatest writers of twentieth-century literature, according to Richard Bernstein, of the *New York Times.*

Babel was a "son of the ghetto." He grew up under an aura of official anti-Semitism and pogroms. His father, a Jewish tradesman, insisted that his son study Hebrew, the Bible, and the Talmud. Babel attended the Commercial High School, where a teacher instilled in him a love of French classics. Later, Gorky would publish a few of Babel's stories, an act that literally started him on the road to fame.

During World War I, Babel first fought with the Tsarist Army. But in 1917, he went over to the Bolsheviks. By 1923, he had become a literary success, as a result of the publication of his *Odessa Stories,* a group of vivid sketches of Russian Jewish life.

The *Odessa Stories* covers the prerevolutionary and revolutionary period in Odessa, and describes "the Jewish proletarian and underworld of the city."

Another of his famous works, published in 1926, was *Red Cavalry,* written out of his cavalry experiences with General Semyon Budyonny, of the Red Army, during the Polish campaign of 1920. *Red Cavalry* "is about men and what they expect of one another in the way of honor, physical courage, love of horses, abuse of women, and Jews. It's about a young man, a Russian, too, but to them a foreigner, who is falling in love with their bravery and suffering," wrote Grace Paley, in an introduction to A.N. Pirozhkova's book *At His Side: The Last Years of Isaac Babel.*

Lionel Trilling, author, says Babel wrote about Jews who were generally crowded into the already overcrowded suburbs, especially in the Moldavanka section of Odessa. Preobrazhenskaia Street was the dividing line between the city center and the suburbs of Moldavanka, Peresyp, and Slobodka Romanovka. And in Moldavanka, the most popular Jewish neighborhood and the best-known suburb, were the famous Jewish gangs.

In 1927, Babel visited his first wife, Evgeniya Gronfein, and his daughter, Nathalie, in Paris. His wife lived in France from 1925 until her death in 1957. She also had a brother who emigrated to the U.S. in 1919.

After 1935, Babel would not be permitted to leave the Soviet Union again. He entered a common-law marriage with Antonina Nikolayevna Pirozhkova, an attractive 23-year-old construction engineer. Their daughter Lidya was born in January 1937. She and her mother lived in Moscow until they moved to the U.S. in 1996. Babel also had a son, Misha, who lives in Moscow.

Babel, who was constantly revising his work, was reluctant to publish original works during the Stalinist terror of the 1930s. That's why he was "singularly unprolific." His complete works would not even exceed two volumes.

Babel would fall victim to the great purges. His friendship with Nikolai Yezhov, the arrested chief of the Soviet secret police, probably sealed his fate. For many years it was not known how or when he died. However, recent disclosures indicate he was arrested on May 15, 1939. His sentence was handed down on January 26, 1940; he was only 45 years old. He was probably shot the next day. Babel was posthumously rehabilitated by the Soviet Supreme Court in 1954.

Simon Frug (1860-1916). Frug was the first poet to treat a Jewish theme in Russian verse. One of his famous songs was composed after the Kishinev pogrom of 1903. In it, Frug, who lived in Odessa, pleads for Jews to "return to productive labor on their ancestral soil."

David Frischmann (1859-1922). Frischmann was a major writer in modern Hebrew literature. While living in Odessa during World War I, he wrote beautiful lyrical poems.

Moses Leib Lilienblum (1843-1910). Lilienblum was a Hebrew writer, critic, and political journalist who moved to Odessa in 1869. One of the founders of the Odessa Committee in 1883, he said one way to end Jewish difficulties was for Jews to stop being aliens in their country of residence and settle in Palestine, the ancient Jewish homeland.

Menachem Mendel Ussishkin (1863-1941). Ussishkin was also a founder of the Odessa Committee. He served as its chairman from 1906 until the Soviets abolished the Committee during the Revolution. Ussishkin was the Hebrew secretary of the first World Zionist Congress in Basel in 1897. He bitterly opposed Herzl's Uganda scheme, the name given to the proposal the British made to the Zionist movement to set up an autonomous Jewish colony, British East Africa, now Kenya. In 1917, he organized a mass demonstration in Odessa of more than two hundred thousand people, including many non-Jews, to celebrate the Balfour Declaration, which called for the establishment of a Jewish state in Palestine. In November 1919, he settled in Palestine. For nearly 20 years he headed the Jewish National Fund. Indeed, for 60 years, "no Zionist or Jewish national activity took place on which he had not left his own unique stamp," says JNF literature.

Meir Dizengoff (1861-1937). Dizengoff, who would later serve as the first mayor of Tel Aviv in 1921, settled in Odessa in 1897. He went into business and became active in the Zionist movement. Dizengoff visited Palestine before he finally settled in Israel in 1905 in Jaffa. He served as mayor of Tel Aviv from 1921 to 1928, and then again from 1929 until he died in 1937.

Osip Rabinovitch (1817-1869). Rabinovitch was the editor of the Odessa *Razsvet,* the first Jewish journal in the Russian language, in which he championed equal rights for Jews. In his short stories he depicted the "reign of terror" that would over-take Russia. But like many others, the pogrom of 1871 in Odessa weakened his faith in assimilation.

Dr. Chaim Tchernowitz (1871-1949). Tchernowitz was a great scholar of the Talmud, a Hebrew writer, and formerly the chief rabbi of Odessa. His yeshiva attracted numerous Jewish intellectuals, including Chaim Nachman Bialik and Joseph Klausner. The *Encyclopedia Judaica* calls him a writer, orator, and physician. He settled in the U.S. in 1923 and taught Talmud at the Jewish Theological Seminary in New York City.

Leon Pinsker (1821-1891). In 1881, in Odessa, Leon Pinsker, an Odessa physician, was probably the first European ideologue of Zionism. His book, *Auto Emancipation,* helped give rise to the Zionist movement. The former editor of *Sion* in Odessa, he was a founder of the Odessa branch of the Society for Enlightenment in 1867. A future leader of the Hovevei Zion, he wrote that the Jews would have to emancipate themselves in their own land. Mikhail Beizer says that Pinsker's book was a rallying call of a Russian Jew to his fellow Jews. Pinsker declared that "Jews could not attain real equality of rights among other peoples simply by the gaining of civil rights." Pinsker wanted Jews to play a part in establishing their own future.

Ahad Ha'am (1856-1927). His real name was Asher Ginsberg, but we know him by the pen name of Ahad Ha'Am, (one of the people). He was among the Lovers of Zion who emerged in the 1890s in Odessa. He wrote Yiddish and Hebrew essays calling on the Lovers of Zion groups to establish agri-cultural settlements in Palestine, which he wanted to be a Hebrew-speaking cultural center of world Jewry. He argued that the "national center has to serve as a secure sanctuary, not for Jews but for Judaism." He remained in Odessa until 1907.

Mendele Mokher Seforim (1836-1917). His real name was Sholem Yankev Abramovich. We translate his name as "Mendel the bookseller." He has also been called the "Grandfather of

Neo-Hebrew Literature," "der Zeide of Yiddish literature," and "the Lion of Odessa Jewry." He lived in many of the cities cited in this book, such as Zhitomir, Berdichev, and Odessa. His younger followers were Peretz and Sholom Aleichem. Seforim was the chief star in the firmament of modern Yiddish letters. His Yiddish classics were *Die Kliatsche* and *Yudel.* Also well-known were *The Call Up* and the Hebrew story *The Hidden Place of Thunder.* After the 1905 pogroms, he moved to Geneva; in 1908, he returned to Odessa, where he continued to write and also compiled his memoirs.

Chaim Nachman Bialik (1873-1934). Some have called him the greatest Hebrew poet of modern times. He was also an essayist, storywriter, translator, and editor. Known as "the poet of the National Awakening," he exercised a profound influence on modern Jewish culture. He was born in Zhitomir, but when he was only six years old, he attended the yeshiva of Volozhin in Lithuania. In 1900, he obtained a teaching position in Odessa, the center of modern Jewish culture in southern Russia, where he lived for a short time. In that year, Maxim Gorky interceded with the Soviet government to persuade the government to permit a group of Hebrew writers to leave the country. Bialik was one of them. He settled in Tel Aviv. He later died in Vienna, where he had gone to seek medical treatment.

Saul Tchernichowsky (1875-1943). A physician in a small Russian village, he became one of the early great Hebrew poets. At age 14, Tchernichowsky was sent to Odessa to further his education. Drawn to Zionist circles, and interested in language, he translated poetry from these languages into Hebrew. A famous portrait of Saul Tchernichowsky was painted by Leonid Pasternak, the father of Boris Pasternak. Both Bialik and Tchernichowsky "fructified" the field of Jewish poetry.

Vladimir Ze'ev Jabotinsky (1880-1940). "One of the stormiest figures in Jewish political life," says Levin. "One does not have to share the views of Jabotinsky in order to recognize the scale of his personality and his energy from political activity to the most difficult of poetic translations," writes Beizer. Jabotinsky was the founder of Revisionist Zionism, and the mentor of Menachem Begin, the late Israeli prime minister.

Scott Richman, JDC desk executive for the Former Soviet Union, is shown in front of the birthplace of Vladimir Ze'ev Jabotinsky, the founder of the Revisionist Movement of Zionism. (Photo credit: Scott Richman)

Jabotinsky was born in Odessa, where he went to secular high-school gymnasium before studying law at the Universities of Rome and Bern. He began his literary career at the age of 19, and was first published in the Russian liberal press. Levin notes that as a young man, Jabotinsky had a reputation as a fighter, an able journalist, and a brilliant speaker. However, very few American Jews knew about him until after Menachem Begin became prime minister of Israel.

Joseph Trumpeldor (1882-1920). There is a Hebrew lament, "Trumpeldor has fallen." He was a celebrated soldier who fought in the Russo-Japanese War and who received all four degrees of the Cross of St. George, the highest decoration for valor in the Russian army. Joseph Trumpeldor was the only Jewish commissioned officer in the Russian army before the Revolution. The Revolutionary Government was in favor of raising a Jewish army against Turkey, but the Bolshevik coup d'ètat put an end to Trumpeldor's plan. As chairman of Hehalutz, the pioneering youth movement and organization, his aim was to prepare young people for settlement in Israel. He visited Odessa many times and helped organize an underground railroad system that sent many young Zionists to Palestine via the Black Sea and Turkey. He himself reached the settlement of Tel Hai, where he was killed by armed Arabs. His last words were in Hebrew, *"Tov lamut be'ad artzenu,"* or "It is good to die for our country." In 1934, a memorial by the sculptor A. Melnikov was erected at Tel Hai in honor of Trumpeldor. It is a lion of Judah. The youth movement Berit Trumpeldor (Betar) was also founded in his memory. One of its later members was Menachem Begin.

Odessa Jewish Community:

The Jewish population in Odessa is estimated to be around fifty thousand. Visitors to Odessa can obtain further information as to events and programs by contacting the community groups listed here, or the synagogues, or the Odessa Jewish Cultural Society, as well as the JDC office in this port city.

For those who would like kosher food, it is suggested that they contact, in advance, the Central Synagogue of Odessa, which is listed next. Also, travel agencies organizing your tour can be consulted ahead of time to arrange kosher food.

Central Synagogue of Odessa and the Odessa Jewish Religious Community (Shomrei Shabbos), Osipov Street 21. Tel: (380-482) 218-890. Fax: (380-482) 247-296. Rabbi Avraham Wolff is chief rabbi of Odessa and southern Ukraine.

Osipov Street was once called Remeslennaya Street, and featured three synagogues. Now only this synagogue remains. It was fully restored, thanks to the efforts of Rabbi Ishay Gisser.

The Former Great Synagogue of Odessa, Yevreyskaya Street, (Yevreyskaya means Jewish) 25. Tel: (380-482) 243-694. Rabbi Shlomo Baksht is the spiritual leader. Efforts are being made to restore this building. Also located here is the **Jewish Religious Community,** or "Sameah." Tel: (380-482) 243-694.

Odessa Jewish Cultural Society, Malaya Amautskaya Street 46A. Tel: (380-482) 226-590. Fax:(380-482) 246-197. This building also serves as a community center. Also located here is the **International Association of Ghetto Survivors,** Tel: (380-482) 240-022; the **Odessa Association of Jewish Culture;** the **Association of the Jewish Historical Society,;** the **Jewish Education and Arts Center** (known as Migdal), and the **Association of Former Prisoners of Ghettos and Concentration Camps.** Migdal can be contacted by telephone at (380-482) 226-590, and by fax at (380-482) 246-197. Kira Verkhovskaya is director of Migdal. Her home phone number is (380-482) 268-086. Besides its Jewish school, Migdal puts on programs in both Hebrew and Yiddish at its Odessa Jewish Musical Theater.

Jewish Library, Pionerskaya Street 5A. Tel: (380-482) 635-404. Veta Maximova is the director. Her home telephone is (380-482) 242-955. As hard as it is to believe, this library, located in the Municipal Building, where groups meet to discuss Jewish heritage, literature, and religion, once housed the KGB. The **Lovers of Yiddish Club** also meets here. The club room is decorated with posters and photos of Jewish leaders, such as former Israeli Prime Minister David Ben-Gurion.

The remodeled Central Synagogue of Odessa is located at 21 Osipow Street. (Photo credit: Scott Richman)

For those who just love libraries, the author being one of them, it is important to repeat that a very high proportion of Russians and Ukrainians love libraries. There are four Jewish libraries in Odessa. They are located at **Migdal School, the Jewish Community Center, the Jewish Agency,** and the **Israel Fund.**

JDC, for instance, has developed a series of libraries in the former Soviet Union, and has sent 730,000 books there. There are about 153 libraries in 104 towns. Libraries also serve as community centers.

Odessa Judaic Community, Odary Street 5. Tel: (380-482) 232-443 and (380-482) 324-019.

Odessa Jewish Welfare Center, known as Gmilus Hesed, Troitzkaya Street 41/8. The director is Vladimir Goldman. Tel/Fax: (380-482) 229-065, (380-482) 253-232, and (380-482) 259-153.

Or Sameah, Jewish Day School for Boys, M. Roskovoy Street 5/7. Tel: (380-482) 325-744.

Or Sameah, Jewish Day School for Girls, Industrianaya Street 34. Tel: (380-482) 325-867.

American Jewish Joint Distribution Committee, Osipova Street 5, Apt. 5. Tel: (380-482) 221-856, (380-482) 287-039, and (380-482) 246-005.

Jewish Agency, (also known as Sochnut), Tolstoy Street 30. Tel: (380-482) 267-467 and (380-482) 264-727. Fax: (380-482) 219-015.

Israel Information Center, Paster Street 11. Tel: (380-482) 230-205, (380-482) 234-411, and (380-482) 234-080.

Since the collapse of the Soviet Union in 1991, volunteers from Israel and the U.S. have helped open Jewish community centers, schools, and theaters here, and the activities of groups such as the Yiddish Club suggest that Jewish life in Odessa may thrive once again.

Suggested Reading:

Allen, W. E. D., *The Ukraine, A History.* New York: Russell & Russell, Inc., 1993.

Anatoli, A., (Kuznetsov), *Babi Yar*. New York: Washington Square Press, 1970.

Ascherson, Neal, *Black Sea*. New York: Hill and Wang, 1995.

Baron, Salo, *The Russian Jew under Tsars and Soviets*. New York: The Macmillan Company, 1994.

Ben-Ami, (Arie L. Eliav), *Between Hammer and Sickle*. Philadelphia: Jewish Publication Society, 1967.

Clark, Alan, *Barbarossa: The Russo-German Conflict, 1941-1945*. New York: Morrow, 1965.

Dawidowicz, Lucy S., *The Golden Tradition, Jewish Life and Thought in Eastern Europe*. New York: Holt, Rhinehart and Winston, 1967.

Ehrenburg, Ilya and Grossman, Vasily, *The Black Book, The Ruthless Murder of Jews by German-Fascist Invaders Throughout the Temporarily-Occupied Regions of the Soviet Union and the Death Camps of Poland During the War of 1941-1945*. New York: Holocaust Library, 1980.

Eliach, Yaffa, *There Once Was A World, A Nine-Hundred-Year Chronicle of the Shtetl of Eishyshok*. Boston, New York, London: Little, Brown and Company, 1998.

Erickson, John, *The Road to Stalingrad, Stalin's War with Germany, Vol. I*. New York: Harper & Row, Publishers, 1975.

Figes, Orlando, *A People's Tragedy: A History of the Russian Revolution*. New York: Viking, 1997.

Florinsky, Michael T., *Russia*. 2 Vols., New York: Macmillan, 1961.

Gilbert, Martin, *Holocaust Journey, Traveling in Search of the Past*. New York: Columbia University Press, 1997.

Gilbert, Martin, *The Jews of Russia, Their History in Maps and Photographs*. London: National Council for Soviet Jewry of the United Kingdom and Ireland, 1976.

Herlihy, Patricia, *Odessa: A History, 1794-1914*. Cambridge, MA: Harvard University Press, 1986.

Hough, Richard, *The Potemkin Mutiny*. New York: Pantheon Books, 1961.

Levitats, Isaac, *The Jewish Community in Russia, 1772-1884*. New York: Octagon Books, 1970.

Lindemann, Albert S., *Esau's Tears: Modern Anti-Semitism and the Rise of The Jews*. New York: Cambridge University Press, 1997.

Pirozhkova, A.N., *At His Side: The Last Years of Isaac Babel.* South Royalton, VT: Steerforth Press, 1996.

Reid, Anna, *Borderland: A Journey Through the History of Ukraine.* London: Weidenfeld & Nicolson, 1997.

Ripp, Victor, *From Moscow to Main Street, Among the Russian Emigres.* New York: Little, Brown and Company, 1984.

Ro'i Yaacov, *Jews and Jewish Life in Russia and the Soviet Union.* Ilford, England: Frank Cass & Co., Ltd.,1995.

Slonim, Marc, *Soviet Russian Literature, Writers and Problems, 1917-1977.* New York, Oxford: Oxford University Press, 1977.

T'homi, Abraham, *Between Darkness & Dawn: A Saga of the Hehalutz.* New York: Bloch Publishing Co, Inc., 1986

Volkogonov, Dmitrii, *Trotsky: The Eternal Revolutionary.* New York: The Free Press, 1996.

Wolfe, Bertram D., *Three Who Made a Revolution, A Biographical History.* New York: The Dial Press, 1964.

Yahil, Leni, *The Holocaust: The Fate of European Jewry, 1932-1945.* New York, Oxford: Oxford University Press, 1990.

Zipperstein, Steven J., *The Jews of Odessa: A Cultural History, 1794-1881.* Stanford, CA: Stanford University Press, 1985.

Index